Lonely Planet Publications
Paris

Sara Benson

Toronto

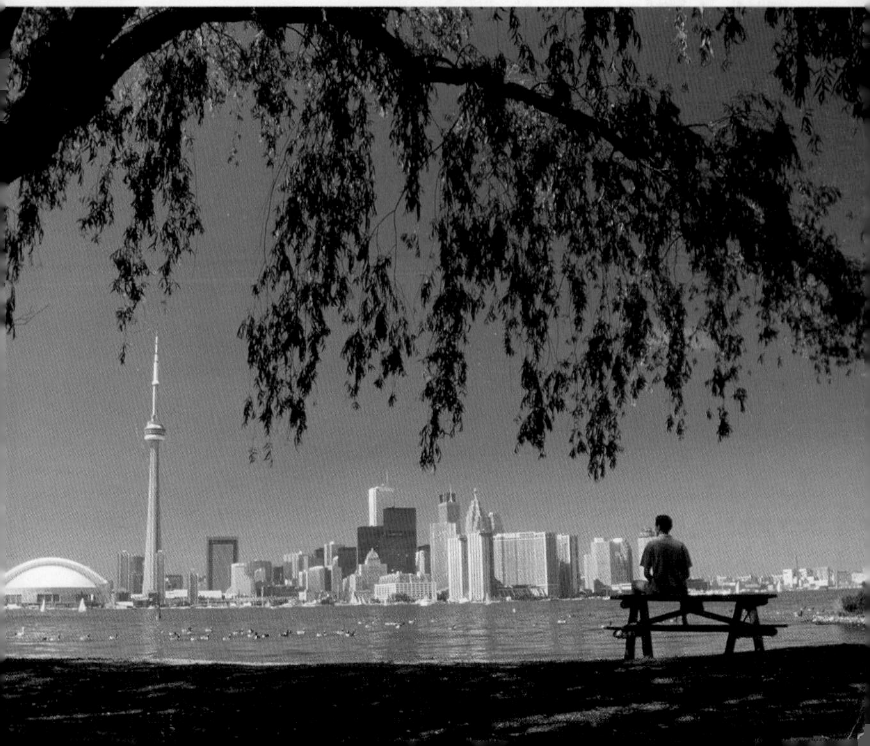

The Top Five

1 Royal Ontario Museum
A trove of ancient civilizations, natural history and art (p56)

2 Toronto Islands
Ferry over to visit beaches and sandbar bohemians (p64)

3 Casa Loma
Secret passages and skyline views inside a mock medieval tower (p58)

4 Niagara Falls
Barrel jumpers and millions of honeymooners (p176)

5 CN Tower
The highest free-standing structure in the world (p44)

Contents

Published by Lonely Planet Publications Pty Ltd
ABN 36 005 607 983

Australia Head Office, Locked Bag 1, Footscray, Victoria 3011, ☎ 03 8379 8000, fax 03 8379 8111, talk2us@lonelyplanet.com.au

USA 150 Linden St, Oakland, CA 94607, ☎ 510 893 8555, toll free 800 275 8555, fax 510 893 8572, info@lonelyplanet.com

UK 72–82 Rosebery Ave, Clerkenwell, London, EC1R 4RW, ☎ 020 7841 9000, fax 020 7841 9001, go@lonelyplanet.co.uk

France 1 rue du Dahomey, 75011 Paris, ☎ 01 55 25 33 00, fax 01 55 25 33 01, bip@lonelyplanet.fr, www.lonelyplanet.fr

Printed through Colorcraft Ltd, Hong Kong.
Printed in China

The Authors

SARA BENSON

Sara (nickname 'Sam') Benson first crossed the US–Canada border on a quest to find the wild heart of the Great White North, but along the way she got sidetracked by the Megacity's funky urban fashion, fusion food and film festivities. She has found herself drawn back to Canada surprisingly often, especially since signing on with Lonely Planet many moons ago. She has taken her readers from the mountains of Whistler to the wine country of the Niagara Peninsula, as well as hiking atop Hawaiian volcanoes, trekking through the Malaysian jungle and riding into the tangled backstreets of Okinawa. Already the veteran author of multiple Lonely Planet city guides, this is her second edition of Lonely Planet's *Toronto*.

CONTRIBUTING AUTHOR

MONICA BODIRSKY

Monica wrote the boxed text 'First Nations Foundations' (p33) in the History chapter. She is currently the coordinator of the Toronto Native Community History Project at the Native Canadian Centre of Toronto (p58).

PHOTOGRAPHER

COREY WISE

For photographer Corey Wise, a month-long stint in Europe visiting a friend unleashed a hopeless case of travel addiction and led to lengthy forays around the Middle East, Asia and South America. The camera became a means to document the journey. Toronto was a welcome change of venue, but Corey found plenty that was exotic, thanks to the city's extremely large immigrant population and architectural exuberance.

Lonely Planet books provide independent advice. Lonely Planet does not accept advertising in guidebooks, nor do we accept payment in exchange for listing or endorsing any place or business. Lonely Planet writers do not accept discounts or payments in exchange for positive coverage of any sort.

Introducing Toronto

Here in Canada's boldest metropolis, citizens of the Megacity know they've got the world at the cost of a subway token, the most inventive cuisine dangling from the edge of every fork, kaleidoscopic multicultural festivals that attract millions of people and a string of jewel-like islands and beaches. What, you were imagining the Great White North? Welcome to the new millennium, and Toronto's great spring thaw.

Like hypnotized subjects, many visitors can't say exactly what makes Toronto so satisfying. The spicy corners of the city's markets call, as do the beachfront boardwalks. Summer festivals seize you with their fervor, and a living mosaic of historical and ethnic neighborhoods will inspire wanderlust. You can disappear for a day in the crystal galleries of the Royal Ontario Museum or at Tommy Thompson Park, an oasis of wildlife on the shores of Lake Ontario. Toronto's very own islands lie in the waters of the lake, facing off against the downtown skyline. The longest transcontinental rail route in Canada starts here. Just beyond the city limits are the fertile vineyards of the Niagara Peninsula and, of course, the mighty falls themselves.

Diversity is what Toronto rightly uses to define its character. Since WWII this 'icebox' city has been melted by waves of Portuguese, Greek, Italian, Latin American, Chinese, Southeast Asian, Indian and Caribbean immigrants, their transplanted cultures largely undiminished by translation. Tolerance is a reigning virtue.

Yet the pages of Toronto's history have been engraved with rebellion, and the wildness of new world democracy. In 1837 the radical William Lyon Mackenzie led a farmers' militia down Yonge St against the Loyalists' tyrannous rule over Toronto. Almost 150 years later the 'sandbar bohemians'

Lowdown

Lazy pronunciation of Toronto, aka the Megacity tuh-*rah*-nuh

Population 2.5 million

Number of languages spoken at city hall Over 100

Time zone Eastern (EST/EDT)

Tim Horton's donut 80c

Coffee $1

TTC subway ride $2.25

Pint of local brew $3.50

Three-star hotel room $100 or so nightly

Distance covered by underground PATH shopping arcades 27km on Toronto Islands stood their ground against a municipal government that was evicting them from their island homes, and the rebels won.

And that's Toronto in a nutshell. Fiercely proud, enlightened and always going against the cultural grain. If Torontonians are united by anything, it's in their passionate debates about how to make life in 'Toronto the Good' even better. So hurry up and pack your suitcase, before someone lets the cat out of the bag. Visiting Toronto is the next best thing to a round-the-world ticket, after all.

SARA'S TOP TORONTO DAY

After a quick breakfast at the **St Lawrence Market** (p47), I stroll down to the **Harbourfront** (p41) and catch the ferry over to **Centre Island** (p65). I cycle along the boardwalk, then stop to admire the flower gardens on **Ward's Island** (p66) and take a perfect skyline photo of downtown. Back on the mainland, I'll ride the subway north from grand **Union Station** (p197). It's a short stroll to leafy **Baldwin Village** (p52), where I put up my feet at an outdoor café. As I wait for lunch to arrive, I flip through *Toronto Life* to find out about exhibitions at the **Art Gallery of Ontario** (p53), the **Royal Ontario Museum** (p56) or the quirky **Bata Shoe Museum** (p55). Once I've gotten my culture fix, I alight from the streetcar on **Queen West** (p61) for eclectic shopping and an artful dinner, followed by dessert from **Dufflet Pastries** (p107). With the alternative weekly *Now* in hand, I connect with a few local friends, maybe to see a live music show, attend a **Cinematheque Ontario** (p115) screening, or knock back a couple of pints at **C'est What** (p117) pub. I finish off with a free improv set at **Second City** (p128) before heading to bed, so I can wake up early and drive to the **Niagara Peninsula wine country** (p182) tomorrow.

Essential Toronto

- **Royal Ontario Museum** (p56)
- **Toronto Islands** (p64)
- **St Lawrence Market** (p47)
- **Harbourfront** (p41)
- **Queen West** (p61)

City Life

City Life

TORONTO TODAY

Backslapped by a string of bad luck at the beginning of the new millennium, Canada's Megacity is very Nietzschean in its adopted attitude that whatever doesn't kill it, only makes it stronger. Voters recently kicked out the conservative Tory government; brought in the Rolling Stones, AC/DC and the Flaming Lips for a relief concert after the outbreak of SARS; stopped construction of a new bridge to the Toronto Islands airport that would have changed the islanders' way of life forever; and tacked another first onto their already progressive resume by becoming the first city in North America to legalize same-sex marriage. Meanwhile life for most Torontonians just keeps getting better, with a rainbow of festivals, fashion and fantastic food just around every street corner. Even better news for residents, the economy looks ready to bounce back any day now. So what are you waiting for? Dive right into T.O.

CITY CALENDAR

Peak season runs from Victoria Day in late May to Labour Day in early September, during which time the squeeze on accommodations and lines at major attractions can become unreal. Everywhere stays open later during summer, and there are festivals on the streets each weekend. Other busy times are Easter, Thanksgiving, Christmas and New Year's, as well as during major special events, such as **Caribana** (p10) or the **Toronto International Film Festival** (p22).

July is the hottest, most humid month. Many Torontonians escape to the Harbourfront, Toronto Islands or the Beaches where, even if the ambient temperature is only a few degrees cooler, strong lakefront winds make it bearable. Subarctic winds blow in January, when many folks traverse the city using Toronto's underground PATH system (p88).

Public Holidays

New Year's Day January 1
Good Friday March/April
Easter Monday March/April
Victoria Day Monday preceding May 25
Canada Day July 1
Simcoe Day (Civic Holiday) August 1
Labour Day 1st Monday in September
Thanksgiving 2nd Monday in September
Remembrance Day November 11
Christmas Day December 25
Boxing Day December 26

JANUARY & FEBRUARY

WINTERCITY FESTIVAL

☎ 416-395-0490; www.city.toronto.on.ca/special_events

From late January through mid-February, the city pulls out all the stops to urge folks to defy the cold, offering free outdoor concerts, fireworks, arts and cultural events, special tourist packages and even a barbecue outside City Hall at **Nathan Phillips Square** (p50).

MARCH & APRIL

CANADA BLOOMS

☎ 416-447-8655; www.canadablooms.com

Heralding the arrival of spring, this is one of the most amazing horticultural expos in North America. Held in early March.

ONE OF A KIND SPRING SHOW & SALE

☎ 416-960-3680; www.oneofakindshow.com

Held in **Exhibition Place** (p41) in late March to early April, this show attracts fine artists, craftspeople and fashion designers.

MAY

DOORS OPEN TORONTO

www.doorsopen.org

Architectural treasures open their doors to the public during this festival (p26).

MILK INTERNATIONAL CHILDREN'S FESTIVAL OF THE ARTS

☎ **416-973-4000; www.harbourfront.on.ca/milk**

Around Victoria Day weekend, hundreds of kiddies take over the Harbourfront Centre (p129) for international puppetry, theater, dance and musical performances, as well as deliciously messy art workshops, outdoor games and storytelling events.

JUNE & JULY

TORONTO INTERNATIONAL DRAGON BOAT FESTIVAL

www.torontodragonboat.com

In a 2000-year-old Chinese tradition, these large, brightly decorated 'dragon' canoes are raced in waters around the **Toronto Islands** (p64) in mid-June. Over 120 teams compete to represent Canada internationally.

NORTH BY NORTHEAST (NXNE)

☎ **416-863-6963; www.nxne.com**

An independent music and film festival to rival South by Southwest (SXSW) in Austin, Texas. A $25 wristband gets you in to any of 400 new music shows at over two dozen clubs, all squeezed into one long weekend in mid-June.

NATIONAL ABORIGINAL DAY

Although not a statutory holiday, Canada's heritage of First Nations, Inuit and Métis cultures is celebrated on 21 June (the first day of the summer solstice) at many public places, including a powwow and cultural arts fair outside City Hall in **Nathan Phillips Square** (p50).

PRIDE WEEK

☎ **416-927-2433; www.pridetoronto.com**

Larger and more flamboyant every year, Pride Week climaxes in late June with an out-of-the-closet Dyke March and an outrageous Pride Parade, with the festival's G-spot in the **Church-Wellesley Village** (p54). Pick up an alternative weekly for a schedule of LGBTTIQ (lesbian, gay, bisexual, transsexual, transgender, intersex and queer!) events, most of which are free.

DU MAURIER DOWNTOWN JAZZ FESTIVAL

☎ **416-928-0233; www.tojazz.com**

For 10 days in late June and early July, jazz blazes in the streets, clubs and concert halls of the city centre, with musical workshops, film screenings and harbor cruises, too. Expect anyone from Wynton Marsalis to gospel choirs, with blues and world beat influences in the mix.

CARAVAN

☎ **416-977-0466; www.caravan-org.com**

A nine-day cultural exchange between ethnic groups, offering music, dance and food that is native to their homelands. A $25 passport entitles you to visit 25 different pavilions around the city in late June and early July.

SCREAM IN HIGH PARK

☎ **416-466-8862; www.thescream.ca**

Sit on a blanket under the stars and listen to local poets, novelists, storytellers and other wordsmiths from across Canada perform on the **Dream in High Park** (p124) stage, as well as at events around town. It all happens between late June and mid-July.

Hot Conversation Topics

- Dear God, what disaster awaits us next? Torontonians have had momentously bad luck recently, with outbreaks of West Nile virus and SARS, then the Great Blackout of 2003. But the city just keeps on kicking. Some residents even relish the chance to overthrow the city's reputation of 'Toronto the Good' for something more like 'Toronto the Badass.'
- Who cares about TIFF? When the **Toronto International Film Festival** (p22) comes to town, locals jump on the bandwagon to roundly abuse it as overly commercial, too much like Hollywood etc. But then who are those hundreds of star-watchers eagerly camped out by the red carpets? Surely they can't all be tourists.
- Can the Libs really be trusted? After almost a decade of Tory rule, the Liberal Party has been swept back into power across the province. But is it too little, too late? Are the Libs serious about solving social problems and cleaning up the environment? Or are they a kinder, gentler version of the old regime?
- What happened to the **Maple Leaf Gardens** (p54), eh? After standing empty on the auction block for a while, this Toronto landmark, where the Maple Leafs had played hockey since the 1930s and Elvis sang, was recently bought by Loblaws, a grocery chain. Loblaws intends to respect history as it redevelops the stadium. We'll see.

Top Five Quirky Events

- Canadian National Exhibition (right)
- Caribana (below)
- Milk International Children's Festival of the Arts (p9)
- Toronto International Dragon Boat Festival (p9)
- WinterCity Festival (p8)

MOLSON INDY

☎ 416-966-6202, 866-670-4639; www.molsonindy.com

Drivers from the international circuit compete in front of large crowds during the two days of practice and qualifying trials in mid-July, with the big race on the third day at **Exhibition Place** (p41). You'll hear the noise pollution everywhere.

BEACHES INTERNATIONAL JAZZ FESTIVAL

☎ 416-410-8809; www.beachesjazz.com

Going strong for more than 15 years, this high-caliber jazz festival in mid-July puts on free performances along Queen St E, at **Kew Gardens** (p64) and in the **Distillery Historic District** (p46). You may hear Chicago jazz cat Kurt Elling or an all-star local swing band.

TORONTO STAR BLUESFEST

☎ 416-489-2583; www.torontobluesfest.com

For most of a week in late July, major blues headliners from the south of the border and the west coast of Canada get together down at **Exhibition Place** (p41) with a late-night series at the intimate **Silver Dollar Room** (p123).

AUGUST

CARIBANA

☎ 877-673-2742; www.caribana.ca, www.caribana.com

This major Caribbean festival is held from late July through the beginning of August. The finale is a weekend of reggae, steel drum, and calypso music and dance with a huge carnival parade along Lake Shore Blvd W featuring outrageous costumes à la Rio. It can take five hours or more in passing – damn, that's some party!

TASTE OF THE DANFORTH

☎ 416-469-5634; www.tasteofthedanforth.com

Modeled on the Taste of Chicago, this multicultural food-and-music festival takes over the streets of Greektown in early August. Look for beer gardens, food booths, cooking demos, fashion and flamenco shows.

CANADIAN NATIONAL EXHIBITION (CNE)

www.theex.com

The Ex claims to be the oldest and largest annual exhibition in the world, dating from 1879 when admission cost just 25¢. Over 700 exhibitors put on agricultural shows, lumberjack competitions, outdoor concerts, carnival games and rides at **Exhibition Place** (p41). This is topped by an air show and fireworks for two weeks prior to, and including, Labour Day.

SEPTEMBER

TORONTO INTERNATIONAL FILM FESTIVAL (TIFF)

☎ 416-968-3456; www.bell.ca/filmfest

Toronto's prestigious 10-day celebration is one of the world's best film festivals (p22).

Canadiana 101: Top Five Books & Websites

- American's Guide to Canada (www.culture.ca) – all the facts about Canada, including what Royal Mounties actually do out there on the prairies, straight from the federal government's mouthpiece
- Canada's Cultural Gateway (www.icomm.ca/emily) – a sassy look at the critical differences between the USA and its northern neighbor (eg which one has more doughnut shops per capita)
- *Canuck Chicks and Maple Leaf Mamas: Women of the Great White North* by Ann Douglas (2002) – a romp through two centuries of Canadian 'herstory'; browse excerpts online at www.canuckchicks.com
- *Mondo Canuck* by Geoff Pevere (1996) – an encyclopedia of Canadian pop culture, including why Canadian TV sitcoms just aren't funny
- *Why I Hate Canadians* by Will Ferguson (1999) – this provocatively titled book decimates the myth of making love in a canoe, and the author is even a true-blooded Canuck; he also wrote *Bastards and Boneheads: Canada's Glorious Leaders, Past and Present* (1999) and *How to Be a Canadian: Even If You Already Are One* (2001), coauthored by his brother Ian Ferguson

WinterCity Festival (p8)

CABBAGETOWN CULTURAL FESTIVAL

☎ 416-921-0857; www.oldcabbagetown.com

A family-friendly celebration held the first weekend after Labour Day, featuring corn roasts, pancake breakfast (yes, with Canadian maple syrup), a minifestival of film and video, performing arts events and historic home tours.

OCTOBER

INTERNATIONAL FESTIVAL OF AUTHORS

☎ 416-973-4000; www.readings.org

Part of the **Harbourfront Reading Series** (p127), the festival brings over 100 acclaimed authors from Canada and abroad to the **Harbourfront Centre** (p129) for readings, panel discussions, lectures, awards and book signings.

NOVEMBER & DECEMBER

CANADIAN ABORIGINAL FESTIVAL

☎ 519-751-0040; www.canab.com

This is a multiday celebration of dancing, drumming, artisan crafts, new films and traditional teachings, as well as a lacrosse competition at **SkyDome** (p45). Takes place late November.

CHRISTMAS & NEW YEAR'S EVE

☎ 416-392-8674; www.city.toronto.ca/culture

In the weeks leading up to Christmas, traditional celebrations light up **Casa Loma** (p58), **Mackenzie House** (p50), **Black Creek Pioneer Village** (p77) and other cultural venues. The **Church of the Holy Trinity** (p50) puts on a musical Christmas pageant that's not to be missed. Right before the New Year, **First Night Toronto** (☎ 416-341-3143; www.firstnight.toronto.com) organizes family-friendly shows inside **SkyDome** (p45).

CULTURE

IDENTITY

Like most Canadians, Toronto residents more easily define themselves by what they are *not* (eg not Americans, or not Québecois), rather than positively defining who they actually are.

The English modernist Wyndham Lewis said of Toronto, 'O for a half-hour of Europe after this sanctimonious icebox!' Indeed, the long-standing tag of 'Toronto the Good' has been hard to shake. From its beginnings as a safe haven for Loyalists fleeing the American Revolution, the town was ruled by a conservative British colonial society of first families led by politically savvy Anglican clergy. In 1906 the Lord's Day Act was passed, which forbade working and most socializing on Sunday: Eaton's department store drew its curtains to guard against 'sinful' window shopping and city playgrounds were chained up and locked. Shockingly, these antivice laws remained on the books until 1950.

Today Toronto is Canada's most culturally diverse city, with more than 70 ethnic groups residing here and over 100 languages spoken. About half of the city's residents were born outside Canada. The urban sprawl beyond the new Megacity boundaries, known as the Greater Toronto Area (GTA), accounts for one in seven Canadians, and continues to swell with new immigrants who arrive steadily from every corner of the globe. Just about the only thing that can be said of all Torontonians is that they absolutely insist on identifying their city as 'world class,' and rightly so.

Canadians are more lax about religious practice than their US counterparts, and generally don't mix religion with politics. Tolerance is a way of life, with a high number of 'affirming' congregations that ordain, marry and welcome the lesbigay community. There are also many places such as downtown's **Church of the Holy Trinity** (p50), where most members come for the social activism and not the Sunday service. Historically, Jews have been a strong presence in Toronto. Buddhism predominates among Asian communities, with a small but notable Tibetan Buddhist presence.

Free for All

A random sampling of a few days' worth of community events in the Megacity as they appeared in the free weekly *Now Toronto* (p204):

- 'Out to Play,' a social night for queer Asian youth.
- Free university lecture on international migration to the Americas.
- A songwriting workshop with a local musician at a café.
- Weekly dharma talk and walking meditation at Tengye Ling Tibetan Buddhist Temple.
- A mock tribunal by antipoverty activists to virtually 'evict' prodevelopment forces.
- A Harbourfront fair for bookbinders and booksellers.
- Screenings of procycling films organized around the theme of 'Divorcing Your Car'.
- Guided tours of world's last standing double-decker theater.
- A forum on sustainable-living practices led by a wind-energy expert.
- Local muralists' demonstrations of 'Wild Aerosol Street Art' at a shopping mall.

Toronto's Aboriginal population, comprised mostly of First Nations people, is only just over 10,000 people. Although a 1997 Supreme Court ruling stated that Aboriginal people have legitimate title to their lands, based on their oral histories, and that government has a 'moral duty' to negotiate with them, it hasn't helped Aboriginal groups without a land base, such as those in urban areas like Toronto. The nearest established community is Brantford's Six Nations of the Grand River Territory, near the Niagara Peninsula. *Back on the Rez: Finding the Way Home* (1996) by Brian Maracle is a true account of one Torontonian's return to life on the reserve after 40 years away.

LIFESTYLE

Describing the city in 1984, Jan Morris wrote that the people here were 'incoherently polite' and that 'even the imminent explosion of a nuclear bomb would not induce its citizens to ignore a red light at a pedestrian crossing.'

In general, Torontonians are still very mannerly, if a bit standoffish. Torontonians think seriously about how to live their daily lives, meaning everything from recycling to how to treat one's neighbor to the future of indie music.

Although Torontonians are less hesitant to speak their mind than other Canadians, especially when it comes to criticizing Americans, tolerance remains a virtue. Most welcome the city's multiculturalism, especially with its attendant festivals, vibrant arts scene and fusion cuisine. Eating and drinking are major pursuits, with life lived outdoors as much as possible, especially during summer.

Quiet residential blocks scattered throughout the city centre boast shady trees, one-way streets (called 'traffic calming zones') and Victorian row houses, all making Toronto a particularly pleasant place to live.

Top Five Chefs to Dine For

Chefs jump from restaurant to restaurant, and their reputation travels with them. Read the fine print on the menu to see if you're feasting on the inventive creations of:

- David Chrystian – skipping from Cafe Societa to reign over Patriot, a short-lived Canadiana restaurant on Bloor St, Chrystian is now tackling another adventure: running the dining room at the resurrected Drake Hotel on bohemian Queen West
- Chris Klugman – once Geena Davis' personal chef, Klugman has worked in the kitchens of **Oro** (p101) and the **Rosewater Supper Club** (p95), but has dropped out of the power-dining scene to run a quirky gourmet grocery, the Summerhill Market, up in Rosedale
- Susur Lee – welcomed home like a prodigal son after a stint in East Asia, this ponytailed Hong Kong chef reigns supreme serving imaginative cuisine at **Susur** (p107)
- Pascal Ribreau – after languishing in middling French kitchens, Ribreau has struck out on his own at sparkling **Celestin** (p111), a success made all the more triumphant since it comes after he survived a paralyzing car accident in the late 1990s
- Dufflet Rosenberg – Toronto's 'Queen of Cake' started her pastry biz at home in 1975; today her storefront, **Dufflet Pastries** (p107) on Queen West, is divine

FOOD & DRINK

When traveling you want to try the local cuisine. Except in Canada, because what's there to try? A bit of charred moose? Maple syrup pie? Once upon a time there was only Québecois cuisine, but all that has changed. Be careful not to think Yukon Gold potatoes are anything more than just plain potatoes, or that seafood labeled as being from Prince Edward Island is necessarily anything special. Actual Canadian nouveau cuisine combines unusual, fresh (often organic) local ingredients with classic French stylings and daring fusion from Asia. In essence, it's a bit like Californian cuisine, but fleshed out with northern game and continental-inspired sauces.

Most Torontonians are epicureans, and the names of local chefs roll off their tongues as easily as the names of movie stars. People here are as comfortable with chopsticks in a bowl of *pho* as they are using proper silver during afternoon tea at the **Windsor Arms** (p166). *Toronto Life* devotes several pages every month to restaurant reviews. What's more, the city's high-flying restaurants have some of the top tables in North America, and many of these belong to the Oliver Bonacini group, including **Canoe** (p94) and **Auberge du Pommier** (p111).

Another influence on the local cuisine is the bountiful Niagara Peninsula wine country (p182). You should not miss out on trying some ice wine vintages (p185). However, the classic cocktail of a Bloody Caesar – basically a Bloody Mary, but made with clamato juice – can be skipped. Happily, microbrew culture is alive and well in Toronto, with several pubs and bars serving beers made in the city and around Ontario, as well as from Québec and British Columbia. Of late bubble tea shops with tapioca pearls have overtaken coffeehouses in popularity, and juice bars like **Fresh by Juice for Life** (p98) are seriously good.

Top Five Cookbooks

- *The ACE Bakery Cookbook* by Linda Haynes and James Chatto (2003) – by a beloved local artisan bakery that supplies many top hotels
- *The Chef's Table* by Lucy Waverman (2000) – beautifully records the creations of top chefs during the annual **Toronto Taste** (p111), with superb background color on the city's culinary scene
- *Great Canadian Cuisine* by Anita Stewart (1999) – features recipes collected from Canadian Pacific railway luxury hotels across the nation, including Toronto's own **Fairmont Royal York** (p161)
- *Niagara Flavours: Recipes from Southwest Ontario's Finest Chefs* by Brenda Matthews and Linda Bramble (2003) – a contemporary guide to wine country cooking
- *Wanda's Pie in the Sky* by Wanda Beaver (2002) – the next best thing to visiting her eponymous Yorkville café (p103)

FASHION

Toronto's sense of fashion is a fascinating hybrid, with tastes of international designers on Bloor St, a treasure trove of vintage wear in Kensington Market and local fashion mavens setting up shops on Queen West. Fashion weeks in the spring and fall bring out the best of cutting-edge native talent, like clothing artist **Annie Thompson** (p155) and Damzels in This Dress designs. Now owned by Estée Lauder, the MAC makeup collections (with its slogan 'All ages. All races. All genders.') also started in Toronto. Past spokespeople have included RuPaul and alt-country musician kd lang. Every year the company donates millions to AIDS research. Meanwhile, younger designers have banded together to open places such as **Fresh Collective** (p156), one of several co-op boutiques. New businesses, such as **Modrobes** (p148), stake their success on niche marketing, while others use artistic innovations to make their mark, such as the silk screenings done by **Peach Berserk** (p156). Re-crafted vintage clothing is found at **Preloved** (p156) and celebrity knitwear at **Fresh Baked Goods** (154). Tattoos and piercings are just as much of a fashion statement, too, as are haircuts by Montréal cult salon **Coupe Bizzarre** (p141).

By the Numbers

Canadian immigrants who settle in Toronto 1 out of every 4

Tibetan Buddhist temples in the Megacity 3

Unemployment rate 8%

Number of municipal beaches 14

Percentage of the US population within a day's drive of Toronto 50%

Number of bridges 535

Population density per sq km 3800

Total length of city sidewalks 7060km

Median family income $64,000

Estimated number of visitors during Pride Week 1 million

SPORTS

Despite the fact that the Toronto Maple Leafs hasn't won the Stanley Cup since 1967, the city is still mad for hockey all winter long. Toronto's most legendary player is none other than Wayne Gretzky, the greatest hockey player who ever lived, according to Canadians. In summer you can catch amateur indoor hockey games at arenas around the greater Toronto area, especially in Etobicoke. An ice-resurfacing machine, called a Zamboni, always makes an appearance.

Observed by a Jesuit missionary during the 1600s, when teams of up to hundreds of First Nations warriors placed goals miles apart and competed from sunrise to sundown, lacrosse is often called 'the fastest game on two feet.' Modern matches are played on an indoor hockey rink, where players use a modified stick with an attached basket to score goals. The blazing Toronto Rock has won the National Lacrosse League's championship four times.

When the Toronto Blue Jays won the World Series (twice!) in the early 1990s, they became the only non-US team ever to win Major League Baseball's highest prize. The struggling Toronto Raptors belong to the Central Division of the NBA's Eastern Conference, along with such illustrious basketball teams as the Chicago Bulls and the Detroit Pistons.

Canadian football is an odd duck, and as for its differences from American-style football, think 'longer, wider and faster.'

If you want to visit the racetrack where Secretariat ran his last race turn to p135. If you would prefer to play golf at Glen Abbey, where Tiger Woods clinched the Triple Crown in 2000, turn to p136.

MEDIA

Toronto is the centre of English-language publishing in Canada. Although newsstands aren't generally found on the street, the city has an abundance of magazine shops, such as **La Maison de la Presse Internationale** (p151), to fulfill residents' voracious appetites for news. Toronto is also a centre for TV, film and radio production. Downtown you'll find the

Newspaper boxes

English-language headquarters of the **Canadian Broadcasting Corporation** (p48), as well as the ever-expanding empire of **Citytv** (p22) run by Moses Znaimer. Whatever the mainstream media lacks in diversity, the city's myriad alternative weeklies, monthly magazines, multicultural radio stations and foreign-language newspapers more than make up for. Turn to p204 for a thumbnail guide to local print media and p205 for a rundown of radio stations.

LANGUAGE

We challenge you to tell us of a language that isn't spoken in the Megacity. Official notices from City Hall are printed in Chinese, English, French, Greek, Italian, Polish, Portuguese, Spanish, Tagalog and Tamil. Unlike those in the rest of Canada, most of Toronto's bilingual signs are written in English and Chinese, not French. Those few French signs are most visible near the US border, as if Ontario wants to hit arriving Americans over the head with the message, 'We are Canadian! We are bilingual! Voilà!'

In practice, the city is predominantly Anglophone. Residents may not exactly speak the Queen's English, but many British terms and spellings (eg 'centre' instead of center) are in common use. The proper pronunciation of the city's name (and many of its streets) troubles visitors. You can pick out the newbies by how they enunciate each syllable of 'toh-*rawn*-toh,' while natives often slur it into almost a grunt, 'tuh-*rah*-nuh.'

As a quickly glossary of Canuck (Canadian) slang, 'ski-doo' means snowmobile, a 'toque' (rhymes with duke) is a winter hat, 'peameal bacon' is cured (not smoked) pork loins (similar to what US citizens aptly call Canadian bacon), a 'Newfie' is someone

The Oracle of the Electronic Age

One of the great critics hailing from the University of Toronto was Marshall McLuhan, a cultural commentator who preached on the 20th-century explosion of electronic media and its ability to hypnotize us into passivity. His most famous book, *The Medium is the Massage*, propelled McLuhan to the forefront of 1960s counterculture. John Lennon, Yoko Ono and other pilgrims all came to visit him during his tenure as the director of UT's Centre for Culture and Technology. Today McLuhan is best remembered for his outlandish wordplay, evidenced by statements like 'the future of the book is the blurb,' and his prediction that TV would unite us all in a global village.

hailing from the province of Newfoundland (a source of much amusement to many Canadians) and a 'hoser' is a beer-drinking idiot.

For a full explanation of the ubiquitous tag 'eh?,' we refer you to Will and Ian Ferguson's book *How to Be a Canadian: Even if You Already Are One* (p10).

ECONOMY & COSTS

From its colonial roots in the fur trade, Toronto has grown to be pivotal in Canada's economy. The Toronto Stock Exchange, which opened in 1937, conducts over $100 million worth of business each day from its high-rise tower just west of Bay St. Canada's five largest banks are headquartered in the Financial District. The city has the nation's busiest airport, serves as a central port for the Great Lakes and straddles two industrial powerhouses, one of which is the 'Golden Horseshoe' along Lake Ontario's horseshoe-shaped western shore from Niagara Falls to Hamilton and the other is the Québec–Windsor corridor.

At the beginning of the 20th century, Britain was Canada's strongest trading partner, but in the 21st century the USA snaps up more than three-quarters of Canada's exports, especially raw materials. Since the passage of the Free Trade Agreement (what Americans call NAFTA), the border has become ever more porous. Alarmists decry the 'brain drain' of highly educated Canadian professionals who leave for higher-paying jobs in the south. The 2003 outbreak of SARS cost the city a billion dollars in lost revenue from tourism, airport fees and retail sales.

Arguably the most expensive city in Canada, for US and European visitors Toronto may seem like a bargain travel destination. Families can take advantage of discounted admission at museums and attractions, and kids stay free at many hotels. The most expensive item in anyone's budget is likely to be their plane ticket and, after that, accommodations. Sleeping at a B&B, eating at neighborhood restaurants and allowing yourself freedom with your entertainment dollar costs $100 or so per day for each of two people traveling together. Anything more (say you had an unlimited expense account) and you could choose the **Fairmont Royal York** (p161), sky boxes at **SkyDome** (p45) and dinner at **Canoe** (p94).

How Much?

Airport shuttle $15

B&B room with private bathroom $85

Glass of wine $6

Harbor cruise $20

Liter of gasoline 70¢

Metered parking $2 per hour

Movie ticket $10

Museum admission $5 to $15

Peameal bacon sandwich $3.50

Short taxi ride $8

GOVERNMENT & POLITICS

Once the capital of Canada, today Toronto is the capital of Ontario province (although Ottawa is only a short plane hop away). Relations between the three levels of government – municipal, provincial and federal – are Byzantine with overlapping responsibilities, as well as gaps where no one seems to be minding the store.

The mayor presides over the city council, which has 44 members who hail from the city's different wards. The city council is the primary legislative body. Watching the council in session can be like watching a Shakespearean drama, with mad ravings and fools letting insults fly.

When Charles Dickens visited the city in the 1840s, he decried its 'rabid Toryism,' and the Union Jack still appears on the provincial flag. But the Tories were long out of power until Mike Harris' promises of tax cuts and reduced social spending returned them to power with a majority in 1995. After being elected, the Tories slashed government jobs, shut down hospitals and weakened labor laws.

Toronto politics have been traditionally progressive, but these right-wing provincial politics shifted the political climate of the city as a whole. In 1997 the amalgamation of the

Megacity (p30) created a strong new suburban voting bloc that swept Mel Lastman, the former mayor of North York, into power. Although mayors traditionally aren't required to announce a party affiliation, Lastman was clearly comfortable with the Tories.

But Torontonians weren't comfortable with him. Shortly after the Liberal Party was returned to power in provincial elections during 2003 with Dalton McGuinty as the new premier, voters elected David Miller, a former councilman from High Park, as the new mayor. Whether he can live up to his promises of cleaning up the city's environment and corruption at City Hall is anyone's guess.

ENVIRONMENT

THE LAND

Ontario is separated from the prairies of western Canada by the massive Canadian Shield, a stretch of Precambrian rock more than 1600km long and formed by a prehistoric glacier. Toronto itself was once under the waters of Lake Iroquois. This ancient sea extended as far north as the rise upon which **Casa Loma** (p58) sits today, where the old shore cliffs eroded over millennia are still visible. Today the modern city sits beside Lake Ontario, part of the chain of Great Lakes shared between Canada and the USA. The **Toronto Islands** (p64), originally a 9km-long sandbar peninsula, were created by a violent 19th-century storm. The sandbar itself was first formed by drifting erosion from the **Scarborough Bluffs** (p75), massive heights formed by over five different eras of glacial deposits, found farther east. Overall, the land around Toronto is flat, making it easy for walking.

GREEN TORONTO

On the streets of Toronto today, recycling bins are as common as garbage cans. Toronto is not Los Angeles, but visitors to the **CN Tower** (p44) will still notice haze problems. Although many residents are progressive cyclists, there are still too many vehicles on the streets. City Hall has even enacted a bylaw to prevent motorists from idling their cars more than a few minutes.

Financial District (p43)

Torontonians do love their lakefront beaches and recreational paths. Even old shipping quays have been converted along the Harbourfront, for example into the **Toronto Music Garden** (p43). Almost every square block of the city core, whether it's a tree-lined residential street or a small conservatory tucked between skyscrapers, utilizes its green space, and river ravines have largely been left wild.

URBAN PLANNING & DEVELOPMENT

Toronto had been tinkering with its environment even before it decided to push around the Don River during the construction of the parkway during the 1950s. During the past few decades, the Toronto & Region Conservation Authority has wisely based its conservation acts on sounder ecology, evidenced in the astounding success of **Tommy Thompson Park** (p63) and the regeneration of natural wetlands at **Grenadier Pond** (p77).

Community groups play an active role in fighting against ill-planned urban development, largely driven by explosive population growth. Most battles over development focus on the Harbourfront area, where City Hall's optimistic 'Making Waves' plan outlines 40,000 new housing units (mostly high-rise condos), even as it allows for just 40 acres of open space.

One of the city's recurring environmental nightmares is the toxic water conditions along the shoreline of Lake Ontario. Any sudden, heavy rains cause sewage treatment plants to overflow, which sends all of the garbage and bacteria (such as *E coli*) straight out into the lake. Summer beach closures are regularly announced on TV.

Arts

Arts

Toronto's arts scene is as diverse as its population, with a heritage of world-class fine arts stretching back to its early years as the colonial town of York. Toronto is a wellspring of Canadian literature, and its theater scene is overshadowed only by New York's and London's. But the city is best known for its celebration of cinema, particularly the wildly popular Toronto International Film Festival. The North by Northeast indie music festival is another magnet for indie-music fans. Visual artists have resurrected a few Victorian-era industrial complexes around town, while masterpieces from decades past hang in the galleries. And the city's architecture is a work of art unto itself, sometimes haphazard but always ready with beautifully restored gems and innovative new designs.

CINEMA & TELEVISION

Toronto is unquestionably the Hollywood of the North, despite the fact that Torontonians tend to favor more independent cinema. The **Toronto International Film Festival** (TIFF; p22) has a sterling reputation and draws an international crowd. More international film stars and directors come from this region than you might think. Many of them are completely assimilated into the Hollywood culture south of the border, so let's just call 'em crypto Canadians. Check out www.northernstars.ca to unmask a few.

Just like their Vancouver and Montréal cousins, locals are actually used to tripping over film sets and trailers as they go about their business (or perhaps where they actually *do* business). On any given day you will find as many as 40 movies, TV shows and music videos shooting around town. Entire blocks are merrily roped off and traffic rerouted, all for the sake of the gigantic contributions that film crews and the **Toronto Film and Television Office** (TFTO; www.city.toronto.on.ca/tfto) make to the city's economy.

ON LOCATION

The city has represented more than half of the United States on film, as well as several countries in Europe. To cover the hundreds of titles filmed on location here would take a guidebook of its own, so we'll just cover a few highlights.

The TV series *Queer as Folk* is based in the **Church-Wellesley Village** (p54), and has also shot scenes at the **Art Gallery of Ontario** (p53) and Seduction sex shop on the Yonge Street Strip.

Top Five Films

Innumerable films have been shot in Toronto, but very few movie storylines are set here (with a few bizarre exceptions). Torontonian directors, on the other hand, are pretty prolific.

- *Adventures of Bob & Doug McKenzie: The Strange Brew* directed by, and starring, Rick Moranis and Dave Thomas (1983) – a wacky cult romp that spoofs the touchstones of Canadian pop culture: doughnuts, hockey and beer
- *Hollywood North* directed by Peter O'Brian (2003) – a satirical look at the Canadian film industry and its tangled love affair with Hollywood, set in the 1980s; north-of-the-border viewers will appreciate the insider jokes
- *Last Night* directed by Don McKellar (1998) – a bizarre end-of-the-world fantasy, with Toronto denizens going on a violent rampage, overturning TTC streetcars and making suicide pacts; David Cronenberg has a bit part
- *M Butterfly* directed by David Cronenberg (1993) – often depraved and called a 'baron of blood,' director David Cronenberg occasionally reaches for higher ground in challenging film adaptations, such as this beautiful failure starring Jeremy Irons and John Lone
- *The Sweet Hereafter* directed by Atom Egoyan (1997) – another poignant film by Atom Egoyan, this one is loosely based on a true story, focusing on the aftershocks of a fatal school bus accident that rips apart a small town

When Minnie Driver and Matt Damon go shopping in *Good Will Hunting* (1997), they're at the **Ontario Specialty Co** (133 Church St) – ask to see the autographed movie stills under the front counter.

Xavier's academy from the movie *X-Men* (2000) was filmed inside **Casa Loma** (p58). Keanu Reeves sped through **Allan Gardens** (p62) and **Union Station** (p197) in *Johnny Mnemonic* (1995), while the **Elgin & Winter Garden Theatre Centre** (p124) appeared in *Blues Brothers 2000* (1998). More recently, scenes from *Bulletproof Monk* (2003) and *Chicago* (2002) were shot here. Digging back further into the past, *The Black Stallion* (1979), with Francis Ford Coppola as the executive producer, was set at the **Woodbine Racetrack** (p135).

Almost any other T.O. tourist attraction has also appeared in countless movies and TV shows, including the **RC Harris Filtration Plant** (p64). Go to www.to-ontfilm.com for an online gallery of film locations – you'll recognize some of them right away.

Toronto Reference Library (p56)

LOCAL HEROES

The director of way-out-there films such as *Videodrome* (1983), *The Fly* (1986), *Naked Lunch* (1991) and *eXistenZ* (1999), David Cronenberg was born right here in Toronto and graduated from the University of Toronto (UT). Cronenberg has a predilection for playing unusual bit parts in all sorts of TV series, most recently a surgeon on the spy drama *Alias*.

Atom Egoyan, another renowned Canadian director, starting making movies while a student at UT. His works, including *Exotica* (1994) and *Ararat* (2002), are often big doses of bitter reality. Egoyan also writes screenplays and once directed a production of *Salome* for the Canadian Opera Company. And yes, he was named in honor of a nuclear reactor built in Egypt, from where his Armenian family immigrated to Toronto.

Another UT alumnus, Toronto-born Norman Jewison worked as a director and producer at the CBC during television's 'Golden Age' before moving to the US to launch *Your Hit Parade* and make feature films. He got his big break when he was called in to finish Sam Peckinpah's *The Cincinnati Kid* (1965), but his crowning achievement was directing the Academy Award–winning *In the Heat of the Night* (1967), a film about racial tensions in the US. It was in part his success that revived the Canadian film industry during the 1960s. Jewison's recent titles include *The Hurricane* (1999), a biographic drama starring Denzel Washington, and *The Statement* (2003), a thriller about a hunted Nazi war criminal and the Catholic church.

When it comes to actors, Toronto has churned out comedy stars by the dozen. Those who got their start at legendary **Second City** (p128) include Gilda Radner, Dan Aykroyd and Mike Myers, all of whom moved on to New York's *Saturday Night Live* TV show. If you ever wondered why the doughnut shop was such a big deal in 'Wayne's World' skits, blame it on Mike Myers being a true Canuck. He grew up in suburban Scarborough and remains to this day a die-hard Toronto Maple Leafs fan.

Another successful Ontario comedian, but one who took a different career path, is Jim Carrey. After working as a factory janitor during his teens, Carrey began doing open-mic performances at the comedy club **Yuk Yuk's** (p128). His physical routines and wild impersonations went over so well that he took off with his newfound fame to LA, where Rodney Dangerfield finally 'discovered' him.

Toronto's dirty little secret is that Keanu Reeves, who was born in Beirut, Lebanon, actually grew up in T.O.

Hollywood o' the North

Every September as autumn winds start to gust, the film world starts its annual migration to the Great White North, all for the sake of the acclaimed Toronto International Film Festival (TIFF). For 10 days, the city is turned into a cinephile's paradise. Red carpets roll out for the stars such as Nicole Kidman and Sofia Coppola, while adoring fans stalk the limo drivers outside the **Four Seasons** (p165) hotel in hope of an autograph or a quickie photo op. Almost a dozen cinemas show films nonstop, from early-morning show times into the 'Midnight Madness' hour. Film critics dart around like spies to a dozen movies a day, while ingénues stare at their festival ticket books, looking a tad lost, yet ecstatic just to be here.

It all started off as an idea tossed around over lunch nearly three decades ago by two unlikely candidates, a lawyer and a mayoral assistant. Except that the lawyer was already a fixture at the Cannes film festival and the assistant was a film producer. They weren't the first to dream up a potent media cocktail of Toronto and movies. But it wasn't until 1976 – when their 'Festival of Festivals' opened with *Cousin, Cousine* at Ontario Place's **Cinesphere** (p114) – that an embryonic international film festival got rolling. At first it was run on a hope and a prayer: films were delivered by bicycle, creditors were put off and there were wild rumors of stars who never showed. Back then it cost $150 for the VIP treatment. Nowadays, gold packages that include invites to all the galas with stars cost $3000 – and they sell out.

Critics and the film industry acknowledge that Toronto's festival has grown into one of the most prestigious and influential in the world, perhaps second only to Cannes. In 2003 over half of the 339 films from 55 countries screened over 10 days were premieres. Toronto festival films have won hundreds of Academy Awards over the years. Along the way the festival has been instrumental in launching local directors like Atom Egoyan and helping to revive the entire Canadian film industry. Designs already have been unveiled for a brand-new **Festival Tower**, which will have a film library, year-round screening rooms and a rooftop terrace, at King and John Sts in the Entertainment District.

Each year over 1000 volunteers help make it all happen. Festival themes change, but noteworthy series include 'Contemporary World Cinema,' 'Real to Reel' documentaries, boundary-breaking 'Visions' and, of course, the cult favorite, 'Midnight Madness.' Tickets (☎ 416-968-3456; www.bell.ca/filmfest) go on sale in early July by phone, fax or on-line. The early-bird pass costs $350 ($145 for a daytime pass), and coupon books for 10 ($115) or 30 ($275) movies can be bought separately. Festival-goers show up a week before opening night in late August to pick up a program, submit ticket request orders for the lottery and cross their fingers to get the shows they want to see. Single tickets for what's left are sold afterward for $14.50. Same-day tickets ($15.50) may be available from the theaters one hour before the first show of the day; rush tickets are sold five minutes before show time, but do not guarantee a seat and you'll usually have to queue in advance. Check the free weeklies and major newspapers for film festival miniguides, or snag the *Festival Daily* newspaper from festival cinemas.

In the interests of getting the most bang for your buck, here are some TIFF tips:

- The magic number – don't attempt to see more than three movies a day
- Feast on the buffet – don't settle for just one genre or one region of the world
- Support indie filmmakers – don't pick movies that are going into wide release anyway
- Relax, don't read 'the bible' – only the most intrepid film geeks read the festival program guide cover to cover, so relax
- You're not a superhero – don't schedule back-to-back screenings at cinemas across town
- No one can live on popcorn alone – bring along some trail mix, Red Bull, power bars – whatever it takes to sustain you through a 12-hour day of movie viewing
- Even if it's your 35th film of the week, please don't yap through it

THE SMALL SCREEN

Although addicted to the silver screen, Torontonians are also enamored of their TV sets. Moses Znaimer, a television visionary, is the cofounder of the continually expanding Citytv world, which includes over a dozen specialty channels. The downtown **Chum/Citytv Complex** (p49) is home to MuchMusic (a sort of Canadian MTV), the Bravo! arts channel and upstart Citytv (http://toronto.citytv.com), which broadcasts outtakes from **Speakers Corner** (p49). Znaimer's personal collection of vintage television sets forms the nucleus of the **MZTV Museum** (p50).

Global cable station imports all of the prime-time gems as well as the dross from south of the border (ie the USA). *Will & Grace* stars Eric McCormack, who was born in Toronto and attended theater school at Ryerson University. *Queer as Folk*, another gay-themed series that can be as much of a guilty pleasure as *Sex and the City*, actually films in Toronto. The public **Canadian Broadcasting Corporation** (CBC) also does a lot of filming around the city, based out of its English-language radio and TV production headquarters downtown.

LITERATURE

As the de facto English-language capital of Canada, Toronto has been fertile ground for as many homegrown writers as it has authors in exile. Each year the **Harbourfront Reading Series** (p127) puts together the **International Festival of Authors** (p11), a veritable who's who of Canadian letters. Look for local literati at the **Scream in High Park** (p9). The spoken word scene is fired-up year-round and mixes with sketch comedy, video and performance art. Cabarets and bars are the venues of choice (p127).

More than a few Canadian literary giants have studied at UT, including Margaret Atwood (1939–) and Ceylon-born Michael Ondaatje (1943–). Ondaatje became famous for his novel *The English Patient*, but his earlier fiction and poetry are equally moving for their tales of lyrically broken lives, postcolonial cultural clashes and the loss of identity. Literary lioness Margaret Atwood, for better or for worse, has become synonymous with modern Canadian literature. A long bibliography of novels, short fiction, poetry, children's books and screenplays includes *The Handmaid's Tale*, an allegedly feminist story set in a future world of straw men. It is now quite dated, but remains her most famous work.

On the pop fiction front, 'Toronto the Good' was the original publishing home of none other than the Harlequin Romance series. Modern potboilers and historical fiction by Rosedale boy Timothy Findley (1930–) are set mostly in Toronto. The beloved children's writer, city poet laureate Dennis Lee (1939–) penned the lyrics to the theme song for the TV show *Fraggle Rock* here. And don't miss the visual ('concrete') poem by bp Nichol (1944–88) drilled into bp Nichol Lane, running north off Sussex Ave between Huron and St George Sts. It's inscribed beside the historic Coach House Press, which was associated with the avant-garde *Open Letter* poetry journal of the 1970s and '80s. Today the press publishes much of its catalogue on-line (www.chbooks.com), where you can leave tips for authors.

Top 10 Books

Although Toronto is a place where great works are penned, not too many great works of literature actually feature the city. Our favorite works of imagination either about Toronto or by famous Torontonians include:

- *Alligator Pie* by Dennis Lee (1974) – these magical rhyming nonsense poems have wormed their way into the brains of two generations of youngsters
- *The Blind Assassin* by Margaret Atwood (2002) – this richly layered novel is a tale of two Canadian sisters in the aftermath of WWII. It won Atwood the prestigious Booker Prize
- *Cabbagetown* by Hugh Garner (1950) – a classic reminiscence of growing up in Toronto's working-class Irish neighborhood during the Depression
- *Headhunter* by Timothy Findley (1993) – for fans of the absurd, a reinterpretation of Joseph Conrad's *Heart of Darkness*, with Kurtz as a psychiatrist who 'goes native' in Toronto's urban jungle
- *In the Skin of a Lion* by Michael Ondaatje (1987) – working-class life and love in Toronto during the construction of the 'Palace of Purification' and the Bloor St viaduct, with glimpses of *The English Patient* characters
- *The Martyrology* by bp Nichol (1972–92) – a nine-book poem written over two decades, it brings the interplay of text, context and design to the forefront of meaning, and a quest for selfhood
- *O Canada!: Travels in an Unknown Country* by Jan Morris (1992) – more aptly described by its Canadian title *City to City*, these sharp profiles vividly capture the 1980s, an era of rapid change in Toronto, Montréal and Ottawa
- *Strange Fugitive* by Morley Callaghan (1928) – Callaghan's first published work is a sparsely written gangster novel set in Prohibition-era Toronto; it's a hard-boiled exception to his overtly moralistic canon
- *This Ain't No Healing Town: Toronto Stories* edited by Barry Callaghan (1995) – two dozen dark, macabre and seamy short stories by famous Canadians and local authors. Barry is Morley Callaghan's son
- *The Wild Is Always There: Canada Through the Eyes of Foreign Writers* edited by Greg Gatenby (1993) – an omnibus anthology of short stories, travel essays, poems and comic pieces by a diverse group, including Ernest Hemingway, Willa Cather, Mark Twain and William Faulkner

William Gibson (1948–), although an American by birth, now lives in Canada and has spent long stretches of time in Toronto, especially **Kensington Market** (p60) environs. In earlier years the city hosted Dickens, Yeats, Arthur Conan Doyle and Walt Whitman, who loved the omnibuses and thought Toronto 'a wild dashing place.' More critical guests included Oscar Wilde, who lambasted the city's architecture in 1882 during his 'The House Beautiful' North American tour, but was welcomed anyway because he was Irish. The English modernist Wyndham Lewis got stranded here during WWII and had nary a good word to say about the city he considered 'a sanctimonious icebox.'

Ernest Hemingway got his start as a cub reporter with the *Toronto Star,* where he penned such smartly titled masterpieces as 'Before You Go on a Canoe Trip, Learn Canoeing.' After joining Hemingway and other expatriates in Paris, local writer Morley Callaghan (1903–90) returned home to Toronto to write several acclaimed novels. His novels often wrestle within a framework of Roman Catholicism to find meaning in modern urban life. He won the Governor General's Literary Award in 1951.

ARCHITECTURE

When the town of York was founded in 1793, colonials constructed many of their churches and mansions in the solid Georgian style. Warehouses and factories were built along Front St; one of these processed pigs, giving rise to the nickname Hogtown. Brewing and distilling whiskey were also popular, with the famous Gooderham and Worts Distillery (1832) anchoring today's **Distillery Historic District** (p46).

Toronto's wealthier Victorian citizens built fanciful Italianate and Romanesque villas, Gothic manors and grand Queen Anne row houses. Also appearing at about this time was the city's distinct 'bay-and-gable' style, which typically consisted of two semidetached dwellings, each with a round bay window and a pointy Victorian gable, sharing a front garden. **Cabbagetown** (p61) has the city's best-preserved collection of Victorian houses and bungalows (see p85 for an architectural walking tour).

Around the beginning of the 20th century, the great civic buildings of a burgeoning Edwardian metropolis were constructed, including **Old City Hall** (p50), the **Royal Ontario Museum** (p56) and **Union Station** (p197). Many were worked on by EJ Lennox, often called the 'Architect of Toronto,' who also designed the **Provincial Legislature** (p58) and **Casa Loma** (p58). These Edwardian masterpieces were all part of a 'City Beautiful' scheme that envisioned parkways radiating from downtown, but the city managed to build only University Ave before the Depression hit.

Keep in mind that the great fires of 1849 and 1904 didn't destroy as much of the city as they might have otherwise done, seeing as earlier legislation had mandated that buildings should made of brick. Strict zoning limitations were finally lifted in 1905, and at last taller buildings began to rise on the city's horizon. However, most skyscrapers were molded in the dull 'form follows function' International Style, which was popular throughout the 1950s.

Top Five Books about Architecture

- *Doors Open Toronto: Illuminating the City's Great Spaces* by John Sewell (2002) – an illustrated guide to beloved buildings and secret places, with text written by a former mayor of Toronto
- *Edward James Lennox: 'Builder of Toronto'* by Marilyn Litvak (1995) – part of the Canadian Master Architects series, it's a biography of the city's most flamboyant turn-of-the-20th-century architect
- *Lost Toronto* by William Dendy (1993) – a bittersweet guide to demolished and disappeared buildings, with some photographs, by a noted architectural scholar
- *Toronto: No Mean City* by Eric Arthur (2003) – a strident 1960s call for historical preservation by a UT professor, this remains the classic study of Toronto's architectural past; the newly revised edition features updates and essays by cultural mavens
- *TSA Guide Map: Toronto Architecture 1953–2003,* Toronto Society of Architects (2003) – carry beautiful shots of the most controversial and creative Toronto buildings of the last half-century in your pocket

The most refreshing architecture in contemporary Toronto is being done by the firm of **Moriyama & Teshima** (www.mtarch.com), cofounded by Vancouver-born architect Raymond Moriyama, who believes in 'healthy' architecture that is both harmonious and ecologically sound, and involves community cooperation at the design stage. Much of the firm's work shows an elegance and clarity of Japanese influences, reminiscent of Frank Lloyd Wright's Prairie School, but these designs are more dynamic, less predictable. Public projects include the **Bata Shoe Museum** (p55); the **Ontario Science Centre** (p75), which has great glass windows overlooking the Don River ravine; and the **Toronto Reference Library** (p56), with its burbling interior fountains.

Top 10 Controversial & Notable Buildings

- **Bata Shoe Museum** (p55)
- **Casa Loma** (p58)
- **City Hall** (p50)
- **CN Tower** (p44)
- **Design Exchange** (p45)
- **Flatiron Building** (p46)
- **Osgoode Hall** (p52)
- **Roy Thomson Hall** (p48)
- **SkyDome** (p45)
- **Toronto-Dominion Centre** (p45)

Recently many of Toronto's museums have embarked upon remarkably ambitious renovation and expansion projects; the revamped **Royal Ontario Museum** (p56) and **Art Gallery of Ontario** (p53) should be especially eye-catching when work is finished. ROM is offering architectural tours of its reconstruction efforts, and the AGO has recruited renowned architect Frank Gehry, who also designed the Guggenheim museum in Bilbao, Spain, and LA's Walt Disney Concert Hall, to spearhead its transformation. It is Gehry's first project in Canada, even though the AGO is just a short walk from his childhood home. Another great institution for contemporary architecture and design is the University of Toronto's **Eric Arthur Gallery** (p59), named for a UT professor and cofounder of the Architectural Conservancy of Ontario.

The **Ontario Heritage Foundation** (☎ 416-325-5000; www.heritagefdn.on.ca) has been instrumental in protecting and restoring some of the city's 19th- and early-20th-century architectural treasures, such as the **Elgin & Winter Garden Theatre Centre** (p124), as well as the **Niagara Apothecary** (p190) in Niagara-on-the-Lake. The wonderful **St Lawrence Hall** (p47) now houses the offices of **Heritage Toronto** (☎ 416-338-0684; www.heritagetoronto.org), which also promotes historical site preservation efforts, cosponsors **Doors Open Toronto** (p26) and organizes free **walking tours** (p40).

THEATER

After London and New York, Toronto can claim the third-largest theater scene in the English-speaking world. Although at times overshadowed by prestigious festivals in **Stratford** (p187) and **Niagara-on-the-Lake** (p189), the city keeps a full house of productions running, with an average of 75 per month. That's enough to satisfy any theatrical taste, whether you're into Broadway musicals, international premieres or provocative new works by Canadian playwrights. Over seven million people attend plays in Toronto each year, and about half are visitors.

SkyDome (p45)

Toronto's theatrical history is mirrored by the topsy-turvy fortunes of the double-decker **Elgin & Winter Garden Theatre Centre** (p124). In the heyday of live vaudeville acts, the likes of George Burns and Gracie Allen, Milton Berle and Sophie Tucker all performed on the Elgin and Winter Garden stages. (In fact, patrons paid only 15¢ to stay all day if they

Doors Open Toronto

Have you ever wanted to open up the door of some eye-catching building and walk right in? That's what the **Doors Open Toronto** (www.doorsopen.org) festival is all about. Doors Open is based on a wildly successful festival that started in Glasgow over a decade ago, an idea that has now spread to more than 40 countries in Europe.

Millions of people across Canada and in the USA have participated in Doors Open events. But in May 2000 Toronto was the first city in North America to adopt the festival, when its architectural treasures, both famous and forgotten, were flung open to the public. Now for one weekend every spring, over 200,000 enthusiastic Torontonians and tourists queue to peek inside the prestigious Arts & Letters Club on Elm St or to hear the Italian consulate's tales of hidden mosaics and a secret passageway leading to the house of the ex-ambassador's mistress.

Who knew that Torontonians had an appetite for architecture? Mostly the city has shown a lack of respect for its past. Many of its finest historic buildings have been torn down since the 1950s, when the Guild Inn started collecting pieces of discarded urban architecture on its front lawn. Those venerable buildings left standing often have private citizens such as 'Honest Ed' Mirvish or nonprofit groups to thank for their survival, not the government, even though City Hall's sponsorship of Doors Open Toronto is a boost.

This extremely popular festival's two days seem all too short, considering it only happens once a year. But take heart, it's now part of the much larger **Doors Open Ontario** (☎ 800-668-2746; www.doorsopenontario.on.ca) celebrations from April to October, which include a binational event in the Niagara Falls region. And in this city alone, next year's selection of buildings will be even greater, with equally intriguing doors to knock on. If you're lucky, maybe the city will open the ghostly subway station rumored to still exist underneath Bay St.

liked.) But the advent of 'talkies' in the 1920s closed the fantastic Winter Garden theater and sadly converted the Elgin into a movie house. After TV was invented, even the Elgin went into a tailspin, later declining into a kung-fu and dodgy XXX cinema.

When 'Honest Ed' Mirvish restored the **Royal Alexandra Theatre** (p125) in the 1960s and brought on productions of big musicals with international casts, such as *Godspell* and *Hair,* live theater in Toronto finally began to revive. The Broadway musical trend gained momentum with Mirvish's building of the **Princess of Wales Theatre** (p125) two decades later. By the time that the Ontario Heritage Foundation started restoring the Elgin and Winter Garden theaters in the '90s, it was able to mount an all-Canadian production of *Cats* that was a sell-out for months. Then the Mirvish family joined forces with big business to save another venue, the old Pantages vaudeville theater, just down the street. Renamed the **Canon Theatre** (p124), it hosted sell-out shows of *The Producers* into 2004.

However, Toronto audiences don't just favor big-time musicals. Since the 1970s, experimental and new dramatic works by Canadian playwrights have burst onto the scene. Many groundbreaking small theaters have made their home here, including **Theatre Passe Muraille** (p125), aka Theater Without Walls; the **Factory Theatre** (p124), with 100% Canadian content; and queer-oriented **Buddies in Bad Times Theatre** (p124). The contemporary **Canadian Stage Company** (p124) is known for major Canadian and international premieres, as well as the popular **Dream in High Park** (p124).

MUSIC

Toronto is still struggling to build an adequate opera house, but its classical music scene is thriving. First there's the **Toronto Symphony Orchestra** (p130), but the city also has a jewel box of small chamber orchestras and choirs, with the most critically acclaimed being **Tafelmusik** (p130). Many others perform downtown at the **Glenn Gould Studio** (p129), which spotlights young musicians and offers free noontime concerts. Meanwhile the respected **Canadian Opera Company** (p129) has been known to do some innovative things, such as handing over a production of the opera *Salome* to film director Atom Egoyan.

Switching to a completely different genre, folk artists Joni Mitchell and Gordon Lightfoot performed (or before that, washed dishes and served) at the 1960s bohemian coffeehouses of Yorkville. Neil Young, the Band and Rush all started in Toronto, as did the Tragically Hip (who some say are the definitive Canadian rock band), the Cowboy Junkies and modern

Top Five CDs to Listen For

- *Beautiful: A Tribute to Gordon Lightfoot* by various artists (2003) – a who's who of Canadian folk and modern rock acts do renditions of essential Canadiana composed by the folk musician Gordon Lightfoot
- *Glenn Gould: A State of Wonder,* Sony Classical (1955 and 2002) – both of Gould's Goldberg Variations albums, which were recorded 25 years apart in the same NYC studio, plus a rare interview with the artist just before his premature death
- *In Violet Light* by The Tragically Hip (2002) – a solid return to the band's original sound of idiosyncratic poetry and manic emotion, akin to other college-town bands like REM, and simply gorgeous cover art besides
- *Stunt* by Barenaked Ladies (1998) – showing more strains of pop and less biting sarcasm than the band's earlier releases (such as *Gordon*), but the rapid-fire hit single 'One Week' topped the charts, even abroad
- *The Trinity Sessions* by Cowboy Junkies (1988) – this haunting album of ballads was recorded inside Toronto's **Church of the Holy Trinity** (p50) in just one day with only a single microphone

rockers Our Lady Peace. The Barenaked Ladies (two of whose members started out playing in a Rush tribute band in suburban Scarborough) were once barred from performing in **Nathan Phillips Square** (p50) because of their 'scandalous' name. All was forgiven when they were symbolically handed the keys to the city after being invited back to give a concert in 2000.

Downtown you can catch free concerts by the likes of Nickelback, a hard-rockin' Vancouver band, in **Dundas Square** (p49), a newly revitalized space near Eaton Centre, as well as at **SkyDome** (p45) and the innovative **Harbourfront Centre** (p127). Every year, the **North by Northeast** (NXNE; p9) festival is Canada's answer to the famous Austin indie music festival, South by Southwest. Now going strong for over a decade, NXNE lets you hear indie bands and break-out artists not just from Canada, but from the rest of the world.

Great live acts often favor smaller venues, such as pubs, bars and legendary neighborhood rock clubs. Classic dives such as the **Horseshoe Tavern** (p122) and the **360** (p121) give local bands their first shot, and any kind of sound draws crowds on bohemian **Queen West** (p61). Toronto also has some renowned places to hear acoustic, folk, jazz and blues, including **Healey's** (p121), owned by Canadian blues-rock guitarist Jeff Healey. Blind since he was a young child, Healey invented a unique technique for playing the guitar across his lap, a method that has now become his musical trademark. Elsewhere there's the jazzy **Rex** (p123), inside an old hotel; the **Silver Dollar Room** (p123) blues joint; intimate **nia** (p122) acoustic lounge; and the Celtic music sessions at **Dora Keogh** (p117).

Of course, everyone knows someone who's a DJ here, and Toronto's club scene (p125) both grows and imports some heavy-hitting sounds. You'll find dance bars popping up along Queen West and the more mainstream Entertainment District, aka Clubland.

So relax, it's not all about Céline Dion here. Remember, she's from Québec. However, Ontarians do have to admit their responsibility for country star Shania Twain and skater rock darling Avril Lavigne.

A Magical Number

The Canadian landscape painters known as the 'Group of Seven' first came together in the 1920s. Fired by an almost adolescent enthusiasm, this all-male gung-ho group of artistic talent spent a lot of time traipsing the wilds of northern Ontario, capturing the rugged Canadian wilderness through the seasons and under all weather conditions. The energy they felt joyfully expressed itself in vibrant, light-filled canvases of mountains, lakes, forests and provincial townships.

Although he died before the group was officially formed, the painter Tom Thompson was considered by other members as the group's leading light. An experienced outdoorsman, Thompson drowned in 1917 just as he was producing some of his most powerful work. His deep connection to the land can be clearly seen in various works hanging at the **Art Gallery of Ontario** (p53). His rustic cabin has been moved onto the grounds of the **McMichael Collection** (p186), the best place to view esteemed works by the Group of Seven.

A Silent Stage May Be Golden

Glenn Gould is one musical star Toronto can proudly claim as its own. Born in the Beaches community in 1932, this eccentric piano genius was a distant relation of the composer Edvard Grieg. He started composing at the age of five, took lessons at the Royal Conservatory of Music just five years later and debuted with the Toronto Symphony Orchestra before his 16th birthday.

But Gould despised the cult of the virtuoso. Later in life he came to strongly believe that young musicians should not have to compete against one another, and that live performances would quickly become outmoded in the modern age. After his famous 1955 recording of JS Bach's Goldberg Variations, he toured in Europe and, for a short time, the Soviet Union (note this was during the Cold War era). Abruptly after a concert in Los Angeles a few years later, he retired from performing in public. He was 32.

Gould never considered himself to be primarily a pianist. His real fascination lay with new sound technologies, and he spent the rest of his life writing, composing music, recording scores of albums and making radio documentaries for the Canadian Broadcasting Corporation (CBC). *The Idea of North* (1967), part of Gould's *The Solitude Trilogy* albums, was originally a 60-minute broadcast on CBC radio, for example. It featured an 'oral tone poem' of documentary interviews that Gould had personally conducted with Canadian train passengers about the romance, reality and uncertainty of life in the nation's northern lands.

Shortly before his death in 1982, Gould made another recording of the Goldberg Variations. He did this because he had come to think differently about Bach's music over the years, but also to take advantage of advances in sound recording technology. Up to the end of his life, he sincerely believed that recording artists, not live performers, could achieve the most intimate connection with audiences. Today Gould's recordings of the Goldberg Variations have become his legacy, which perhaps proves his point.

VISUAL ARTS

Toronto doesn't seem to quite grasp the importance of public art. In the 1960s when the new City Hall was being built, the English sculptor Henry Moore offered to practically donate his work to the city, yet the city council at first turned him down. Apart from a few abstract sculptures in the Financial District and the murals adorning the **Flatiron (Gooderham) Building** (p46) and the **St Lawrence Market** (p47), the city barely has any outdoor art installations, even today. Halfhearted attempts at city-funded art projects are limited to such things as the odd metalwork along the Spadina streetcar line.

Indoors it's an entirely different story. Toronto has an active contemporary art gallery scene, mostly focused in converted industrial buildings around downtown, including the labyrinthine **401 Richmond** (p53) and **Art at 80** (p53) complexes, as well as the revitalized **Distillery Historic District** (p46). Many of the upscale galleries are further north in Bloor-Yorkville, and beyond. For an art gallery walking tour of Toronto, see p83.

When it comes to First Nations art, you'll be hard-pressed to find anything apart from museum exhibits, mostly imported from British Columbia and Arctic Inuit nations. An exception is the **McMichael Collection** (p146) in suburban Kleinburg, one of the country's finest museums for both traditional and contemporary Aboriginal art. A handful of shops around the city also sell high-quality First Nations art and crafts, including the **Bay of Spirits Gallery** (p145), **Arctic Nunavut** (p145) and the simpler **Cedar Basket** (p151).

Contemporary Canadian artisans are thriving in Toronto, starting with the studios at **York Quay Centre** (p43) and in the **Distillery Historic District** (p46). Shops for contemporary crafts, many of them Ontario-centric, include **Proud Canadian Design & First Hand Canadian Crafts** (p145) and the **Guild Shop** (p150).

Top Five Museums & Gallery Complexes

- **401 Richmond** (p53)
- **Art Gallery of Ontario** (p53)
- **Distillery Historic District** (p46)
- **McMichael Collection** (p146)
- **York Quay Centre** (p43)

History

History

THE RECENT PAST

THE MEGACITY

In 1998 when five sprawling suburbs were incorporated into the Megacity, Toronto became the largest city in Canada and the fifth largest in North America. That's certainly a long way from its beginnings as 'Muddy York,' the second-choice prize after Niagara.

Yet the Megacity was not a wildly popular proposition. Many residents felt that amalgamation would result in worse city services, especially to outlying neighborhoods that would now have to shoulder more than their fair share of City Hall's financial burdens. When a referendum was held in 1997, voters in the proposed Megacity municipalities soundly rejected the plan. But former Ontario Premier Mike Harris introduced legislation that forced the Megacity merge through anyway, making an awful lot of folks unhappy.

Overnight the population of Toronto jumped from 650,000 to well over two million people. Millionaire 'Bad Boy' appliance salesman Mel Lastman, formerly the mayor of North York, assumed the reins at City Hall. He was a flamboyant character, known for riding on a fire truck in Toronto's Pride Parade and begging Ginger Spice to rejoin the Spice Girls. Lastman also accurately reflected the schizophrenia of the new Megacity: ruthlessly prodevelopment, yet with a guilty social conscience.

Detail of statue, University Ave (p57)

Despite having an annual operating budget greater than that of some Canadian provinces, Toronto had a recession in the 1990s that led to social spending cuts resulting in increased homelessness and environmental neglect. Meanwhile development was pushed forward, with condominiums edging out affordable housing, new subway lines being built (never mind that they don't go anywhere useful) and historic structures coming under the wrecking ball.

Considering what was about to happen, a salesman like Mayor Lastman may have been exactly what was needed to drive the Megacity into the 21st century.

THE 21ST CENTURY

Although Toronto is still 'the city that works,' an admiring nickname gained for its urban planning successes, the new millennium has delivered a lot of headaches so far.

First, Toronto lost its bid to host the 2008 Summer Olympics. Then it was smacked by successive outbreaks of West Nile Virus and Severe Acute Respiratory Syndrome (SARS), and experienced

TIMELINE	1615	1649	1787
	Voyageur Etienne Brûlé arrives at the 'Carrying Place' by the Humber River	League of the Iroquois attacks local Huron tribes	The British purchase Toronto from the Mississauga tribes

the Great Blackout of 2003, when power plants failed across northeastern US and Canada, leaving Torontonians in the dark for days. Chinatown vendors quickly began selling 'Toronto Survivor' T-shirts and pundits joked about 'Toronto the Bad' becoming 'The City That Works You Over,' even as the tourist board embarked on an optimistic new ad campaign, 'Toronto: You Belong Here.'

But the Megacity has a new mayor, David Miller, elected on a platform vision of Toronto returning to its roots: a patchwork city of neighborhoods. He has pledged to make Dundas Square a public space worthy of NYC's Times Square, clean up corruption at City Hall and make environmental healing a priority. Miller is also a strong proponent of civil rights for all of the minorities populating the Megacity, including the disabled, gay and lesbian citizens, and various ethnic groups. He recently established a Racial Diversity Secretariat, a crucial step for a city where interethnic gang violence is rife.

Only time will tell. But in spite of recent challenges, there is every reason for enthusiasm about Toronto's future. Today one out of every two Torontonians is a recent immigrant, who brings fresh ideas, perspectives and a wealth of diversity to the Megacity on a daily basis. More than 100 languages are spoken on the streets. It's an experimental city just finding its feet, and nothing is static. Toronto is a city in evolution.

FROM THE BEGINNING

ARRIVAL OF THE FRENCH

When Etienne Brûlé first arrived in 1615 at what voyageurs came to call 'The Carrying Place,' he was on a mission from French explorer Samuel de Champlain, who had already founded a settlement at Québec. The new site at the mouth of the Humber River was called Toronto, an Aboriginal word that perhaps means 'meeting place,' since it was located at the convergence of several key trading and portage routes. These were historically used by First Nations tribes and later by French fur traders as shortcuts between Lake Ontario and Georgian Bay or the upper inland lakes. It wasn't until around 1720 that the French were able to establish a fur-trading post and mission near the Humber River. In 1750 they built Fort Rouillé – also known as Fort Toronto, on the site where **Exhibition Place** (p41) now stands – one in a series of forts set up to control navigation on the Great Lakes and links with the Mississippi River.

Haunted by the Past

Even as things change in the newborn Megacity, Toronto's famous ghosts have chosen to remain. As you amble about town, you're likely to visit more than a few of the city's most haunted sites. It's said that on certain nights at the **Mackenzie House** (p50), the 19th-century-style print shop machines in the basement can be heard working when no one else is around. The hand-operated elevators in the **Elgin & Winter Garden Theatre Centre** (p124) have been known to move of their own accord, too. Poltergeist activity has been reported in the **Distillery Historic District** (p146), where one of the distillery's original owners drowned in a well (either accidentally or as a suicide) shortly after his wife died during childbirth. On the islands, the **Gibraltar Point Lighthouse** (p65) is haunted by the ghost of its first keeper, a bootlegger who is thought to have been murdered. Red-coated guards still wander the grounds of **Fort York** (p41) and elegantly dressed apparitions float through the **Grange** (p53). The souls of the last men hanged in Canada are heard still moaning inside **Old City Hall** (p50), while the former jail cells in the basement of the **Courthouse Market Grille** (p95) are almost as chilling.

'MUDDY YORK'

After years of hostility with the French on both sides of the Atlantic, the British took over all of New France, including the area around Toronto, under the Treaty of Paris in 1763. Montréal had already been captured three years earlier. However, it wasn't until after

1793	1813	1832	1837
Lieutenant Governor of Upper Canada John Graves Simcoe founds the town of York	Americans invade during the War of 1812 (which actually lasted until 1814)	Cholera epidemics devastate the old town of York	William Lyon Mackenzie raises the Rebellion of Upper Canada against the Family Compact's oligarchy

Top Five Toronto History Books

- *Accidental City: The Transformation of Toronto* by Robert Fulford (1995) – an engaging interpretation of how a changing landscape of modern architecture, lakefront development and natural ravine lands has resulted in one of North America's most livable cities
- *A Magical Place: Toronto Island and Its People* by Bill Freeman (1999) – takes readers effortlessly through the islands' turbulent history, historic sites and even lighthouse ghosts
- *Muddy York Mud: Scandal and Scurrility in Upper Canada* by Chris Raible (1992) – dishes the dirt on players in the old town of York – the Baldwins, the Mackenzies et al – through a retelling of the famous 1826 Types Trial
- *Niagara: A History of the Falls* by Pierre Berton (1992) – for all the tales of tightrope walkers and daredevils in barrels
- *Toronto Then and Now* by Mike Filey (2000) – a photographic portrait of the city's evolution from virgin woods into thriving neighborhoods

the American Revolution that Loyalists fleeing the United States arrived and settlement began in earnest. The British paid £1700 to the Mississauga nation for the Toronto Land Purchase of 1787, although the 'official' deed was suspiciously left blank. Four years later the provinces of Upper Canada (now Ontario) and Lower Canada (Québec) were created.

Soon afterward, in 1793, John Graves Simcoe, the new Lieutenant Governor of Upper Canada, moved the provincial capital from Niagara-on-the-Lake to a more defensible position at Toronto, which he founded as the town of York. This colonial town was laid out on a 10-block grid with such patriotic street names as King, Queen, George and Duke. The lieutenant governor's men also constructed a trail, which later became Yonge St, leading 48km straight north through the wilderness to the borders of the original Toronto purchase. (Today the *Guinness Book of World Records* calls Yonge St 'the longest road in the world,' because it winds for over 1800km along Hwy 11 all the way to Rainy River, Ontario.)

The inhospitable muddiness of the new capital gave rise to its notorious nickname 'Muddy York,' but Simcoe reasoned this made it all the less likely that York would be attacked should the Americans decide to invade. Which, of course, they did anyway during the War of 1812. On April 27, 1813, the American forces reached Fort York and after a short struggle overcame the British and Ojibwa troops. The Americans looted and razed York but held it for only six days before Canadian troops kicked them out and chased them all the way back to the US political headquarters in Washington. Enraged Canadian forces even burned the White House, allegedly so named for the white paint that was later used to cover the charred bits.

After the 1814 Treaty of Ghent ended the hostilities between the USA and Canada, the British no longer saw the Iroquois nations as valuable allies and quickly subjected them to increased government control. At the same time, the city of York began to expand and, in 1828, the first stagecoach service began on Yonge St. British and then Irish immigrants began to arrive in Upper Canada in still larger numbers, quadrupling the population to about 10,000 people.

FROM REBELLION TO UNITY

By 1824 firebrand William Lyon Mackenzie had started publishing his *Colonial Advocate,* an outcry against the oligarchic Tory government that ruled York. Termed the 'Family Compact,' these Loyalist families, including the Jarvises, Baldwins and Strachans, had come to power as advisers to Lieutenant Governor Simcoe, who before departing Upper Canada had limited the province's legislative powers as a means of avoiding an American-style revolution.

1849	1856	1867	1886
First great fire starts in the stables behind Covey's Inn on King St	First railway carries passengers between Toronto and Montréal	Ontario, Québec, Nova Scotia and New Brunswick unite in the Confederation of Canada	Women first admitted to classes at the University of Toronto

First Nations Foundations *by Monica Bodirsky*

Chances are, anywhere you step in Toronto, you are walking on the bones of First Nations ancestors. Toronto has been continually occupied by Aboriginal people for the past 11,000 years, and beneath its towers of concrete and steel, the foundations of this city may lie obscured, yet not eradicated.

Several place names that travelers encounter are clues to the true history of our sprawling Megacity and continue to honor its First Nations origins. Mississauga scholar AR Bobiwash interpreted 'Toronto' as a Wendat (Huron) word for a fishing weir, a group of sticks placed together at the mouth of a river to gather fish. It was this etymological understanding that gives Toronto its description as 'The Gathering Place.' An equally valid Aboriginal perspective on the meaning of the city's moniker is offered by Mohawk historian and architect William Woodworth of Ontario's Six Nations of the Grand River Territory. Woodworth understands that 'Toron:to' (pronounced 'Delondo') is derived from the Mohawk word for log. He believes that the name may refer to a fallen log that had a deep spiritual and ceremonial purpose. 'Trees grew to heights that defy our imagination,' he says. 'There were white pines as tall as 100m then.' Interpretations of language, as with many other things, are subjective. In keeping with the Aboriginal concept of all perspectives being equal, and the practices of tolerance and respect, the important thing to remember is that the name 'Toronto' is Aboriginal.

Spadina Ave, which runs from Lake Ontario north to Bloor St and continues as Spadina Rd up to Roselawn Ave, was originally known as 'Ishpaadiina' (ish-*pah*-dee-nah), which is an Anishnawbe word meaning 'to go up the hill.' The hill being referred to is still part of the city's landscape and today leads to **Casa Loma** (p58). Five thousand years ago, the original shoreline of Lake Ontario reached the top of that same hill. At that time it was a campground for Iroquois people. When the glacier receded, what is now known as Davenport Rd became a lakefront trail. Instead of being moved, this trail was just paved over. As many travelers will notice, it meanders off Toronto's typical urban grid.

St George St and its subway station are generally thought to have been named after St George, the patron saint of England and famed dragon slayer. However, they were actually named after Clinton St George, an Aboriginal fur trader who did business regularly between Toronto and Rama, north of the city off Lake Huron. He was involved with the influential Baldwin family, who gained much of their wealth through the fur trade. One of the Baldwin family's houses, **Spadina House** (p59; located next to Casa Loma) still stands to this day, and has been turned into a museum.

Not far from Spadina Ave is Queen's Park, home of the **provincial legislature** (p58). It has been noted with some irony that this was the original site of the city's first insane asylum. Unfortunately, at the time of construction, no consideration was given to the Mississauga people who had been using the grounds at Queen St to hold council. An appeal was made to the governor with no resolution, and the Mississauga land claim is still being resolved today.

The Toronto Islands remain a sacred part of Aboriginal history in Toronto. With a spectacular view of Lake Ontario and the city skyline, the islands have long been used as a spa by Aboriginal people, who came here to camp seeking solitude and rest. Dr Peter Martin (Oronyatek:ha) was a noted Six Nations physician who lived in a house north of Allan Gardens, just east of downtown. He was a renowned 19th-century philanthropist. When he passed away in 1907, his body lay in state in **Massey Hall** (p51) for three days. A newspaper account at the time noted, 'The drawn blinds, the bared heads and the sorrowful faces formed a tribute of respect such as is paid to few men in either life or death.'

Stop by the **Native Canadian Centre of Toronto** (p58) to get a better understanding of what lies beneath Toronto's towers of concrete and steel.

Monica Bodirsky is the coordinator of the Toronto Native Community History Project at the Native Canadian Centre of Toronto. This article was written in memory of Mississauga scholar and historian A Rodney Bobiwash (Wacoquaakmik, 1959–2002). Chi miigwetch *(Thank you) Rodney.*

During 1834 Mackenzie got himself elected as the first mayor of the new city of Toronto, but the Family Compact's continuing political influence proved much too strong for him. Finally out of options, Mackenzie initiated the shortest-lived rebellion in Canadian history on December 5, 1837. Mackenzie and an assorted band of around

1892	1904	1906	1907
First electric streetcar runs on Church St	Second great fire	Lord's Day Act prohibits work and social activities on Sunday	Toronto's youngest millionaire builds the Royal Alexandra Theatre

600 disgruntled citizens marched down Yonge Street and confronted the Loyalist troops that were directed by Sheriff Jarvis. Shots were volleyed, confusion and panic ensued and both sides broke and ran. Mackenzie went into temporary exile in the USA while unluckier rebels were hanged.

Another newspaperman, George Brown, the publisher of the *Globe* since 1844, became a key political player in Toronto politics in Mackenzie's absence. Brown forged a new liberal party and was also a driving force behind the confederation of Canada during 1867, to which most voters agreed more out of fear of another US invasion than any nationalistic ideals. Their fears were not unfounded, considering that Fenian raids (below) were still being launched across the border. By the time of confederation, the railway had already brought the coalescing nation much closer together. Toronto gained prominence as the capital of the newly renamed Ontario, even though the city was still economically in the shadow of Montréal.

O Brother, Where Art Thou?

What do Irish Republicans, African Americans, Mohawk tribes and Québec radicals have in common? They all hate the British – or at least they did during the mid-19th century. Although the resultant Fenian raids (tacitly approved but not acknowledged by the US) are a side note to Canadian history, their epic goals are worth recounting.

A series of border incursions organized by the Fenian brotherhood, made up of Irish Americans loyal to the Republican cause, had as their goal the harassment of British forces and the eventual capture of Canada's major cities, Toronto and Montréal. Why? The fiendish Fenian brethren planned to hold both cities hostage until Britain agreed to free Ireland. Veteran fighters from the US Civil War, including a company of African American soldiers, along with 500 Mohawk warriors and French sympathizers in Montréal, rallied to the cause.

Everything went tragicomically awry when the raids began in 1866. Although one detachment of Fenians quickly overran Fort Erie, a deadly combination of fever outbreak, poor planning, even laziness on the part of their brethren – along with efficient spying by British military scouts – stopped the major brunt of the attack. When those Fenians at Fort Erie attempted to retreat across the Niagara River, they were arrested by a US warship, convicted and sentenced in a New York court later, then quietly released. Prisoners-of-war taken to Toronto fared far worse; nearly two dozen were executed. Nevertheless, the Fenian border raids continued sporadically into 1871.

TORONTO THE GOOD

Throughout the Victorian era of the late 1800s, there was seemingly nothing but progress for Toronto. Eaton's and Simpson's department stores opened on Yonge St, the city was wired for electricity and the first national exhibition was held. By the end of the century, more than 200,000 folks called Toronto home. Masterpieces of Edwardian architecture arose downtown, and the first Italian and Jewish immigrants arrived. Like many big cities, Toronto had already had its great fire, in 1849, but it had another in 1904, when about 20 acres of the inner city burned, leveling 100 buildings. Miraculously, no one died.

Around this time the city became known as 'Toronto the Good,' a tag that only began to fade a few decades ago. Conservative politicians voted for prohibition (outlawing the production and sale of alcoholic beverages) and strong antivice laws (it was illegal to rent a horse on Sunday) that culminated in the Lord's Day Act of 1906. Eaton's department store drew its curtains to prevent 'sinful' window shopping and playground sets were chained and locked.

Meanwhile businessmen such as Sir Henry Pellat of Casa Loma fame were amassing their fortunes, and by the 1920s Bay St was booming, in part because gold, silver and uranium

1918	1920	1927	1931
Women are given the federal right to vote	Group of Seven exhibits paintings at the Art Gallery of Toronto	Union Station opens on the nation's 60th birthday	First hockey game played at Maple Leaf Gardens

Provincial legislature building (p58)

mines had been discovered in northern Ontario. Everything stopped short during the Depression era, sparking ethnic hostilities. Chinese immigration was banned, anti-Semitic riots exploded in Christie Pits Park and during WWII, Canada interned citizens of Japanese ancestry in camps, as did the USA. Widespread prejudice against African Canadians was all the more lamentable for Ontario having been a safe haven for Harriet Tubman and other escaped slaves on the Underground Railroad.

THE WHOLE WORLD IN A CITY

After WWII, the city breathed a sigh of relief. As thousands of European immigrants began arriving, they gifted the city with an influx of new tongues, customs and food. Enclaves like Kensington Market began showing signs of diversity that have become the city's hallmark, and a subway line was opened in 1954 to handle a burgeoning population. Starting in the 1960s many people moved from the suburbs back into the city and began restoring fine old Victorian homes. Bohemian folk-music coffeehouses opened in Yorkville, patronized not least by US citizens looking to avoid the Vietnam War draft.

It was the building of the controversial new City Hall in 1965 that really gave Toronto its boost into modernity, however. Into the '70s and beyond, Portuguese, Chilean, Greek, Southeast Asian, Chinese and West Indian immigrants rolled over the city in waves. The redeveloped Harbourfront and new skyscrapers sprang up as Toronto finally overtook Montréal in terms of population, becoming one of the fastest-growing cities in North America.

1941	1960s	1972	1976
The government conducts secret anti-U-boat technology research at Casa Loma	US exiles arrive fleeing the Vietnam War draft; folk music coffeehouses open in Yorkville	Pride Week celebrated with Queen's Park march and picnic at Hanlan's Point	CN Tower opens

The city's optimism and pride expressed themselves in the building of the **CN Tower** (p44) in 1976, continuing right through the 1980s economic boom on Bay St and the city's sesquicentennial in 1984. However, not everyone shared the 'progressive' outlook of City Hall. In 1980 'sandbar bohemians' on Toronto Islands stood their ground against eviction by the municipal government. And of course, the economy had to go bust sometime, which it did with a bang during the '90s.

1980	1998	1999	2003
Standoff between city officials and remaining residents on Toronto Islands	Protests in Queen's Park over birth of the Megacity	City council legalizes 'clothing optional' status of Hanlan's Point beach	Toronto legalizes same-sex marriage, survives an outbreak of SARS and the Great Blackout

Neighborhoods

Neighborhoods

To tell the truth, Toronto is a very walkable city. You don't need to worry if your stamina gives out, though, because the subway is quick, safe and simple to navigate. So are the old-fashioned streetcars that run along many of the major thoroughfares. Each of the following sections contains transport details and there's further information in the Directory (p195). Downtown is clasped on almost all sides by a hodgepodge of bohemian, ethnic and historic neighborhoods, with the remaining southern edge crisply defined by Lake Ontario. Most visitors start by taking long strides along the lakeshore in the Harbourfront area just a short ferry ride from the Toronto Islands. Back downtown, Union Station is the gateway to the skyscrapers of the Financial District and to Old York, a historic neighborhood upon which the city was founded. On King St the Theatre Block stands within the giant Entertainment District, aka Clubland. Further north, Queen St parades east past City Hall toward Eaton Centre, near Dundas Square. The Yonge Street Strip, with its parallel universe of the gay Church-Wellesley Village, leads north to chichi Bloor-Yorkville. Over on the west side is quaint Baldwin Village and Toronto's biggest Chinatown, which borders vibrant Kensington Market and the University of Toronto (UT) campus around the Annex, a student-dominated neighborhood.

A short stroll from the market is Little Italy, which runs parallel to the bohemian strip, Queen West. Spreading from Cabbagetown across the river into Greektown (The Danforth), East Toronto reaches further out toward the Beaches community. The city tends to sprawl throughout the Greater Toronto Area (GTA), where Yonge St (pronounced 'young'), the main north–south artery, begins at Lake Ontario and heads north to the city's boundaries, and beyond.

Top Five Downtown

- **Distillery Historic District** (p46)
- **Art Gallery of Ontario** (p53)
- **Hockey Hall of Fame** (p45)
- **St Lawrence Market** (p47)
- **Elgin & Winter Garden Theatre Centre** (p50)

Peak summer season runs from Victoria Day in late May to Labour Day in early September. Note that opening hours for most attractions and services are reduced out of season.

ITINERARIES

One Day

Start your day along the **Harbourfront** (p41), strolling along the shores of Lake Ontario and the quays, then hop on a quick harbor cruise or a ferry over to the **Toronto Islands** (p64). Back in the afternoon, head up to **Bloor-Yorkville** (p55) for its excellent museums or over to bohemian **Queen West** (p61) for eclectic shopping. Take a leisurely dinner with cocktails in **Little Italy** (p61), then catch a live music show (p121) anywhere around town to cap off the night.

Three Days

On the morning of your second day, pick a major sight – like the **Royal Ontario Museum** (p56), **Hockey Hall of Fame** (p45), **Art Gallery of Ontario** (p53) or **Casa Loma** (p58) – then lunch at the **St Lawrence Market** (p47), unique **Baldwin Village** (p52) or **Kensington Market** (p60). Spend the afternoon taking one of our walking tours (p39) or go out to the **Beaches** (p63). Make plans to attend a performing arts event that evening, perhaps an intimate jazz set at **Montréal Bistro** (p95) or a major theater production (123). Have late-night mezes and drinks in **Greektown** (p107). On your last day, rent a car to visit **Niagara Falls** (p176) and the **Niagara Peninsula Wine Country** (p182).

ne Week

Vith more time to spare, you'll get a chance to enjoy the full flavor of Toronto's neighborhoods. pend almost a full day in the **Annex** (p57), touring the **University of Toronto Campus** (p59), noshing in hinatown (p52) and shopping in **Markham Village** (p58) or around downtown. Take another morn-ng to explore **Old York** (p46) or **East Toronto** (p61), then unwind at a luxury spa (p139), enjoy some easonal outdoor activities (p135) or score tickets for a game at **SkyDome** (p45) or the **Air Canada entre** (p44). Also be sure to see the **McMichael Canadian Art Collection** (p187) or explore **Tommy Thompson ark** (p63). Families should visit one of the city's kid-friendly attractions, such as the **Ontario Science entre** (p75), **Black Creek Pioneer Village** (p77) or **Paramount Canada's Wonderland** (p78).

RGANIZED TOURS

oat Trips

everal companies run boat tours around he harbor and Toronto Islands roughly be-ween May and September. Most boats de-art from the Harbourfront beside Queen's Quay Terminal or further west beside York Quay Centre. For shorter harbor excursions, ou can often just show up and buy a ticket t the quay, though reservations are recom-nended for brunch and dinner cruises.

Keep in mind that ferries to and from the **ronto Islands** (p64) offer spectacular views of he city that are cheap in comparison with he private boat tours.

Yorkville (p55)

GREAT LAKES SCHOONER COMPANY

Map pp228-30

☎ 416-203-2322, 800-267-3866; www.greatlakesschooner.com; 90min cruise adult/child/senior $20/11/18; 1-3 departures Jun–Labour Day; streetcar 509, 510

The dashing three-masted *Kajama*, a 1930s trading schooner launched in Germany, towers 55m above water. It's moored behind the Power Plant at the foot of Simcoe St, but there's often a seasonal ticket kiosk beside Queen's Quay Terminal. Discounts for on-line booking are available.

MARIPOSA CRUISE LINES Map pp228-30

☎ 416-203-0178, 800-976-2442; http://mariposacruises.com; Queen's Quay Terminal, 207 Queens Quay W; tour $15-60; streetcar 509, 510

One-hour harbor tours depart several times daily. More leisurely three-hour dinner cruises include a buffet, cash bar and dancing. Sunday brunch cruises sail between May and September.

TORONTO TOURS LTD Map pp228-30

☎ 416-868-0400; www.torontotours.com; 145 Queens Quay W; 1hr harbor cruise adult/child 2-12 $20/10; streetcar 509, 510

Harbor cruises depart every half-hour from 10am until 6pm between April and November. There's one-hour evening cruises during June, July and August. The dock is at the foot of York St.

Bus Tours

Bus tours are convenient, but with TTC day passes (p198) being so cheap, a do-it-yourself tour also makes sense.

GRAY LINE TOURS Map pp226-7

☎ 416-594-3310, 800-353-3484; www.grayline.ca; departs Metro Toronto Coach Terminal, 610 Bay St; 2-day pass adult/child under 12/senior $34/18/30; departures hourly; subway Dundas

Reliable Gray Line runs basic two-hour, double-decker bus tours of central Toronto. Buy tickets for these hop-on, hop-off tours on board the bus at **Nicholby's Sports & Souvenirs** (Map pp228-30; 123 Front St W), which is the main departure point. Passengers who book in advance can request pick-ups from downtown hotels and hostels.

ROMBUS Map pp231-3

☎ 416-586-5797; www.rom.on.ca; 100 Queen's Park; full-day tour $80; subway Museum

The **Royal Ontario Museum** (p56) leads monthly bus tours arranged around historical, architectural and cultural themes, perhaps surveying Islam in Toronto or exploring art-deco sights. Advance reservations are necessary.

TORONTO HIPPO TOURS Map pp228-30

☎ 416-703-4476, 877-635-5510; www.torontohippotours.com; 151 Front St W; 90min tour adult/child 3-12/youth/senior $35/23/30/30; hourly departures 11am-6pm May-Nov

Amusing 40-passenger 'floating boats' take families on narrated tours of downtown before splashing into the city's harbor; the driver of your amphibious bus is also a marine captain.

Walking & Cycling Tours

Most folks' favorite way to experience Toronto is on foot or by bicycle. For University of Toronto campus tours, see p59.

A TASTE OF THE WORLD

☎ 416-923-6813; www.torontowalksbikes.com; 2-3½hr tour $15-35; year-round

Quirky, well-qualified guides lead over a dozen different off-beat walking and cycling tours of Toronto's nooks and crannies; one delves into the culinary wonders of Chinatown, whil another tries to unveil the ghosts of Yorkvill Prices vary depending on whether bike rent and snacks or full-fledged meals are include Make reservations.

CIVITAS CITY WALKS

☎ 416-966-1550; http://ourworld.compuserve.com/homepages/civitas; 2hr tour $12, child under 12 free; May-Oct

Civitas offers three main walks, focusing o either colonial, Victorian or modern architectur along with tales of scandal and disaster throw in. Call between 8am and 10pm to reserve spot and check meeting times and places.

HERITAGE TORONTO

☎ 416-338-3886; www.heritagetoronto.org; 1½-3hr tour free; usually weekends late Apr–mid-Oct

Over three dozen historical, cultural and natur walks are led by museum docents and neighborhood historical society members. Eac uniquely designed tour is given only onc during the summer. Recent walks investigate the groovy 1960s musical heritage of Yorkvill re-imagined battles at Fort York and hiked th city's ravines and wilderness parks. Reservations are not required.

ROMWALKS

☎ 416-586-8097; www.rom.on.ca; 1-2hr tour free; usually Sun afternoons & Wed evenings May–mid-Se

Volunteers from the **Royal Ontario Museum** (p4 lead free historical and architectural walkin tours, rain or shine. No advance reservatior are necessary for most of these interestin tours. Check current schedules on-line or pic up a brochure at the museum.

WinterCity

How do folks survive winter in Toronto? From November to March the wind whips down Bay St and chills the bones. Many shops, restaurants and attractions reduce their hours or even close. Still, the coldest day can be made bearable by a fireside pint, and don't forget – it's hockey season. Ice-skating (p136) is another favorite pastime. Victorian-style Christmas celebrations abound at various attractions, and when the gas lamps are lit on Toronto St during a snowfall, romantic souls will be transported to another century. After New Year's, **WinterCity Festival** (p8) comes alive during the subzero months.

On winter days when frostbite is a possibility (usually when the wind-chill factor dangerously low) you'll know about it. Everyone discusses the freezing cold, and radio stations broadcast warnings and state how many minutes it's safe to expose your skin. That's your cue to scuttle below ground into Toronto's PATH system (p88) or delight in one of the city's museums, galleries, tropical conservatories, the enclosed **St Lawrence Market** (p47) or a rejuvenating spa (p139).

Many residents won't wear heavy down jackets, even when it's 30°C below zero outside, just so they still look hip, although hats (called 'toques,' and pronounced 'tukes') can be a fashion statement unto themselves. Even in winter, pack a bathing suit, which weighs next to nothing, for heated indoor pools and saunas. Bring a good, sturdy pair of walking shoes that won't slip on the ice, because the city can put a lot of mileage on your tootsies. And, remember, this *is* the Great White North still, so get psyched to brave the elements if you decide to visit the city at its most winterlicious time.

ꞁARBOURFRONT

ating p93; Shopping p145; Sleeping p161; Walking & Cycling 'ours p81

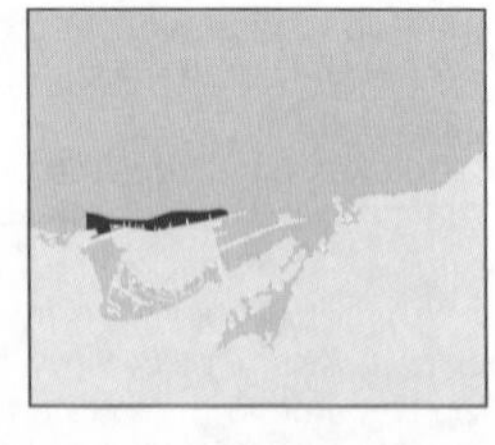

'he Harbourfront area was once a run-down district of ware-ıouses, factories and docklands along Lake Ontario. Once lated for redevelopment, Queens Quay W gained galleries, ultural centers and outdoor entertainment venues, most f them springing up between Yonge St and Spadina Ave. Iowever, construction has been allowed to run amok: much f the waterfront has been blighted by ugly condos. The lakeshore may seem underutilized o those visitors from other great lakefront cities such as Chicago, but any further progress ıas previously been stymied by wrangling among governmental bodies.

Nevertheless, on weekends the Harbourfront is quite popular for walks and harbor cruises hat take advantage of the lakeshore breezes. A few ex-shipping terminals now contain shop-ing malls and indoor/outdoor performing and visual arts venues. So the area is well worth visit, especially combined with a ferry trip ver to the **Toronto Islands** (p64). Attractions or families abound, especially beyond the uays at Fort York and at Ontario Place, nd there are many special events at **Exhibition lace** (p41), where the **Canadian National Exhibition** CNE; p10) is held every year. A laidback troll, cycle or blade along the waterfront **Aartin Goodman Trail** (p135) is another bonus.

Transportation

Subway & Streetcar From Union Station, board either the 509 Harbourfront or 510 Spadina streetcars along the quays. For outlying destinations further west, take the 509 Harbourfront streetcar, which joins up with the 511 Bathurst streetcar line at Bathurst St.

Bicycle & Skates The Martin Goodman Trail is a paved recreational path connecting all of the Harbourfront sights. In the Queen's Quay area, it shares the sidewalk with pedestrians.

Car Parking in the area is a headache. Private lots charge at least $10 per day (no hourly rates). The municipal lot at 10 York St normally charges $1 per half-hour (daily maximum $8.50). All rates jump during special events.

)rientation

'he main Harbourfront area centers on the oot of York St, just a short walk south of Jnion Station. Most of the foot traffic fol-ows Queens Quay W either west toward kyDome or east toward the Toronto Is-ands ferry terminal by the Westin Harbour otel and Yonge St Strip. Outlying attrac-ions are just a 15-minute streetcar ride west f the main quay area, beyond Bathurst St.

EXHIBITION PLACE Map p225

☎ 416-263-3600; www.explace.on.ca; off Lake Shore lvd W, btwn Strachan Ave & Dufferin St; ⌚ event chedules vary; streetcar 509, 511

:ach year these historic grounds are revived or their original purpose: the **Canadian National xhibition** (CNE; p10). During 'The Ex' millions of visitors flood the midway for carnival rides, umberjack competitions and more home-rown fun. The beaux-arts Victory statue over he **Princes' Gate** has flown aloft since 1927, when Canada celebrated its 60th birthday.

Other special events held at Exhibition 'lace throughout the year include the **Molson ndy** (p10), the **Royal Agricultural Winter Fair** and an nergetic variety of sports and design shows.)therwise the grounds are often bereft of visi-ors, apart from conventioneers and a few die-ıard fans visiting the **Canada Sports Hall of Fame** (☎ 416-260-6789; admission free; ⌚ 10am-4:30pm) or the humble **Scadding log cabin**, Toronto's oldest building (c 1795), built by an estate clerk of Colonial Lieutenant Governor John Simcoe (p32).

FORT YORK Map p225

☎ 416-392-6907; Garrison Rd, off Fleet St W, east of Strachan Ave; admission & tour adult/child/youth 13-18 $5/3/3.25; ⌚ 10am-5pm Jun-Aug, 10am-4pm Sep-May, tours hourly, closed mid-Dec–early Jan; streetcar 509, 511; Ⓟ

Established by the British in 1793 to protect the town of York, as Toronto was then known, this fort was almost entirely destroyed during the War of 1812 (p32), when a small band of Ojibwa warriors and British troops couldn't stop the US fleet. Invading American troops went on to raze and loot the capital city but were kicked out after just six days. The fort was quickly rebuilt.

Today a handful of the original log, stone and brick buildings have been restored. In summer, men decked out in 19th-century British military uniforms carry out marches and drills, and fire musket volleys – kids much prefer running around the fort's embankments with wooden rifles. If you get lost looking for the fort, just look for the old Union Jack waving in the breeze.

ONTARIO PLACE Map p225

☎ 416-314-9900, 866-663-4386; www.ontarioplace.com; 55 Lake Shore Blvd W; all-day pass adult/child $29/15, grounds admission only before/after 5pm $13/5; 🕑 10am-8pm daily late June-early Aug, Sat & Sun only May & Sep; P $5-10

Built on three artificial islands offshore from Exhibition Place, this 40-hectare recreation complex is an easy way to beat the heat during summer. A 'Play All Day' pass entitles you to most of the thrill rides and attractions, including Soak City waterpark and walk-up seating at the **Cinesphere**, where 70mm IMAX films are shown on a six-story-high curved screen.

Parents should know about the H_2O Generation Station, a popular children's soft-play climbing area where you can let 'em go nuts. Additional attractions, such as the human-sized MegaMaze and House of Blues concerts at the **Molson Amphitheatre** (☎ 416-260-5600), must be paid for separately. Discounted passes may be available after 5pm and for grounds-only admission. On rainy days, many of the activities, restaurants and rides do not operate. A free red trolley picks up Ontario Place visitors by the clock tower on the Front St side of Union Station, running every half-hour from 8:30am until 7pm, but only on weekends. Otherwise, take the streetcar to Exhibition Place, trek through the grounds and over the Lakeshore Bridge.

POWER PLANT Map pp228-30

☎ 416-973-4949; www.thepowerplant.org; 231 Queens Quay W; adult/child under 12/student/senior $4/free/2/2, admission free 5-8pm Wed; 🕑 noon-6pm Tue-Sun, noon-8pm Wed; streetcar 509, 510

The Power Plant is an art gallery celebrating contemporary Canadian art, just one artist at a time. Its focus is painting, sculpture and large-scale installations, which can be hit-and-miss. However, free talks by visiting artists and curators, and tours led by the gallery director, should aid your appreciation. The gallery is in a renovated power station by the du Maurier Theatre Centre, which has taken over the old icehouse.

QUEEN'S QUAY TERMINAL Map pp228-30

☎ 416-203-0510; www.toronto.com/queensquay; 207 Queens Quay W; 🕑 most shops 10am-6pm; streetcar 509, 510; P 2hr free with $50 purchase

Start your Harbourfront stroll at this refurbished 1926 warehouse filled with skylights, arts-and-crafts shops and also the **Premier Dance Theatre** (p130). Vociferous ticket sellers hawk harbor cruises outside (p39).

Top Five Harbourfront

- **York Quay Centre** (p43)
- **Ontario Place** (left)
- **Toronto Music Garden** (p43)
- **Steam Whistle Brewing** (below)
- **Queen's Quay Terminal** (above)

REDPATH SUGAR MUSEUM Map pp228-30

☎ 416-366-3561; 95 Queens Quay E; self-guided tour free; 🕑 usually 10am-noon & 1:30-3:30pm Mon-Fri; bus 6, 75; P

The working Redpath Sugar Mill is a descendant of the original refinery opened in Montréal 150 years ago. Inside, a small museum examines the history of the Caribbean slave trade, the now-defunct Ontario sugar beet industry and, most intriguingly, sugar's role as a muse for artistic design. An educational short film is teasingly titled *Raising Cane*. Enter via the west gate by Yonge St and follow the museum signs.

STEAM WHISTLE BREWING Map pp228-30

☎ 416-362-2337, 866-240-2337; www.steamwhistle.ca; 255 Bremner Blvd; admission free, 30min tour $4; 🕑 noon-6pm Mon-Sat, tours 1, 2, 3 & 4 pm; streetcar 509, 510

Downhill from SkyDome this microbrewery specializes in a crisp European-style Pilsner. In fact, that's all it makes! During snappy tours of the premises, guides will actually blow the railway roundhouse's historic steam whistle. Tours include free tastings at the brewery's retail store and a souvenir glass or bottle opener. Call to check hours and tour schedules, which are subject to change.

TORONTO MUSIC GARDEN Map p228-30

475 Queens Quay W; admission free; ⌚ dawn-dusk; streetcar 509, 510

Delicately strung along the western Harbourfront, this sculpted garden was designed in collaboration with famed cellist Yo-Yo Ma. It aims to express Bach's *Suite No 1 for Unaccompanied Cello* through landscape, with an arc-shaped grove of conifers, a swirling path through a meadow and a grass-stepped amphitheatre where free summer concerts are held. Contact the Harbourfront Centre box office in **York Quay Centre** for performance schedules. Musical audio tours are available from the **Marina Quay West office** (rental $5; ⌚ tours 10am-8pm) on the pier immediately south of the garden.

YORK QUAY CENTRE Map pp228-30

Harbourfront Centre information desk ☎ 416-973-3000, box office ☎ 416-973-4000; www.harbourfront.on.ca; 235 Queens Quay W; ⌚ most galleries Tue-Sun; streetcar 509, 510

Throughout the summer, especially during the weekends, the **Harbourfront Centre** (p129) puts on a kaleidoscopic variety of performing arts events at the York Quay Centre, many especially for kids and some are even free. Performances sometimes take place on the covered outdoor concert stage beside the lake. Also outside are the unusual **Artists' Gardens**. Admission to the indoor galleries, including the **Photo Passage** and **Craft Studio** (p145), is free.

FINANCIAL DISTRICT

Eating p93; Shopping p145; Sleeping p161; Walking & Cycling Tours p88

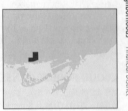

Today the area around **Union Station** is kept busy night and day with briskly paced executives, lost tourists trying to orient themselves to the CN Tower and fresh faces from outlying suburbs and provincial towns who have just arrived for hockey night at the Air Canada Centre. Designed in part by the great Montréal architects Ross and MacDonald, Union Station's classical revival style means to signify progress and prosperity. After over a decade of construction delays due to WWI and bureaucracy, the station was finally opened in 1927. Standing opposite is the **Fairmont Royal York** (p161), one of many grand chateau-like hotels built by the Canadian Pacific Railroad all across the nation to accommodate rail passengers.

From Union Station, you can walk into the windy corridor of Bay St, Canada's premier **Financial District**. About $100 billion worth of stocks are bought and sold each year at the high-tech Toronto Stock Exchange, which relocated to King St's **Exchange Tower** during Toronto's boom years, but not too long before the big market crash of 'Black Monday' on October 19, 1987. Dominating the district are the three stark, black skyscrapers of the **Toronto-Dominion Centre**, which was designed in the International Style and overseen by Ludwig Mies van der Rohe, the German prophet of the Modernist movement in architecture. When IM Pei, who also designed Paris's Pyramide du Louvre and the Rock and Roll Hall of Fame and Museum in Ohio, drew up plans for the **Commerce Court** across the street, he was careful to make it one story taller than the TD Centre.

Naturally banks make up the bulk of the Financial District's remaining landmarks. Dignified **Scotia Plaza** has art-deco bas reliefs and is the city's second-tallest skyscraper after **First Canadian Place**. Fancifully built of arches that resemble dinosaur ribs, a glass atrium connecting the two towers of **BCE Place** is the work of Spanish architect and

Transportation

Subway Union subway station is adjacent to Union train station.

Walking The underground PATH system (p88) connects Union Station with many of the surrounding sights.

Car Parking lots and garages are plentiful, but expensive. Most charge at least $2.50 per hour, although early-bird specials (say, in before 7:30am) keep the daily maximum around $10 to $15. The municipal garage at 40 York St charges $1.50 per half-hour (daily maximum $17), but only $7 on evenings and weekends. Daily maximum rates are lower at the St Lawrence Garage at 2 Church St and other municipal lots along Lakeshore Blvd W, which are further away.

engineer Santiago Calatrava. Inside stands a restored 1845 Bank of Montréal building facad
from Kingston, the town in eastern Ontario that once aspired to being Canada's capital o
commerce. Nearby the triangular towers of the **Royal Bank Plaza** are covered in gold leaf, an
with 2500oz of 24-carat gold baked into the glass, they are bedazzling in sunlight.

Orientation

Union Station is the city center's transport hub, standing on Front St just north of th
Harbourfront. The Financial District gobbles up much of the downtown core, taking u
over a dozen city blocks between the subway lines along Yonge St and University Ave. I
stops short at Queen St, which defines the district's northern edge.

AIR CANADA CENTRE Map pp228-30

☎ 416-815-5982; www.theaircanadacentre.com; 40 Bay St; tour adult/child under 13/student/senior $12/8/10/10; subway Union

Guided tours of the home of the Toronto Maple Leafs hockey team take you where the players go (even into the dressing room sans players), but you'll enjoy the arena more if you can actually score tickets to a game (p135). Tours run hourly, events permitting.

CLOUD FOREST CONSERVATORY

Map pp228-30

☎ 416-392-1111; btwn Richmond & Temperance Sts, east of Yonge St; admission free; 🕒 10am-3pm Mon-Fri; subway Queen

The Cloud Forest Conservatory is an unexpected sanctuary in the downtown core. Built vertically as a 'modernist ruin,' it has exposed steel, creeping vines, a waterfall and a mura depicting the trades of construction worker Avoid the area after dark, however, since th adjacent park attracts some pretty unsavor types.

CN TOWER Map pp228-30

Canadian National Tower; ☎ 416-868-6937; www.cntower.ca; 301 Front St W; main observation deck adult/child 4-12/senior $19/14/17, SkyPod deck extra $5; 🕒 10am-10pm, later in summer; subway Union

Even if we tell you not to bother, you'll probably feel obligated to take a gander at thi city icon which, since 1976, has been th highest freestanding structure (553m) in th world. Its primary function is radio and T communications, but relieving every tourist o as much cash as possible is another priority

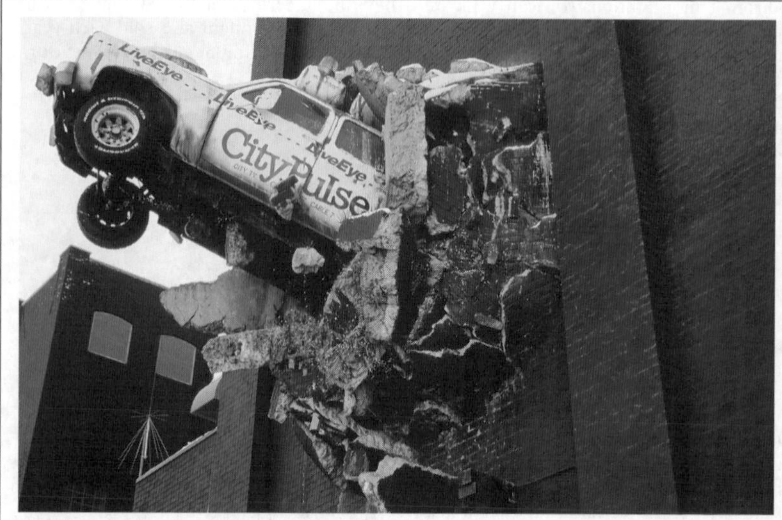

Citytv (p49)

glass elevators whisk you up the outside to observation decks at the top. For extra thrills, one deck has a glass floor, and the other is a windy, vertigo-inducing outside platform. If it's hazy, however, you won't be able to see a thing. Summer queues for the elevator can be up to two hours long – going up *and* coming back down. For those with reservations at the award-winning revolving restaurant, **360** (☎ 416-362-5411; prix fixe dinner adult/child $65/37.50; ⌚ lunch May-Dec, dinner daily), the elevator ticket price is waived.

DESIGN EXCHANGE Map pp228-30

DX; ☎ 416-216-2160; www.dx.org; 234 Bay St; admission free, surcharge for special exhibitions; ⌚ 10am-6pm Mon-Fri, noon-5pm Sat & Sun; subway King

The streamlined *moderne* Design Exchange building served as the original Toronto Stock Exchange starting in 1937, and its opening pushed Toronto ahead of Montréal as Canada's financial center. Note the frontal art-deco stone friezes and the medallions on the stainless steel doors depicting toilers in the nation's industries. Inside are eye-catching temporary exhibits of contemporary industrial design, attached to a unique gift shop. Also on site is the restaurant **Kubo DX** (p94).

GOETHE-INSTITUT GALLERY Map pp228-30

☎ 416-593-5257; www.goethe.de/uk/tor/enindex.htm; 163 King St W; admission free; ⌚ 10am-5pm Mon-Thu, 10am-4pm Fri & Sat; subway St Andrew

Below street level inside this respected German cultural center, you can peruse temporary exhibitions of contemporary fine arts emphasizing the avant-garde from Europe and across Canada. German film screenings with English subtitles cost just $5 per person. The center also sponsors concerts and dramatic readings around the city.

HOCKEY HALL OF FAME Map pp228-30

☎ 416-360-7765; www.hhof.com; BCE Pl, 30 Yonge St, lower concourse; adult/child under 4/youth 4-13/senior $12.50/free/8/8; ⌚ 10am-5pm Mon-Fri, 9:30am-6pm Sat, 10:30am-5pm Sun, till 6pm during summer; subway Union

In a gorgeous, gray stone rococo Bank of Montréal building (c 1885), this shrine gives hockey fans everything they could possibly want. You can attempt to stop Wayne Gretzky's winning shot (in virtual reality) or have your photo taken with hockey's biggest prize – the one and only Stanley Cup. After being overwhelmed by interactive multimedia exhibits and nostalgic hockey memorabilia, even visitors unfamiliar with the game may come to an understanding of Canada's passion for this, one of the fastest (and most violent!) of sports.

SKYDOME Map pp228-30

☎ 416-341-2770; www.skydome.com; 1 Blue Jays Way; 1hr tour adult/child 5-11/youth 12-17 $12.50/7/8.50; ⌚ tour schedules vary, French-language tours Jul & Aug; subway Union

As technically awe-inspiring as the CN Tower, the SkyDome sports stadium opened in 1989 with the world's first fully retractable dome roof. Made mostly of concrete, this feat of engineering moves at a rapid 22m per minute, taking just 20 minutes to completely open. That beats Montréal's Olympic Stadium, which opened just once and failed to ever do so again.

Tours are pricey for what you get. After watching a 10-minute introductory film, the tour sprints up to a box suite, takes in the view from the stands and press section, and briefly walks through a locker room (without athletes). Did you know that eight 747s would fit on the playing field and that the stadium uses enough electricity to light the province of Prince Edward Island?

A cheap seat to a Blue Jays baseball game (p134) is the least expensive way to see the SkyDome. When no game is on, the SkyDome's own **Hard Rock Café** runs as a regular sports bar; you can simply go in for a hamburger and a beer and have a look at the playing field. During games, tables with views must be paid for. Rooms overlooking the field can be rented at the SkyDome's own hotel, the **Renaissance Toronto** (p162).

Before leaving, look for the faces of Michael Snow's *Audience* sculptures gazing back at you from their perch high up on SkyDome's northern exterior.

TORONTO DOMINION GALLERY OF INUIT ART Map pp228-30

☎ 416-982-8473; Maritime Life Tower, 79 Wellington St W, ground fl & mezzanine; admission free; ⌚ 8am-6pm Mon-Fri, 10am-4pm Sat & Sun; subway St Andrew

A fourth Toronto-Dominion Centre tower stands on the other side of Wellington St from the original trio of skyscrapers. Inside is an exceptional gallery of Aboriginal carvings and sculptures in stone and bone, worthy of display in any museum, and free for public viewing.

OLD YORK

Eating p94; Shopping p146; Sleeping p162; Walking & Cycling Tours p80

A few blocks east of Union Station along Front St, many of the city's oldest and best-preserved buildings come into view. If you miss out on seeing this district, you'll miss out on the keys to Toronto's past.

Established by Captain John Simcoe in 1793, the historic town of York (p32) was bounded by Duke, Front, George and Berkeley Sts. Although a few of the street names have changed, this neighborhood stil boasts the city's greatest concentration of historic sites dating from early colonial times In 1834 York was officially swallowed up by the newly established city of Toronto, bu remained a center of social, political and economic life, especially at the **St Lawrence Marke** (p47).

Over the centuries, the district has continually been an odd mix of posh and run-dowr areas. The first parliament buildings of Upper Canada, which were burned to the grounc by American troops during the War of 1812, were built here, as were the homes of many distinguished colonial citizens. But Old York also served as the province's first red-ligh district, ground zero for cholera epidemics and also for the city's first great fire in 1849. During the 1960s, many of its grand Victorian and Edwardian structures were torn down but a few like the **Flatiron (Gooderham) Building** (below), **St Lawrence Hall** (p47) and quaint Torontc St buildings, near the **Le Royal Meridien King Edward** (p162) and the **Courthouse Market Grille** (p95) survived razing. So did the **Mackenzie House** (p50), which is located by **Dundas Square** (p49). Some of the old warehouses still stand vacant, but the **Distillery Historic District** (below) has beer wonderfully revitalized. Pubs abound, too, for example **C'est What** (p117).

Neighborhoods – Old York

Orientation

Historically speaking, the old town of York comprises just 10 square blocks. But today i extends east of Yonge St all the way to the Don River, and from Queen St south to the waterfront Esplanade.

DISTILLERY HISTORIC DISTRICT

Map pp238-9

☎ 416-866-8687; www.thedistillerydistrict.com; 55 Mill St; admission free, tour $5-6; 🕑 10am-6pm Tue-Sun, later in summer; streetcar 503, 504

At the 1832 Gooderham and Worts distillery, this rousing new arts complex is full of cobblestone streets and Victorian warehouses converted into soaring galleries, artists' studios, design shops, coffeehouses and restaurants, even a brewery. Self-guided audio tours aren't very riveting, so instead join one of the more lively guided tours departing from the visitors' center on Trinity St, just south of the main gates.

ENOCH TURNER SCHOOLHOUSE

Map pp238-9

☎ 416-863-0010; www.enochturnerschoolhouse.ca; 106 Trinity St; admission free; 🕑 call for schedules; streetcar 503, 504

Dating from 1848, this restored one-room classroom is where kids are shown what the good ol' days were like. Wealthy brewer Enoch Turner opened it as Toronto's first free schoo so children of poorer citizens could learn the three Rs. Visiting is free, but is only permittec when school tours are not scheduled.

FLATIRON (GOODERHAM) BUILDING

Map pp228-30

49 Wellington St E; streetcar 503, 504

As the headquarters of the Gooderham distillery family in the 1890s, the Flatiron is famous for its unusual triangular shape, dictated by the angle at which Old York's grid system intersects the waterfront. An exterior trompe l'oeil mural mimics the restored 19th-century warehouses with their cast-iron facades across Front St.

ST JAMES CATHEDRAL Map pp228-30

☎ 416-364-7865 ext 233; www.stjamescathedral.on.ca; 65 Church St; admission by donation; 🕑 7:30am-5:30pm Sun-Fri, 9am-3pm Sat, services daily, museum & archives 1-4pm Tue & Wed; streetcar 503, 504

Erected after the Great Fire of 1849, this venerable Gothic Revival cathedral is graced by Tiffany stained glass, a grand organ, lovely gardens and the tallest spire in Canada. A small religious museum and historical archives are kept in the parish house.

ST LAWRENCE MARKET & HALL

Map pp228-30

☎ 416-392-7120; www.stlawrencemarket.com; South Market, 2 Front St E; admission free; 🕑 8am-6pm Tue-Thu, 8am-7pm Fri, 5am-5pm Sat; streetcar 504

Old York's market has been a neighborhood meeting place for over two centuries. The restored **South Market** building, which houses specialty food vendors (p96), dates back to Toronto's 1845 city hall. Inside the old council chambers upstairs, the **Market Gallery** (Map pp228-30; ☎ 416-392-7604; admission free; 🕑 10am-4pm Wed-Fri, 9am-4pm Sat, noon-4pm Sun) is now the city's exhibition hall, with rotating displays of paintings, photographs, documents and historical artifacts. On the opposite side of Front St, the **North Market** comes alive with a Saturday **farmers' market** (p96) and an **antique market** (p146) on Sunday. After being sadly neglected, it was rebuilt around the time of Canada's 100th birthday in 1967. A few steps further north, the glorious **St Lawrence Hall** (1849), topped by a clock tower that can be seen for blocks, is considered one of the city's finest examples of Victorian classicism.

Transportation

Subway Both Union and King subway stations are about a 500m walk from the Old Town of York.

Streetcar The 504 King streetcar runs along King St, stopping within a block or two of every sight. The 503 Kingston Rd streetcar line makes a useful loop onto Wellington St E, just east of Yonge St, but only runs during weekday morning and evening rush hours.

Walking With sturdy footwear, you can cover much of the district on foot.

Car Metered on-street parking is rarely available, except during the early morning and late evening. Pay lots and garages are not difficult to find, however. The municipal St Lawrence Garage at 2 Church St charges $1.25 per half-hour (daily maximum $8).

TORONTO'S FIRST POST OFFICE

Map pp238-9

☎ 416-865-1833; www.townofyork.com; 60 Adelaide St W; admission by donation; 🕑 9am-4pm Mon-Fri, 10am-4pm Sat & Sun; streetcar 503, 504

Dating from the 1830s, the old post office is now a living museum. After you have written your correspondence with a quill pen and ink, costumed staff will seal the letter with wax and send it postmarked 'York-Toronto 1833' for a small fee. Self-guided tour pamphlets are available by the front door, where a gift shop sells Victorian-style writing materials. Famous folks like William Lyon Mackenzie and the Baldwins once rented postal boxes here. At the back of the old-fashioned reading room are interesting historical displays about the Old Town of York and a model of Toronto c 1873. To find the post office, look for the British and Canadian flags flying out front, just west of the Bank of Upper Canada building.

THEATRE BLOCK & ENTERTAINMENT DISTRICT

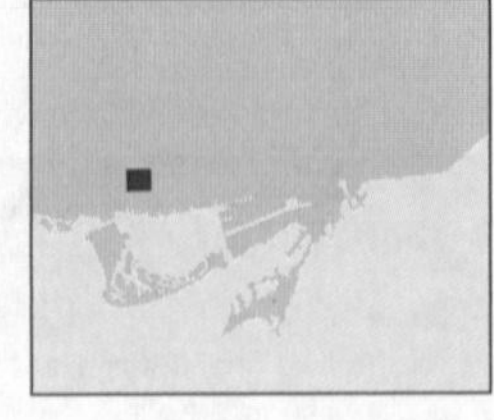

Eating p96; Shopping p147; Sleeping p164; Walking & Cycling Tours p86

West of the Financial District along King St is Toronto's revitalized theater district, called the Theatre Block. In the 19th century, however, the corner of King and Simcoe Sts was nicknamed 'Education, Legislation, Salvation and Damnation.' Why? Because Upper Canada College, the lieutenant governor's house, a church and a rowdy tavern (respectively) faced off on opposite corners. Only salvation remains standing today at **St Andrew's** (p48). The focal point of the Theatre Block is the beaux-arts **Royal Alexandra Theatre** (p125). Nicknamed the 'Royal Alex,' it was built by Toronto's youngest millionaire, Cawthra Mulock, in 1907. Mary Pickford, Fred Astaire, Humphrey Bogart and Edith Piaf performed here before the stage lights started to flicker out. It was saved from demolition in the 1960s by discount-shopping entrepreneur 'Honest Ed' Mirvish, who restored the Royal Alex's velvet, brocade and crystal Edwardian luxury and put on productions of *Hair* and *Godspell* that woke up the entire district. Two decades later Mirvish and his son David commissioned the **Princess of Wales Theatre** (p125) for *Miss Saigon*. Princess Di herself attended the ceremonial opening in 1983. Inside over 929 sq meters of murals by Frank Stella adorn the walls

The Theatre Block is part of the ever-expanding galaxy of the Entertainment District (nicknamed Clubland). Pay your respects to legendary **Second City** (p128), which shares its name with another comedy club in Chicago. The common moniker refers to how each city has been thought of as playing second fiddle in the past, Chicago to the Big Apple (New York City) and Toronto to Montréal (in the prideful eyes of Montréalers, that is).

Orientation

The so-called Theatre Block actually takes up two blocks of King St W, between John St and Simcoe St. Most of the Entertainment District's bars and clubs are further north, concentrated on a few square blocks of Adelaide St W and Richmond St W, between John St and Spadina Ave. Second City is one of a few venues on Peter St, headed south via Blue Jays Way toward SkyDome.

CANADA'S WALK OF FAME Map pp228-30

☎ 416-367-9255; www.canadaswalkoffame.com; John, King, Simcoe & Front Sts; subway St Andrew

True to its moniker 'Hollywood of the North,' Toronto has its own walk of fame, with concrete stars straggling beside Roy Thomson Hall featuring only a few names you'll recognize (including some you'll wish you didn't know), and even fewer born in Toronto. On the roll call are comedian Mike Meyers, country singer Shania Twain, supermodel Linda Evangelista, the rock band the Tragically Hip and, yes, even zany Cirque du Soleil.

CANADIAN BROADCASTING CENTRE Map pp228-30

☎ 416-205-8605; ww.cbc.ca; 250 Front St W; 1hr tour adult/student/senior $7/6/6, museum admission free; ⏲ tour schedules vary, museum 9am-5pm Mon-Fri, noon-4pm Sat; streetcar 504, subway Union

The Canadian Broadcasting Centre, which we fancy King Kong made out of Lego blocks, serves as the headquarters for English-language public radio and TV programming across Canada. The French-language production facilities are in Montréal, which leaves the president, in a truly Canadian spirit of compromise, stranded in an executive office in Ottawa.

You can take a peek at the radio newsrooms anytime or attend a free noontime concert in the world-class **Glenn Gould Studio** (p129). For a dose of Canadian pop culture nostalgia, visit the miniature-sized **CBC Museum** or enjoy some classic TV shows in the **Graham Spry Theatre**. Be warned that the CBC's public tours don't take you much 'behind the scenes.'

ROY THOMSON HALL Map pp228-30

☎ 416-872-4255; www.roythomson.com; 60 Simcoe St; subway St Andrew

Looking like an inverted ballerina's tutu, the controversial design of this concert hall has been called neo-expressionist or 'deconstructionist.' Some might say it's a pity that no one has yet knocked this place down, it's so ugly. You may recognize its futuristic interior from the 2000 film *X-Men*.

ST ANDREW'S PRESBYTERIAN CHURCH Map pp228-30

☎ 416-593-5600; www.standrewstoronto.org; cnr Simcoe & King Sts; admission by donation; ⏲ 8:30am-3pm Mon-Sat, services 10:30am Sun, 12:15pm Thu & 8:30am weekdays; streetcar 504

Built in 1876, it's as much Scottish as it is Norman Romanesque – note the twisted barley on certain interior columns and the grand French Classic–style organ decorated with Scottish thistle motifs. Pick up a self-guided tour pamphlet by the entrance.

Transportation

Streetcar The 504 King streetcar runs along the Theatre Block. The 501 Queen and 510 Spadina lines border Clubland.

Subway St Patrick and Osgoode stations on the University line are a short walk east of the neighborhood.

Car Avoid driving here, especially during the evening and on weekends. Private lots charge extortionate rates. Fees vary at the underground garage at Roy Thomson Hall; it's open 6am to 12:30am, except holidays.

QUEEN STREET & DUNDAS SQUARE

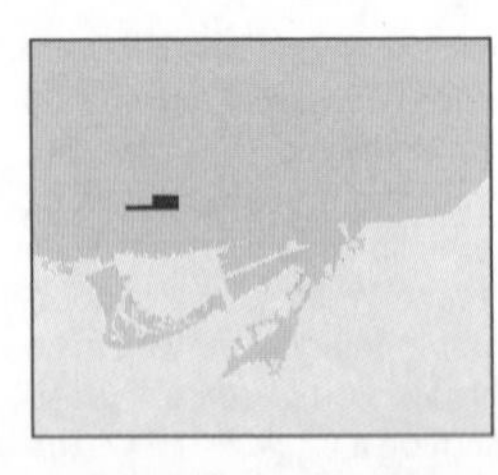

Eating p97; Shopping p147; Sleeping p163; Walking & Cycling Tours p88

In 1869 historic Eaton's department store was established on Yonge St by enterprising Timothy Eaton. His dry-goods business succeeded with the 'revolutionary' sales policies of fixed prices, cash only and refunds for dissatisfied customers. Eaton's went bankrupt in 1999, but the gargantuan **Eaton Centre** (p148) shopping complex still stands today. You would be forgiven for thinking it's still under construction, since renovations are ongoing and no attention has been paid whatsoever to the exterior, but inside it's all sweetness and light, with trees and sculpted Canada geese by Michael Snow suspended from the galleria's glass roof. Interestingly, the mall was built around Trinity Square, which houses a Victorian-era church.

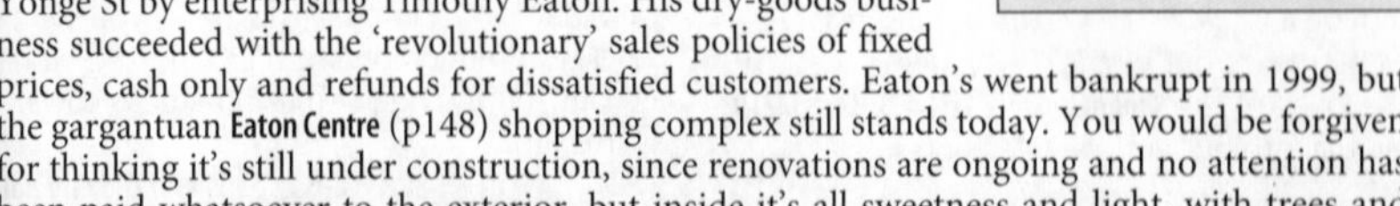

Just northeast of Eaton Centre, **Dundas Square** aims to be the city's newest public space with an outdoor concert stage right in the heart of downtown. Local radio station Q107 broadcasts from a ground-floor studio just across the street at the Hard Rock Café, which has a patio overlooking the square for drinks. In the same vein of entertainment, further south on Yonge St very well-heeled patrons mill around outside the **Canon Theatre** (p124), a 1920s vaudeville and cinema venue, and the venerable **Elgin & Winter Garden Theatre Centre** (p124). This half a block has become the city's secondary theater district, after the popular Theatre Block (p47).

Orientation

Dundas Square is often better known for the nearby landmark, Eaton Centre. The shopping mall sprawls between Queen and Dundas Sts. Both are located south of the main Yonge Street Strip and east of the Queen St shopping district. City Hall and many other governmental buildings sit on Queen St, west of University Ave.

CAMPBELL HOUSE Map pp226-7

☎ 416-597-0227; 160 Queen St W; tour adult/child/student/senior $4.50/2/2.50/3; 9am-4:30pm Mon-Fri mid-Feb–mid-Jan, noon-4pm Sat & Sun in summer, closed mid-Jan–mid-Feb

This formal Georgian mansion dating from 1822 was one of the city's first brick buildings. It belonged to Chief Justice William Campbell, the same judge who presided over the famous Types Trial of 1826. It has been beautifully refurbished in 19th-century style by the Advocates' Society, which now uses the premises as its clubhouse. Interestingly, it took six hours to move the house from its original location on Adelaide St, just 1.5km away.

Transportation

Subway Queen and Dundas stations are on the Yonge subway line. A few blocks further west, Osgoode (at Queen St W) and St Patrick (at Dundas St W) are stops on the University line.

Streetcar 501 Queen and 505 Dundas streetcars serve the area.

Walking Eaton Centre and City Hall are part of downtown's underground PATH system.

Car The municipal garage at 25 Dundas St E charges $1.50 per half-hour (daily maximum $13). Parking at Nathan Phillips Square or the municipal garage at 37 Queen St E costs $6 maximum after 6pm weekdays or before 6pm on weekends.

CANADA LIFE BUILDING Map pp226-7

330 University Ave; subway Osgoode

Walk north of Queen St to the monumental Canada Life building. At the lobby security desk, pick up a weather card that explains the mysteries of the 1950s beacon tower on top. If it's flashing white, everyone knows that snow is on the way.

CHUM/CITYTV COMPLEX Map pp226-7

☎ 416-599-7339; www.mztv.com; 277 Queen St W; museum adult/student/senior/family $6/4/4/18; museum tours 11am, 2pm & 4pm; streetcar 501

At the corner of John St there's a public video booth, the infamous **Speakers Corner**. Anyone can step inside and, for just a loonie ($1), record themselves saying or doing pretty much anything. Creative and controversial segments are broadcast on Canada's original reality TV show, called *Speakers Corner*. At the adjacent studios of **MuchMusic**, the Canadian version of MTV, you might see pop stars dashing inside from their limos as teen fans cheer à la Beatlemania; every Wednesday afternoon, club kids decked out in full-on gear wait in line to get picked as dancers on *Electric Circus*. Above the east parking lot, a CityPulse news truck spins its wheels as it crashes out of the Citytv studio walls. At the back of the **ChumCityStore** (p147), the **MZTV Museum** exhibits vintage television sets.

CHURCH OF THE HOLY TRINITY

Map pp226-7

☎ 416-598-4521; www.holytrinitytoronto.org; 10 Trinity Sq; admission by donation; ⌚ 10am-3pm Mon-Fri, services 9am & 10:30am Sun, noon Wed; subway Queen

On the west side of Eaton Centre is Trinity Square, named for this welcoming Anglican church. When it opened in 1847, it was the first church in Toronto not to charge parishioners for pews, thanks to an anonymous Englishwoman who was reportedly quite taken with the bishop. Today it's a cross between a house of worship, small concert venue (p129) and a community drop-in center – everything an inner-city church should be. Don't miss the wonderful Christmas pageant if you're in town in December.

Nearby at No 6 Trinity Square is the well-preserved **Henry Scadding House** (1862), which some believe is haunted by the benign ghost of the first rector, who wrote works of literature, religion and history here.

CITY HALL Map pp226-7

☎ 416-392-7341; www.city.toronto.on.ca; admission free; ⌚ 8:30am-4:30pm Mon-Fri; 100 Queen St W; subway Queen

Much-maligned City Hall was Toronto's first jump into architectural modernity. Its twin clamshell towers, with a flying saucer–style structure between them at the bottom, were completed in 1965 to Finnish architect Viljo Revell's award-winning design. Frank Lloyd Wright had called it a 'headmarker for a grave,' and in a macabre twist of fate, Revell died before construction was finished. When sculptor Henry Moore first offered to sell *The Archer*, a piece located in the gardens, out of his own collection and at a low price, the city council (unbelievably) refused. Ask for a self-guide tour pamphlet (available in eight languages) at the info desk in the lobby.

Out front is **Nathan Phillips Square** a meeting place for skaters, demonstrators and office workers on their lunch breaks. In summer, look out for a Wednesday **farmers' market** (10am to 2:30pm), free concerts and special events. Canada's rock band Barenaked Ladies were once banned from playing here but were later invited back in a conciliatory gesture. The fountain pool becomes a popular ice-skating rink during winter (p136). Don't feel intimidated if you are a novice – you won't be alone. Immigrants from around the world are out there gingerly making strides toward assimilation.

On the other side of Bay St is the **Old City Hall** (1899). It was the definitive work of Toronto architect EJ Lennox, the same man who built **Casa Loma** (p58). Lennox was chastized for inscribing his name just below the eaves here. Now housing legal courtrooms, this distinctive Romanesque hall has an off-center bell tower, painted murals and an allegorical stained-glass window. First-floor exhibits are open to the public.

ELGIN & WINTER GARDEN THEATRE CENTRE Map pp226-7

☎ 416-314-2871; www.heritagefdn.on.ca; 189 Yonge St; tours adult/student/senior $7/6/6; ⌚ tours usually 5pm Thu & 11am Sat; subway Queen

A restored masterpiece, the Elgin & Winter Garden represents the last operating double-decker theater in the world. In 1913 the breathtaking Winter Garden was built as the flagship for a vaudeville chain that never really took off, while the downstairs Elgin was converted into a movie house in the 1920s.

The Ontario Heritage Foundation saved both theaters from being demolished in 1981. During its $29-million restoration effort, bread dough was used to uncover original rose-garden frescoes, the Belgian company that made the original carpeting was contacted for fresh rolls, and the beautiful foliage hanging from the ceiling of the upstairs Winter Garden Theatre was replaced, leaf by painstaking leaf. Seats were bought from Chicago's infamous Biograph Theater.

Entertaining public tours, worth every penny, are given by the same passionate volunteers who staff the theaters' ongoing restoration efforts. See p123 for box office information.

MACKENZIE HOUSE Map pp226-7

☎ 416-392-6915; www.city.toronto.on.ca; 82 Bond St; adult/child under 13/student/senior $3.50/2.50/2.75/2.75; ⌚ noon-5pm Tue-Sun, closing 4pm weekdays Sep-Dec, weekends only Jan-Apr; subway Dundas

This gaslit Victorian home was owned by William Lyon Mackenzie, the city's first mayor and the leader of the failed Upper Canada Rebellion of 1837. It's well furnished with antiques; notice the brass door knocker, presented to Mackenzie in 1859 after his return from exile in America. Handmade 19th century printing-press items, such as 'Mackenzie: Rebel with a Cause' T-shirts, and reproductions of the 'Ye Olde' variety are sold in the museum shop.

MASSEY HALL Map pp226-7

www.masseyhall.com; 178 Victoria St; subway Queen

Landmark Massey Hall was given to the city in 1894 by industrial baron Hart Massey. Orators, explorers and other famous faces (including Oscar Wilde, Enrico Caruso, George Gershwin, Charlie Mingus and the Dalai Lama) have all appeared on its stage. The acoustics are superb, and that's why the **Toronto Symphony Orchestra** (p130) occasionally plays here.

What's Free?

Here's a quick rundown of things to do when your wallet is running on empty! See City Calendar (p8) for free-for-all festivals and celebrations. Most architectural sights, cemeteries and cathedrals are also free for entry. So are many gardens, conservatories and parks (for more on outdoor activities, turn to p135).

Almost Any Day

Allan Gardens Conservatory (p62)
Casa Loma gardens (p58; 4pm-dusk summer only)
CBC Museum (p48)
City Hall (p50; closed Sat & Sun)
Cloud Forest Conservatory (p44)
Frisbee Golf on Ward's Island (p66)
High Park (p77)
Market Gallery (p47)
Metro Toronto Police Museum (p54)
Museum of Contemporary Canadian Art (p77)
National Film Board Mediatheque (p116)
Provincial legislature (p58)
Redpath Sugar Museum (p42; closed Sat & Sun)
Riverdale Farm (p62)
Scarborough Bluffs (p75)
Steam Whistle Brewing (p42; closed Sun)
Tengye Ling Tibetan Buddhist Temple (p138) Dharma talk & walking meditation.
Tommy Thompson Park (p63)
Toronto Dominion Gallery of Inuit Art (p45)
Toronto Music Garden (p43)
Toronto's First Post Office (p47)
University of Toronto Campus (p59)
York Quay Centre (p145; most galleries closed Mon & Tue)

Tuesday

Bata Shoe Museum (p55; 1st Tue of month)
Gardiner Museum of Ceramic Art (p56; 1st Tue of month)

Wednesday

Art Gallery of Ontario (p53; 6-8:30pm)
Power Plant Art Gallery (p42; 5-8pm)
Textile Museum of Canada (p52; 5-8pm)

Friday

Royal Ontario Museum (p56; 4:30-9:30pm)

Sunday

Sivananda Yoga Vedanta Centre (p138) Afternoon yoga.

Special Events & Exhibitions

Church of the Holy Trinity (p50)
Eric Arthur Gallery (p59)
Glenn Gould Studio (p129)
Goethe-Institut Gallery (p45)
Harbourfront Centre (p129)
Heritage Toronto (p40)
Japan Foundation (p56)
Music Gallery (p122)
Osgoode Hall (p52)
ROMWalks (p40)
St James Cathedral (p46)
Second City (p128)
UT Art Centre (p59)

OSGOODE HALL Map pp226-7

☎ 416-947-3300; www.osgoodehall.com; 130 Queen St W; admission free; 🕑 tours usually 1:15pm Mon-Fri Jul & Aug; subway Osgoode

Built in many phases during the Victorian era, this august classical hall became a showcase for elite colonials, many of whom were lawyers. The peculiar wrought-iron 'cow gates' out front were said to have been put up to keep out wandering bovines, a common street problem in the 1860s. Inside the hall a grand staircase leads up to the Ontario superior courts and the Great Library, with miles of books, twisting stairways and 12m-high vaulted ceilings. Free tours are given by students of the Law Society of Upper Canada, whose members have been pacing the grounds for 170 years.

TEXTILE MUSEUM OF CANADA Map pp226-7

☎ 416-599-5321; www.textilemuseum.ca; 55 Centre Ave; adult/child under 5/student/senior/family $8/free/6/6/22, 5-8pm Wed admission by donation; 🕑 11am-5pm Tue-Fri, 11am-8pm Wed, noon-5pm Sat & Sun, gallery tours usually 2pm Sun; subway St Patrick

Although quite obscurely situated, this small museum will delight anyone with even the slightest interest in handmade textiles and tapestries. The exhibits draw upon a permanent collection of almost 10,000 items from Latin America, Africa, Europe, Southeast Asia and India, as well as contemporary Canada. Workshops teach batiking, weaving, knitting and more.

CHINATOWN & BALDWIN VILLAGE

Eating p98; Sleeping p164

Toronto's principal **Chinatown** is right in the city centre. A brilliantly vermilion twin dragon gate stands on Spadina Ave, just north of Dundas St W, marking the epicenter. The whole area looks more like Little Saigon or Bangkok every year, as Vietnamese and Southeast Asian immigrants continue to arrive. Like its counterparts around the world, Chinatown offers rock-bottom prices on clothes, everyday goods, groceries and imports. There are naturally tons of restaurants here, but also traditional herbalists, bakeries, tea rooms and other places selling mysterious items recognizable only to the initiated. Vendors set up in summer along the sidewalks, so you can wander down and buy a fresh coconut or some spiky rambutan. If you're brave, crack open a stinky, prickly oval durian and scoop out its sweet custard-like fruit.

Another good place for noshing is shady **Baldwin Village**, a short stroll north of the **Art Gallery of Ontario** (p53). As evidenced by the Yiddish sign at No 29, the village has Jewish roots. But the bohemian air comes from counterculture US exiles who decamped here during the Vietnam War era. Today discovering Baldwin St feels like stumbling onto a Manhattanesque movie set, complete with Italian sidewalk cafés. Cultural spillover from Chinatown makes things even more interesting, with Malaysian bistros, South Asian kitchens and Chinese seafood joints joining the epicurean throng. During summer every restaurant's patio is full to bursting with neighborhood denizens, romantic couples and a few lucky tourists.

Transportation

Streetcar 510 Spadina streetcars run from Spadina subway south through Chinatown, while the 505 Dundas line cuts east–west. The 506 College or 501 Queen streetcars are within walking distance of Baldwin Village and Chinatown.

Subway Baldwin Village is 500m from St Patrick station.

Car Driving around Chinatown is a headache – avoid it at all costs. Instead use the municipal garage at 40 Larch St, which charges $1 per half-hour (daily maximum $6), or Dragon City garage at 521 Dundas St W, which charges slightly more. Residential streets around Baldwin Village are either metered or restricted, but you might find space to park for an hour or two.

Orientation

Chinatown originally ran along Dundas St W, but today the main thoroughfare is Spadina Ave, roughly running between College and Queen Sts. Baldwin Village is one short block of Baldwin St between Beverly and McCaul Sts, about 300m east of Spadina Ave.

401 RICHMOND Map pp228-30

☎ 416-595-5900; www.401richmond.net; 401 Richmond St W; admission free; ⏲ most galleries Tue-Sat; streetcar 510

Admirers have called it a 'city within a city,' and this sprawling arts complex certainly lives up to the moniker. Inside an early 20th-century lithographer's warehouse, 401 Richmond is bursting with diverse contemporary art and design galleries for painters, holographers, photographers, printmakers, sculptors, milliners and other arty folks. It has a glass elevator, ground-floor artists' café and roof garden, too. Afterward swing by **Art at 80** (Map pp228-30; 80 Spadina Ave; ⏲ Tue-Sat), another varied contemporary gallery complex, just two blocks away.

ART GALLERY OF ONTARIO Map pp226-7

AGO; ☎ 416-979-6648; www.ago.net; 317 Dundas St W; adult/youth 6-15/student/senior/family $12/6/9/9/25, 6-8:30pm Wed admission free, surcharge for special exhibitions; ⏲ 11am-6pm Tue-Fri, 11am-8:30pm Wed, 10am-5:30pm Sat & Sun; streetcar 505

The AGO's art collections are excellent, and unless you have a lot of stamina, you'll need more than one trip to see it all. Highlights include rare Québecois religious statuary, First Nations and Inuit carvings, and major Canadian works by Emily Carr and the Group of Seven. The museum is known for its Henry Moore sculpture pavilion, which has benches with sit-down listening stations (one recounts the controversy over City Hall's acquisition of Moore's work).

Looking out onto its own park, the **Grange** is a restored Georgian house that's actually part of the AGO and is included in the admission price. Authentic mid-19th-century furniture and staff in period dress present life in a 'gentleman's residence' of the time, staying in character without so much as a snicker. Note the Grange may be open shorter hours than the AGO.

For schedules of free gallery tours, art play for kids, special events and films at the **Cinematheque Ontario** (p115), call ☎ 416-979-6649, check at the information desk or go to the museum's website, which also has updates on Transformation AGO, a project of extensive gallery renovations and expansion overseen by famed architect Frank Gehry (p25).

Dragon sculpture, Chinatown (p52)

Toronto for Kids

Special events for children take place throughout the year, and two of the best are the **Milk International Children's Festival of the Arts** (p8) and the **Canadian National Exhibition** (p10). During summer it's easy (if expensive) to keep 'em entertained at **Ontario Place** (p42) or **Paramount Canada's Wonderland** (p75) amusement parks. At any time of year, interactive exhibits at the **Ontario Science Centre** (p75), **Royal Ontario Museum** (p56) and the **Children's Own Museum** (go to www.childrensown museum.org for reconstruction updates) are always winning ideas. Explore the **Harbourfront** (p37), **Toronto Islands** (p75), the **Beaches** (p62) and **High Park** (p77), then turn to p133 for more outdoor activity ideas. Then give your little city slickers a taste of rural life at **Riverdale Farm** (p62) or **Black Creek Pioneer Village** (p77). For entertainment, drop by storytime at the **Toronto Public Library – Lillian H Smith Branch** (p59) or attend a performance at the innovative **Lorraine Kimsa Theatre for Young People** (p124). Specialty stores include **Kidding Awound** (p151), **Science City** (p51) and cozy **Parentbooks** (p152). See p96 for recommended restaurants and p199 for an overview of traveling with kids in Toronto.

YONGE STREET STRIP & CHURCH-WELLESLEY VILLAGE

Eating p100; Shopping p149; Sleeping p162

Often called the 'longest road in the world,' **Yonge St** actually seems to be the start of the world's longest, most unrelenting strip of porn theaters, exotic-dance venues and XXX lingerie boutiques. Once a humble oxcart trail, it roughly follows the journey taken by First Nations tribes and colonial traders as they portaged their canoes north, to avoid risking the exposed waters of the Great Lakes.

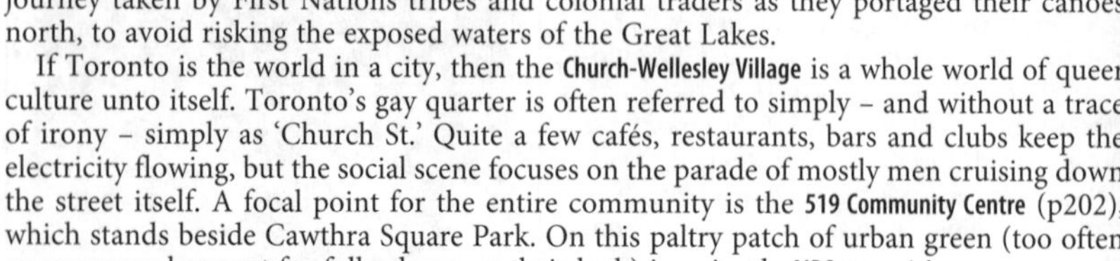

If Toronto is the world in a city, then the **Church-Wellesley Village** is a whole world of queer culture unto itself. Toronto's gay quarter is often referred to simply – and without a trace of irony – simply as 'Church St.' Quite a few cafés, restaurants, bars and clubs keep the electricity flowing, but the social scene focuses on the parade of mostly men cruising down the street itself. A focal point for the entire community is the **519 Community Centre** (p202), which stands beside Cawthra Square Park. On this paltry patch of urban green (too often an unsavory hangout for folks down on their luck) is a simple **AIDS memorial.**

Orientation

Although another pocket of shops and entertainment is found on Yonge St around Eaton Centre and Dundas Square, the main Yonge Street Strip falls between College and Bloor Sts. One long block east is Church St, where a rainbow flag–festooned village has its epicenter at the intersection of Church and Wellesley Sts.

MAPLE LEAF GARDENS Map pp231-3

60 Carlton St; subway College

The hallowed Maple Leaf Gardens hockey arena was home to the Toronto Maple Leafs (p135) for over half a century, starting with the opening game against the Chicago Blackhawks in 1931. Although the Leafs lost that game, they went on to win nearly a dozen Stanley Cup championships and play a record-breaking number of sold-out seasons before moving to the **Air Canada Centre** (p44) in 1999. Over the years, Elvis Presley, Frank Sinatra and the Beatles all performed at the Maple Leaf Gardens.

Rumors that this much-loved piece of city history was to be torn down are only partly true: some of the original facade will remain intact, and a hockey souvenir shop is likely to open inside. The gardens are being redeveloped into a shopping complex. Nostalgic sports fans may also want to drop by the **Canadian Boxing Hall of Fame** (Map pp231-3; ☎ 416-921-5225; 782 Yonge St; admission by donation; usually 4-9pm Mon-Fri; subway Bloor-Yonge).

Transportation

Subway Useful stops off Yonge St are College, Wellesley and Bloor-Yonge.

Streetcar The 506 College (westbound) and 506 Carlton (eastbound) streetcars run along the area's southern edge, but aren't as convenient as the subway.

Car On-street parking is either metered or severely restricted. You may find a free spot for an hour or two on residential side streets east of Yonge St. The **municipal lot** (15 Wellesley St E) charges $1.50 per half-hour (daily maximum $12).

METRO TORONTO POLICE MUSEUM

Map pp231-3

☎ 416-808-7020; www.torontopolice.on.ca/museum; 40 College St; admission free; 10am-4:30pm Mon-Fri; subway College

Inside the monumental Toronto police headquarters, this nonprofit museum has a small but diverting collection of equipment, uniforms and crime-related paraphernalia from 1834 to the present day. Aspiring CSIs can learn about how a murderer's DNA is traced from a simple cigarette butt. At the back, a row of glass cubes exhibit macabre evidence taken from noteworthy cases: the personal effects of the last man hanged in Canada during the 1960s, and legends of the Boyd Gang, a group of bank robbers who escaped from the Don Jail twice before being caught for good.

BLOOR-YORKVILLE

Eating p101; Shopping p150; Sleeping p165

Once Toronto's version of Greenwich Village or Haight-Ashbury, the old countercultural bastion of **Yorkville** has become the city's trés glamorous shopping district, done up with art galleries, glitzy nightspots, exclusive restaurants and outdoor cafés for eyeing the passing parade of Jaguars, Bentleys and classic convertibles. Long gone are the penny-pinching rooming houses and bohemian cafés where Joni Mitchell and Neil Young got their starts. Today towering condo complexes and five-star hotels define the neighborhood demographics. Yet antique shops in well-preserved Victorian houses and atmospheric **Old York Lane** do provide glimpses of yesteryear, as does the 650-ton Precambrian rock sitting in Yorkville's park off Cumberland St. The colonial village of Yorkville (itself named after the old town of York, which officially met its demise when the city of Toronto was born) was founded by brewer Joseph Bloor and Sheriff William Jarvis in the 1830s. Present-day **Bloor St** is a gold-card shopper's paradise for high-end international chains like Chanel, Tiffany's and MAC, as well as Canada's own upscale Holt Renfrew department store. Also stationed here are several embassies and some of Toronto's top museums, handily adjacent to the UT campus.

Orientation

In Yorkville, which officially stretches from Yonge St west to Avenue Rd, the busiest streets are Yorkville Ave, Cumberland St and Hazelton Ave, all found just north of Bloor St. In practice, the neighborhood extends a few blocks further west along Bloor St W into the Annex. The neighborhood's northern edge is Davenport Rd.

Transportation

Subway Convenient stations include Bloor-Yonge, St George and Museum, which are stops along the Bloor-Danforth and Yonge-University lines. Bay station has a confusing number of entrances, so read the exit signs carefully before emerging from underground to save yourself some walking, especially in winter.

Car On-street parking is metered or restricted. Spaces are rarely available, except maybe on Scollard St. The municipal garage at 37 Yorkville Ave charges $1.50 per half-hour with a daily maximum $9 and is cheaper than those at 76 Yorkville Ave and 9 Bedford Rd.

BATA SHOE MUSEUM Map pp231-3

☎ 416-979-7799; www.batashoemuseum.ca; 327 Bloor St W; adult/child 5-14/student/senior/family $6/2/4/4/12, 1st Tue each month admission free; 🕑 10am-5pm Tue-Wed & Fri-Sat, 10am-8pm Thu, noon-5pm Sun; subway St George

Designed by famed architect Raymond Moriyama (p25) to resemble a stylized shoebox, this innovative museum stands on fashion-conscious Bloor St. It has much more to offer than you might at first imagine. Over 10,000 'pedi-artifacts' from every corner of the globe were hunted down by Sonja Bata, of the same family that founded Canada's famous shoe company. Children and adults will gaze in fascination at the museum's 19th-century French chestnut-crushing clogs, Aboriginal Canadian polar boots and famous modern pairs worn by Elton John, Indira Gandhi and Pablo Picasso.

Beginning with a replica set of footprints almost four million years old, the permanent exhibits cover the evolution of the shoemaking craft, as well as human footwear, both gruesome or gorgeous, with a focus on how shoes have signified social status throughout human history. Rotating exhibitions on special topics are just as thoughtfully curated. On the 3rd floor, you can peek through glass windows at curators effecting shoe restoration. In case you miss out on visiting, the website lets you view some of the museum's treasures on-line.

FIREHALL NO 10 & YORKVILLE LIBRARIES Map pp231-3

22 & 34 Yorkville Ave; subway Bay

Yorkville's historic 19th-century fire hall nobly bears the old town hall's coat of arms, which symbolically depicts the occupations of the elected councilors: a brewer, a brick maker, a carpenter, a blacksmith and a butcher, all united under a patriotic Canadian beaver. Next door is the Toronto Public Library's Yorkville Branch, one of hundreds of bold 'Carnegie Classical' libraries funded by philanthropist Andrew Carnegie in the early 1900s.

Close by is the **Toronto Reference Library** (Map pp231-3; ☎ 416-395-5577; 789 Yonge St; 🕓 10am-8pm Mon-Thu, 10am-5pm Fri & Sat, also 1:30-5pm Sep–mid-Jun; subway Bloor-Yonge), a refreshingly modern space designed by architect Raymond Moriyama (p25). Inside are spiraling staircases, a five-story atrium and a noncirculating collection of millions of books.

Top Five Bloor-Yorkville, UT & the Annex

- **Bata Shoe Museum** (p55)
- **Royal Ontario Museum** (right)
- **Casa Loma** (p58)
- **University of Toronto – St George Campus** (p59)
- **Provincial legislature** (p58)

GARDINER MUSEUM OF CERAMIC ART Map pp231-3

☎ 416-586-8080; www.gardinermuseum.on.ca; 111 Queen's Park; adult/student/senior/family $10/6/6/24, 1st Tue each month admission free, surcharge for special exhibitions; 🕓 10am-6pm Mon, Wed & Fri, 10am-8pm Tue & Thu, 10am-5pm Sat & Sun; subway Museum

Opposite the Royal Ontario Museum, this small museum was founded by philanthropists who were passionate collectors themselves. The museum's excellent collections of ceramics are spread over two floors and cover several millennia of art history, focusing on pre-Columbian wares from Mexico, Central and South America; Italian Renaissance majolica; 17th-century English tavern ware; and blue-and-white Chinese porcelain designed for export to European markets.

Admission is steep, but includes a free audioguide. On certain days you can take a guided tour or drop in at the Clay Pit for hands-on pottery demonstrations; call for schedules. The museum gift shop has free exhibitions by contemporary Canadian potters that are well worth browsing, too. Upstairs is **á la Carte** (p102). Note the museum is closed for renovations until fall 2005.

JAPAN FOUNDATION Map pp231-3

☎ 416-966-1600; www.japanfoundationcanada.org; the Colonnade, 131 Bloor St W, 2nd fl; admission usually free; 🕓 schedules vary, closed Sun; subway Bay, Museum

Among the Bloor St embassies, this Japanese cultural center offers temporary multimedia exhibitions, special events (such as dramatic readings of medieval Japanese comedies and contemporary film retrospectives) and artistically inspired rest rooms that deserve design awards. Advance reservations are required for some events.

ROYAL ONTARIO MUSEUM Map pp231-3

ROM; ☎ 416-586-8000; www.rom.on.ca; 100 Queen's Park; adult/child 5-14/student/senior $15/10/12/12, 4:30-9:30pm Fri admission free, surcharge for special exhibitions; 🕓 10am-6pm Mon-Thu & Sat, 10am-9:30pm Fri, 11am-6pm Sun; subway Museum

The multidisciplinary ROM was already Canada's largest museum, even before embarking upon Renaissance ROM, an ambitious building project due to be completed in late 2005. Meanwhile the museum remains open. After renovations are complete, the museum will boast a panoramic restaurant, eye-catching 'crystal' galleries overlooking Bloor St and new space for international traveling exhibitions.

ROM's collections are weighty, filling five floors with natural science, ancient civilization

Bata Shoe Museum (p55)

and art exhibits. The Chinese temple sculptures, Gallery of Korean Art and costumery and textile collections are some of the best anywhere in the world. Kids will be mesmerized by the dinosaur rooms, Egyptian mummies and a replica of an immense bat cave found in Jamaica. Also worth searching out are four towering cedar crest poles carved by First Nations tribes in British Columbia; the largest pole (85m) was shipped from the West Coast by train, then lowered through the museum roof, leaving only centimeters to spare. Other highlights include the Institute of Contemporary Culture's temporary media and design exhibits, perhaps featuring Frank Lloyd Wright furniture or modern photography.

All of this said, the ROM is not always as impressive as it sounds. For most people, a quick walk-through suffices. The best time to visit is on Friday night, when admission is free and there's always a lively special event. Check the website for other museum programs, lectures and organized tours (p40). If you're driving here, ask the front desk for discount vouchers, which are valid at the 9 Bedford Rd municipal lot.

TORONTO HELICONIAN CLUB

Map pp231-3
35 Hazelton Ave; subway Bay

Nudged between the art galleries on Hazelton Ave, this former house of worship boasts of Carpenter Gothic Revival–style construction with a unique carved rose window and a wooden spire. The hall originally belonged to Olivet Congregational Church (1875), but was taken over by the Heliconian Club, an association for women in the arts and letters, in 1923.

UNIVERSITY OF TORONTO & THE ANNEX

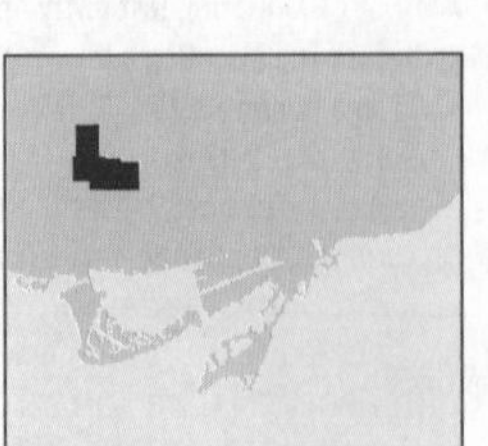

Eating p103; Shopping p151; Sleeping p166

Toronto is arguably the center of English-language education in Canada. Founded in 1827, the prestigious **University of Toronto**, or just 'UT' for short, is Canada's largest university with almost 40,000 full-time students, over 10,000 faculty and staff members and a whopping annual budget of a billion dollars. Its venerability is obvious after just a quick wander around the central St George campus with its distinct college quadrangles.

UT has long been a guardian and wellspring of Canadian literature and the arts, counting Margaret Atwood and Michael Ondaatje among its alumni, as well as filmmakers David Cronenberg and Atom Egoyan. The university's 'best' claim to scientific fame rests with Dr Charles Herbert Best and Sir Frederick Banting who, along with Collip and Macleod, discovered insulin in 1920. They received a Nobel Prize for their efforts, and the university has been joyfully bragging about it for almost a century.

West and north of the UT campus lies the **Annex**, a residential neighborhood populated primarily with students and professors. It overflows with pubs, organic grocery stores, global-minded eateries and spiritual venues, such as the musical **Trinity-St Paul's United Church** (p130) and **Tengye Ling Tibetan Buddhist Temple** (p138). Around the outer edges of the Annex, like so many satellite moons, are still more eclectic and ethnic communities, including **Markham Village** (p58) and Koreatown. **Chinatown** (p52), **Kensington Market** (p60) and **Little Italy** (p61) are all within easy striking distance.

Orientation

On University Ave, just north of College St, is UT's principal St George campus, which runs north to the museums along Bloor St and east to Queen's Park, where you'll find the provincial legislature buildings. The main drag of the Annex, which lies mostly west of Spadina Ave, is Bloor St W, although Harbord St also has a few restaurants and shops. On its north side, the Annex is bounded by Dupont St and to the west by Bathurst St. Markham Village is a short block of Markham St, south of Bloor St. Koreatown begins further west of Bathurst St, stretching all the way to Christie St.

Transportation

Subway Spadina and Bathurst stations are handy.

Streetcar The subway connects to the 510 Spadina and 511 Bathurst streetcar lines, while the 506 College streetcar runs along the south side of campus.

Car Metered on-street parking is rarely available. Parking on residential side streets is usually free, but strict time limits apply. Private lots charging $6 per day are found on Spadina Ave, just north of Bloor St. The municipal parking lot at 465 Huron St charges $1 per half-hour (daily maximum $10).

CASA LOMA Map p225

☎ 416-923-1171; www.casaloma.org; 1 Austin Tce; adult/child 4-13/youth 14-17/senior $12/6.75/7.50/7.50; 🕑 10am-5pm, last entry 4pm, gardens free 4pm-dusk Tue May-Oct; subway Dupont; P per hr $2.75, maximum $8.25

Literally the 'House on a Hill,' this mock medieval castle proudly juts up above the Annex proper. It's best reached on foot via the scenic Baldwin Steps, leading up from Spadina Ave, north of Davenport Rd, past flowering gardens with benches. Casa Loma's towers offer views of the city that rival the **CN Tower** (p44). This eccentric 98-room mansion was built after 1910 for Sir Henry Pellat, a wealthy financier whose fortunes derived from his exclusive contract to provide Toronto with electricity. He later lost everything he had in land speculation, which resulted in foreclosure and forced Sir Henry and his wife to move out. Later the castle briefly reopened as a luxury hotel, but its famous big-band nightclub attracted far more patrons than the hotel ever did guests, and it too failed.

During the Depression era, the charitable Kiwanis organization bought the castle and have operated it as a tourist site ever since. Self-guided audio tours (available in eight languages) lead you through the sumptuous interior. The conservatory where the Pellats did their entertaining is lit by an Italian-made chandelier with electrical bunches of grapes. Rugs are done in the same patterns as Windsor castle. It is said that the original castle kitchen had ovens big enough to cook an ox, and secret panels abound. It might thrill you to know that the stables were used by the Canadian government as a secret laboratory for WWII research into anti-U-boat technology.

MARKHAM VILLAGE Map pp236-7

www.markhamvillage.com; Markham St, south of Bloor St; 🕑 farmers' market 8am-1pm Sat May-Sep, most galleries closed Mon; subway Bathurst

As you approach the corner of Bloor and Bathurst Sts, you may think you're in Las Vegas, but it's just zany **Honest Ed's** (p153), Toronto's most colorful, gaudy discount-shopping emporium. Giant signs say things like 'Don't just stand there, buy something' and 'Only our floors are crooked!' You won't believe the queues before opening time. Owner Ed Mirvish has earned kudos as Toronto's most beloved theater impresario, too. The revival of nearby **Markham St**, an artists' lane of shops, bookstores and galleries, is partly thanks to both Ed and his son, David Mirvish.

NATIVE CANADIAN CENTRE OF TORONTO Map pp236-7

☎ 416-964-9087; www.ncct.on.ca; 16 Spadina Ave; 🕑 schedules vary; subway Spadina

As well as managing the **Cedar Basket** (p152) gift shop, this community center hosts Thursday night drum socials, seasonal powwows and elders' cultural events that promote harmony and conversation between tribal members and non-First Nations peoples. You can also drop by the Toronto Native Community History Project, or make reservations to join one of their 'Great Indian Bus Tours' of Toronto to get a better understanding of the area's Aboriginal history (p33).

Nearby the **Alliance Française** (☎ 416-922-2014; www.alliance-francaise.com; 24 Spadina Rd; 🕑 gallery 9:30am-6pm Mon-Thu, 9:30am-3pm Fri & Sat) offers French cultural events, language classes and a free gallery of contemporary photography.

PROVINCIAL LEGISLATURE Map pp231-3

☎ 416-325-7500; www.ontla.on.ca; Queen's Park, north of College St; admission free; 🕑 tours usually 10am-4pm Mon-Fri year-round, also 9am-4pm Sat & Sun in summer, legislature usually in session Mon-Thu Mar-Jun & Sep-Dec; subway Queen's Park

The seat of Ontario's provincial legislature resides is an 1893 pinkish sandstone building in Queen's Park. You'll usually find a few hospital employees picnicking on the lawn or a few stray demonstrators writing up sandwich boards, then determinedly picketing the front steps. For some home-grown entertainment, head for the visitors' gallery when the adversarial legislative assembly is in session. Attending a session is free, but security regulations are in full force. You may not smoke, write, read or even applaud as the honorable members heatedly debate such pressing issues as Ski-Doo safety. Free tours of the legislative building depart frequently from the information desk, but call ahead or go on-line to check schedules ahead of time.

SPADINA HOUSE Map p225

☎ 416-392-6910; www.city.toronto.on.ca; 285 Spadina Rd; grounds admission free, tours adult/child 6-12/youth 13-18/senior $6/4/5/5; 🕑 noon-5pm Tue-Sun May-Aug, noon-4pm weekdays Sep-Dec, Sat & Sun only Jan-Apr; subway Dupont

Far quieter than nearby **Casa Loma** (p58) this gracious mansion was built in 1866 as a country estate. It's still lit by Victorian gaslights, and the interior contains fine furnishings and art collected over three generations. Begin with a short film by the basement historical exhibits, then hear all about the history of the Austin family and the neighborhood on the tour, which points out 1905 Tiffany lamps and a stunning art-nouveau frieze in the billiards room. The working kitchen seasonally hosts cooking demonstrations by costumed workers. Afternoon teas, strawberry festivals and summer concerts are held in the apple orchard, while the beautiful Edwardian and Victorian gardens are perfect for a stroll or a snooze.

TORONTO PUBLIC LIBRARY – LILLIAN H SMITH BRANCH Map pp231-3

☎ 416-393-7753; www.tpl.toronto.on.ca; 239 College St; admission free; 🕑 10am-8:30pm Mon-Thu, 10am-6pm Fri, 9am-5pm Sat, also 1:30-5pm Sun Sep-Jun, special collections till 6pm weekdays; streetcar 506, 510

Architecturally speaking, this children's library is worth a peek look for its fairy-tale interior with bronze griffins flanking the front entrance. Special collections archive precious picture books, original artwork and manuscripts, poetry, letters and early movable (pop-up) books. Storytime and puppet shows are free.

UNIVERSITY OF TORONTO – ST GEORGE CAMPUS Map pp231-3

switchboard ☎ 416-978-2011, visitor information ☎ 416-978-5000; www.utoronto.ca; Nona Macdonald Visitors' Centre, 25 King's College Circle; admission free; 🕑 tours usually weekday mornings & afternoons, also weekend mornings Sep-May; streetcar 506, 510

Campus life focuses on the grassy expanse of **King's College Circle**, where students study on blankets, kick around soccer balls and dream of graduation day in domed **Convocation Hall**. Dating from 1919, sociable **Hart House** (☎ 416-978-2452; www.harthouse.utoronto.ca; 7 Hart House Circle) is an all-purpose art gallery, music performance space, theater, student lounge and café. The **Soldiers' Tower**, a memorial to students who gave their lives during World Wars I and II, is next door.

A nearby mid-19th-century Romanesque Revival building houses the **UT Art Centre** (☎ 416-978-1838; www.utoronto.ca/artcentre; 15 King's College Circle; admission free; 🕑 noon-6pm Tue-Fri, noon-4pm Sat Sep-Jun, noon-6pm Tue-Fri Jun-Aug), a contemporary art gallery for Canadian and world culture.

You will also find some thought-provoking exhibitions south of King's College Circle inside the boldly designed **Eric Arthur Gallery** (☎ 416-978-5038; www.ald.utoronto.ca; 230 College St; admission free; 🕑 usually 9am-5pm Mon-Fri, noon-5pm Sat), curated by the university's Faculty of Landscape, Architecture and Design.

The most famous of the UT colleges is the ultra-starched, traditional **Trinity College** (☎ 416-978-2651; www.trinity.toronto.edu; 6 Hoskin Ave), where entering collegians are anachronistically required to wear academic robes to meals and classes. It's worth looking around the traditional quadrangle and the **Anglican chapel**, which was designed by Sir Gilbert Scott, the same man responsible for Britain's ubiquitous red telephone booths. Pick up a self-guided tour pamphlet from the tract rack near the chapel door. Finally, the green **Philosopher's Walk** leads north along the east side of Trinity College toward the stone-and-iron **Alexandra Gates**, which stand on Bloor St just east of the **Royal Conservatory of Music**.

Free university walking tours of the historic St George campus cover many of these sights.

Top Five Places to Escape the Crowds

- **Financial District** Toronto Dominion Gallery of Inuit Art (p45)
- **Chinatown** Roof Garden at 401 Richmond (p53)
- **Harbourfront** Toronto Music Garden (p43)
- **Dundas Square** Church of the Holy Trinity (p50)
- **Bloor-Yorkville** Gardiner Museum of Ceramic Art (p56)

Student tour guides may also tell you of the haunted love triangle involving the stonemasons who worked on the neo-Romanesque **University College**, then elsewhere point out how the campus' old cannons aim toward the **provincial legislature** (p58) buildings, which are only a stone's throw (or one good shot) east of campus.

KENSINGTON MARKET

Eating p104; Shopping p153; Sleeping p168

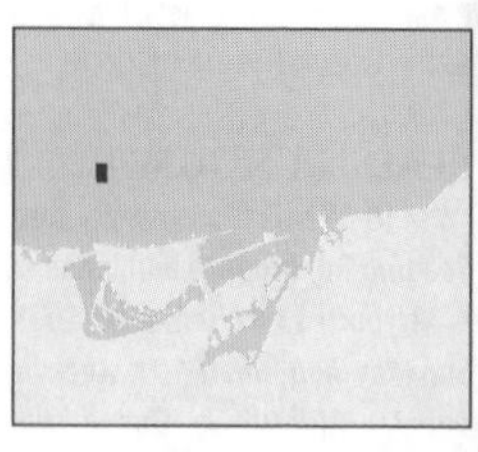

Despite its tattered edges, Kensington Market represents multicultural Toronto at its most authentic. The first Jewish merchants in Toronto arrived in the early 1900s from rural Orthodox communities in Eastern Europe and Russia. After World War II, this historic Jewish quarter was transformed by immigrants from Hungary, Italy, Portugal and Ukraine. In the 1970s waves of Chinese arrived, followed by Latin Americans, East and West Indians, Koreans, Vietnamese, Malay and Thai citizens. This historic market neighborhood still draws new immigrants every day, along with plenty of bohemians, punks and anarchists who make it their chosen home. Wander by on a busy Saturday morning, when the open-air vendors crowd the sidewalks and myriad shops have their colorful front doors flung open to the world. Market specialties include ethnic food, fresh produce and baked goods, along with vintage and discount clothing. Whether it's an army surplus jacket, rare retro duds, imported cheeses or an ooey-gooey Nanaimo bar, you're sure to find it here.

Orientation

Kensington Market isn't indoors. Its shops line a few narrow streets west of Spadina Ave, bounded by College St on the north and Dundas St W on the south side, where the neighborhood merges into Chinatown. The main drags are Baldwin St, Augusta Ave and Kensington Ave, the last of which has the majority of vintage clothing shops. The market is just a short walk from Little Italy or the UT campus.

ANSHEI MINSK SYNAGOGUE

Map pp234-5

☎ 416-595-5723; www.pdora.com/~minsk; 10-12 St Andrew St; admission by donation; daily prayer 7:30am, regular services 7:30pm Fri & 9:30am Sat; streetcar 510

This Russian Romanesque masterpiece will once again be a real gem after restoration work is complete. Sadly, the synagogue was vandalized by arson in early 2002, when thousands of its holy books were damaged. You may still be able to take a peek inside if the doors are unlocked. Orthodox Jewish services have been held here since the 1920s, and the synagogue's shared kosher meals on Friday nights are popular with everyone, from long-time market denizens to travelers to UT students

Transportation

Streetcar The 506 College and 510 Spadina lines border the market area.

Walking By far the best way to explore the market is on foot.

Car On-street parking is metered, but spaces are rarely available. Instead use the municipal garage at 20 St Andrews St for $1 per half-hour (daily maximum $5).

Kensington Market (above)

LITTLE ITALY & QUEEN WEST

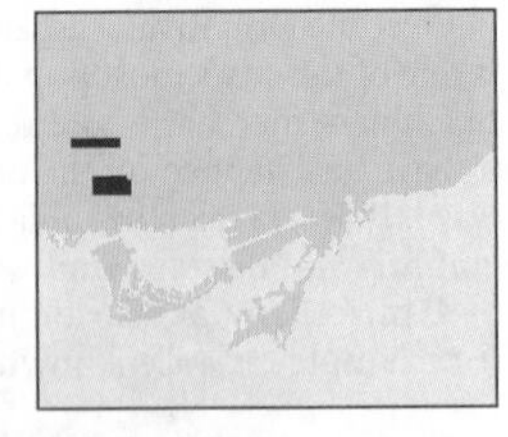

Eating p105; Shopping p154; Sleeping p168

Although Little Italy and Queen West may not have any sights to speak of, they effect a siren's call nonetheless. What both of these areas have in common is that each possesses a distinct community identity that's essential to the vibe of present-day Toronto. In either neighborhood you can expect to shop avariciously, dine deliciously and rock out or shake your booty all night long.

Little Italy is an established trendsetting strip of outdoor cafés, bars and small restaurants that are almost always changing hands – the well-heeled clientele is notoriously fickle. However, the further west you go, the more traditional it all becomes, with aromatic bakeries, sidewalk *gelaterias* and fine *ristoranti*. (Incidentally, there's another Italian area north of downtown called **Corso Italia** on St Clair Ave W, west of the Dufferin St intersection. Here you'll find Italian cinemas, smoky espresso cafés and pool halls.)

Nearby is Portugal Village. Many of the houses here are decorated with traditional painted ceramic tiles, and the bakeries, fish shops and markets are enticing. The old men sitting inside the sports bars don't appear to have moved much since the day they arrived from the old country.

Many of the city's bohemians and more impecunious artists have moved south to Queen West, which is roughly (and we mean rough – it can be an unruly neighborhood) based along Queen St W in the old garment district. It's a Canadian version of NYC's SoHo arts district, although not as affluent yet. A range of creative, upstart restaurants, hip boutiques, second-hand antique stores, Zen-styled tea rooms, industrial design shops, cool clubs and old-world fabric stores all unite here. The local goths, vampires and punks also parole the area.

Orientation

These three neighborhoods are west of Spadina Ave, although the real action doesn't start until Bathurst St. Little Italy runs along College St W, while Queen West is based along Queen St W and a burgeoning new strip along King St W, too. Trinity Bellwoods Park is a shady expanse of green, near the end of the main Queen West strip, stretching up toward the Portugal Village. Portugal Village is south of College St and north of Queen St, running along Dundas St W all the way to Dufferin St.

EAST TORONTO

Eating p107; Shopping p157; Sleeping p168

The district east of Parliament St to the Don River was settled by Irish immigrants fleeing the potato famine of 1841. It became known as **Cabbagetown** because the sandy soil of the area provided ideal growing conditions for cabbages. Since the 1970s there has been considerable gentrification of this once run-down area, although it's still a haven for artists. Today Cabbagetown has possibly the richest concentration of fine Victorian architecture in North America, and it's worth a stroll to peek at some of the beautifully restored houses and their carefully tended gardens.

Just north is **Rosedale**, one of the city's wealthiest areas for nearly 100 years. It was first settled by Sheriff William Jarvis, who built a country villa here. Later his wife named it after the wild roses growing nearby. The subway station was named after **Castle Frank**, the summer colonial residence of Toronto's founder, Lieutenant Governor John Simcoe, and his artistic wife, Elizabeth. Unfortunately, the majestic house that once stood here on the banks of the Don River burned down almost two centuries ago. But today the area boasts some of Toronto's most luxurious homes. As in Cabbagetown, many of them are architectural treasures.

Over the Don River, east along Danforth Ave, is **Greektown**. Often called just the Danforth, this is one of the city's most popular restaurant districts. By the river further south there's a pocket of Chinese merchants and restaurants, called **Chinatown East**; most of the immigrants here seem to have just stepped off the boat (or plane), and almost everything is in Chinese. Also out this way is **Little India** (aka the India Bazaar), studded with subcontinental food vendors, gorgeous sari emporia and blaring Hindi video-music shops. The scent of spices is in the air everywhere.

A miscellany of eclectic neighborhoods lies along Queen St E en route to the Beaches, for example **Leslieville**, known for its antique and design shops.

Orientation

The borders of Cabbagetown are disputed, but for our purposes the main drag is Parliament St, running north of Gerrard St E up to Bloor St E. Cabbagetown also extends east to the Don River, which is the dividing line between Rosedale and Greektown (The Danforth). The residential area of Rosedale lies north of Bloor St and sprawls west to Sherbourne St, although the main business strip is along Yonge St, north of Bloor St. Greektown is based on Danforth Ave, east of Broadview Ave to Coxwell Ave and beyond. Little India is found further south along Gerrard St E, just west of Coxwell Ave, while Chinatown East lies closer to the Don River, centered on the intersection of Gerrard St E and Broadview Ave. Leslieville lies along Queen St E, roughly from Carlaw Ave east to Coxwell Ave.

ALLAN GARDENS CONSERVATORY

Map pp238-9

☎ 416-392-7288; http://collections.ic.gc.ca./gardens; 19 Horticultural Ave; admission free; 9am-4pm Mon-Fri, 10am-5pm Sat & Sun; streetcar 506; P

The jewels of this scruffy city park are its early-20th-century greenhouses, filled with huge palms and trees from around the world divided into arid, cool and tropical plantings. Limited free parking is available off Horticultural Ave. After dark the entire area is dangerous enough to be not recommended, and that includes even taking a shortcut through the park.

NECROPOLIS Map pp238-9

☎ 416-923-7911; www.mountpleasantgroupofcemeteries.ca; 200 Winchester St; 8am-5:30pm; streetcar 506

Many of the remains of Toronto's colonists, including the city's first mayor William Lyon Mackenzie, were transferred to this wickedly named cemetery in the 1850s because the old potter's field burial ground near **Todmorden Mills** (p75) was contaminating the town. A road leads off Winchester St through the gates of the Necropolis, passing by its high Victorian gothic chapel.

RIVERDALE FARM Map pp238-9

☎ 416-392-6794; www.friendsofriverdalefarm.com; 201 Winchester St; admission free; 9am-5pm Nov-Apr, 9am-6pm May-Oct, farmers' market 3:30-7pm Tue May-Oct; streetcar 506

Riverdale Farm is the site of the original Toronto Zoo, where prairie wolves used to howl at night and scare the Cabbagetown kids. It's now run as a working farm museum, with two barns to wander through, a summer wading pool and also pens of waterfowl and animals, some of which may permit a pat or two. It's a great place to head with kids in tow.

Transportation

Subway From Rosedale's Castle Frank station, you can walk south into Cabbagetown. Stops along the Bloor–Danforth subway convenient to Greektown are Broadview, Chester and Pape.

Streetcar The 506 streetcar line heads east of downtown into the Cabbagetown district and across the river to Chinatown East and Little India. The 504 King and 505 Dundas lines turn north after crossing the Don River, connecting through Chinatown East en route to Broadview subway station. The 501 Queen line runs from downtown to the Beaches via Leslieville and other communities, all of which are also on the 502 Downtowner and 503 Kingston Rd (weekday rush hours only) lines.

Bus TTC bus lines run north–south along most major streets, which is handy for connecting between neighborhoods. Useful routes include 65 Parliament, 72 Pape and 75 Sherbourne.

Car Metered on-street parking is not difficult to find. You may be able to score a free spot in the residential side streets, especially in Cabbagetown, where daytime parking is not restricted. Most municipal lots charge 50¢ to 75¢ per half-hour (daily maximum $5). You'll find them along Danforth Ave, Queen St E, in Cabbagetown at 51 Aberdeen Ave and near Allan Gardens at 405 Sherbourne St.

ST JAMES CEMETERY Map pp238-9

☎ 416-964-9194; www.stjamescathedral.on.ca; 635 Parliament St; 🕑 8am-5pm Nov-Mar, 8am-8pm Apr-Oct; subway Castle Frank

Many of Toronto's founding families lie buried in this historic cemetery, which belongs to **St James Cathedral** (p129). Its Gothic Revival-style **Chapel of St James-the-Less** (1860) is a national historic site. Reminiscent of an English countryside church, it has justifiably been called one of the most beautiful buildings in Canada.

TOMMY THOMPSON PARK Map p224

☎ 416-661-6600; www.trca.on.ca; cnr Leslie St & Unwin Ave; admission free; 🕑 9am-4:30pm Sat-Sun & holidays Nov-Mar, 9am-6pm Apr-Oct; streetcar 501, 502, 503, then bus 83; P

Often still known as the Leslie St Spit, this artificial peninsula found along the Harbourfront, just west of the Beaches neighborhood, extends further out into Lake Ontario than the Toronto Islands. Managed by the Toronto & Region Conservation Authority (TRCA), this landfill site has unexpectedly become a phenomenal wildlife success. It is one of the world's largest nesting places for ring-billed gulls, as well as being a haven for terns, black-crowned night heron and other colonial waterbirds.

This 'accidental wilderness,' a narrow, paved 5km-long strip, is open to the public on weekends and holidays. Pets are prohibited. Summer schedules of free interpretive programs and guided walks, which often have an ecological angle, are posted at the front gate. Songbirds fly in during the spring and fall migrations; in winter, you'll observe several species of owl here, including the great horned and snowy varieties. At the end of the path, there is a lighthouse and skyline views of the city.

The park is at the foot of Leslie St, off Lake Shore Blvd E. No vehicles are permitted, but many people use bicycles and in-line skates – the Martin Goodman Recreational Trail runs by in both directions. By public transport, take any streetcar east along Queen St to Jones Ave, then transfer to the 83 Jones bus southbound. Get off at Commissioners St, from where it's a 500m walk south to the park's main gate. Note this bus does not run on Sunday or some holidays. Call the conservation authority for information on van shuttles from the gate into the park between early May and mid-October.

THE BEACHES

Eating p110; Shopping p157; Sleeping p170

To residents, 'The Beach' is a rather wealthy, mainly professional neighborhood down by the lakeshore. To everyone else, it's part of 'The Beaches' – meaning the area, the beaches and the parklands along Lake Ontario. The area was first settled in the late 18th century by the Ashbridge family, Loyalists who had fought on the side of the British during the American Revolution and lost. Today the bay is still named after them.

Development took off during the '70s and the onslaught of beachfront construction has not stopped since then. Thankfully, many of the side streets east of Woodbine Ave still have gardens bursting with color and quaint lakeside houses. The beaches are good for sunbathing and picnicking, and the 3km boardwalk, which edges the sand, is perfect for strolling. There's also a recreational path for cycling, running and in-line skating.

But travelers should think twice before jumping into the waters of Lake Ontario. Every summer the city periodically closes its public beaches due to toxic levels of pollution. Since these closures aren't signposted well, travelers who miss the TV news announcements may not know whether the water is safe or not. When in doubt, keep your tootsies out.

After a day at the beach, the Beaches offers plenty of places to dine, drink or shop along Queen St E. What you'll notice most about the neighborhood is that absolutely everyone seems to be a dog owner, and also there's a coffeehouse on nearly every block.

Orientation

The Beaches neighborhood extends from Woodbine Ave east to Victoria Park Ave. Most of the recreational areas are along the lakefront, one long block south of Queen St. To reach the Beaches from downtown, take the streetcar east; the journey takes about 30 minutes.

Transportation

Streetcar 501 Queen streetcars run along Queen St E, terminating at the filtration plant.

Car On summer weekends and holidays, every pay lot will be full. The biggest private lot is off Lake Shore Blvd E, near Woodbine Beach; rates vary depending upon demand. The municipal lot at 192 Boardwalk St charges 75¢ per half-hour (daily maximum $4). Residential areas have free on-street parking, but spaces are usually only available at the east end of the neighborhood, near Victoria Park Ave.

BEACHES & PARKS Map p240

☎ **416-392-8186; www.city.toronto.on.ca; dawn-dusk; streetcar 501**

Kew Beach is the most popular section of sand. The boardwalk runs by the Silverbeach Boathouse, which doesn't actually have boats, but does rent sports equipment and beach toys during summer. Adjacent Kew Gardens offers restrooms, snack bars, a skate rink, a lawn bowling club and benches for kicking back; at the west end near Woodbine Beach, there's an excellent Olympic-size public swimming pool. The **Martin Goodman Trail** (p135) leads past Ashbridge's Bay Park, where you'll find a lighthouse and the historic **Leuty Life Saving Station**. Off Queen St, **Glen Stewart Ravine** is a patch of wilder green leading north to Kingston Rd.

RC HARRIS FILTRATION PLANT Map p240

☎ **416-392-2932; 2701 Queen St E; streetcar 501**

Commanding heavenly views of the lakefront, the RC Harris Filtration Plant is a modern art-deco masterpiece that has appeared in countless movies and TV shows, as well as in Michael Ondaatje's *In the Skin of a Lion* (p23). Originally residents disparagingly dubbed it the 'Palace of Purification,' due to the burden of its costly construction during the Depression era.

TORONTO ISLANDS

Eating p110; Sleeping p170; Walking & Cycling Tours p86

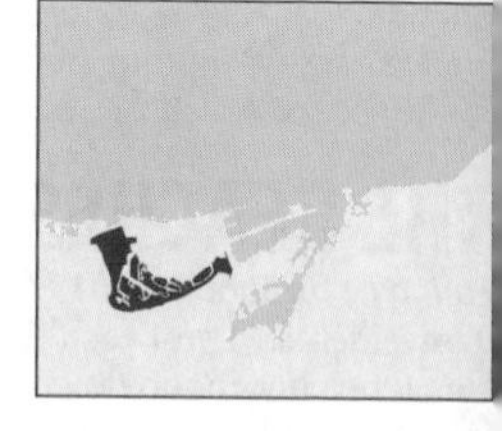

Once upon a time, there were no Toronto Islands. There was only an immense sandbar, stretching 9km out into the lake from the foot of present-day Woodbine Ave. Early colonials flocked here to take advantage of the lakeshore breezes, as did First Nations peoples, who had treated the area as a spa and campground for centuries. Later on they simply called it 'the Peninsula,' a name taken on by the premier Victorian resort hotel built here. On April 13, 1858, however, a hurricane-force storm cut through the sandbar, swallowed the hotel and created the Gap (now known as the Eastern Channel), forming Toronto's jewel-like islands.

Present-day **Centre Island** gets hundreds of visitors each weekend, but has no residents. During the 1960s the city began steadily evicting all of the 'sandbar bohemians' who had been living here for more than a generation. The remaining residents on other islands struggled for over 20 years to keep their homes and unique way of life. It all boiled down to a dramatic standoff in 1980, after which the city granted 99-year leases for year-round residents under a land trust administration arrangement. Once you see the small artistic communities living on **Algonquin Island** and **Ward's Island** for yourself, you may be jealous. They've got peace, little pollution and incredible skyline views of the city.

Orientation

All of the islands are interconnected by bridges or footpaths. The cool breezes are great on a sticky humid day, and ambling along the islands' paved paths and the boardwalk on the southern shore aren't bad ways to spend some time. Bring along a picnic lunch, as most of the islands' fast-food outlets are overpriced.

Most ferries dock at Centre Island Park, which has the majority of outdoor amusements and hosts all of the islands' major events, such as the **Toronto International Dragon Boat Festival** (p9) in June. Next to the ferry terminal is a bridge leading to **Olympic Island** with its outdoor stage, where concerts are held. Beaches all along the southern shores of the nain islands are favored for picnicking, beach volleyball and just lazing about like a izard in the sun.

If you only plan to explore one island, you can get around on foot easily enough. Otherwise, you'll need to rent a bicycle. For general information on the Toronto Islands, contact **oronto Parks and Recreation** (☎ 416-392-8195; www.city.toronto.on.ca) or stop by the seasonal ourist information booth on Centre Island. The **community website** (http://torontoisland.org) s a flavorful slice of island life.

CENTRE ISLAND PARK Map p241

From the ferry terminal, head past the information booth and first-aid station to quaint **Centreville Amusement Park** (☎ 416-203-0405; www.centreisland.ca; grounds admission free, rides 75¢, day-pass $17-23; 10:30am-5pm Mon-Fri & 10:30am-8pm in summer, weekends only early May & Sep, weather permitting). Squeezed together on a few hundred acres are an antique carousel, goofy golf course, miniature train rides, sky gondola and even a petting zoo, **Far Enough Farm**.

Head south over the bridge toward the splashing fountains and gardens, where you'll find an English-style **hedge maze** and ticket booths for **tram tours** (30-minute ride per adult $5, child $2, student or senior $4) of the island. On the south shore are changing rooms, lockers (rental $2), snack bars, bicycle rentals and a pier leading out into the lake.

To the east is a **boathouse**, where canoes, kayaks and paddleboats can be rented ($15 to $25 per hour). Nearby is **St Andrew-by-the-Lake Church** (☎ 416-203-6164; services 10am Sun) a petite Anglican house of worship dating from 1884. Often known simply as 'The Island Church,' it holds heart-warming traditional Christmas celebrations each year and a blessing of the harbor boats every June.

GIBRALTAR POINT Map p241

Gibraltar Point was selected by Captain John Simcoe as the most easily defensible point in the harbor, and a British fort was promptly built in 1800. It was destroyed just 13 years later during the American raid on York. A ways inland stands the picturesque **Gibraltar Point Lighthouse** (1809), just 25m tall, built with grey limestone quarried at the village of Queenston on the Niagara escarpment. The lighthouse was the first of its kind on the Great Lakes and used sperm oil to light its lamp. Its first keeper, JP Radan Muller, disappeared mysteriously in 1815. Years later human bones were dug up

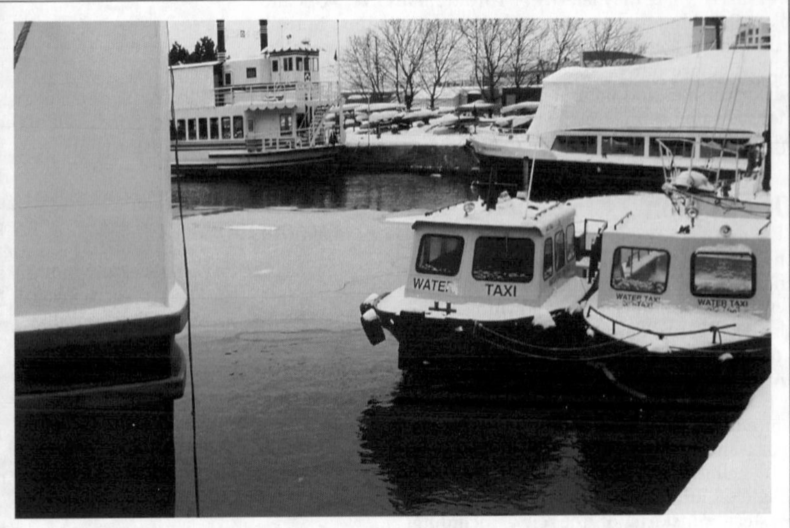

Harbourfront (p41)

Transportation

Ferry From the foot of Bay St, near the Westin Harbour Castle hotel, catch a ferry (p197) to Centre Island, Hanlan's Point or Ward's Island. These quick cruises are as good as harbor tours.

Bicycle & Skates Bicycles are allowed on some ferries (p195). Bicycle rentals are available on Centre Island (p135). You can also rent bicycles and in-line skates along the Harbourfront (p136) before boarding the ferry.

nearby, which supported the theory that he was murdered by soldiers for refusing to share his bootleg American whiskey.

HANLAN'S POINT Map p241

At the west end of Centre Island by the Toronto City Centre Airport (TCAA) is sporty Hanlan's Point, named after world-champion sculler 'Ned' Hanlan, a member of the first family to settle here year-round. Interestingly, the point was once known as the 'Coney Island of Canada.' Babe Ruth hit his first professional home run here in 1914 while playing minor-league baseball – sadly, the ball drowned in Lake Ontario. The sport of iceboating atop the frozen lake was at its peak until the 1940s; it's hard to believe, but winters nowadays are too mild for it.

Following the paved paths past picnic tables and barbecue pits brings you near **Hanlan's Point Beach**, the best on the islands. Popular for years, especially with gay men, the 'clothing optional' status of this beach was finally legalized by the city council in 1999. Civic-minded island volunteers distribute 'naked-beach etiquette' flyers to new arrivals. Officially the beach is only supervised during July and August.

WARD'S ISLAND Map p241

At the west end of Ward's Island is a **Frisbee golf course** and a groovy **children's fort**, both free. An old-fashioned boardwalk runs all along the south shore of the island, passing the back gate of the **Rectory** (p110) café.

GREATER TORONTO AREA

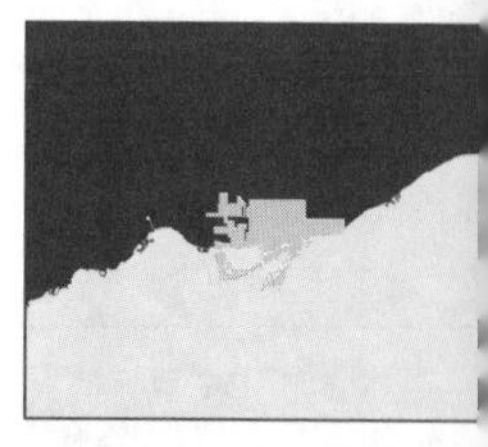

Eating p111; Sleeping p171

Many of the towns surrounding Toronto have been incorporated into the Megacity (p30), which is just as monstrous as it sounds, at least when it comes to navigation by visitors. But this is where the majority of Torontonians live, work and play. Reaching these areas can be often rewarding, but it'll take a large chunk of your day if you don't have a car. The following are our picks among myriad outlying museums, historical sites and natural areas in the Greater Toronto Area (GTA). While some attractions are almost must-dos, especially for families traveling with younger children, one of the historic sites is probably enough for anyone who isn't a total colonial-history buff.

Orientation

It would take an encyclopedia to list all of the suburbs, towns and communities making up the GTA, but visitors will only need a few reference points. East of downtown and the Beaches are Toronto's quieter lakefront communities, such as Scarborough. Affluent neighborhoods north of downtown are an entirely different story, with vast amounts of wealth concentrated in North York and at the intersection of Yonge St and Eglinton Ave, nicknamed 'Young and Eligible.' Ethnic neighborhoods crowd the western outskirts of the city, including those communities near High Park: multicultural Bloor Village, on Bloor St west of

Transportation

Subway & Bus TTC subway lines will take you to many outlying sights, although a free transfer to a local bus may be required to reach your destination.

Car If you want to really explore, rent a car. Parking at most attractions is plentiful, although a surprisingly steep fee may be charged. The fastest routes out of the city center are to take the Don Valley Parkway north to Hwy 401, or take the Gardiner Expressway west to Hwy 427, then head north.

(Continued on page 75)

1

kyline **2** City Hall (p50)
on (Gooderham) Build-
5)

2

3

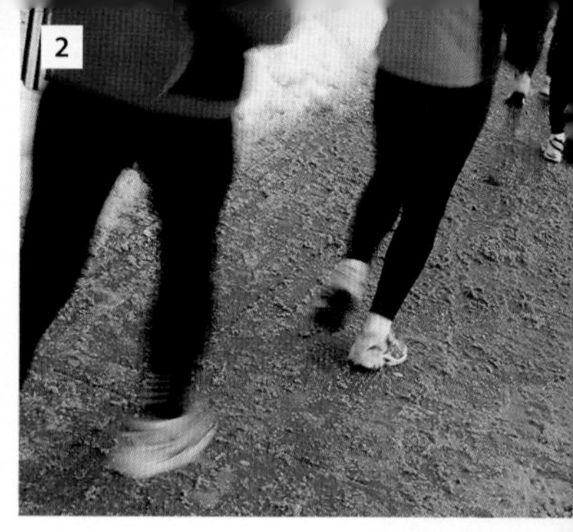

1 Ice skating, Nathan Phillips Square (p136) **2** *Joggers, Bloor-Yorkville (p55)* **3** *Hockey fans at a Toronto Maple Leafs game (p135)* **4** *WinterCity Festival (p8)*

1 *Marche Mövenpick (p94)*
2 *Gypsy Co-op (p106) & Hooch (p127)* **3** *Chinatown (p98)*

1 *Madison Avenue Pub (p117)*
2 *Steam Whistle Brewing (p42)*
3 *Cineforum (p115)* **4** *Air Canada Centre (p44)*

1 *Bata Shoe Museum (p55)*
2 *Blanket hanging by Fran Hunt, Bay of Spirits Gallery (p145)*
3 *Dinosaur exhibit, Royal Ontario Museum (p56)*

1 *Peach Berserk (p156)* ***2*** *Shop window, Bloor-Yorkville (p150)* ***3*** *Sam the Record Man (p149)* ***4*** *Fresh Collective (p156)*

__1__ Toronto Islands (p64) __2__ Allan Gardens Conservatory (p62) __3__ Colborne Lodge, High Park (p77) __4__ Autumn oasis, Financial District (p43)

1

2

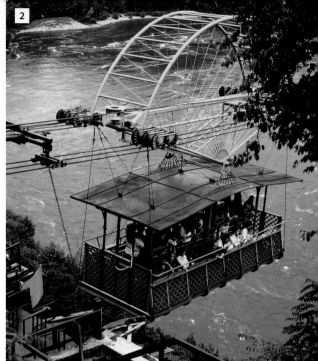

1 Clock Tower, Niagara-on-the-Lake (p189) 2 Whirlpool Aero Car over Niagara River (p179) 3 Wintertime at Niagara Falls (p176)

3

(Continued from page 66)

Keele St to Jane Ave, and Eastern European–flavored Roncesvalles Village, running along Roncesvalles Ave between Queen St W and Dundas Ave W. Suburban Etobicoke lies further west of downtown toward the airport.

EAST

ONTARIO SCIENCE CENTRE Map p225

☎ 416-696-3127, tickets ☎ 416-696-1000; www.ontariosciencecentre.ca; 770 Don Mills Rd; adult/child 4-12/youth 13-17/senior $14/8/10/10; 10am-5pm; subway Eglinton, then bus 34; P $8

Where can you climb a rock wall, catch a criminal with DNA fingerprinting and race an Olympic bobsled, all in one day? Answer: at this excellent, ever-evolving museum containing over 800 totally interactive, high-tech science exhibits and live demonstrations that will wow most kids (and even some adults). It's worth driving by just to admire the structure, designed by the innovative architectural firm of Moriyama & Teshima (p25). You won't want to miss the beaver pond out back, either. On weekends there are hundreds of kids running around like mad, but children under 12 must be accompanied by an adult. Combined discount tickets with Omnimax films are available. Check the museum's website for special family events, including theme-night sleepovers ($46, reservations required). The science center is located in a small ravine on the corner of Eglinton Ave E and Don Mills Rd.

SCARBOROUGH BLUFFS Map p224

Toronto Parks & Recreation ☎ 416-392-8186; off Kingston Rd (Hwy 2), Scarborough; admission free; dawn-dusk; P

A few kilometers east of the Beaches neighborhood, these cliffs of glacial deposits (commonly known as till) tower over the lakeshore. When Elizabeth Simcoe came here in 1793, she named this spot Scarborough after the town in Yorkshire, England, also famed for its cliffs. If you want to be atop the cliffs (and you do), there are several parks that will give you access to footpaths, sweeping views of the bluffs and panoramas of Lake Ontario, as well as ways of getting down to the water.

From Kingston Rd (Hwy 2), turn south at Cathedral Bluffs Dr to reach an excellent vantage point, **Cathedral Bluffs Park**. It's the highest section of the bluffs (at 98m) and once belonged to the Sisters of St Joseph, whose property extended from Kingston Rd to the lake. These bluffs were not named after the former convent, but because of geology: at the top of the cliffs, erosion has created oddly beautiful formations resembling cathedral spires, and simultaneously revealed full-profile evidence of five different glacial periods. On-street parking is severely limited here.

Below, in the lake itself, landfill has been used to form **Bluffer's Park** (☎ 416-338-3278; Brimley Rd; subway Victoria Park, then bus 12; P), a boat-mooring and recreational area for walking and beach activities during July and August. Access to Bluffer's Park is from Brimley Rd, running south off Kingston Rd, less than 1km west of Cathedral Bluffs Dr. The park is a 10-minute walk south of the nearest bus stop.

A 15-minute drive east of the bluffs is the quirky **Guild Inn** (☎ 416-392-8188; www.guildwood.on.ca; 201 Guildwood Parkway, off Kingston Rd; subway Kennedy, then bus 116; P), an Arts & Crafts-style mansion dating from 1914, set in serene lakefront parklands with walking trails. An artists' colony was formed here during the Great Depression, and in the front garden there's a collection of sculptures, Ionic columns and gargoyles rescued from condemned and half-destroyed city buildings during the 1950s.

Top Five GTA

- **Ontario Science Centre** (left)
- **Scarborough Bluffs** (below)
- **Paramount Canada's Wonderland** (p78)
- **Black Creek Pioneer Village** (p77)
- **David Dunlap Observatory** (p76)

TODMORDEN MILLS Map p225

☎ 416-396-2819; www.toronto.ca/todmorden; 67 Pottery Rd; adult/child 6-12/youth/senior $3/1.50/2.25/2.25; 11am-4:30pm Tue-Fri, noon-5pm Sat & Sun, Wed-Sun only Oct-Dec, closed Jan-Apr; subway Broadview, then bus 8, 62, 87, 100; P

Quietly set by the Don River, this was the location of a late 18th-century sawmill, turned gristmill and then paper mill. Just as importantly to early Canadian colonists, beer and whiskey also flowed from here. Historical exhibits are found inside the Brewery Gallery, where eager guides await to show visitors around the old millers' houses and petite Don train station, relocated here in the 1960s. Nature paths start near the bridge and wind back to a secluded wildflower garden. For urban hikers, one of the city's **Discovery Walks** (p136) runs by here. Otherwise from Broadview station, take any bus northbound a few blocks to Mortimer Ave, then walk west less than 1km.

NORTH

DAVID DUNLAP OBSERVATORY Map p174

☎ 905-884-2672; www.astro.utoronto.ca/DDO; 123 Hillsview Dr, Richmond Hill; tour adult/child 7-12/senior $6/4/4; tour schedules vary; P

Just north of the Toronto city limits, the David Dunlap Observatory offers 40-minute introductory talks on modern astronomy, followed by a bit of stargazing through Canada's biggest optical telescope (the reflector measures 1.9m) if skies are clear. Tickets are sold on a first-come, first-served basis (cash only). Tours usually run twice nightly every Friday and Saturday between May and early October, and also on Friday evenings (which are especially family-friendly) during July and August, but call ahead to check current schedules. Children under seven years old are not permitted, due to safety concerns. The website shows how many seats have already been reserved by groups. On some clear-sky nights, the Royal Astronomical Society of Canada brings its own telescopes and sets up informal (and free!) viewing for the public outside, too.

To reach the observatory, drive for about 30 minutes up Bayview Ave past 16th Ave to Hillsview Dr, turn left onto Hillsview Dr and drive 1km west until you see the white dome on your left. If you're on Bayview Ave and reach Major Mackenzie Dr, you've gone too far. Alternatively take the TTC subway north to Finch station, the northern terminus of the Yonge line. Walk underground to a nearby transit terminal and catch the No 91 Bayview bus operated by **York Region Transit** (☎ 905-762-2100, 866-668-3978; www.yorkregiontransit.com). This bus stops upon request at Hillsview Dr, from where it's a 1km walk to the observatory. The entire trip costs $2.25, with a free transfer from the subway station.

GIBSON HOUSE Map p224

☎ 416-395-7432, events line ☎ 416-338-3888; www.city.toronto.on.ca; 5172 Yonge St; adult/child 2-12/youth 13-18/senior $2.75/1.75/2.25/2.25, mid-Nov–Dec extra 50¢; noon-5pm Tue-Sun Oct-Aug, closed Sep; subway North York Centre; P

Scottish immigrant David Gibson, a successful surveyor and politician who helped to tame the wild Canadian colonies, built this gorgeous Georgian-style house after his return from exile in the USA, which had been an unfortunate result of his stirring role in the Upper Canada Rebellion of 1837. Costumed workers offer tours of the house between 11am and 3pm as well as cooking demonstrations on some weekends and holidays. The Gibson House is in the far northern part of the city, north of Sheppard Ave, next to a small park. If you're driving, limited parking is only accessible via a small laneway off southbound Yonge St.

MT PLEASANT CEMETERY Map p224

☎ 416-485-9129; www.mountpleasantgroupofcemeteries.ca; 375 Mt Pleasant Rd; admission free; 8am-8pm in summer, 8am-5:30pm rest of year; subway Davisville; P

North of Moore Ave, between Yonge St and Bayview Ave, this 19th-century cemetery is the final resting place of many of Toronto's brilliant and best (or at least richest) citizens

Osgoode Hall (p52)

lere you'll find the graves of Glenn Gould, the vorld-famous classical musician; former prime ninister William Lyon Mackenzie; Timothy aton, founder of Eaton's department store; itanic survivor Arthur Godfrey Peuchen; and oster Hewitt, Canada's 'Voice of Hockey,' he sportscaster who coined the phrase, 'He hoots, he scores!' The most arresting sight s the castle-like Massey mausoleum. Guide naps are available from the cemetery office ear the south gate, on the east side of Mt 'leasant Rd, which cuts through the middle f the cemetery.

MUSEUM OF CONTEMPORARY CANADIAN ART Map p224

10CCA; ☎ 416-395-7430; www.mocca.toronto.on.ca; oronto Centre for the Arts, 5400 Yonge St; admis-ion free; ⌚ noon-5pm Tue-Sun; subway North York entre

ormerly the Art Gallery of North York, MOCCA s the city's only museum mandated to collect nd promote works by living Canadian visual rtists. The permanent holdings only number bout 400 works created since 1985, but ward-winning temporary exhibitions focus on new artists from Nova Scotia to British Columbia. The galleries are open during most evening performances at the Toronto Centre or the Arts, which is on the same site.

WEST

BLACK CREEK PIONEER VILLAGE

Map p224

☎ 416-736-1733, 888-872-2344 ext 5400; www.blackcreek.ca; 1000 Murray Ross Pkwy, Downsview; adult/child 5-14/student/senior $10/6/9/9; ⌚ 10am-4pm May-Dec; subway Finch, then bus 60; P $5

Toronto's most popular historical attraction for amilies re-creates rural life in 19th-century Ontario. Here workers in period costume care for the farm animals, play fiddlin' folk music and demonstrate country crafts and skills using authentic tools and methods. Shops sell the artisans' handiwork, which consists of everything from tin lanterns to fresh bread to woven throw rugs. Souvenir postcards can be mailed from the old-fashioned post office. Holidays are often the best time to visit; traditional Victorian 'Christmas Remembered' celebrations start in mid-November. The village is on the southeast corner of Steeles Ave and Jane St, a 40-minute drive northwest of downtown.

HIGH PARK Map p224

☎ 416-392-1111; www.city.toronto.on.ca; 1873 Bloor St W; admission free; ⌚ dawn-dusk; subway High Park, streetcar 501, 506, 508; P

The city's biggest park is a popular escape, whether for a little picnicking, cycling, skating or sitting in the flower gardens and watching the sunset. Some parts are left as natural woods, but those looking for serious outdoor pursuits should look elsewhere. Near the north gates are **tennis courts** and an outdoor **swimming pool** (☎ 416-392-0695). The main road winds around south through the park; another road branching to the east takes you to the **Dream in High Park** (p124) stage. Further south, past the Grenadier Restaurant, are the refreshing **Hillside Gardens** overlooking **Grenadier Pond**, where people ice-skate in winter (p136). The road continues downhill past the **animal paddocks** (a small children's zoo) to **Colborne Lodge** (Map p225; ☎ 416-392-6916; Colborne Lodge Dr; adult/child under 13/youth 13-18/senior $3.50/2.50/2.75/2.75; ⌚ noon-4pm Tue-Sun Oct-Dec, noon-5pm May-Sep, Sat & Sun only Jan-Apr), a Regency-style cottage built in 1836. Once belonging to the Howards, the founders of High Park, it still contains original furnishings, including Ontario's first indoor flush toilet.

High Park's north entrance is off Bloor St W at High Park Ave. Bus 30B picks up at High Park subway station, then makes a loop through the park on weekends and holidays from mid-June to Labour Day. Otherwise it's a 200m walk to the north gates. The 506 High Park streetcar drops off on the east side of the park. If you exit the park by Colborne Lodge at the south gates, walk down to Lake Shore Blvd W and catch any streetcar back east to downtown.

MONTGOMERY'S INN Map p224

☎ 416-394-8113; www.montgomerysinn.com; 4709 Dundas St W, Etobicoke; adult/child under 13/youth 13-18/senior/family $3/1/2/2/8; ⌚ 1-4:30pm Tue-Fri, 1-5pm Sat & Sun; subway Islington, then bus 37; P

Built in 1832 by an Irish military captain of the same name, Montgomery's Inn is a fine example of Loyalist architecture and has been faithfully restored to its heyday era in the late 1840s. Staff in period dress answer questions and serve afternoon tea (p92). Contemporary and traditional art exhibits and cooking classes are often hosted here.

You may also want to visit formal **James Gardens** (Map p224; Edenbridge Dr, east of Royal York Rd; admission free; ⌚ dawn-dusk; subway

Royal York, then bus 73; P), 3km away on the west bank of the Humber River.

PARAMOUNT CANADA'S WONDERLAND Map p174

☎ 905-832-7000, events line ☎ 905-832-8131; www.canadas-wonderland.com; Hwy 400 & Rutherford Rd, Vaughan; 1-day pass adult/child 3-6/senior $45/26/26; 🕒 10am-10pm in summer, Sat & Sun only late Apr–late May & early Sep-early Oct; P $7.50

Wonderland is a state-of-the-art amusement park with over 60 rides, including some killer roller coasters (don't miss Canada's first 'flying' coaster) and the Cliffhanger super-swing, which slams through water walls and allows riders to experience zero gravity. Wonderland has an exploding 'volcano,' a 20-hectare Splash Works water park (bring a bathing suit), Nickelodeon Central and Hanna-Barbera Land for the young 'uns. Queues can be lengthy, except on overcast days, and most rides operate rain or shine.

Wonderland is about a 45-minute drive northwest of downtown Toronto on Hwy 400. Exit at Rutherford Rd, about 10 minutes north of Hwy 401. Alternatively, from Yorkdale subway station, catch a **GOTransit** (☎ 416-869-3200; www.gotransit.com) 'Wonderland Express' bus ($4.25).

Walking & Cycling Tours

Walking & Cycling Tours

No doubt about it, the best way to explore Toronto's leafy neighborhoods, compact city centre and revitalized Harbourfront is to strike out on your own, either on foot or by bicycle. We've included all sorts of options for you here, from historical and architectural walks to beachfront bike rides to art gallery hopping on the subway and streetcars. We've even thrown in an underground tour of downtown, for when nasty winter weather arrives, just so you'll have no excuse not to get out there and explore the teeming streets of the Megacity. For organized group tours, see p39.

ROYAL YORK TO OLD YORK WALK

Overshadowed by the skyscrapers of downtown, you can almost feel what were once the streets of 'Muddy York' slipping beneath your feet.

Where else to begin but at **Union Station 1** (p197). Exit from the grand lobby onto Front St, crossing over to the **Fairmont Royal York 2** (p161). Enter the hotel, then turn around to look up above the doors at a fresco landscape of Canadian history, from arctic Inuit to voyageurs in their canoes. Walk east through the lobby, past the stone lions and down the stairs back onto Front St. On your left the **Royal Bank Plaza 3** (p44) rises. At Bay St, cross over and walk a few steps north to enter the stunning atrium of **BCE Place 4** (p43), also housing the **Hockey Hall of Fame 5** (p45). At Yonge St, backtrack a half-block west on Front St to admire the museum's stone exterior and whimsical statues by the bench.

Resume walking east on Front St. At Scott St, a small park affords the best views of the trompe l'oeil mural on the **Flatiron**

Walk Facts

Best time Any morning or afternoon, except Monday.

Start Union Station (subway Union Station).

End Toronto's First Post Office Museum (streetcar 504).

Distance 2.5km.

Time One to 1½ hours.

Food en route **Marche Mõvenpick** (p94), **Spring Rolls** (p96), **St Lawrence Market** (p96), **Courthouse Market Grille** (p95).

Drinks en route **Library Bar** (p120), **C'est What** (p117).

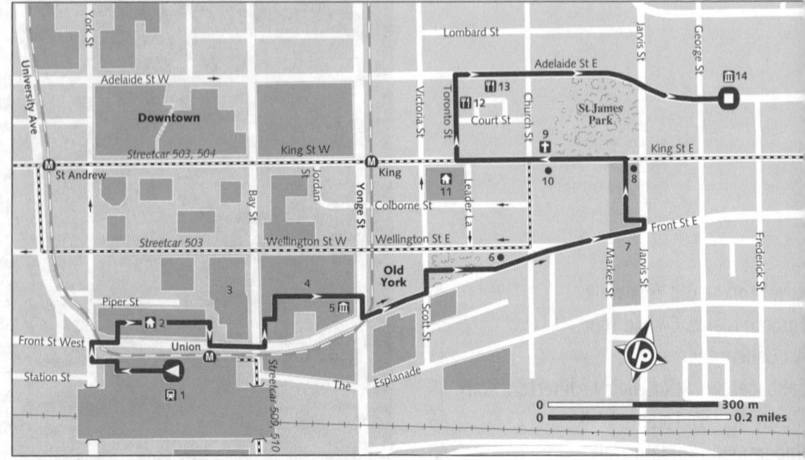

Gooderham) Building 6 (p46). Stroll along the south side of Front St to the **St Lawrence Market 7** (p47), then cross over to the north side of the street and use the pedestrian walkway on the west side of the North Market building, passing **St Lawrence Hall 8** (p47) en route to **St James Cathedral 9** (p129), with its beautiful gardens.

Almost opposite, the **Toronto Sculpture Garden 10** doesn't contain much art worth looking at, but it opens up grand vistas of the downtown skyline. Heading west on King St, pause inside the lobby of the **Le Royal Meridien King Edward 11** (p162), then pay your respects to the city by strolling up Toronto St, a narrow road full of elegant triple-story office buildings built in the 19th century. Note the heraldic lion and unicorn atop No 10 and the gas lamp outside the **Rosewater Supper Club 12** (p95). Turn the corner for the historic **Courthouse Market Grille 13** (p95). Three blocks further east on Adelaide St is **Toronto's First Post Office 14** (p47), which is now a museum and just a block north of the 504 King streetcar line.

TORONTO ISLANDS CYCLING TOUR

A short sail from the Harbourfront brings you to paradise, the Toronto Islands (p64). The islands are a vehicle-free escape from the crush of downtown. Whether you come for an afternoon or the whole day, it's sure to be a highlight of your trip.

From the Centre Island ferry terminal, follow the crowd past **Centreville Amusement Park 1** (p65), over the bridge by the **hedge maze 2** (p65) to the south shore, where you'll find **Centre Island Bicycle Rental 3** (p136). Hop on your quaint metal steed and turn left onto the paved recreational path, cycling parallel to Centre Island Beach all the way to **Hanlan's Point 4** (p66), by Toronto City Centre Airport.

Tour Facts

Best time Summer.

Start Centre Island Ferry Terminal.

End Centre Island Pier.

Distance 11km.

Time 1½ to two hours.

Food & drinks en route Rectory (p110).

Before reaching the ferry terminal, loop back around, pausing to read the historical plaques. Backtrack south along the paved path, from where signs point the way to clothing-optional **Hanlan's Point Beach 5** (p66). Next on the right is missable Gibraltar Point (p65). Look

Union Station (p197)

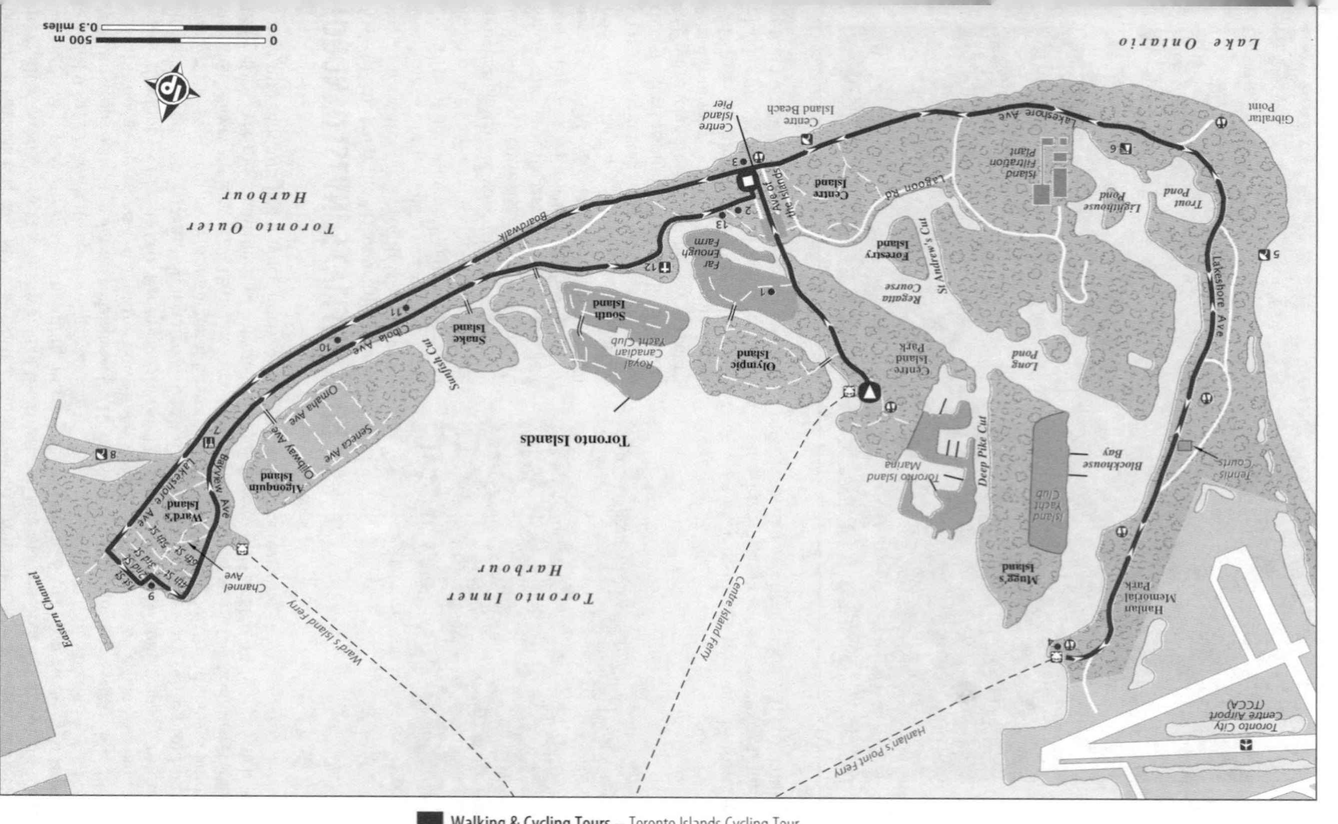

Eastern Channel
1st St
2nd St
3rd St
4th St
5th St
6th St
Channel Ave
Ward's Island
Lakeshore Ave
Bayview Ave
Ward's Island Ferry
Algonquin Island
Ojibway Ave
Omaha Ave
Seneca Ave
Toronto Inner Harbour
Toronto Outer Harbour
Cibola Ave
Sunfish Cut
Snake Island
Boardwalk
Toronto Islands
Royal Canadian Yacht Club
South Island
Centre Island Ferry
Olympic Island
Far Enough Farm
Centre Island Pier
Ave of the Islands
Centre Island
Centre Island Beach
Centre Island Park
Toronto Island Marina
Regatta Course
Forestry Island
St Andrew's Cut
Lagoon Rd
Deep Pike Cut
Long Pond
Island Filtration Plant
Mugg's Island
Island Yacht Club
Blockhouse Bay
Lighthouse Pond
Hanlan's Point Ferry
Hanlan Memorial Park
Trout Pond
Tennis Courts
Toronto City Centre Airport (TCCA)
Gibraltar Point
Lake Ontario
0
500 m
0
0.3 miles
1
2
3
4
5
6
7
8
9
10
11
12
13

nland for the **Gibraltar Point Lighthouse 6** (p65), which is rumored to be haunted (p31). Keep ;oing east. Back at Avenue of the Islands, zoom by Centre Island Bicycle Rental and follow he paved shoreline path onto the boardwalk, which goes for a little over a kilometer right o the back gate of the **Rectory 7** (p110), not far from sweet little **Ward's Island Beach 8**. Take the oardwalk until you can go no further east and cut back onto 1st St. At the corner of Channel ve is a gorgeous **flower garden 9** framing perfects views of the Toronto skyline. From there, it's short distance west to the Ward's Island Ferry Terminal, where you join paved Bayview Ave. ollow it west past the bridge to residential Algonquin Island, the **Frisbee golf course 10** (p66) nd **children's play fort 11** (p66). Veer right as the Royal Canadian Yacht Club comes into view, ollowing a smaller paved path toward **St-Andrew-by-the-Lake Church 12**. Cycle past the **boathouse 3** back to the pier at Centre Island Beach, where you rented your bicycle.

ART GALLERY TOUR

f you're jonesing for a fix of art, but can't ear the thought of traipsing through yet nother museum, take in Toronto's varied ;allery scene instead. Buy a TTC day pass p198), since you'll be on the subway and treetcars quite a bit.

The tour starts just west of Union Station at he **Bay of Spirits Gallery 1** (p145). Then head east o the basement concourse of the train station o catch the 509 Harbourfront or 510 Spadina treetcar along the Harbourfront. Get off at **Queen's Quay Terminal 2** (p42) to visit Arctic Nunavut (p145) and Proud Canadian Design & First Hand Canadian Crafts (p145). Walk west o the craft studios, art galleries and artist-nspired gardens of **York Quay Centre 3** (p43).

Tour Facts

Best time Any morning or afternoon, except on Sunday or Monday.

Start Bay of Spirits Gallery (subway Union Station).

End Streetcar 504.

Distance Varies.

Time All day.

Food & drinks en route **Le Gourmand** (p98), **Mövenpick's Bistretto & La Pêcherie** (p102), **Sassafraz** (p102), **Mill St Brewery** (p116).

Elgin & Winter Garden Theatre Centre (p50)

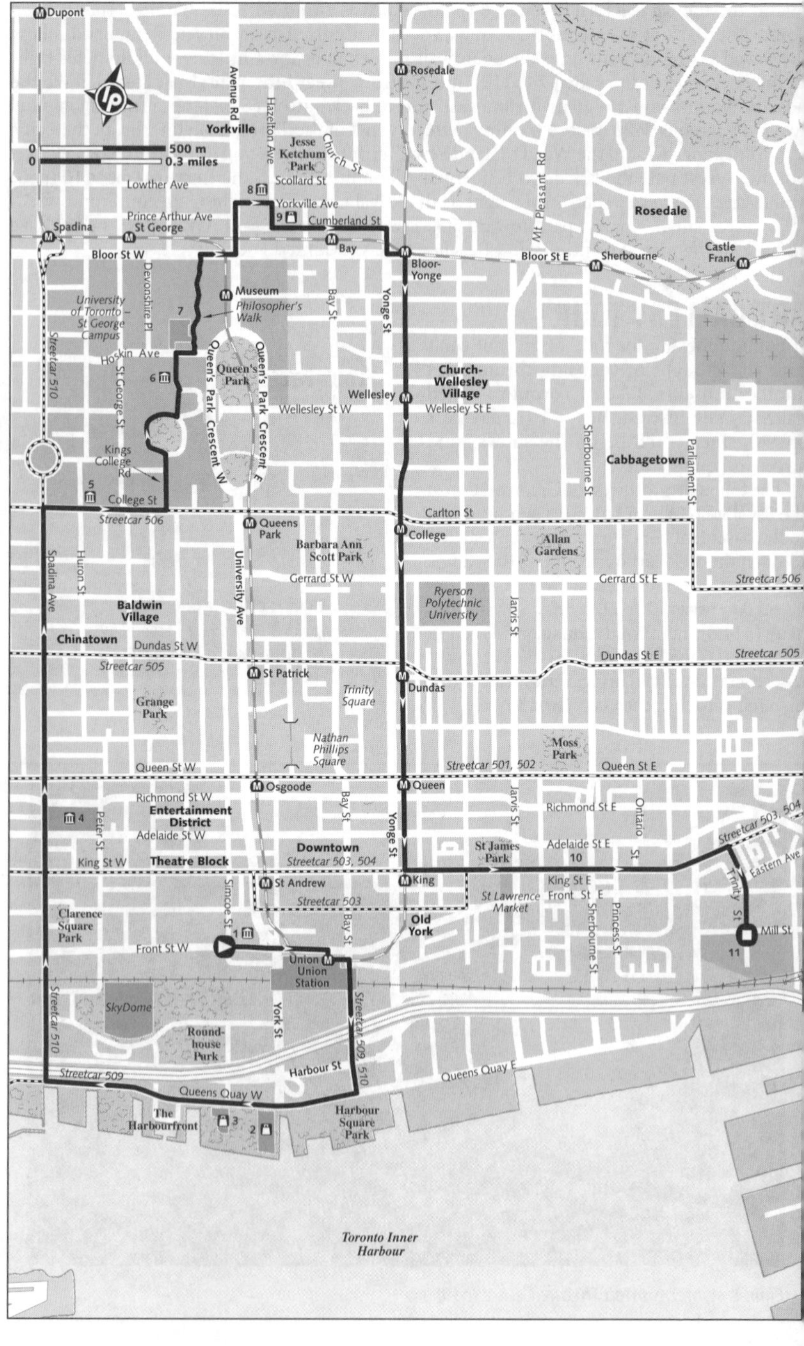

Dupont
Rosedale
Yorkville
Avenue Rd
Hazelton Ave
Jesse Ketchum Park
Church St
Scollard St
Yorkville Ave
Cumberland St
Lowther Ave
Prince Arthur Ave
St George
Spadina
Bay
Bloor-Yonge
Bloor St W
Bloor St E
Sherbourne
Castle Frank
Rosedale
Mt Pleasant Rd
Museum
Philosopher's Walk
University of Toronto – St George Campus
Devonshire Pl
Hoskin Ave
St George St
Queen's Park
Queen's Park Crescent W
Queen's Park Crescent E
Bay St
Yonge St
Church-Wellesley Village
Wellesley
Wellesley St W
Wellesley St E
Kings College Rd
College St
Streetcar 506
Streetcar 510
Cabbagetown
Sherbourne St
Parliament St
Carlton St
Queens Park
College
Barbara Ann Scott Park
Allan Gardens
Gerrard St W
Gerrard St E
Ryerson Polytechnic University
Spadina Ave
Huron St
University Ave
Baldwin Village
Chinatown
Dundas St W
Dundas St E
Streetcar 505
St Patrick
Dundas
Trinity Square
Jarvis St
Grange Park
Nathan Phillips Square
Moss Park
Queen St W
Streetcar 501, 502
Queen St E
Osgoode
Queen
Richmond St W
Richmond St E
Entertainment District
Adelaide St W
Adelaide St E
Peter St
Ontario St
King St W
Theatre Block
Downtown
Streetcar 503, 504
St James Park
King St E
King
St Andrew
Streetcar 503
St Lawrence Market
Front St E
Eastern Ave
Trinity St
Simcoe St
Old York
Princess St
Clarence Square Park
Front St W
Union
Union Station
Mill St
SkyDome
York St
Roundhouse Park
Streetcar 509, 510
Harbour St
Streetcar 509
Queens Quay W
Queens Quay E
The Harbourfront
Harbour Square Park
Toronto Inner Harbour
0
500 m
0
0.3 miles
1
2
3
4
5
6
7
8
9
10
11

Catch another 510 Spadina streetcar heading west, then north on Spadina Ave to **401 Richmond 4** (p53), an art gallery complex at the corner of Richmond St. When you've seen the rooftop garden and refueled at the coffee shop, get back on the 510 Spadina streetcar heading north through Chinatown (p52) to the University of Toronto (p57). Hop off at College St, then swing by the **Eric Arthur Gallery 5** (p59) and **UT Art Centre 6** (p59) before heading up to **Trinity College 7** (p59), where you can pick up the Philosopher's Walk (p59). The walk brings you onto fashionable Bloor St, just east of the Bata Shoe Museum (p55). Walk east to the corner of Avenue Rd, where you'll spy the Royal Ontario Museum (p56), but turn left instead. Join the moneyed set in Yorkville where contemporary Canadian and Aboriginal art galleries, found along Hazelton Ave and Scollard St, include **Feheley Fine Arts 8** at No 14 Hazelton Ave. Don't miss the **Guild Shop 9** (p150), either.

Meander east, ending up at Bloor-Yonge subway station. Assuming you've still got some time to spare, take the subway line back downtown to King station, then the 503 Kingston Rd or 504 King streetcar east along the **Design Strip 10** (p145), hopping off just after Parliament St to visit the **Distillery Historic District 11** (p146), where you can browse more galleries and artisan shops, and grab a free swig of beer at Mill St Brewery (p116).

CABBAGETOWN & ROSEDALE ARCHITECTURE WALK

Formerly St Enoch's Presbyterian Church, the **Toronto Dance Theatre & School 1** (p131) is a soaring red-brick Romanesque Revival building (1891) with a distinctive weather vane. A stone's throw south at No 37 is the **Italianate Villa 2**, which incidentally once belonged to the president of the Brilliant Sign Company; when an apartment complex was built next door to his home in 1910, he transferred all of its finest details, such as classical Ionic columns and carved stone lions, to the Metcalfe St façade.

Continue south to **Trinity Mews 3**, originally part of the Trinity College Medical School (1859). Peek into its courtyard, patterned with bricks, for the best views. Walk east to Sackville St, turning north toward No 377, the **Shields House 4**. It's identical to every mansard-roofed Second Empire building in the neighborhood, except for its distinguished gray stone facing. At the end of the block, turn right and look for **No 320 Carlton St 5**, a plump example of the architectural style Toronto is best known for, the bay-and-gable home (p24).

Head east and loop through the working class–style **Geneva Ave Cottages 6**, then walk up Sumach St next to Riverdale Park. On the left at No 384 is the **Witches' House 7**, so nicknamed for its gingerbread appearance and the gargoyle on its front face. At the corner is quaint **Winchester Cafe 8** (p109). Turn right and go as far as the **Riverdale Farm 9** (p62). On the north side of Winchester St, a road leads through the cemetery gates into the **Necropolis 10** (p62). Backtrack, then continue north to Wellesley St, where you'll come upon a sampler of all the different Cabbagetown architectural styles. The most famous are the hidden **Alpha Ave Cottages 11** and **Wellesley Cottages 12**, all originally built for workers in the 19th century but now occupied by urban professionals. Further west, **No 314 Wellesley St 13** is a whimsical delight of terra-cotta and carved Victorian ornamentation, including a full serpent carved under the highest gable.

Turn right on Parliament St, and it's just a few steps north to **St James Cemetery 14** (p63). Continue up to Bloor St, then walk east past the **former site of Castle Frank 15**, by a subway station (p61). Here you'll cross an invisible line over into the wealthy enclave of Rosedale. Walk north up Castle Frank Rd, stopping to view the terra-cotta picture-frame ornamentation on the **James Ramsey House 16**, the shaped hedges of the stately white Georgian home at **No 65 Castle Frank Rd 17** and, finally, **No 43 Castle Frank Rd 18**, where each 'clinker brick' (misshapen seconds) is differently colored.

As the road curves around, next to the redeveloped **Hawthorn Gardens 19** with its restored coach house, is a sign pointing to the petite **Craigleigh Gardens 20**. Castle Frank

Walk Facts

Best time Any morning or afternoon.

Start Toronto Dance Theatre & School (streetcar 506).

End Bramstone Hall (subway Sherbourne).

Distance 4.5km.

Time 1½ hours.

Food en route **Peartree** (p109), **Winchester Cafe** (p109), **Rashnaa** (p109).

Drinks en route Java at **Jet Fuel** (p131).

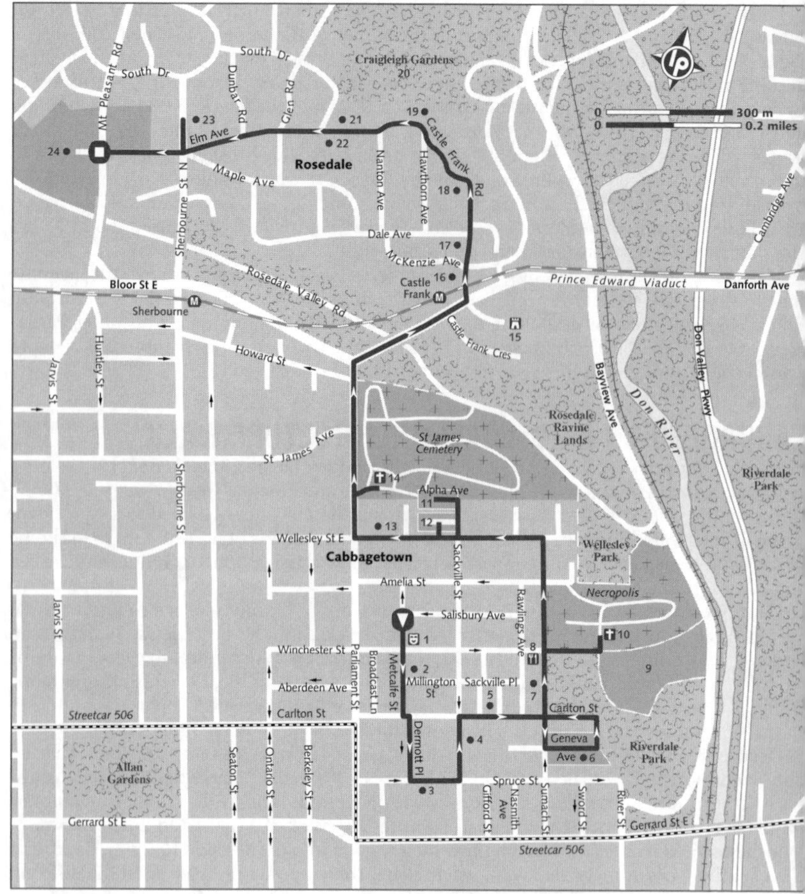

Rd leads to Elm Ave, where nearly every house is listed by the Ontario Heritage Foundation as being of architectural or historical significance. They are all most impressive, but particularly noteworthy are **No 88 Elm Ave** 21, which won an architecture prize in 1921, and **No 93 Elm Ave** 22 with its ornamental iron porch. Turn north onto Sherbourne St, toward the charmingly unkempt **Edward Gooderham House** 23 at No 27. This Georgian home was built for the same distillery family that had its offices in the **Flatiron (Gooderham) Building** (p46) and **Distillery Historic District** (p46).

Finally, backtrack and walk to the western end of Elm Ave. These are the original houses of Rosedale, where a group of Victorian manors has been joined together as a private school, impressive **Bramstone Hall** 24. They can be found on both sides of the road. It's a 10-minute walk south to Sherbourne subway station.

MOSTLY MODERN TORONTO WALK

To glimpse Toronto in all its glory, start this walk in the late afternoon or just before sunset, as the city's neon lights start to come on and even a few ghosts come out of the woodwork.

Hop off the 504 King streetcar on the Theatre Block (p47) at the corner of John and King Sts. Walk east past the **Princess of Wales Theatre** 1 (p125) and the **Royal Alexandra Theatre** 2 (p125). Look to your right for a perfect view of the CN Tower (p44) before reaching the corner of 'Education, Legislation, Salvation and Damnation.' At Simcoe St, cross over to **Roy Thomson Hall 3** (p48) and **Canada's Walk of Fame 4** (p48). If it's still early enough, peek inside **St Andrews Presbyterian Church 5** (p48), then continue west past the **Goethe-Institut Gallery 6** (p45). Turn right at York St, left onto Wellington St for the **Toronto Dominion Gallery of Inuit Art 7** (p45).

Continue walking to Bay St, turning north toward the **Design Exchange 8** (p45). Wander north along Canada's Wall Street, taking note of the financial powerhouses at **First Canadian Place 9** (p43) and **Scotia Plaza 10** (p43). As you approach Temperance St, on your left is the **Canada Permanent Building 11**, another art-deco effort. Walk east on Queen St, then head up Yonge St to the historic **Elgin & Winter Garden Theatre Centre 12** (p50).

Walk Facts

Best time Any afternoon or evening.

Start Theatre Block (streetcar 504).

End City Hall (streetcar 501).

Distance 3km.

Time One hour.

Food en route **Canoe** (p94), **Bymark** (p94), **Kubo DX** (p94), **Mercatto** (p94), **Senator Restaurant** (p97).

Drinks en route **Reds** (p118), **Top O' the Senator** (p123).

Detour onto Shuter St toward **Massey Hall 13** (p51). At Bond St, turn left by **St Michael's Catholic Cathedral 14** and walk up to the **Mackenzie House 15** (p50), said to be haunted (p31). Cut through the garden walkway into a parking lot. Look up for the mural on the south facade of the **Senator Restaurant 16** (p97). At the sidewalk, turn right and walk by **Top O' the Senator 17** (p123) and circle around **Dundas Square 18** (p49) to the west side of Yonge St. Walk south and pass through **Eaton Centre 19** (p148) to Trinity Square, where you'll find the **Church of the Holy Trinity 20** (p50) and its outdoor labyrinth. Cross over Bay St to **City Hall 21** (p50) and Nathan Phillips Square.

From here, it's just a short streetcar ride to Clubland (p27) in the Entertainment District.

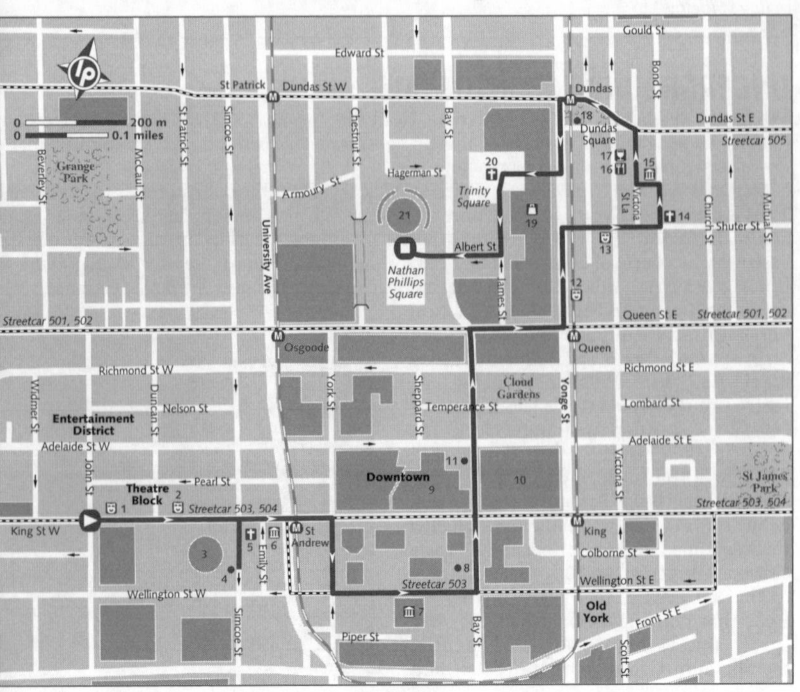

Bay St (below)

UNDERGROUND TORONTO WALK

When the weather outside is frightening, head for Toronto's underground PATH system (p198), an accidental labyrinth of mostly subterranean corridors, which connect many downtown sights, skyscrapers and shops.

Start at **Union Station 1** (p197) Follow the SkyWalk signs over the railroad tracks to the **CN Tower 2** (p444), next to **SkyDome 3** (p45). Retrace your steps to Union Station, then cross under Front St into the **Fairmont Royal York 4** (p161) for a quick look around the lobby upstairs. Back inside the basement concourse of Union Station, head for the double doors at the back leading to the **Air Canada Centre 5** (p44), which has interesting architectural displays near the Bay St entrance.

Retrace your steps back to Union Station one last time, then follow the color-coded arrows to **BCE Place 6** (p43) and the **Hockey Hall of Fame 7** (p45). Wander through Commerce Court en route to the **Toronto-Dominion Centre 8** (p43). After passing the electronic stock market displays, turn left toward 220 Bay St, but instead go up the escalators into the **Design Exchange 9** (p45). Back below the TD Centre, follow the signs for the Maritime Life Tower to visit the **Toronto Dominion Gallery of Inuit Art 10** (p45). Backtrack to the TD Centre, then start looking for signs that point toward Exchange Tower (p43), the Richmond-Adelaide Centre, the Sheraton Centre Toronto (p164) and

Walk Facts

Best time Weekday mornings in winter.

Start Union Station (subway Union).

End Trinity Square (subway Dundas).

Distance 5km.

Time 2½ hours.

Food en route **Marche Mövenpick** (p94), **Kubo DX** (p94), **Canoe** (p94), **Bymark** (p94), countless food courts.

Drinks en route Afternoon tea at **Epic** (p92).

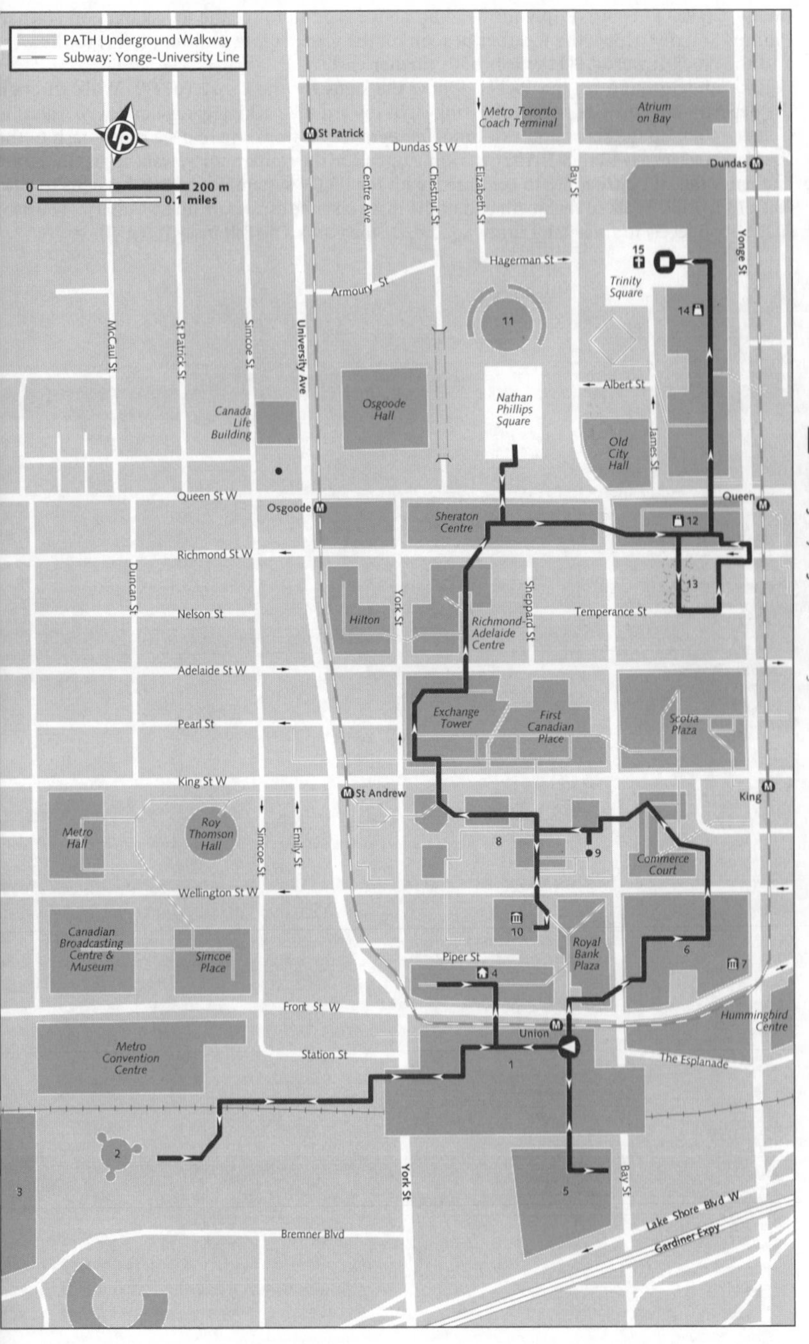
PATH Underground Walkway
Subway: Yonge-University Line
0 200 m
0 0.1 miles
St Patrick
Dundas St W
Metro Toronto Coach Terminal
Atrium on Bay
Dundas
Centre Ave
Chestnut St
Elizabeth St
Bay St
Yonge St
Hagerman St
15
Trinity Square
Armoury St
11
14
McCaul St
St Patrick St
Simcoe St
University Ave
Osgoode Hall
Nathan Phillips Square
Albert St
Canada Life Building
Old City Hall
James St
Queen St W
Osgoode
Sheraton Centre
Queen
12
Richmond St W
Duncan St
York St
Sheppard St
13
Nelson St
Hilton
Richmond-Adelaide Centre
Temperance St
Adelaide St W
Exchange Tower
First Canadian Place
Scotia Plaza
Pearl St
King St W
St Andrew
King
Metro Hall
Roy Thomson Hall
Simcoe St
Emily St
8
9
Commerce Court
Wellington St W
10
Canadian Broadcasting Centre & Museum
Simcoe Place
Royal Bank Plaza
6
7
Piper St
4
Front St W
Union
Hummingbird Centre
Metro Convention Centre
Station St
1
The Esplanade
2
York St
5
Bay St
3
Lake Shore Blvd W
Gardiner Expy
Bremner Blvd

finally, **City Hall** 11 (p50). Pop your head up above ground to see the ice-skaters on Nathan Phillips Square (p136), the weather beacon on the Canada Life Building (p49) to the west and the clock tower of **Old City Hall** (p50) further east.

Back underground on the PATH, follow the signs for the **Bay** 12 (p147). Walk through the department store basement, diverting right toward the parking garage and Bay-Adelaide Centre. Walk up the stairs and exit onto Temperance St, from where it's a quick dash to the **Cloud Forest Conservatory** 13 (p44). After warming up inside the conservatory, walk across the street and enter the Bay once more to reconnect with the PATH system, following the signs to **Eaton Centre** 14 (p148). Walk to the north end of the mall, take the escalators up by Ontario Tourism (p206) two levels to finish at Trinity Square, by the **Church of the Holy Trinity** 15 (p50).

Eating

Eating

America calls itself a 'melting pot,' but Canadians prefer the term 'mixed salad' for themselves. The metaphor is never more apt than when applied to the Megacity's flavorful dining scene. What chefs at five-star Michelin restaurants are finally admitting, Torontonians have known for decades – fusion is the future of food. So it's no surprise to find miso or Thai lemongrass sprinkled across the contemporary bistro menus here, but keep in mind the lingering British influences, too. A pint with lunch, and afternoon high teas, are still much-loved traditions. Residents savor every last ray of summer by dining out on rooftops, in shady backyards and on jostling sidewalk patios. In winter, crackling fireplaces are the soundtrack to many hearty meals. You'll find high-powered restaurants in the **Financial District** and many traditionalists in **Old York**, plus a new world of choices in **Baldwin Village**, near Kensington Market. Toronto's most kinetic restaurant strips are **Little Italy** and **Queen West**, with **Greektown (The Danforth)** and other neighborhoods almost as busy.

High Time for Tea

For traditional Victorian afternoon tea, the **Windsor Arms** (p166) has all the accoutrement: tinkling ivories, starched tablecloths, overstuffed chairs and crackling fireplaces. At the venerable **Café Victoria** (p95), Buckingham Palace shortbread is served amid palm trees and Victorian-print chairs. Meanwhile **Epic** restaurant, just off the lobby of the **Fairmont Royal York** (p161) has been making a name for itself with its variations on traditional tea service, such as 'Tea and Tarot Thursdays' and special children's teas of caffeine-free fruit and herbal brews. Reservations are advised for any of these hotel tea rooms, costing $20 to $30 per person.

Scattered around the city are more eclectic small tea rooms, each just about perfect for an afternoon's retreat. On Queen West, the **Red Tea Box** (p107) serves pan-Asian afternoon teas (from $12) inside its small shop, which has more in common with a Malaysian tea plantation bungalow than Olde England. At the Beaches, whimsy abounds at **La Tea Da Salon de Thé** (Map p240; ☎ 416-686-5787; 2305 Queen St E; afternoon tea $10-20; 🕒 11am-6pm Wed-Fri, noon-6pm Sat & Sun; streetcar 501), where fresh-baked scones are served. Further flung **Montgomery's Inn** (p77) has a tea room full of history that's open 2pm to 4:30pm daily, except Monday.

It's also worth phoning ahead to find out about special Edwardian teas at **Spadina House** (p59), afternoon tea tours of the **provincial legislature** (p58) and glorious operatic teas sponsored by the **University of Toronto Faculty of Music** (p130). Advance reservations are essential for all of these events.

Opening Hours

Restaurants are usually open for lunch on weekdays from 11:30am until 2:30pm and serve dinner daily from 5pm until 9:30pm, sometimes later on weekends. A few also serve weekend brunch, usually 11am to 2:30pm. For those that serve breakfast, the time is around 7:30am until 10am. If restaurants take a day off, it's Monday. Some restaurants may close early or on additional days in winter, then stay open later during summer.

How Much?

Prices are low for what most visitors from the US and Europe are used to, so eating out can be a high point of your trip. Stretch your budget even further by eating well at lunch, when most restaurants charge about half as much for a meal as at dinner – often for exactly the same menu. Otherwise at dinner, expect to pay around $20 (before taxes and tip) at a mid-range establishment, and $50 or more at a top-end restaurant. Our Cheap Eats category at the end of each neighborhood section reviews places offering meals under $10. Some coffeehouses (p131) and pubs (p116) also serve great food.

Booking Tables

As a general rule of thumb, the higher the prices are on the menu, the more strongly reservations are advised. Without a reservation, you should try to show up for an early or late seating, say, before 5:30pm or just after 9pm. It's most difficult to score a free table around downtown in the Financial District, Old York, the Theatre Block and the Entertainment District, as well as trendy neighborhoods like Little Italy, Queen West and the Beaches.

Self-Catering

The indoor **St Lawrence Market** (p47) and the shops found around **Kensington Market** (p60) are each as much of a sightseeing experience as a destination for take-out meals, snacks and picnic goodies. Natural food stores and organic groceries are your best bet for vegetarian, vegan and nondairy eats, including hot and cold buffet delights. Greektown's **Big Carrot Natural Food Market** (Map pp238-9; ☎ 416-466-2129; www.thebigcarrot.ca; Carrot Common, 348 Danforth Ave; ⌚ 9:30am-8pm Mon-Wed, 9:30am-9pm Thu-Fri, 9am-7pm Sat, 11am-6pm Sun; subway Chester) is the grandmother of them all. Its streetfront café has fresh organic juices, a salad bar and a few tiny tables. Some others worth trying include:

Baldwin Natural Foods (Map pp226-7; ☎ 416-979-1777; 20½ Baldwin St; streetcar 501, 502)

Kensington Natural Bakery (Map pp236-7; ☎ 416-534-1294; 460 Bloor St W; subway Bathurst)

Lennie's Whole Foods (Map pp238-9; ☎ 416-967-5196; 489 Parliament St; streetcar 506)

Noah's Natural Foods (Map pp231-3; ☎ 416-968-7930; 322 Bloor St W; subway Spadina)

Wholesome Market (Map pp240; ☎ 416-690-9500; 2234 Queen St E; streetcar 501)

Taxes & Tipping

With such a feast of tables and cuisines to choose from, the one sour note is taxes. A hamburger and beer priced at $9.95 on the menu will actually cost you $13, including taxes and a tip of 15% (equal to the total amount of tax on your bill, or calculate 20% for excellent service), by the time you get out the door. Either discreetly leave the tip behind on the table or hand it directly to your server. A few restaurants may include a service charge for large parties; no tip should be added in these cases.

HARBOURFRONT

HARBOUR SIXTY STEAKHOUSE

Map pp228-30 *Steakhouse/Seafood*

☎ 416-777-2111; 60 Harbour St; dinner $27-50; ⌚ 11.30-1am Mon-Fri, 5pm-1am Sat & Sun; streetcar 509, 510

Inside the stately 1917 Toronto Harbour Commission building, an opulent baroque dining room glows with brass lamps. Sink into a gold brocade banquette and order from an eminent variety of steaks, sterling salmon ($29) or seasonal Florida stone-crab claws and broiled Caribbean lobster tail. The only sour note? Side dishes, from Lyonnaise potatoes to fire-roasted peppers, are overpriced ($7 to $10). Arrive early to get started on an award-winning wine list of European and New World vintages, then stay late and linger over chocolate soufflé with Grand Marnier creme anglaise ($15).

FINANCIAL DISTRICT

High-powered and traditional restaurants encircle the Financial District, a location convenient for many shoppers and hotel guests.

BIFF'S

Map pp228-30 *French Bistro/Pre-Theater*

☎ 416-860-0086; 4 Front St E; dinner $22-32; ⌚ lunch Mon-Fri, dinner; streetcar 503, 504

A short jump from the Hummingbird Centre for the Performing Arts, Biff's can provide whatever your heart (or your stomach) desires: a high-powered business lunch or even a romantic full-course meal spent lingering over champagne on the sidewalk patio. Modern French dishes are dressed with New World additions, such as PEI mussels and heirloom tomatoes.

BYMARK Map pp228-30 *Fusion*

☎ 416-777-1144; Toronto-Dominion Centre, 66 Wellington St W; dinner $30-50; ⌚ lunch Mon-Fri, dinner Mon-Sat; subway St Andrew

Chef Mark McEwan of **North 44°** (p224) brings his sophisticated menu of Asian-inspired continental cuisine downtown to a bilevel modern space, where he proffers a terrine of foie gras with maple balsamic glaze ($25), lobster salad in caviar cream ($24) and a warm chocolate torte with roasted banana ice cream ($13), each with its own suggested wine or beer pairing.

CANOE Map pp228-30 *Contemporary Canadian*

☎ 416-364-0054; Toronto-Dominion Centre, 66 Wellington St W; dinner $36-42; ⌚ lunch & dinner Mon-Fri; subway St Andrew

Toronto's definitive dining space may still be Canoe, and what a space it is, situated on the 54th floor of the Toronto-Dominion Bank Tower. Sweeping views of Lake Ontario and the Toronto Islands stand out along with regional Canadian haute cuisine – maybe a plate of Bay of Fundy scallops with pumpkin and kumquats ($18) or Nunavik caribou steak ($42).

KUBO DX Map pp228-30 *Asian Fusion*

☎ 416-368-5826; 234 Bay St; dim sum lunch $10, mains $9-14; ⌚ 11:30am-9pm Mon-Fri; subway King

Inside the **Design Exchange** (p45), sharply styled Kubo offers a happy sight for artistic eyes, gastronomic pleasures in a hurry and a lot of laughter upon reading the menu. Snack on Dumb & Dumplings with spicy soy dipping sauce or the Grill of a Lifetime steak wrap with orange-peppercorn marinade and fiery onions.

MARCHE MÖVENPICK

Map pp228-30 *International/Late Night*

☎ 416-863-0108; BCE Pl, 42 Yonge St, street level; buffet lunch $10, mains $8-25; ⌚ 7:30-2am Sun-Thu, 7:30-4am Fri & Sat; subway Union

An innovative market-style restaurant dreamt up in Switzerland, Mövenpick will satisfy anyone's taste buds. Wander between the fresh-food stations, merrily filling up your tray with such treats as Atlantic salmon and potato rösti, Belgian waffles topped with cherries, signature maple ice cream or fresh juices, baked goods and salads. It's great fun for kids, but watch the price stamps on your check-out card because they add up quickly.

Also inside BCE Place, **Mövenpick's Caffé Bar & Masquerade** (Map pp228-30; ☎ 416-363-8971) serves Italian pasta and other specialties. Smaller branches around downtown include **Marchelino Mövenpick** (Map pp226-7; ☎ 416-351-8783; Eaton Centre, 220 Yonge St; subway Queen) and **Mövenpick Palavrion** (Map pp228-30; ☎ 416-979-0060; 270 Front St W; streetcar 504), specializing in rotisserie grill fare and seafood, near SkyDome.

TASTING ROOMS Map pp228-30 *International*

☎ 416-362-2499; First Canadian Pl, 100 King St W; breakfast & lunch $7-15, 3-course dinner $30; ⌚ 7am-10pm Mon-Fri, 5-11pm Sat; subway King

Here, the menu is as far-flung as the dining room, which spills over into a wine library, lodge bar and elevated patio. Later in the day the cuisine becomes more adventurous with your choice of tasting-sized portions – maybe seared blue tuna with yellow curry or Ontario venison pie. Wine flights and hors d'oeuvre platters are ideal for pre-theatre dining or celebratory groups.

Cheap Eats

Ever wonder where bike couriers go when they're on standby? The answer is **Temperance Society Breadspreads Bar** (Map pp228-30; Temperance St, cnr Yonge St; items $1-5; ⌚ Mon-Sat; subway Queen). If a sweet ending is what you're after, the **Nutty Chocolatier** (Map pp228-30; ☎ 416-363-9009; 144 Yonge St; items start from $1.50; ⌚ Mon-Sat; subway Queen) serves up Belgian specialties in Victorian tins.

MERCATTO Map pp228-30 *Italian Café*

☎ 416-306-0467; 330 Bay St; meals $4-10; ⌚ 7am-8pm Mon-Fri; subway King

A delightful string of Italian deli cafés, Mercatto hand crafts its creative panini, pasta and pizzas while DJ music flows. You'll find magazine racks, friendly faces and a cappuccino bar as well. There's a busier branch in **Old York** (Map pp228-30; ☎ 416-366-4567; 15 Toronto St; subway King).

OLD YORK

On the streets of the Old Town of York, just east of Yonge St, wonderful dining inside some of the city's most distinguished historic buildings can be easily had, even for just a few dollars.

Dinner & a Movie

Feeling under the weather? Or is it just too cold to go outside? You can pick up a full night's entertainment at **Dinner+DVD** (Map pp228-30; ☎ 416-703-0383; http://dinnerdvd.com; 263 King St W; streetcar 504), where the menu changes daily (call ahead for special orders). A gourmet take-out meal for two plus the rental DVD of your choice will run about $35. You can even have it delivered straight to your downtown hotel room.

CAFÉ VICTORIA

Map pp228-30 *Continental/Pre-Theater*

☎ 416-863-4125; King Edward Hotel, 37 King St E; mains $17-35; ⌚ breakfast, lunch & dinner, closed Mon; subway King

A baroque-styled dining room fringed by palm fronds, Café Victoria serves pre-theater set meals. Sunday brunch and afternoon teas also enjoy elegant service.

COURTHOUSE MARKET GRILLE

Map pp228-30 *Steakhouse Grill*

☎ 416-214-9379; 57 Adelaide St E; dinner $15-33; ⌚ lunch Mon-Fri, dinner Mon-Sat; subway King

Toronto's last public execution took place here, and the downstairs bathrooms are set amid old jailhouse cells, one of which is now an ice-wine cellar. Macabre jokes aside, this distinguished 19th-century building boasts fireplaces, marble fixtures and grilled meats and seafood that are perfectly done. Around the corner is the imposing **Rosewater Supper Club** (Map pp228-30; ☎ 416-214-5888; 19 Toronto St; pastas $18-32, mains $30-42; ⌚ lunch Mon-Fri, dinner Mon-Sat).

MONTRÉAL BISTRO & JAZZ CLUB

Map pp238-9 *Québecois Bistro*

☎ 416-363-0179; 65 Sherbourne St; mains $10-23; ⌚ lunch Mon-Fri, dinner Mon-Sat; streetcar 503, 504

This jazz club (p123) does not rate its food in second place. Heavily influenced by Québecois cooking, the chefs whip up seafood cocotte, grilled Atlantic salmon and roasted lake duck, all served to tête-à-tête tables lit by boudoir lamps.

NAMI Map pp238-30 *Japanese*

☎ 416-362-7373; 55 Adelaide St E; mains $16-33; ⌚ dinner Mon-Sat; subway King

The name means 'wave' – look for the neon version on the sign outside. Bustling about the sleek, black lacquered interior are kimono-clad matrons and intense-looking sushi chefs, who make only small concessions to North American palates. *Robatayaki* grilling is a specialty.

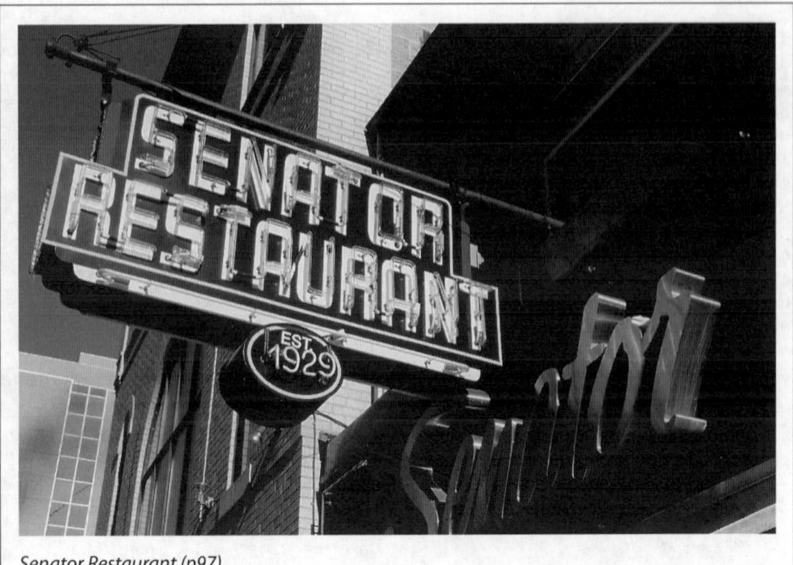

Senator Restaurant (p97)

SPRING ROLLS Map pp228-30 *Pan-Asian*
☎ **416-365-7655; 85 Front St E; mains $7-13;**
🕑 **11am-11pm; streetcar 503, 504**
Spring Rolls has settled into a new dining space bedecked with Chinese warriors, Buddha's and a shark aquarium. Bowls of Vietnamese *bún* (rice vermicelli), spicy Sichuan noodles and *pad thai* (stir-fried noodles) are backed by grilled sea bass ($15) and banana fritters. An energetic after-work crowd often unwinds at sidewalk tables.

Cheap Eats

ST LAWRENCE MARKET

Map pp228-30 *Specialty/Take-out*
☎ **416-392-7120; South Market, 2 Front St E;**
🕑 **8am-6pm Tue-Thu, 8am-7pm Fri, 5am-5pm Sat; streetcar 503, 504**
Classical musicians often perform at the city's beloved indoor market, where you will be amazed by the range and quality of the produce, baked goods and imported foodstuffs on offer. Faves include **Carousel Bakery**, **Future Bakery**, **St Urbain** for Montréal-style bagels and, on the lower level, **Mustachio's** chicken sandwiches that are said to be 'about as big as your head.'

Toronto's historic **farmers' market** (since 1803) is held in the North Market, starting at 5am every Saturday.

THEATRE BLOCK & ENTERTAINMENT DISTRICT

For pre-theatre dining, there's a line-up of places on King St, just west of John St and the Theatre Block. Although most give indifferent service and serve worse food, people keep coming back. Shiny new restaurants (some ferociously passé even as they open) are found in the fickle, expanding galaxy, south of Queen St W, that is often referred to as the Entertainment District.

Top Five Restaurants for Kids

- **Marche Mövenpick** (p94)
- **St Lawrence Market** (p47)
- **Bright Pearl** (p98)
- **White Bros Fish Co** (p110)
- **Phil's Original BBQ** (p105)

ASAKUSA Map pp228-30 *Japanese*
☎ **416-598-9030; 389 King St W; mains $8-13;**
🕑 **lunch daily, dinner Mon-Sat; streetcar 504, 510**
Once you know that the Japanese chef-owner worked for three decades in Tokyo's top hotel kitchens, it's worth the long wait. Service is gracious, bringing traditional sushi and sashimi, tempura, noodles and authentic appetizers straight to your table.

AVALON Map pp228-30 *Eclectic*
☎ **416-979-9918; 270 Adelaide St W; mains $25-40;**
🕑 **lunch Thu, dinner Tue-Sat; streetcar 504**
Chef-owner Chris McDonald's nightly tasting menu may sound deliciously controversial, yet rest assured it always delivers both fresh ingredients and fusion accents. Discreetly tucked into a brash neighborhood, Avalon's superb service, stained glass windows and seasonal fireplace are noteworthy accompaniments, too.

FEZ BATIK Map pp228-30 *International*
☎ **416-204-9660; 129 Peter St; mains $12-16;**
🕑 **11am-10pm; streetcar 501**
Flowery murals bedeck the walls, and the patio sprawls into the lap of the Entertainment District. A tame menu belies the crazy come-on, showing Italian pastas, Asian main dishes and Southwestern sandwiches. Order a flourless mocha torte or maple butter tart ($7.50) for that perfect pre-clubbing sugar rush.

MONSOON Map pp228-30 *Asian Fusion*
☎ **416-979-7172; 100 Simcoe St; dinner $20-36;**
🕑 **lunch Mon-Fri, dinner Mon-Sat; subway St Andrew**
Clean Zen lines and mid-century modern designs mix harmoniously in this lounge below street level. Monsoon's tasting menu ($88/60 with/without wine pairings) goes all out, listing the likes of halibut seared in ginger-saké sauce or Bangkok bouillabaisse along with lemongrass sorbet to refresh your palate between glorious courses.

N'AWLINS
Map pp228-30 *Cajun-Italian/Pre-Theater*
☎ **416-595-1958; 299 King St W; mains $16-37;**
🕑 **dinner; streetcar 504**
A saving grace near the Theatre Block is N'Awlins, where the food leans more toward Italian than Deep South, but service is courteous and prompt. Live jazz and blues take the stage nightly, except Monday (no cover).

RAIN Map pp228-30 *Asian Fusion*

☎ 416-599-7246; 19 Mercer St; mains $18-35; 🕑 5:30-11pm Mon-Sat; streetcar 504, 510

'atrons may be forgiven for expecting to ee a waterfall or bamboo grove around very corner at Rain. An A-list crowd loves he artistic and fanciful food concepts, but he menu items only seem challenging and exotic.

SEN5ES Map pp228-30 *Eclectic*

☎ 416-961-0055; 318 Wellington St W; breakfast & unch $5-17, dinner $32-45; 🕑 breakfast & lunch, dinner Wed-Sun, lounge 5pm-1am daily; treetcar 510

'his truly divine caterer's creation reigns over he ground floor of the **SoHo Metropolitan Hotel** p163). In the sun-drenched airy café, breakfast brings an impeccable cappuccino and roissant with chocolate butter, while the leek modern dining room harbors a chef's able, offering lobster ravioli or an ocean ot plate with citrus-ginger dipping sauce it night. Take your dinner in the lounge to ample from the same amazing menu for ınder $25 per plate.

WAYNE GRETZKY'S

Map pp228-30 *Family Restaurant*

☎ 416-979-7825; 99 Blue Jays Way; mains $8-15; 🕑 11:30-1am Mon-Thu, 11:30-2am Fri & Sat, 11:30am-11pm Sun; streetcar 504

Near SkyDome and named after the Canadian hockey legend, Wayne Gretzky's is a sports bar, estaurant and rooftop patio serving pastas, alads and burgers. Most people pop in here on a pilgrimage to view the hockey memorabilia. Walk around to the building's Mercer St side to see how No 34 thanks his fans with a huge outdoor mural.

YYZ RESTAURANT & WINE BAR

Map pp228-30 *Asian Fusion*

☎ 416-599-3399; 345 Adelaide St W; mains $26-33; 🕑 dinner; streetcar 510, 504

Formerly of Mercer Street Grill, chef Chris Zielinski has reincarnated his daring fusion fare at this mod 1960s-style moon lounge, which stole its name from Toronto's airport abbreviation. A recent 'winterlicious' menu featured sweet potato–chipotle–lime soup paired with pan-seared Atlantic salmon and scallops, plus a side of sesame-encrusted sushi rice, all crowned by a royal coconut and banana mousse.

QUEEN STREET & DUNDAS SQUARE

You can shop till you drop on Queen St, but eventually you'll need to refuel. Avoid a dining disaster by going perhaps just a few steps out of your way to find these culinary shining stars.

JULES RESTAURANT TARTERIE

Map pp234-5 *French*

☎ 416-348-8886; 147 Spadina Ave; meals $6-13; 🕑 11:30am-9pm Mon-Fri, noon-5pm Sat; streetcar 510, 501

Some of the best pick-me-up lunches are had at this straightforward French café, where sunshine splashes across wooden tables. Crepes, quiches and salads abound. Efficient service means there may be time for apple tart or crème brûlée.

LE SELECT BISTRO Map pp226-7 *French*

☎ 416-596-6405; 328 Queen St W; dinner $17-30; 🕑 11:30am-11pm Mon-Thu, 11:30am-midnight Fri & Sat; streetcar 501

Cute bread baskets hang above patron's table. Parisian bistro classics, such as cassoulet or goat cheese tart, appear on the three-course prix fixe French menu ($29). An extensive wine list draws from just shy of 1000 bottles. Call after-hours to hear the crazy, triumphant answering machine message.

QUEEN MOTHER CAFÉ

Map pp226-7 *International*

☎ 416-598-4719; 208 Queen St W; mains $8-15; 🕑 11:30am-midnight Mon-Sat, 11:30am-11pm Sun; subway Osgoode

Another Queen St institution, Queen Mother Café is beloved for its cozy, dark wooden booths and surprisingly good pan-Asian dim sum. You'll also find some great Canadian comfort food here. **Dufflet Pastries** (p107) delivers desserts here.

SENATOR RESTAURANT

Map pp226-7 *Diner*

☎ 416-364-7517; 249 Victoria St; mains $6-18; 🕑 7:30am-3pm Mon-Fri, 8am-3pm Sat & Sun, 5pm-7:30pm Wed-Sat; subway Dundas

This authentic '30s luncheonette sits beside the **Top O' the Senator** (p123) jazz club. Weekday breakfast specials are a good deal, and so is the time-honored diner fare and Canadian comfort food.

TIGER LILY'S NOODLE HOUSE

Map pp226-7 *Pan-Asian/Vegetarian*

☎ 416-977-5499; 257 Queen St W; mains $8-13; 11:30am-9pm Mon-Fri, noon-10pm Sat & Sun; subway Osgoode

This atmospheric tea room seems to embody one of its signature dishes, the 'love nest' (a stir-fry with walnuts over noodle cake, $12). Creative dim sum brunch and Vietnamese coffee ensure patronage, but service can be sloppy.

Cheap Eats

FRESH BY JUICE FOR LIFE

Map pp226-7 *Vegetarian/Take-out*

☎ 416-599-4442; 336 Queen St W; items $4-8; 8:30am-6:30pm Mon-Fri, 9am-6:30pm Sat, 10:30am-6:30pm Sun; streetcar 501, 510

Everything is made fresh at this city fave. A wholesome and tasty menu includes kaleidoscopic salads and 'Free Tibet' rice bowls, plus smoothies, shakes and 'vital fluids' to cure whatever ails. There are other branches of Fresh By Juice For Life in the **Annex** (Map p236-7; ☎ 416-531-2635; 521 Bloor St W; subway Bathurst) and **Queen West** (Map pp234-5; ☎ 416-913-2720; 894 Queen St W; streetcar 501).

LE GOURMAND

Map pp234-5 *Specialty Café/Take-out*

☎ 416-504-4494; 152 Spadina Ave; meals $5-10; 7am-9pm Mon-Fri, 9am-6pm Sat, 9am-4pm Sun; streetcar 510, 501

A nirvana for foodies, the upmarket grocery store Le Gourmand stocks Napa Valley mustards and rare chocolates made in Mexico. You should peruse the deli case and pastry shelves, or at least pop by for a foamy cappuccino and dish of homemade gelato. As for breakfast, can we tempt you with a warm chocolate-banana-nut bread pudding topped by fresh fruit, cream and maple syrup ($8)?

CHINATOWN & BALDWIN VILLAGE

Chinatown is home to scores of restaurants serving Cantonese, Szechwan, Hunan and Mandarin cuisine. As ever more well-off Chinese restaurateurs pack up and leave for the suburbs, Thai and Vietnamese kitchens take their place.

Located near the Art Gallery of Ontario, secretive Baldwin St is not a place that many out-of-towners discover on their own. It's a culinary wonderland of tastes from Europe, the Americas and Asia. As a bonus, summer outdoor patios flourish here.

> **Top Five Romantic Restaurants**
>
> - **Harbour Sixty Steakhouse** (p93)
> - **Montréal Bistro & Jazz Club** (p95)
> - **Celestin** (p224)
> - **Café Brussel** (p118)
> - **Mata Hari Grill** (p99)

BRIGHT PEARL

Map pp226-7 *Cantonese/Dim Sum*

☎ 416-979-3988; 346-8 Spadina Ave; dim sum from $1.50, dinner for 2 $37; 9am-11pm, dim sum 9-11am daily & 1:30-4pm Mon-Fri; streetcar 510

Walk by the stone lions up onto the 2nd floor of Hsin Kuang shopping center and discover this Cantonese-style banquet hall. It's especially popular for dim sum, when dozens upon dozens of dishes (including vegetarian) are offered.

EATING GARDEN

Map pp226-7 *Chinese Seafood*

☎ 416-595-5525; 41-43 Baldwin St; mains $8-15; lunch Mon-Fri, brunch noon-5pm Sat & Sun, dinner 5pm-midnight; streetcar 505

A glass-fronted kitchen inspires confidence in this clean, bright dining room hung with chalkboard menus. Some classics, like fresh seafood in garlic, appear on the menu, but so does satay sauce and other pan-Asian flair. Repeat diners at Eating Garden are loyal to the great value two-for-one lobster specials ($26).

JODHPORE CLUB

Map pp226-7 *Indian*

☎ 416-598-2502; 33 Baldwin St; weekday lunch buffet $8, mains $7-13; lunch Mon-Sat, dinner daily; streetcar 505

Aspiring to serve Indian colonial cuisine, with spicy curries from the beaches of Goa up into the Himalayas, the Jodhpore Club has an excellent lunch buffet (available until 3pm). It's an evocative taste of the raj at much less than a king's ransom.

JOHN'S ITALIAN CAFFE

Map pp226-7 *Italian*

416-596-8848; 27 Baldwin St; pizzas $8-15; 11am-11pm Sun-Thu, 11-1am Fri & Sat; streetcar 505

John's classic joint wouldn't look out of place in New York's Little Italy, or even New Jersey. Its leafy summertime patio is perfect for a bottle of Chianti and a fresh pizza piled high with toppings.

KONNICHIWA Map pp226-7 *Japanese*

416-593-8538; 31 Baldwin St; mains $6-12; 11am-9pm Mon-Sat; streetcar 505

At a Japanese diner favored by nostalgic ex-pats, friendly staff dish up soba noodles, sushi and Sapporo beer. Comfort fare extends to summertime barley tea and individually wrapped *manju* (steamed cakes, $2) sold at the front counter.

LEE GARDEN Map pp226-7 *Cantonese*

416-593-9524; 331 Spadina Ave; mains $8-12; 4pm-midnight; streetcar 510

Longstanding, casual Lee Garden offers an unusually varied menu of Cantonese comfort fare and seafood. It's open late – but you should expect to join the queue of regulars, who rave about the blackboard specials.

MATA HARI GRILL Map pp226-7 *Malaysian*

416-596-2832; 39 Baldwin St; lunch $8-10, dinner mains $11-18; lunch Mon-Fri, dinner; streetcar 505

A romantic hideaway makes perfect sense on Baldwin Street. Revel in a cozy nook with gilt mirrors and richly colored fabrics before diving into fiery beef *rendang* ($15) or 'Chicken Kapitan' curry ($13), an authentic Nyonya (Straits Chinese) dish. Desserts are inspired, and so is the list of ice wines and imported beers.

SWATOW Map pp226-7 *Chinese/Late Night*

416-977-0601; 309 Spadina Ave; mains $6-12; 11-4am; streetcar 510, 505

An extensive menu covers cuisine from Swatow (a city now known as Shantou, on the coast of China's Guangdong province), nicknamed 'red cooking' for its potent use of fermented rice wine; house noodles are fiery. Cash only.

Cheap Eats

A loonie will buy a *bánh mí* (Vietnamese sub sandwich) with meat or tofu filling at **Kim Thanh** (Map pp226-7; 416-979-7928; 336 Spadina Ave; items from $1; streetcar 510). Always bustling **Furama Cake & Dessert Garden** (Map pp226-7; 416-866-7412; 248-250 Spadina Ave; items from $1; streetcar 510) sells lotus seed cakes, almond cookies and curried buns for pocket change. **Ten Ren's Tea & Ginseng** (Map pp226-7; 416-598-7872; 454 Dundas St W; streetcar 505) carries rare Chinese imports.

FRECKLE BEAN CAFE

Map pp226-7 *Contemporary Canadian*

416-595-1943; 132 McCaul St; meals $6-8; lunch & dinner; streetcar 505

Drawing you in with its jazz soundtrack and retro-styled tables, this quiet spot pours strong coffee and keeps microbrews on tap. Sate yourself with imaginative selections like a vegetable-brie sandwich, bison burger or escargot-topped pizza.

GOLDSTONE NOODLE HOUSE

Map pp226-7 *Hong Kong/Cantonese*

416-596-9053; 266 Spadina Ave; meals $4-8; 8-2am Sun-Thu, 8-4am Fri & Sat; streetcar 510, 505

Airy, bright and always jam-packed, you'll easily identify this place by the barbecued ducks (a house specialty) hanging in the windows. Helpings of noodles, rice and vegetable dishes are humongous.

John's Italian Caffe (left)

PHỠ' HU'NG

Map pp226-7 *Vietnamese*

☎ **416-593-4274; 350 Spadina Ave; mains $6-10;**
🕑 **11am-11pm; streetcar 510**

An awesome array of delicious Vietnamese soups with fresh greens, although certain dishes may be a touch too authentic for some (what, don't you like pork intestines and blood?). A fair-weather bonus is the patio. It has another branch in **Bloor-Yorkville** (Map pp231-3; ☎ 416-963-5080; 200 Bloor St W, 2nd floor; subway Museum).

YONGE STREET STRIP & CHURCH-WELLESLEY VILLAGE

Yonge St, although busy night and day, is not one of Toronto's prime restaurant districts; it's swamped with bland franchises and cheap take-out counters. Further east, in the gay Church-Wellesley village, eateries often worry more about the size of their patios than passing any taste tests. Yet turnover in both neighborhoods guarantees you'll find a few gems.

Brunch Hunt

Torontonians are single-minded in their search for the perfect weekend brunch (a combination of breakfast and lunch). Indulge yourself by waking up late (but arrive before 4pm, please) to try pancakes with fresh Ontario peaches and maple syrup or maybe eggs Benedict with smoked salmon.

For contemporary brunches, **Agora** (p102) at the Art Gallery of Ontario has skylights and sculpture. At Le Royal Meridien King Edward Hotel, elegant **Café Victoria** (p95) offers a royal spread.

Eclectic **Bella's Bistro** at **Free Times Cafe** (p122) hosts the Bella! Did Ya Eat? Jewish brunch with live *klezmer* and Yiddish music ($17). **Latitude** (p103) serves spicy Latin brunches, heavy on hot salsa, eggs, cornmeal and fruity sangria, **Xacutti** (p106) does South Asian fusion and **Bright Pearl** (p98) is the place for Cantonese dim sum. Vegetarians, try **Fressen** (p106).

Did you wake up with a hangover headache? Cure it with comfort food at **Insomnia** (p103), **Swan** (p107), **Hello Toast** (p108) or **Edward Levesque's Kitchen** (p108). The **Bedford Ballroom** (p119) has nostalgic, budget-priced brunch items, such as mini-boxes of cold cereal served with cute, cafeteria-sized cartons of milk.

BYZANTIUM

Map pp231-3 *French Fusio*

☎ **416-922-3859; 499 Church St; mains $15-25;**
🕑 **brunch 11am-3pm Sun, dinner 5:30-11pm daily; subway Wellesley**

If you've got a rich boyfriend or girlfrienc suggest Byzantium. Creative main dishes lik thyme-honey encrusted Arctic char are lai out on fine linens, and the bar is known for it playful martinis.

CARMAN'S DINING CLUB

Map pp231-3 *Steakhous*

☎ **416-924-8558; 26 Alexander St; mains $39-46;**
🕑 **5-11pm; subway Wellesley**

Carman's popularity has waxed and wane over the past 40 years, but the profuse flowe gardens out front and its Alexander Woo homestead setting filled with stained glas and antiques still makes patrons gasp. Steak and lobster come with seven famous sid dishes and a minidessert.

ETHIOPIAN HOUSE

Map pp231-3 *Africa*

☎ **416-923-5438; 4 Irwin Ave; mains $7.50-11.50;**
🕑 **11:30-1am; subway Wellesley**

It's a packed and popular place with African inspired murals on the walls, but there's n silverware in sight as *sherro wot* (seasone chickpeas) and *gored-gored* (spiced beef) ar slathered onto moist *injera* (bread). Save tim for a traditional coffee-roasting ceremony when the aroma of frankincense fills the air.

FIRE ON THE EAST SIDE

Map pp231-3 *Eclecti*

☎ **416-960-3473; 6 Gloucester St; dinner $12-22;**
🕑 **11am-midnight; subway Wellesley**

A stone's throw from Yonge St, this ultrachic din ing room feels just like someone's living room A haywire fusion kitchen works variations o African, Caribbean, Acadian French and Caju themes, from spicy crab cakes ($11) to jalapeño vodka pasta ($14). Desserts are chef-made.

FRIENDLY THAI

Map pp231-3 *Tha*

☎ **416-924-8424; 678 Yonge St; mains $7-13;**
🕑 **noon-midnight Mon-Wed, 11:30am-midnight Thu-Sat, 11am-midnight Sun; subway Wellesley**

A favorite among Yonge St's many Southeas Asian eateries, this one's good for a quick lunc of *pad thai*, classic curry or savory salad serve with sticky rice. A few Malay and Indonesia items, such as *gado gado* (cooked vegetable with peanut sauce) and *tofu goreng* (fried tofu have sneaked onto the menu, too.

ORO Map pp226-7 *Contemporary Canadian*
☎ 416-597-0155; 45 Elm St; pastas $18-22, dinner 25-45; lunch Mon-Fri, dinner Mon-Sat; subway Dundas

A showpiece for the contemporary Canadian food creations of chef Dario Tomaselli, elegant Oro successfully grazes the outer limits of culinary creativity. Plates of coffee-dusted bison tenderloin ($40) and birch-lacquered duck breast ($25) are followed by even more surprises, such as a chilled pumpkin soufflé or steamed maple pudding with sour-cream ice cream and candied popcorn. Fresh-cut flowers rest atop polished tables, and contemporary art hangs on the walls.

RETRO ROTISSERIE
Map pp231-3 *Comfort Food*
☎ 416-960-6159; 508 Yonge St; mains $8-13; 11:30am-11pm Mon-Fri, noon-11pm Sat; subway Wellesley

Swing back into the '40s at this upmarket diner. Lean your elbows on a mahogany wood table sturdy enough for steaming platters of rotisserie beef, pork and fowl. Nostalgic desserts (apple pie and velvety carrot cake) fit the bill perfectly. So do the big band tunes, daddy-o.

SAIGON SISTER Map pp231-3 *Vietnamese*
☎ 416-967-0808; 774 Yonge St; mains $7-13; 11am-11pm; subway Bloor-Yonge

Like a stylish and sophisticated younger sister, this Vietnamese restaurant's ambience leaves all others' in its dust. Dine on full portions of classic dishes either in the lounge or outdoors on the umbrella-shaded back patio. Memorable fruit drinks, teas and cocktails are served.

WISH Map pp231-3 *Eclectic/late night*
☎ 416-935-0240; 3 Charles St E; mains $12-20; 11-1am Sun-Mon, 11-2am Tue-Sat; subway Bloor-Yonge

Billowy clouds of white cushions pad this hipster restaurant and lounge, which looks like a winter wonderland year-round. Though the young chef gets mixed reviews and some of the more ambitious menu items still need work, the scene is sexy.

ZELDA'S Map pp231-3
International/Comfort Food
☎ 416-922-2526; 542 Church St; mains $7-17; 11-1am Mon-Wed, 11-2am Thu-Sat, 10-1am Sun; subway Wellesley

Zany Zelda's has a winning combination of familiar food, crazy cocktails and a spacious outdoor patio. A diverse Church-Wellesley crowd adores the brash, colorful and queer atmosphere, especially on drag queen and leather theme nights.

Cheap Eats

Stop by **La Maison du Croissant Tree** (Map pp226-7; ☎ 416-363-3359; 60 Yonge St; 7am-6pm Mon-Fri; subway King) for breakfast on the run. **Just Desserts** (Map pp231-3; ☎ 416-963-8089; 555 Yonge St; 10-1am Mon-Fri, 10-2am Sat, noon-2am Sun; subway Wellesley) is the perfect place for heavenly cheesecake topped with Ontario blueberries or a slice of decadent chocolate cake.

LE COMMENSAL Map pp226-7
Vegetarian Buffet
☎ 416-596-9364; 655 Bay St, entrance off Elm St; buffet $2 per 100g; 11:30am-10pm Mon-Fri, noon-10pm Sat & Sun; subway Dundas

Cafeteria-style Le Commensal sells fresh salads, hot main dishes with international flavors and desserts naturally sweetened with maple syrup or fruit nectars. Most dietary restrictions can be easily accommodated; only a few dishes border on bland. Expect to pay about $10 for a fair-sized meal, before drinks and taxes. Herbal teas, beer and wine are also sold.

PAPAYA HUT Map pp231-3 *Juice Bar/Take-out*
☎ 416-960-0821; 513A Yonge St; items $3-6; 10am-10pm; subway Wellesley

Manhattanites will see this tiny hole-in-the-wall as a long-lost twin of Gray's Papaya in NYC, right down to the silver kegs dispensing tropical juices. But here, the menu takes a healthy vegetarian turn with its soups, sandwiches, smoothies and shakes.

BLOOR-YORKVILLE

Money presents no obstacle to the trendy Yorkville crowd, but worthy dining destinations are few. At many places, it's about making the scene rather than a magnificent meal.

BISTRO 990 Map pp231-3 *French*
☎ 416-921-9990; 990 Bay St; mains $20-40; lunch Mon-Fri, dinner daily; subway Wellesley

Patronized by Toronto film festival stars and celebrities staying at **Sutton Place Hotel** (p166), romantic Bistro 990 unsteadily upholds fine

Mixing with Masterpieces

At the **Art Gallery of Ontario** (p53), contemporary **Agora** (Map p226-7; ☎ 416-979-6612; meals $10-18; ⏰ noon-2:30pm Wed-Fri, 11am-2:30pm Sat & Sun; streetcar 505) is exquisitely placed in a sunny sculpture atrium. Continental-inspired cuisine is served like a work of art, with ice wines and sweets afterward; menus are often exhibit-themed. Reservations are essential.

When Renaissance ROM construction is done, the **Royal Ontario Museum** (p56) expects to open a panoramic restaurant off chichi Bloor St. Or dash across the street to the **Gardiner Museum of Ceramic Art** (p56) where, in a quiet nook upstairs, you will find **à la Carte** (Map pp231-3; ☎ 416-408-5072; mains $9-16; ⏰ 11:30am-4pm Mon-Sat). This caterer's kitchen features the likes of eggplant salad or lamb satay, along with a daily soup and fresh-baked desserts.

French standards by serving classic dishes, such as duck in blackberry *jus* and rabbit fricassee, as well as meticulously made desserts. The wine selection is excellent, but service sometimes misses the mark.

BLOOR STREET DINER
Map pp231-3 *Continental/Canadian*

☎ 416-928-3105; Manulife Centre, 55 Bloor St W; breakfast & lunch $6-14, dinner $15-21; ⏰ 8-2am; subway Bloor-Yonge

Its humble-sounding name belies just how swank this place actually is, with its banquettes, starched tablecloths, formal table service by attentive waitstaff and a Parisian-style patio. You may even catch stars dining here during the film festival. Steaks and rotisserie fare are as distinguished as the bistro's wine list. **Café L'Express** (Map pp231-3) vends drinks, muffins, bagels and take-out sandwiches.

COLONY KITCHEN
Map pp231-3 *Eurasian Fusion*

☎ 416-591-9997; 153 Bloor St W; mains $12-25; ⏰ lunch Mon-Fri, dinner daily; subway Museum

An underground eatery at Club Monaco (p150), Colony Kitchen defines Bloor St cool – at least for the moment, anyway – with an adventurous menu that mixes French and Asian accents. In summer, a gorgeous cocktail bar and sidewalk tables attract quite a sexy crowd.

DUKE OF YORK Map pp231-3 *Pub Grub*

☎ 416-964-2441; 39 Prince Arthur Ave; mains $8-12; ⏰ 11am-midnight; subway St George

Admittedly it's a chain, yet the student-filled Duke of York pub is a classic place for traditional ploughman's lunches, bangers and mash, savory pies and, of course, fish and chips (wrapped in pages from a British daily!) Children are welcome upstairs.

MÖVENPICK'S BISTRETTO & LA PÊCHERIE Map pp231-3 *Seafood/International*

☎ 416-926-9545; 133 Yorkville Ave; mains $13-45; ⏰ 11:30am-midnight Mon-Fri, 8am-2am Sat, 8am-midnight Sun; subway Bay

Another branch of the Mövenpick empire (p94), this restaurant has everyone raving about its seafood. A daily-changing menu is written on a chalkboard, which waitstaff will hoist over to your table before launching into mouth-watering descriptions of the day's feasts. Vegetarian dishes can be made to order. Although the atmosphere is smart it's also family-friendly, especially inside the casual street-level.

OKONOMI HOUSE Map pp231-3 *Japanese*

☎ 416-925-6176; 23 Charles St W; mains $6-13; ⏰ noon-9pm; subway Bloor-Yonge

Authentic Okonomi House is one of the only places in Toronto, let alone North America, dishing up *okonomiyaki,* a savory Japanese cabbage pancake filled with your choice of meat, seafood or vegetables. It's perfect cold-weather comfort food, as Toronto's police force can testify.

SASSAFRAZ
Map pp231-3 *Californian/Continental*

☎ 416-964-2222; 100 Cumberland Ave; dinner $28-40; ⏰ 11:30-2am; subway Bay

With celebrity photographs autographed by Mike Myers ('Yum! Yum!') and Robin Williams ('L'Chaim!'), Sassafraz feels very much like LA, with jazz combos serenading weekend brunches. Despite falling off over the years, recently the food had an infusion of exotic spice from bad-boy Toronto chef Greg Couillard. Sun-drenched sidewalk tables and an indoor garden courtyard are kept busy.

Cheap Eats

Stop by all-natural **Greg's Ice Cream** (Map pp231-3; ☎ 416-961-4734; 200 Bloor St W;

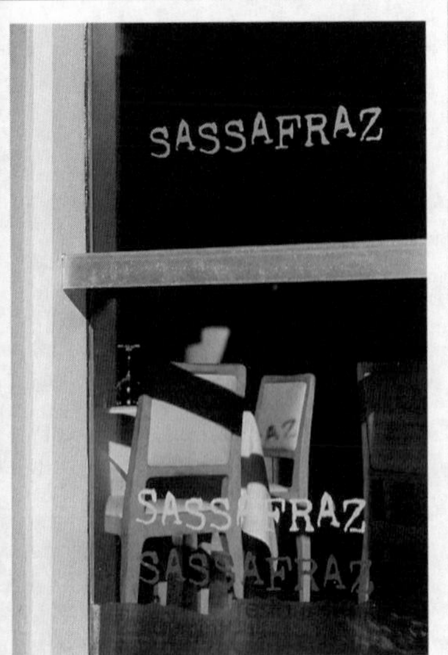

Sassafraz (p102)

ubway Museum) for one of its 'flavors of the moment' (roasted marshmallow, if ou're lucky). Or get an equally delicious coop from **Summer's Ice Cream** (Map pp231-3; ☎ 416-944-2637; 101 Yorkville Ave; subvay Bay), which also stocks nonfat and ondairy varieties.

VANDA'S PIE IN THE SKY
Aap pp231-3 *Bakery Café*
☎ 416-925-7437; 7A Yorkville Ave; meals $5-10; ⏰ 10am-6pm; subway Bay
Be flexible when ordering, since daily specials dvertising a healthy half-sandwich with soup r salad ($6) sell out quickly. A sugar rush is uaranteed by one of Wanda's fantastical desert creations, maybe a slice of Ontario sour herry or Niagara peach pie.

UNIVERSITY OF TORONTO & HE ANNEX
The Annex bursts with eateries, but not nany stand up to the taste test of other than tarving students. On Bloor St west of Honest Ed's, the Annex merges into Koreatown, vhere sushi shops and barbecue grills show a pan-Asian influence.

BY THE WAY
Map p236-7 *Mediterranean/Canadian*
☎ 416-967-4295; 400 Bloor St W; mains $7-11; ⏰ 9am-11pm; subway Bathurst, Spadina
An Annex fixture, this neighborhood bistro has a daily-changing menu of Mediterranean and New World fusion dishes, with plenty of creative choices for vegetarians. Service is A+ and the wine list features Niagara ice varietals and labels from as far away as Oregon and Australia. Why do people forsake the cozy booths inside for the claustrophobic patio?

GOLDFISH Map p236-7 *Italian Fusion*
☎ 416-513-0077; 372 Bloor St W; pasta & pizzas $14-18, dinner $18-28; ⏰ lunch 11:30am-3pm Wed-Fri, brunch 10am-3pm Sat & Sun, dinner from 5pm daily; subway Spadina
Inside a cool fish bowl of aqua-colored windows, diners can fork into mouth-tingling modern mains, such as Cornish hen served with lemon-raisin couscous, which are half the price at lunch.

INSOMNIA Map p236-7 *Comfort Food*
☎ 416-588-3907; 563 Bloor St; mains $6-15; ⏰ 10-2am Sun, 4pm-2am Mon-Thu, 4pm-4am Fri, 10-4am Sat; subway Bathurst
You'll always have company at this arty Internet café, where DJs take over after 10pm. An eclectic menu exhibits real staying power. Roll in early for weekend brunch, perhaps a taste of Heaven on Earth (French toast with wild berries and cream cheese).

LATITUDE Map p236-7 *Latin American*
☎ 416-928-0926; 89 Harbord St; mains $12-20; ⏰ lunch daily, dinner Tue-Sat; streetcar 510
An Uruguayan chef takes care with pan-Latin American fare, and although the menu occasionally speaks of Asia, there's always fried yucca or plantains on the side. Looking for a romantic tree-draped back patio? Walk straight back past the intimate wine bar.

REAL THAILAND Map p236-7 *Thai*
☎ 416-924-7444; 350 Bloor St W; mains $9-16; ⏰ 11:30am-midnight; subway Spadina
Truly authentic Real Thailand must have T.O.'s tiniest patio (and it's carpeted with artificial turf reminiscent of minigolf courses). Appearing on a menu of over 100 items are such standards as *tod mun pla* (fish cakes; $9), spicy *larb* (salads; $9) and for dessert, sticky rice with mangoes and coconut milk ($6).

Cheap Eats

Students flock to **Cora Pizza** (Map p236-7; ☎ 416-922-1188; 656-½ Spadina Ave; streetcar 510) and next-door **Papa Ceo** (Map p236-7; ☎ 416-961-2222; 654 Spadina Ave) for gourmet slices of imaginative pizza creations. In Koreatown, stand outside **Hodo Kwaja** (Map p236-7; 656 Bloor St W; subway Christie) and watch quaint machines pump out tiny little walnut cakes (30¢ each), or get an authentic taste of Mexico at **Tacos El Asador** (Map p236-7; ☎ 416-538-9747; 690 Bloor St W; 🕑 noon-9pm).

FUTURE BAKERY & CAFÉ

Map p236-7 *International/Comfort Food*

☎ 416-922-5875; 483 Bloor St W; meals $5-10; 🕑 8-2am; subway Bathurst

A students' favorite, Future Bakery stays busy selling budget dishes like cheese crepes with sour cream and all-you-can-eat perogies with sauerkraut nights. Bowls of café au lait and glorious cakes and pies make for sweet nightcaps.

HARBORD FISH & CHIPS

Map p236-7 *Seafood/Take-Out*

☎ 416-925-2225; 147 Harbord St; meals $6-10; 🕑 11:30am-9pm; bus 94

This fish-and-chips shack wins big smiles for its generous portions of haddock and halibut, all freshly fried. Get yours wrapped up in newspapers, or eat at outdoor picnic tables while your laundry spins at Coin-O-Rama across the street. Nearby is Jewish-style **Harbord Bakery** (Map p236-7; ☎ 416-922-5767; 115 Harbord St).

KENSINGTON MARKET

Kensington Market is an explosion of Italian butchers, West Indian roti shops, Middle Eastern groceries, fruit markets and home-spun bakeries. It's hot, hectic and fragrant – just the opposite of the St Lawrence Market. Most shops are open daily, but are busiest on Saturday morning.

BAN VANIPHA Map pp234-5 *Thai/Laotian*

☎ 416-340-0491; 638 Dundas St W; mains $7-15; 🕑 lunch & dinner, closed Sun; streetcar 505

This jewel-like downtown outpost of fiery **Vanipha Lanna** (p112) cooks up authentically spicy northern Thai and Lao cuisine. Curried seafood, savory salads and tofu with tamarind sauce all are on hand here.

Round the Clock

Never fear, Cinderella, there's always good foraging after midnight in Toronto. You can depend on **Greektown (The Danforth)** (p62) and **Little Italy** (p105) or stylish restaurants that don't shut their kitchens until midnight or later, and on Spadina Ave in **Chinatown** (p52), glaringly lit noodle shops stay open practically all night. Other late-night restaurants include **Marche Mövenpick** (p94), **Mövenpick's Bistretto & La Pêcherie** (p102), **Bloor Street Diner** (p102), **Fez Batik** (p96), **Sassafraz** (p102) and **Insomnia** (p103).

When even these trusty standbys shut down, hungry night owls turn to Toronto's all-night diners, all serving meals for $10 or less. Retro **Mars** (Map p236-7; ☎ 416-921-6332; Little Italy, 432 College St; 🕑 24hr; streetcar 506, 511) makes famous buttery muffins and waitstaff know regulars by name. Legend has it that classic **Fran's** (Map pp231-3; ☎ 416-923-9867; 20 College St; 🕑 24hr; subway College) diner has never closed since it opened its doors in the 1940s.

Darkly romantic **7 West Café** (Map pp231-3; ☎ 416-928-9041; 7 Charles St W; mains $6-13; 🕑 hr vary; subway Bloor-Yonge) is where lovers' tête-à-têtes over wines by the glass (last call 3am on weekends), knowing it's never too late or too early to whisper sweet nothings in somebody's ear.

CHIENG MAI Map pp234-5 *Tha*

☎ 416-813-0550; 147 Baldwin St; mains $6-10; 🕑 11am-11pm Sun-Thu, 10am-11pm Fri & Sat; streetcar 510

Right on the edge of Chinatown, this charmingl traditional restaurant is run by the same folks a the **Friendly Thai** (p241). Vegetarian dishes run th gamut of soups, salads, curry and noodles.

STREAMS OF BLESSINGS FISH SHACK Map pp234-5 *Caribbean Seafoo*

☎ 416-597-2364; 285 Augusta Ave; mains $6-12; 🕑 10am-10pm Mon-Fri, 10am-11pm Sat & Sun; streetcar 506

A reggae-style seafood kitchen, Streams o Blessings boasts chilled-out couches and a few tables, but the ace-in-the-hole is the food Jamaican-style fish (fried whole and pepperec with incendiary hot sauce), red snapper stev served with a side of plantains and vegetariar coco bun sandwiches ($3).

Cheap Eats

For halal meat and falafel sandwiches, visi **Akram's Shoppe** (Map pp234-5; ☎ 416-979-3116

91 Baldwin St; streetcar 510). If you've got a raving for kitschy chocoholic gifts or freshly nade truffles in unusual flavors, **Chocolate Addict** (Map pp234-5; ☎ 416-979-5809; 185 Baldwin St; streetcar 510) can help.

UMBO EMPANADAS

Map pp234-5 *South American/Take-out*

☎ 416-977-0056; 245 Augusta Ave; items $3-6; 11am-8pm Mon-Sat, 11am-5pm Sun; streetcar 510

Real Chilean empanadas (beef, chicken, cheese or vegetables) and savory corn pie with beef, olives and eggs always sell out early in the day. Bread and salsas are also homemade.

MY MARKET BAKERY Map pp234-5 *Bakery*

☎ 416-593-6772; 172 Baldwin St; items $1-4; 7:30am-7pm Mon-Sat, 8:30am-6pm Sun; streetcar 510

Portuguese buns, focaccia, Vancouver-born Nanaimo bars and loaves of seven-grain bread are baked fresh daily. Its sister shop, **Cheese Magic** (Map pp234-5; ☎ 416-593-9531; 182 Baldwin St), has delicacies like cranberry stilton and gouda galore – ask for free sample slices to taste. Sandwiched in between, **European Quality Meats & Sausages** (Map pp234-5; ☎ 416-596-8691; 176 Baldwin St) hangs bratwurst and debreceni in its windows.

LITTLE ITALY

Stretching along College St, Little Italy is one of the hottest spots for eating and meeting, or just perusing the old-world bakeries and haute restaurants. Many double as bars and clubs after dark, and almost all are fully licensed.

BAR ITALIA Map p236-7 *Italian*

☎ 416-535-3621; 582 College St; sandwiches & pastas $7-12, mains $16-25; 11-1am Mon-Thu, 11-2am Fri, 10:30-2am Sat, 10:30-1am Sun; streetcar 506

Trendsetters come and go, but Bar Italia remains a place to be seen, as well as to relax. Grab an excellent sandwich or lightly done pasta, with a lemon gelato and a rich coffee afterward, and you could while the entire afternoon or evening away. Seats on the convivial streetfront patio are scarcely ever free.

BRASSERIE AIX Map p236-7 *French*

☎ 416-588-7377; 584 College St; mains $12-25; dinner daily, brunch Sun; streetcar 506

Its reputation with the A-list is sealed by a potent mix of chic Paris and sunny southern France. A soaring, subtly toned dining room lends itself to special occasions. The prix fixe dinner ($20), perhaps with red-wine braised beef and a citrus coffee cake, is served from 5pm until 7pm daily.

BRUYEA BROTHERS RESTAURANT

Map p236-7 *Eclectic*

☎ 416-532-3841; 640 College St; pastas $9-14, mains $15-21; 6-11pm Tue-Sat; streetcar 506, 511

Duotone photography from their grandfather's era decks the buffed brick walls, but this joint has an exciting modern culinary outlook and a surprisingly New World wine list. The multicourse 'grazing' menu pours forth curried lobster tarts, peppery rocket salads, caraway gnocchi and a chestnut-stuffed pheasant. After the kitchen closes, drinks and DJs appear.

BUTT'R Map p236-7 *International*

☎ 416-516-4756; 587 College St; small plates $7-16, main courses $14-40; 6pm-2am Tue-Sun; streetcar 506

This elemental modernist lounge is Little Italy's flavor of the moment. Patriotically inspired dishes, such as fresh PEI mussels in a delicate butter sauce of lemon, white wine, garlic and herbs ($14) and Butt'r's triple-crusted mustard chicken supreme with Yukon gold mashed potatoes ($19), are almost lost in a sea of Italian, Cajun and Asian fare. A strong draw is the bar scene, which DJs take over as the night catches fire.

CHIADO Map p236-7 *Portuguese Seafood*

☎ 416-538-1910; 864 College St; mains $20-38; lunch Mon-Fri, dinner daily; streetcar 506

At venerable Chiado, Portuguese specialty dinners for two cost just $40. Start off with the lobster-shrimp bisque, savor a roast pheasant in Madeira wine and citrus sauce and then for dessert order *natas do ceu* in almond liqueur. Service in the formal dining room is nearly faultless.

PHIL'S ORIGINAL BBQ

Map p236-7 *Southern*

☎ 416-532-8161; 838 College St; sandwiches $7, mains $12-20; lunch Mon-Fri, dinner Mon-Sat; streetcar 506

'Real smoke. Real slow. Real good.' Hailing from the barbecue belt of the USA, these folks are passionate about 'cue. At their real-deal storefront, enjoy heartbreakingly tender beef brisket, dry-rub smoked meats and homemade sauces, too.

XACUTTI Map p236-7 *Indian Fusion*

☎ 416-323-3957; 503 College St; small plates $8-15, large plates $20-35; ⌚ brunch 10:30am-3pm Sat, 10:30am-4pm Sun, dinner 6:30pm-midnight Tue-Sat; streetcar 506

Swirls of chocolate brown and jet black come alive with saffron accents, as befits such exotic twists on regional Indian cooking as Goan-spiced duck ($12) or hot tikka baked salmon with tamarind sauce ($12). In a hurry? You won't believe your good luck: the kitchen offers prepared meals for take-out.

Cheap Eats

SICILIAN SIDEWALK CAFÉ

Map p236-7 *Italian*

☎ 416-531-7755; 712 College St; ⌚ till midnight; streetcar 506

For the best *tartufo, zabajone* and specialty desserts in town, don't dally on your way here. Nearby **Nova Era Bakery & Pastry** (Map p236-7; ☎ 416-516-1622; 770 College St) is less mobbed.

SUPERMODEL PIZZA

Map p236-7 *Pizza/Take-out*

☎ 416-533-9099; 772 College St; slice/pizza from $3.50/7; ⌚ 11am-midnight; streetcar 506

The name may be hard to swallow, but its amusing motto is 'Our crust is as thin as a super model.' Creative combos like eggplant with olives and roast peppers are also stuffed into calzone. For imaginatively topped thick-crusted slices, drop by **Amato Pizza** (Map p236-7; ☎ 416-972-6286; 380 College St).

QUEEN WEST

West of Spadina Ave, Queen St W is an experiment in food fusion, with flavors of Asia, Latin America and Europe swirled together in hip surrounds. Also look for new restaurants being birthed along the blocks of King St W, mainly between Spadina Ave and Bathurst St.

CANTENA Map pp234-5 *Fusion*

☎ 416-703-9360; 181 Bathurst St; dinner $12-22; ⌚ dinner 5-2am daily, brunch 10:30am-4:30pm Sat & Sun; streetcar 501, 511

Formerly Azul, glorious Cantena hides on an unsavory street corner. Who would suspect that its motto is 'Damn fine food. Kick-ass cocktails'? Or that the ultracreative menu lives up to its promises? A tapas-style dinner men of platters, meant to be shared by up to fou people, are a steal, and on weekends shov up for the Hangover Helper brunch (serve until 4:30pm).

Top Five Vegetarian & Vegan

The **Toronto Vegetarian Association** (☎ 416-544-9800; www.veg.ca) dispenses free advice about eating out, cooking classes and the annual vegetarian food fair in September.

Our favorites for enlivening atmosphere and inventive vegetarian cuisine are:

- **Susur** (p107)
- **Red Tea Box** (p107)
- **By the Way** (p103)
- **Fressen** (below)
- **Fresh by Juice for Life** (p98)

FRESSEN Map pp234-5 *Eclectic Vegetaria*

☎ 416-504-5127; 478 Queen St W; mains $12-18; ⌚ brunch Sat & Sun, dinner daily; streetcar 501

The city's epitome of haute vegetarian (an vegan) dining, here smiling service and high backed wooden booths make for an enjoyabl night out, even for carnivores. A strong an stylish organic menu picks among the world cuisines, depending on what's seasonal whe you visit.

GYPSY CO-OP

Map pp234-5 *International/Late Nigh*

☎ 416-703-5069; 815 Queen St W; pastas $9-16, mains $14-22; ⌚ noon-3pm & 6-10pm Tue-Sat; streetcar 501

Trendy Queen West eateries come and go but this bohemian spot lives on. Contemporary food at Gypsy Co-op comes wit nouveau twists, for example the black ravio in chipotle-pumpkin sauce ($9 to $13) an the Indian vegan stew ($14). Upstairs is **Hooc** (p127) lounge.

IRIE FOOD JOINT Map pp234-5 *Caribbea*

☎ 416-366-4743; 745 Queen St W; mains $8-16; ⌚ noon-11pm Mon-Thu, noon-midnight Fri, 1pm-midnight Sat, 1-11pm Sun; streetcar 501

A sexy Caribbean dining room, with earth toned chairs and a long bar, it lets DJs spin or some nights. Mussels in ginger-mango-citru cream sauce, jerk chicken wings with a pot c pepper sauce and fresh seafood mains defin succulent.

ALAPEÑO'S Map pp234-5 *Mexican*

☎ **416-216-6743; 725 King St W; lunch special $7, nains $9-15; 🕑 11am-9pm; streetcar 504**

's almost a truism that Toronto doesn't have ny Mexican food worthy of the name. Colorul Jalapeño is an exception. Here you will ind superb regional Mexican specialties like hicken *molé poblano* (spicy sauce with a hint of chocolate) cactus and authentic seafood lishes. Occasionally there's live mariachi music on weekends.

RED TEA BOX Map pp234-5 *Pan-Asian Café*

☎ **416-203-8882; 696 Queen St W; lunch or afternoon ea $15-25; 🕑 10am-6pm Mon & Wed-Thu, 10am-pm Fri & Sat, noon-5pm Sun; streetcar 501**

he jewel-like Red Tea Box has genuine South Asian flair. Handwoven Thai textiles drape the valls and people are willing to queue for their nonthly changing bentō boxes ($25), which eveal a fusion world of taste-bud temptations. Everything's gorgeous, and seasonally inspired. The afternoon tea is exotic and inviting (p92). Reservations are not accepted.

RODNEY'S OYSTER HOUSE

Map pp234-5 *Seafood*

☎ **416-363-8105; 469 King St W; mains $13-24**
🕑 **11-1am Mon-Sat; streetcar 504, 510**

classic seafood bar and restaurant, Rodney's lies in a dozen or more types of fresh oysters harvested from the Pacific and Atlantic Oceans. Dungeness crabs, lobsters, Fundy scallops and eafood chowders swim their way onto the ong daily menu, which ends at a N'awlins-tyle banana flambé. Well-chosen beer and vine pairings are available.

SUSUR Map pp234-5 *Eclectic Fusion*

☎ **416-603-2205; 601 King St W; mains $35-45, tasting menu $70-110; 🕑 6-11:30pm Mon-Sat; streetcar 504, 511**

Star chef Susur Lee will take you on a whimsical journey with his elaborate tasting menus, vhich race from Europe to the New World to Asia and back again. Each plate is a magical tudy in contrasts, complemented by an imaginative wine list. Even vegetarians will find a bounty of culinary goodness here. Make reservations at least several weeks in advance.

SWAN Map pp234-5 *Eclectic Comfort Food*

☎ **416-532-0452; 892 Queen St W; mains $6-18;**
🕑 **lunch noon-4pm Mon-Fri, 10am-4pm Sat & Sun, dinner 5-10:30pm Sun-Wed, 5-11pm Thu-Sat; streetcar 501**

Fickle Queen Westers rave about Swan, a swanky diner just off the beaten path by Trinity-Bellwoods Park. You will find upscale comfort food that is like nothing anyone's family ever cooked; from oyster omelettes to racks of beer-marinated ribs, dishes satisfy both the stomach and the soul.

TERRONI Map pp234-5 *Italian Deli*

☎ **416-504-0320; 720 Queen St W; meals $6-12;**
🕑 **9am-11pm; streetcar 501**

Off-duty Toronto chefs eat at Terroni, a traditional southern Italian grocery store and deli, which has counter stools and a backyard patio. Wines by the glass, wood oven-fired pizzas and fresh panini all approach perfection. There's a second branch **downtown** (Map pp228-30; ☎ 416-855-0258; 106 Victoria St; streetcar 501).

Cheap Eats

All along Queen St W are Indian roti takeout shops where you can get a monster-sized wrap for $5.

DUFFLET PASTRIES

Map pp234-5 *Bakery/Take-out*

☎ **416-504-2870; 787 Queen St W; items from $2;**
🕑 **10am-7pm Mon-Sat, noon-6pm Sun; streetcar 501**

Dufflet's desserts appear at Toronto's most prestigious restaurants; bite into tasty little temptations like sugar cookies, tarts or sinful chocolate cakes here. If French bakery goods are more your style, walk west to **Clafoutí Patisserie et Café** (Map pp234-5; ☎ 416-603-1935; 915 Queen St W), which also serves light meals.

VIENNA HOME BAKERY

Map pp234-5 *Comfort Food*

☎ **416-703-7278; 626 Queen St W; mains $7-14;**
🕑 **10am-7pm Wed-Sat; streetcar 501, 511**

With the kind of checked tiles that your grandmother's kitchen floors may have had, Vienna Home Bakery is cozy. Hop onto a stool at the retro luncheonette counter and eat your fill of hearty contemporary home cooking, especially hot soup.

EAST TORONTO

Most of the places in the Greek area along Danforth Ave, east of the city center, get very busy on summer nights when there's quite a festive air. Casual souvlaki houses and upscale mezes (Greek tapas) restaurants often stay open after midnight. Traditional bakeries and delis take over during the day.

Whether you're staying at a neighborhood B&B or just strolling around the architectural district, historic Cabbagetown also offers a handful of unique places to dine.

Epicurean haunts are sprinkled along Queen St E in Leslieville and other neighborhoods, all found on the streetcar line between downtown and the Beaches.

For a wallet-friendly place with a side order of cultural experience, you can't beat Little India, trailing along Gerrard St E, just west of Coxwell Ave. After dinner, pop into one of the shops for an exotic mouthful of pan, made to order either with or without tobacco. There are also plenty of *chaat* (usually shredded fresh fruit covered in tamarind sauce, sugar and salt) houses and South Indian vegetarian eateries serving *thali* (mixed plate) for under $10.

CAFÉ BRUSSEL Map p238-9 *Belgian Bistro*

☎ 416-465-7363; 124 Danforth Ave; mains $24-30; ⌚ 5-11pm Tue-Sat, 5-10pm Sun; subway Broadview

For the sake of romance, we'll allow a Belgian exception to the Greektown rule. Mussels ($18 per kg with frites) are served 32 ways, from Tahiti to Provençale style. European, Québecois and Belgian microbrews are on hand, while a notable wine list includes over 600 labels.

EDWARD LEVESQUE'S KITCHEN

Map p238-9 *Eclectic Canadian*

☎ 416-465-3600; 1290 Queen St E; breakfast & lunch $4-10, dinner $14-25; ⌚ 9am-4pm Wed-Fri, 9am-3pm Sat & Sun, dinner Tue-Sat; streetcar 501, 502, 503

Inside of a retro-looking diner, chef Edward Levesque creates nouveau Canadian comfort food out of seasonal ingredients, with influences ranging from Asian to Italian. Savor the chicken supreme with 100 bay leaves ($23), avocado-lime vichyssoise ($4) or ricotta mousse with roasted stone fruit and cinnamon ice cream ($6).

GIO RANA'S REALLY, REALLY NICE RESTAURANT Map p238-9 *Italian*

☎ 416-469-5225; 1220 Queen St E; mains $12-20; ⌚ 6-11pm Sun-Thu, 6pm-midnight Fri & Sat; streetcar 501, 502, 503

At this carnivalesque Italian dining room, found inside a former bank building, the neighborhood scene can get riotous, especially later on in the evening. Grilled calamari, polenta, bee carpaccio – you name it, they'll dish it up.

HELLO TOAST

Map p238-9 *Contemporary Canadian*

☎ 416-778-7299; 993 Queen St E; dinner $16-25; ⌚ lunch Tue-Fri, brunch Sat & Sun, dinner Tue-Sun; streetcar 501, 502, 503

Part the velvet curtains and enter an artsy newfangled bistro that's best at weekend brunch, when just $10 buys Eggs Benny or French toast stuffed with cranberries. If there' a long wait for a table, the '40s and '50s déco should keep you amused.

KEG MANSION Map p238-9 *Steakhouse*

☎ 416-964-6609; 515 Jarvis St; mains $25-40; ⌚ 4-11pm Mon-Fri, 5-11pm Sat & Sun; subway Wellesley

For an affordable steak with some class, the Keg sets a standard. Although it's a chain, thi particular branch presides over the historic Massey Mansion, the scene of hundreds of film and TV shoots. Dinner is served only until 11pm, but the upstairs bar stays open late. Children welcome.

MYTH Map p238-9 *Greek/Late Night*

☎ 416-461-8383; 417 Danforth Ave; mezes $5-12, dinner $18-30; ⌚ noon-midnight Sun-Wed, noon-1am Thu, noon-2am Fri & Sat; subway Chester

Inside a converted movie house, Myth serves the most chic mezes on the Danforth, along with possessing a bar, pool table and a high ceilinged dance floor. Small portions of mezes are dearly priced, but its balsamic-marinated octopus with roasted peppers or pasticcio of lamb medallions might be the best you'l ever have.

OUZERI Map p238-9 *Greek*

☎ 416-778-0500; 500A Danforth Ave; mezes $5-10, mains $12-20; ⌚ 11:30am-11pm Sun-Thu, 11:30am-midnight Fri & Sat; subway Chester

More sensibly priced mezes and sophisticated seafood endear this friendly place to local families. Roasted eggplant with a Greek salad and a cold beer will cost around $15. There's live traditional Greek music on some nights.

ΠΑΝ Map p238-9 *Greek*

☎ 416-466-8158; 516 Danforth Ave; mezes $5-13, mains $13-23; ⌚ 5pm-1am Sun-Thu, 5pm-2am Fri & Sat; subway Chester

Comfortable ΠΑΝ serves exceptionally well-prepared meals with traditional Greek flavours ke stuffed quail complimented with green ɪrape sauce and salmon wrapped in phyllo ›astry ($18). Order the delightful chocolate ›aklava for dessert.

'EARTREE

Iap p238-9 *Contemporary Canadian*

☎ 416-962-8190; 507 Parliament St; mains $8-16; 11:30am-11pm Mon-Fri, 1am-11pm Sat & Sun; treetcar 506

'his quiet Cabbagetown bistro is painted in ›lushing colors, and service is demure, yet ·fficient. A pleasantly low-key wine list com›lements a contemporary menu of generously ›ortioned salads, sandwiches and hot pastas.

·EAL JERK Map p238-9 *Caribbean Bar*

☎ 416-463-6055; 709 Queen St E; mains $5-12; 11:30am-10pm or later Mon-Fri, 2pm-1am Sat, ·-10pm Sun; streetcar 501, 502, 503, 504

'his renowned Caribbean kitchen serve clas·ic jerk chicken, oxtail or goat curries, 'rasta ›asta' and Red Stripe beer. Inside it feels just ·ke a huge beach bar, with reggae beats, ropical décor and Jamaican flags hanging ·verywhere.

·ILK ROAD CAFÉ

Iap p238-9 *Chinese/Pan-Asian*

☎ 416-463-8660; 341 Danforth Ave; mains $7-12; lunch Tue-Sat, dinner daily; subway Chester

'ravelers who've been to Asia will be en·hanted by the owners' photos of India and 'ibet hanging on the walls. These days, he con·entrates his creativity on cooking – get your noodles Shanghai-, Bangkok- or Singapore-style, perhaps with some hot Japanese saké or cool Chinese plum wine.

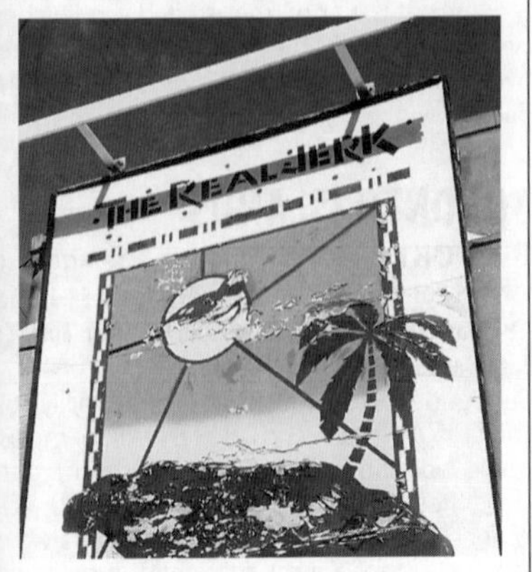

Real Jerk (above)

TOWN GRILL

Map p238-9 *Contemporary Canadian*

☎ 416-963-9433; 243 Carlton St; mains $20-30; 5:30-10pm Mon-Thu, 5:30-10:30pm Fri & Sat; streetcar 506

A posh surprise on a humbler corner of Cabbagetown, this grill and bistro serves sophisticated contemporary Canadian fare. Locals rave about the chef's wizardry with all things related to fowl. Desserts are magical.

WINCHESTER CAFE

Map p238-9 *Contemporary Canadian*

☎ 416-924-4362; 161 Winchester St; meals $8-20; brunch Sun, dinner Wed-Sat, closed winter; streetcar 506

Next to Riverdale Park stands a little cottage eatery with a quaint tea-room atmosphere that's perfect for Sunday brunch or a quiet dinner, maybe of pork tenderloin with apples and garlicky mashed potatoes ($18).

YER MA'S KITCHEN Map p238-9 *Irish*

☎ 416-778-1804; 141 Danforth Ave; mains $8-20; dinner, closed Mon; subway Broadview

Dora Keogh's pub serves amazing Irish fare from an open country-style kitchen at the back. Salmon, potato and green onion cakes served with chile sour cream ($9) are unforgettable. Handwritten menus are put out in the bar from 5pm until whenever the kitchen runs out of food, but you're usually safe arriving before 9pm. Next door **Allen's** (p117) pub reputedly has the best bison burgers ($12) and lamb chops ($20) in town.

Cheap Eats

BAR-BE-QUE HUT Map p238-9 *Indian*

☎ 416-466-0411; 1455 Gerrard St E; mains $6-15; dinner Tue-Sun; streetcar 506

A long-established place, the friendly Bar-Be-Que Hut is also plusher than most Little India restaurants. Among succulent meat and vegetarian dishes, try the half-chicken tandoori, sizzling curry pots or assorted nan, *paratha* and *kulcha* breads. Look for live Bollywood-style music on weekends.

RASHNAA Map p238-9 *South Asian*

☎ 416-929-2099; 307 Wellesley St E; mains $6-10; 11am-11pm; streetcar 506

This out-of-kilter bungalow is full of wonderful surprises, such as South Indian devil curry and Sri Lankan 'String Hopper Rotty.' The prices are unbeatable; only a dollar or two for appetizers like deep-fried lentil dumplings with coconut chutney.

THE BEACHES

At its most crowded on summer weekends, when good weather brings out the beach bum in everyone, the long Queen St E drag between Woodbine Ave and Victoria Park is full of gourmet restaurants, some that flop and some that fly. You can also get upmarket pub grub at **Lion on the Beach** (p117).

Top Five Patios

- **Bar Italia** (p105)
- **John's Italian Caffe** (p99)
- **Sassafraz** (p102)
- **Beacher Café** (p110)
- **Latitude** (p103)

AKANEYA Map p240 *Japanese*

☎ 416-699-0377; 2214 Queen St E; mains $13-26; dinner Tue-Sun; streetcar 501

You'll swear you can feel the ocean breezes when you bite into tender eel sushi and yellowtail sashimi at this modern dining room, which is filled with black lacquer and *shoji* screens. Prices are high, but so is quality. Wander down to family-owned **Otabe** (Map p240; ☎ 416-693-8994; 2326 Queen St E; mains $10-28; dinner Tue-Sun) for a more traditional experience.

BEACHER CAFÉ

Map p240 *Contemporary Canadian*

☎ 416-699-3874; 2162 Queen St E; mains $8-18; 10am-11pm Mon-Fri, 9am-11pm Sat, 9am-10pm Sun; streetcar 501

Looking like a seaside house out of a Virginia Woolf novel, this long-standing café also has a sought-after sidewalk patio. Particularly good are the egg and pancake brunches, and at other times the burgers and seafood are reasonable. Splashes of local artwork change monthly.

BLŪ LOBSTER BISTRO Map p240 *Seafood*

☎ 416-691-0909; 2306 Queen St E; lunch $20-45, dinner $30-55; dinner Tue-Sun; streetcar 501

Swim into a daringly blue room, found on a quiet block of Queen St. Here, spotless white tablecloths are a fitting accompaniment fo grand plates of grilled orange roughy, surf-and turf specials and, of course, the signature dish

NEVADA Map p240 *Canadian/Italian*

☎ 416-691-8462; 1963 Queen St E; brunch $8-12, salads & pastas $11-15, mains $14-17; noon-4pm Mon-Fri, brunch noon-4pm Sat, 11am-4pm Sun, dinner daily; streetcar 501

Painted in warm earth tones, Nevada has a menu that wanders all over the map, from bourbon ribs to pasta with creamy coconu Madras curry. Brunch plates are stacked high maybe with blueberry pancakes or Montréa corned beef hash.

WHITE BROS FISH CO Map p240 *Seafood*

☎ 416-694-3474; 2248 Queen St E; meals $5-15; 4-9pm Tue-Thu, Sat & Sun, noon-9pm Fri; streetcar 501

A fraternal feeling suffuses this storefront which we'll crown the king of all the Beaches fish-and-chip shops. Cheery tables fill up fas as diners demand hearty chowders, citrus seafood salads, grilled calamari, blackened fish and divine scallops.

Cheap Eats

BEST COFFEE HOUSE

Map p240 *Bakery/Deli*

☎ 416-686-3500; 2377 Queen St E; snacks & sandwiches $2-8; 7am-5pm; streetcar 501

They're not kidding around with their name Not only is the freshly brewed organic coffee a draw, but their gourmet stuffed sandwiches will make you lick your lips before the first bite Sweet breakfast pastries and desserts are sold all day long.

TORONTO ISLANDS

RECTORY Map p241 *Canadian/International*

☎ 416-203-2152; 102 Lakeshore Ave; meals $4-16; 11am-5pm Wed-Thu, 11am-8pm Fri, 10am-8pm Sat, 10am-5pm Sun; ferry Ward's I

Set beside the boardwalk on **Ward's Island** (p66) this cozy art gallery and café serves light meals apple cider and weekend brunch in the garden. Reservations are recommended fo brunch and dinner, although you can always stop by just for a quick snack and some liquid refreshment.

A Glorious Harvest

Every April Toronto's famed chefs and epicurean elite get together to hobnob, drink fine wines and dine at the **Toronto Taste** (☎ 416-408-2594; www.torontotaste.ca). For a mere $175, anyone can sample tasting-sized portions of dishes approaching culinary perfection. It's also a guilt-free feast, since all proceeds benefit the charity Second Harvest, which redistributes excess food from restaurants, hotels and grocery stores to social service agencies and people in need.

Over five dozen restaurants show up for Toronto Taste, with a litany of Toronto chefs such as Mark McEwan, Anthony Walsh, Jamie Kennedy and Chris Klugman on hand to whip up concoctions both delicate and daring. The yearly shindig is garnished with a wine auction, netting Second Harvest a half million dollars all told. Kudos! If you're tempted to take a bite yourself, be sure to buy your tickets way in advance.

GREATER TORONTO AREA

Most of Toronto's finest European dining rooms are located far uptown. If you've got the time, it's also worth the trek out to Corso Italia, centered on St Clair West, for authentic Italian food (and more espresso shops). Elsewhere, the spicy Little Portugal area, located west of Ossington Ave on Dundas St W, offers espresso sports bars loaded with machismo, but you'll also find bakeries and Portuguese seafood restaurants.

AUBERGE DU POMMIER

Map p224 *French/Mediterranean*

☎ 416-222-2220; North York, Yonge Corporate Centre, 4150 Yonge St; lunch $17-35, dinner $34-40; lunch Mon-Fri, dinner Mon-Sat; subway York Mills, then bus 97

A classic culinary training ground for many of Toronto's best chefs, the graceful Auberge du Pommier restaurant was built out of a pair of 19th-century woodcutters' cottages. It's far from the city center, just north of the intersection of Yonge St and York Mills Rd, opposite William Carson Crescent. Plates of roast Québec pheasant ($35) or perhaps seared sea scallops and braised oxtail ($38) arrive on the garden terrace in summer. Wine selections naturally focus on French vintages, but you will find that there are also a few Niagara labels.

CELESTIN

Map p225 *French*

☎ 416-544-9035; 623 Mt Pleasant Rd; mains $28-45; 6-11pm Tue-Sat; subway St Clair, then bus 74

Chef Pascal Ribreau's imaginative French cooking triumphs inside a converted bank, where tantalizing *amuse-bouche* (amusements for the mouth) precede artful mains of succulent lamb shank, baked Atlantic salmon with homemade gnocchi or veal sweetbreads. Celestin's atmosphere induces serenity; it has widely spaced tables and superb service by waitstaff who know all about the wines cellared away in the old bank vault.

JOV BISTRO

Map p225 *Eclectic*

☎ 416-322-0530; East York, 1701 Bayview Ave; mains $16-35; dinner Wed-Sun; bus 11

Divining its name from the initials of its chef-owners, sassy JOV Bistro is a space for independent-minded foodies. Reservations for dinner on weekends should be made in advance. But the forethought is worth it, especially for witty French reinterpretations of classic seafood dishes. You'd be best served by taking the chefs up on their Trust Me four-course dinner ($65) with Trust Us wine pairings ($20 to $35).

NORTH 44°

Map p225 *Contemporary Continental*

☎ 416-487-4897; 2537 Yonge St; mains $32-45; 5-11pm Mon-Sat; bus 97

After deluxe renovations of mosaics and sculpted metal, sleek North 44° has again been voted one of North America's top tables. Solid main courses, such as a whole roasted Dover sole in brown butter with capers, citrus, chive-spun potatoes and sweet beets ($38), are paired with selections from a mind-boggling international wine list (17 pages, excluding bibliography). A sleek piano lounge sits on the mezzanine.

SCARAMOUCHE

Map p225 *French*

☎ 416-961-8011; 1 Benvenuto Pl, off Avenue Rd; mains $25-48; 5:30-10:30pm Mon-Sat; streetcar 512

Lording over a hilltop south of St Clair Ave, tried-and-true Scaramouche offers grand views of the downtown skyline. Don't forget your gold card when dining on its top-notch modern French cuisine, with a dash of tasteful invention.

STEAKFRITES Map p225 *French*

☎ 416-486-0090; 692 Mt Pleasant Rd; mains $15-37; ⏰ dinner; subway St Clair, then bus 74

This smart neighborhood bistro by the creators of **Auberge du Pommier** (p224) and **Canoe** (p94) has skyrocketed in popularity. Noteworthy steaks are accented by peppercorn cream or béarnaise sauce, while seafood such as steamed mussels or a delectable trout pâté is definitely worth your attention (and so is the heart-warming chocolate brioche pudding).

VANIPHA LANNA Map p225 *Thai/Laotian*

☎ 416-484-9625; 863 St Clair Ave W; mains $9-14; ⏰ noon-10pm Mon & Wed, 5-10pm Tue & Thu, noon-10:30pm Fri, 1-10:30pm Sat; streetcar 512

A gracious welcome and shimmering textiles are the perfect background for Vanipha Lanna's esteemed cooking, which ranges from fiery seafood creations to familiar noodles. You'll also spy unusual dishes like *khao moak ga* (spiced chicken in banana leaves) on the menu, along with satisfying sampler plates and platters.

Entertainment

Entertainment

Worldly Montréalers may sneer, but Toronto's nightlife artfully keeps everyone busy long after dark, and there's plenty of entertainment going on during the daylight hours, too. Whether it's a Mad Bastard Cabaret, indie film festival, legendary Second City comedy, a world-class concert at the Glenn Gould Studio, radical Canadian theater, a slate of live local bands or a simple brewpub, you'll have no trouble finding it here. There are free outdoor festivals and concerts going on nearly every weekend, especially in summer. The city's most encyclopedic entertainment guide is inside the free alternative weekly *Now*, while *Xtra* and *eye* stay on top of the club, alt-culture and live-music beats. All three daily newspapers (p204) provide weekly entertainment listings, too. Glossy *Toronto Life* magazine (p204) publishes a monthly 'what's on' guide.

Tickets

For an added booking fee, **Ticketmaster** (☎ 416-870-8000; www.ticketmaster.ca) sells tickets for major concerts, sports games, theater and performing arts events. Buy tickets either online or at various city outlets, including **SkyDome** (p45), the **Hummingbird Centre for the Performing Arts** (p129) and T.O. Tix. The classified sections of newspapers and alternative weeklies also list tickets available for every event in town, from opera to Tragically Hip concerts. For a price, any seat is yours.

For half-price and discount same-day rush tickets, **T.O. Tix** (Map pp226-7; ☎ 416-536-6468 ext 40; www.totix.ca; Dundas Sq, 1 Dundas St E; noon-7:30pm Tue-Sat; subway Dundas) has a booth on Dundas Square. These tickets for theater, comedy and dance performances, even as far away as Stratford or Niagara-on-the-Lake, are sold in person on a first-come, first-served basis only. You can check what's available first by calling. Rush tickets may also be available at theater box offices.

What's Free?

ALT.COMedy Lounge (p127) Monday nights at the Rivoli.

Chicago's Diner (p122) No-cover blues, funk and jazz shows.

Glenn Gould Studio (p129) Free noon concerts.

Music Gallery (p122) Free lunchtime concerts.

National Film Board (NFB) Mediatheque (p116) Often has free screenings.

Second City (p128) Free improv after the last show ends on many nights.

Torch Lounge (p123) Where you can eavesdrop on the Top O' the Senator jazz club.

Toronto Music Garden (p43) Free outdoor concerts during summer.

University of Toronto Faculty of Music (p130) Free admission to some performance classes and concerts.

CINEMA

For first-run movies, the Bloor-Yorkville area is full of cinemas often used for film festivals. Elsewhere IMAX movies (play at **Famous Players Paramount** (p115), Ontario Place's **Cinesphere** (Map p225; ☎ 416-314-9900; www.ontarioplace.com; 955 Lakeshore Blvd W; streetcar 509, 511) and the Ontario Science Centre's **Omnimax** (Map p225; ☎ 416-696-1000; www.ontariosciencecentre.ca; 770 Don Mills Rd; subway Eglinton, then bus 34).

Tickets

First-run movie tickets cost $10 to $13 for adults, less for students and seniors. Matinee shows (usually before 6pm weekdays, earlier on weekends) cost from around $7. Tuesday is discount movie day.

Festivals

At any time of year there's always a film festival going on, whether it's the famous **Toronto International Film Festival** (p10) or special-interest series like the **Hot Docs Canadian International Documentary Film Festival** (☎ 416-203-2155; www.hotdocs.ca) starting in late April and the **Inside Out Toronto Lesbian & Gay Film & Video Festival** (☎ 416-977-6847; www.insideout.on.ca) in late May.

ALLIANCE ATLANTIS CUMBERLAND 4 Map pp231-3

☎ 416-646-0444; Bloor-Yorkville, 159 Cumberland St; subway Bay

This pint-sized multiplex shows a mix of independent films and hand-picked Hollywood releases. Moviegoers can swing by the lobby cappuccino bar for some above-par baked goods before the show. Alliance Atlantis' mainstream cinema is at the **Beaches** (Map p240; ☎ 416-646-0444; 1651 Queen St E; streetcar 501, 502, 503; Ⓟ $2).

BLOOR THEATRE Map pp236-7

☎ 416-516-2330; www.bloorcinema.com; The Annex, 506 Bloor St W; nonmember $7, senior & child $3; subway Bathurst

Counted among the city's fave repertory cinemas, this art-deco theater with a two-tiered balcony screens a wonderfully varied schedule of new releases, art-house flicks, shorts, documentaries and vintage films. Buy an annual membership card ($4) and pay just $4 per movie.

CINEFORUM Map pp236-7

☎ 416-603-6643; Little Italy, 463 Bathurst St; adult/child under 15/youth under 24 $20/5/10; streetcar 506, 511

Torontonian character Reg Hartt has ads wrapped around telephone poles advertising his Cineforum, which is actually the front room of a Victorian row house, where he showcases classic and avant-garde films. Animation retrospectives are his specialty, as are rare Salvador Dali prints. Come prepared for entertainingly idiosyncratic lectures, sometimes delivered right while the movies are playing. Bring your own food and drink.

CINEMATHEQUE ONTARIO Map pp226-7

☎ 416-968-3456; www.bell.ca/cinematheque; Baldwin Village, Art Gallery of Ontario, 317 Dundas St W; nonmember/student/senior from $10/5/5; 🕓 closed late Aug & Sep; subway St Patrick

The popular Cinematheque Ontario screens world cinema, independent films and retrospectives of famous directors, sometimes introduced by film critics and Canadian authors. About 400 films are shown annually in the AGO's Jackman Hall. Nonmembers can purchase tickets at the box office 30 minutes before the day's first screening (be sure to show up early, since tickets sell out quickly).

CINEPLEX ODEON VARSITY Map pp231-3

☎ 416-961-6303; Bloor-Yorkville, Manulife Centre, 55 Bloor St W, 2nd fl; subway Bloor-Yonge

This state-of-the-art multiplex shows a respectable range of movies, from Hollywood blockbusters to small-budget indie releases. VIP theaters have extra leg room, tableside refreshment service and smaller screens (but excellent sound). In downtown, **Cineplex Odeon Carlton** (☎ 416-598-2309; Yonge Street Strip, 20 Carlton St; subway College) attracts a more diverse crowd by screening major independent films and some truly bizarre offerings.

DOCKS DRIVE-IN THEATRE Map p225

☎ 416-461-3625; www.thedocks.com; East Toronto, 11 Polson St; adult $13, under 12 $6.50, senior $4; 🕓 Apr-Sep; Ⓟ

This waterfront entertainment complex has space for 500 cars, and skydeck seating for nonmotorists. Double bills feature first-run blockbuster movies, usually on Tuesday, Friday and Saturday evenings, starting around dusk. The Docks also has a minigolf course and nightclubs (p125).

FAMOUS PLAYERS PARAMOUNT Map pp228-30

☎ 416-368-5600, IMAX ☎ 416-368-6089; Entertainment District, 259 Richmond St W; subway Osgoode

Famous Players' gargantuan multiplex features new releases and the latest in IMAX technology, including 3D. It's always screening a dozen movies or more, with some off-beat picks found among the bigger mainstream releases.

FESTIVAL CINEMAS

☎ 416-690-2600; www.festivalcinemas.com; nonmember/student/senior $8/4/4

A few of Toronto's second-run and repertory film houses have got together. Daily schedules include art-house films, including Hong Kong action flicks and cult classics such as Monty Python. Try the **Royal** (Map pp236-7; ☎ 416-516-4845; Little Italy, 608 College St; streetcar 506), Greektown's **Music Hall** (Map pp238-9; ☎ 416-778-8272; 147 Danforth Ave; subway Broadview) or the **Fox** (Map p240; ☎ 416-691-7330; the Beaches, 2236 Queen St E; streetcar 501).

NATIONAL FILM BOARD MEDIATHEQUE Map pp228-30

NFB; ☎ 416-973-3012; www.nfb.ca/mediatheque; Entertainment District, 150 John St; hours vary; subway Osgoode

Aiming to 'reconnect Canadians with thei past, present and future on film,' the NFB ha opened its vast collection of audiovisual gem to the public. Attend a low-cost (or even free film screening in an intimate, 80-seat cinema or try one of the personal touch-screen viewing stations. Rare DVDs and videotapes are available for rent or purchase.

DRINKING

Pub hours are normally 11am to 2am (some bars may not unlock their doors until the late afternoon), but specially licensed clubs stay open until 4am. And who knows how many illega mercurial boozecans there are where drinks can be had at all hours? The city may soon pass strict antismoking bylaws, which will ban lighting up in virtually any indoor public place but for now most bars and pubs have designated smoking areas. As if that weren't enough however, the Liquor Control Board of Ontario (LCBO) strictly limits where and how beer can be sold. But the flagship **LCBO** (Map p225; ☎ 416-922-0403; www.lcbo.com; Rosedale, 10 Scrivener Sq; 9am-11pm Mon-Sat, 11am-6pm Sun, tasting tower noon-8pm Mon-Fri, noon-6pm Sat, noon-5pm Sun; subway Summerhill) is Canada's largest liquor store, and worth a special trip. This prominent building was once the North York train station, built by the Canada Pacific Railroad in the early 20th century. Nowadays it has a wondrous array of Niagara ice wines and over 100 vintages for sampling (nominal fee applies).

A Strange Brew

Anyone who sits down for a beer and tastes the fizzy carbonation of Ontario's usual brews will ask: Is this real ale, or Canada Dry?! You can't blame it entirely on the province's beer-drinkers, though, since they don't really enjoy the right to choose. The **Beer Store** (www.thebeerstore.ca) – no, it's not for souvenirs – is one of only two places where beer can be legally bought. It has scores of outlets around Toronto. It's a private monopoly owned almost exclusively by the major breweries, Labatt and Molson, who limit the number of microbrews sold. **LCBO** (Map p225; ☎ 416-922-0403; www.lcbo.com; Rosedale, 10 Scrivener Sq; 9am-11pm Mon-Sat, 11am-6pm Sun, tasting tower noon-8pm Mon-Fri, noon-6pm Sat, noon-5pm Sun; subway Summerhill)outlets, the only alternative, sell even fewer brands. When the **Toronto Festival of Beer**, co-sponsored by the Beer Store, rolls around at Fort York in August, know that your $25 admission ticket (which includes five samplings and a souvenir tasting cup) goes for a good cause. During the festival almost 20,000 fans turn out to sample products from over 30 local microbreweries.

Otherwise, with the market so tied up, microbreweries have only a few tricks to stay in business. One is to tempt the drinking public to on-site retail stores, such as you can find at **Steam Whistle Brewing** (p42) and **Amsterdam Brewing Co** (p117), which offer tours and a cozy pub and grill. Other brewpubs include redoubtable **C'est What** (p117). The new kid on the block is **Mill St Brewery** (Map pp238-9; ☎ 416-681-0338; www.millstreetbrewery.com; Distillery Historic District, 55 Mill St; 11am-6pm Sun-Wed, 11am-8pm Thu, 11am-10pm Fri, 10am-10pm Sat), which offers free samples of its delicious coffee porter inside a gloriously renovated Victorian distillery.

If you're getting the idea that you have to really know where to look for good beer in Ontario, you're right. Recommended regional brews include Conners Best Bitter, Kawartha Lakes raspberry wheat, Cameron's Cream Ale, Ste André Vienna Lager. Also watch out for **Niagara Falls Brewing Co** (p180), the first folks in North America to make Eisbock, a daredevil of a sweet, malty 'ice' beer with a potency of nearly 10%, which results from freezing off the extra water to increase the concentration of alcohol. Although it doesn't make its own beer, **Allen's** (p117) has an encyclopedic chalkboard list of regional and import brews. The **Esplanade BierMarkt** (p117) and newer **beerbistro** (Map pp228-30; ☎ 416-861-9872;18 King St E; subway King) also deserve honorable mentions.

PUBS

Considering its British heritage, it's odd that Toronto has so many out-of-the-box pub chains with names starting with a generic 'Duke' or 'Bishop' and ending with Newcastle, Firkin or something just as predictable, instead of watering holes with genuine character. In the Annex you'll find plenty of pubs, which also function as procrastination venues for UT students.

ALLEN'S Map pp238-9

☎ 416-463-3086; Greektown, 143 Danforth Ave; subway Broadview

Saloon-style Allen's has daunting beer and whiskey lists, with over 100 types of each. Neighboring **Dora Keogh** (☎ 416-778-1804; 141 Danforth Ave), which has a fireplace and copper-covered tables, is like stepping into a corner pub in the west country of Ireland. Both places host live Celtic music (p27) and have earned quite a reputation for their cooking (p109).

AMSTERDAM BREWING CO Map pp234-5

☎ 416-504-6886; Queen West, 600 King St W; 🕑 11am-11pm Mon-Sat, 11am-6pm Sun; streetcar 504, 511

Toronto's first microbrewery produces cheery batches of cold-filtered beers, including a Belgian-style framboise, Irish stout, Dutch amber ale and the 'Avalanche' (a stunningly strong lager). Signature 'Nut Brown Ale' utilizes four different Canadian and international malts, including a chocolate variety from Belgium. Call the on-site store for **tours** (☎ 416-504-6882; admission $15; 🕑 usually 6pm Fri & 3pm Sat & Sun).

C'EST WHAT Map pp228-30

☎ 416-867-9499; Old York, 67 Front St E; streetcar 504

Over 30 whiskeys and two dozen Canadian microbrews are on hand at this modern pub near the St Lawrence Market. An in-house brewmaster has created a velvety Coffee Porter that is heavenly. So feel free to drink your way across the nation here, or first pop next door to **nia** (p122), a live music lounge.

ESPLANADE BIERMARKT Map pp228-30

☎ 416-862-7575; Old York, 58 The Esplanade; streetcar 504

Recently the BierMarkt has gone upscale; the bouncers behave as if this were a nightclub. But it's still worth stopping by, if only to taste from a beer menu that covers Belgium to South Africa to Trinidad, with more than 150 varieties all told. Be careful to avoid those that are actually brewed in Ontario, losing flavor in their trans-Atlantic translation.

IRISH EMBASSY PUB & GRILL

Map pp228-30

☎ 416-866-8282; Old York, 49 Yonge St; subway King

Calling themselves 'Ambassadors of Irish Hospitality,' this smart-looking pub is loved by all. It holds court inside a distinguished Victorian edifice with stained-glass windows and glowing lamps. A convivial crowd stops by for after-work drinks, footie matches on satellite TV and heartily gourmet pub fare, including ale-battered halibut and Irish stew.

JAMES JOYCE TRADITIONAL IRISH PUB Map pp236-7

☎ 416-324-9400; The Annex, 386 Bloor St W; subway Spadina

A favorite gathering place for students, here the green Christmas lights stay on year-round, and live folk music makes the whole house sway. Further east is multilevel **Brunswick House** (☎ 416-964-2242; 481 Bloor St W), another rollicking student pub.

LION ON THE BEACH Map p240

☎ 416-690-1984; The Beaches, 1958 Queen St E; streetcar 501

An expansive pub that spills out onto the sidewalk (lyin' on the beach – get it?). A respectably long list of beers and hearty pub grub, such as bangers and mash or fried rainbow trout, keeps everyone satisfied. Children are welcome.

MADISON AVENUE PUB Map pp236-7

☎ 416-927-1722; The Annex, 14-18 Madison Ave; subway Spadina

The elegant Madison is built out of three Victorian houses, where antique-looking lamps light the curtained upper floors at night. Wander the elephantine interior, where you'll find a fireplace, jukebox, darts, billiards, live piano music (Thursday to Saturday) and a specialty bar stocking imported beers and scotch. Did we mention there are five patios, too?

PILOT TAVERN Map pp231-3

☎ 416-923-5716; Bloor-Yorkville, 22 Cumberland St; subway Bloor-Yonge

The hoary Pilot got its start during WWII, which explains the aviation-themed décor and why it calls the patio the Flight Deck. Stop by during live jazz sets on Saturday afternoon.

Madison Avenue Pub (p117)

REBEL HOUSE Map p225

☎ **416-927-0704; Rosedale, 1068 Yonge St; subway Rosedale**

North of Yorkville, the merry, rough-and-tumble Rebel House has 16 patriotic Canadian brews on tap, many Ontario wines and well-trained chefs (yes, chefs) in the kitchen. Expect to rub elbows with neighboring patrons here.

WHEAT SHEAF TAVERN Map pp234-5

☎ **416-504-9912; Queen West, 667 King St W; streetcar 504, 508, 511**

At Toronto's longest running pub (since 1849), a host of faithful regulars sit around the dartboards, pool tables, jukebox and a relaxed streetside patio. Although out of the way, it's atmospheric and welcoming.

BARS

On Little Italy's swanky College St, *porto* bars are fast outnumbering all the martini lounges, while new bohemians favor Queen West. Other types of watering holes can be found downtown. Many restaurants also have worthy places for you to imbibe, such as high-flying **Crush** (Map pp234-5; ☎ 416-977-1234; www.crushwinebar.com; Queen West, 455 King St W; 🕑 11:30am-10:30pm Mon-Fri, 5pm-10:30pm Sat; streetcar 504, 510), which offers dozens of varietals by the glass and wine tasting evenings for everyone from novices to experts. Other notable wine lists can be found at **YYZ Restaurant & Wine Bar** (p97) and **Reds** (Map pp228-30; ☎ 416-862-7327; Financial District, First Canadian Place, 77 Adelaide St W; 🕑 lunch Mon-Fri, dinner Mon-Sat; subway King).

BABYLON Map pp231-3

☎ **416-923-2626; Church-Wellesley Village, 533 Church St; subway Wellesley**

A hip martini lounge (with hundreds of imaginative varieties for you to choose from), Babylon rises inside an elegant brownstone in Toronto's Church-Wellesley Village. Lie back upon the couches upstairs where beautiful boys languorously swirl jewel-colored cocktails.

BANKNOTE BAR & SUPERGRILL

Map pp234-5

☎ **416-947-0404; Queen West, 665 King St W; streetcar 504, 511**

Serving high-rise condo dwellers and financiers, the Banknote has an old-fashioned bank vault sitting behind the pool tables, in addition to an upscale grill menu. For some no-fuss drinks, visit the nearby **Wheat Sheaf Tavern** (left).

BEDFORD BALLROOM Map pp231-3
☎ 416-966-4450; Bloor-Yorkville, 232 Bloor St W; subway St George

At this low-key pub, Ontario beers, good grub (p100) and smiling staff can be counted on, and you'll also find that the pool table is often up for grabs. Down the street, urbane and stylish **Bar Mercurio** (☎ 416-960-3877; 270 Bloor St W; 🕒 closed Sun) serves choice cocktails.

BLACK EAGLE Map pp231-3
☎ 416-413-1219; Church-Wellesley Village, 457 Church St; subway Wellesley

Leather, uniform and denim men go here, where strict dress codes are in full effect. Seriously raunchy theme nights include free clothes checks at the door. Another alternative off the beaten path is the **Toolbox** (Map pp238-9; ☎ 416-466-8616; East Toronto, 508 Eastern Ave; streetcar 501), which draws an older male crowd (hey, they've even got euchre).

CASTRO'S LOUNGE Map p240
☎ 416-699-8272; The Beaches, 2116 Queen St E; 🕒 3pm-3am; streetcar 501

An attitude-free zone near the Beach, this bohemian bar has lotsa Canadian microbrews, vintage posters and hardwood tables, around which cluster the local literati, conspiracy theorists, political activists and slacker hangers-on. Occasionally the bar hosts spoken word events and live music.

A Drink with a View

For a free rooftop view of the city, head to **Panorama** (Map pp231-3; ☎ 416-967-1000; Bloor-Yorkville, Manulife Centre, 55 Bloor St W, 51st fl; 🕒 5pm-2am), which has the city's highest licensed patios. It's a bit tricky to find, and a regular beer costs $6 or more (please skip the food). If you stand up, you can see the city over the balcony of the Park Hyatt hotel's **Rooftop Lounge** (Map pp231-3). The bar stools at **Canoe** (p94) restaurant afford awe-inspiring views of Lake Ontario and the Toronto Islands, day or night. Next to the film studios, **Waterside Sports Club** (Map pp238-9; ☎ 416-203-0470; Harbourfront, 225 Queens Quay E; bus 75) has unspoiled lakefront views from the patio. Here you can check out movie stars on a break, young Torontonians fresh off the nearby racquetball courts and middle-aged cruise groupies.

CIAO EDIE Map pp236-7
☎ 416-927-7774; Little Italy, 489 College St; 🕒 closed Sun & Mon; streetcar 506; 511

A subterranean hot spot, Ciao Edie keeps on going with its 1960s mod colors, lighthearted lamps and whimsical décor, and retro tunes spinning in the background. Cocktails are deliciously deadly. It's queer-friendly, too.

COBALT Map pp236-7
☎ 416-923-4456; Little Italy, 426 College St; streetcar 506

Cloistered alcoves, tea lights and ambient DJs make this in-the-know spot a sweet surprise. Closer to Kensington Market than the main drag of Little Italy, the vibe is both eclectic and tony.

CREWS/TANGO/ZONE Map pp231-3
☎ 416-972-1662; Church-Wellesley Village, 508 Church St; subway Wellesley

An elevated front patio is perfect for people-watching. Women kick up the heat at Tango, right next door to the men's bar Crews (nice pun!) and cabaret-style the Zone. Show up for the drag queen and drag king shows or when DJs spin their stuff, usually during the weekends. Nearby, the Victorian-style **Wilde Oscar's** (Map pp231-3; ☎ 416-921-8142; 518 Church St) pub draws a genial, mostly male crowd.

GLADSTONE HOTEL Map p225
☎ 416-531-4635; Queen West, 1214 Queen St W; streetcar 501

A down-at-heel historic hotel on Queen West reveals Toronto's avant-garde arts scene. It's best known for the Melody Bar, a place for karaoke (9pm to 2am Wednesday to Saturday). Other spaces, namely the Art Bar and the Gladstone Ballroom, are taken over by off-beat DJs, 'earresponsible' musicians and odd events like nouveau vaudeville or a 'Pedal to the Metal' craft fair. Cover varies, usually $10 or less.

HEMINGWAY'S Map pp231-3
☎ 416-968-2828; Bloor-Yorkville, 142 Cumberland St; subway Bay

Equal parts sports pub, singles' bar and jazz venue, Hemingway's is undeniably a Yorkville hot spot. Its heated double-deck rooftop patio makes for a vivacious night out with an upwardly mobile crowd of Torontonians.

INDIAN MOTORCYCLE CAFE & LOUNGE Map pp228-30

☎ 416-593-6996; Entertainment District, 355 King St W; streetcar 504, 510

A lounge inside a retail motorcycle shop may be a surprise, but it's not a bad one – except when the bouncers dish out attitude. A mixed crowd is beautifully adorned, draping itself over multiple levels and a dance floor.

LIBRARY BAR Map pp228-30

☎ 416-368-2511; Financial District, Royal York Hotel, 100 Front St W; closed Sun; subway Union

At Library Bar a clubby atmosphere pervades, with rich wood paneling and overstuffed chairs. It's said to have the best classic martinis in town, although wilder combinations appear on the menu – chocolatini or berrytini, anyone?

LOBBY Map pp231-3

☎ 416-929-7169; Bloor-Yorkville, 192 Bloor St W; closed Sun & Mon; subway Museum, St George

On posh Bloor St, where gold cards are de rigueur, this exclusive lounge beckons with its white couches, glittering lamps and hush-hush curtains. Service and food are both killer – once you sweet-talk your way past the serious bouncers.

PADDOCK Map pp234-5

☎ 416-504-9997; Queen West, 187 Bathurst St; streetcar 501

A revamped 1940s spot with Rat Pack cool, this hybrid of a swanky cocktail bar, featuring bakelite art-deco fixtures and leather banquettes, with a regular ol' tavern appeals. Look for sleek, silver lettering over the jet-black doors.

POPE JOAN Map pp238-9

☎ 416-925-6662; Cabbagetown, 547 Parliament St; hours vary; streetcar 506

Another steady favorite for women, the very relaxed Pope Joan bar is found further east in Cabbagetown. A rainbow-colored crowd makes space for dancing, drinking and shooting stick, too. Call for hours, as it's not open daily.

RED SPOT Map pp231-3

☎ 416-967-7768; Church-Wellesley Village, 459 Church St; hours vary; subway Wellesley

You never know what you'll uncover at this queer-oriented multicultural community space, whether it's spoken word and comedy nights, drag shows, karaoke night, live music shows or underground DJs that heat up the house. Cover charges are low.

SLACK ALICE Map pp231-3

☎ 416-969-8742; Church-Wellesley Village, 562 Church St; subway Wellesley

Bridging the divide between gay men, lesbians and straight folks all searching for a little glitz, Slack Alice opens its gorgeous French doors and backlit bar. An eventful monthly calendar features comedy shows, karaoke, live music and fab theme nights.

SMOKELESS JOE'S Map pp228-30

☎ 416-591-2221; Entertainment District, 125 John St; streetcar 501

Buried below street level in Clubland, this friendly, narrow bar vends over 250 different types of bottled beer. Some of the rarest brews aren't sold in stores, so stop by for a pint or two. Above it is the quirky Beatlemania Shoppe.

TRANZAC Map pp236-7

☎ 416-923-8137; The Annex, 292 Brunswick Ave; subway Bathurst

Drop in at the Toronto Australia New Zealand Club (Tranzac), where there's a bar open to all, sports matches on satellite TVs and live music Monday to Thursday (no cover), anything from indie rock to country tunes.

VELVET UNDERGROUND Map pp234-5

☎ 416-504-6688; Queen West, 508-510 Queen St W; closed Tue & Wed; streetcar 501

Here the sign looks like industrial scrap metal, and the crowd may all be extras from *Bladerunner*. This grungy garage bar with its tattered couches, pool tables and found art is nevertheless a Sunday chill-out spot. You may spy DJs or a launch party for a new Canadian band here.

WOODY'S/SAILOR Map pp231-3

☎ 416-972-0887; www.woodystoronto.com; Church-Wellesley Village, 465-467 Church St; subway Wellesley

On any given night, Woody's sells more beer than any other bar in the country. The city's most popular gay bar complex has a full bag of special tricks, from drag shows to leather events to billiards tables, and DJs spin nightly. It has even made cameo appearances on the TV series *Queer as Folk*.

LIVE MUSIC

Mega-tours stop at **SkyDome** (p45), the **Air Canada Centre** (p44) and the **Molson Amphitheatre** (p42) at Ontario Place. Major independent concert halls are **Phoenix** (Map pp238-9; ☎ 416-323-1251; East Toronto, 410 Sherbourne St; streetcar 506), the **Opera House** (Map pp238-9; ☎ 416-466-0313; www.theoperahousetoronto.com; East Toronto, 735 Queen St E; streetcar 501, 502, 503) and **koolhaus** inside the **Guvernment** (p126). Smaller venues for rock, reggae, jazz, blues and alternative sounds are found all over town. Expect to pay anywhere from nothing to a few dollars on weeknights up to $20 or more for breakthrough weekend acts. Under-19s are usually not admitted to bars or clubs where alcohol is served, except during all-ages shows. Opening hours vary, depending on that week's bookings.

Top Five Spots for Live Local Music

- **Horseshoe Tavern** (p122)
- **nia** (p122)
- **Rex** (p123)
- **Silver Dollar Room** (p123)
- **360** (below)

ROCK, REGGAE & ALTERNATIVE

Festivals

Anyone who doubts that Toronto's live music scene measures up should attend **North by Northeast** (p9) in June.

360 Map pp226-7

☎ 416-593-0840; Queen Street, 326 Queen St W; streetcar 501

Local bands often get their first gigs at 360. Full slates of live shows almost nightly feature indie rock bands, from renowned Canadian acts to bizarrely named unknowns.

BIG BOP Map pp234-5

☎ 416-504-6699; Queen West, 651 Queen St W; streetcar 501

There's always a bellicose crowd of goths, punks and hardcore fans with their bad-ass hounds pacing just outside this concert hall. Upstairs **Holy Joe's** is a groovy little room made for acoustic shows, while serious indie bands power up 2nd-floor **Reverb**. The ground-floor **Kathedral** stage also has low-cover acts, and a dance floor.

CAMERON HOUSE

☎ 416-703-0811; Queen West, 408 Queen St W; streetcar 501

Get down with soul, R&B, acid jazz and other alt-music at this veteran Queen West venue. All types of folks – artists, musicians, dreamers and slackers – fill both the front and back rooms here. On Sunday evenings, Mad Bastard Cabaret ('accordion singing about love, lust and Spain') is a big draw, and so are live swing music nights.

EL MOCAMBO LOUNGE Map pp234-5

☎ 416-777-1777; Kensington Market, 464 Spadina Ave; streetcar 510, 506

A palm tree nightclub sign suggests Miami, but it's all local bands at El Mocambo Lounge – alternative rock, hip-hop, funk, jazz and anything else – in the same space where Mick Jagger and the Rolling Stones once writhed as the ex-prime minister's wife stood upon the tabletops.

FEZ BATIK Map pp228-30

☎ 416-204-9660; Entertainment District, 129 Peter St; streetcar 501

In Clubland, Fez Batik restaurant mixes live music and DJs, sometimes scoring a winner. Four floors of lounging, chatting and grooving go along with a full kitchen, Moroccan tea room and streetside patio underneath frisky floral murals. The intimate club **B-Side** has a separate ground-floor entrance.

GRAFFITI'S Map pp234-5

☎ 416-506-6699; Kensington Market, 170 Baldwin St; streetcar 510

This diverse bohemian bar has credible acoustic rock, roots, blues and jazz acts, as well as open-stage nights and 'cabarets' that could (and almost certainly will) talk about anything. Performances mirror the multicultural crowd.

HEALEY'S Map pp234-5

☎ 416-703-5882; Queen West, 178 Bathurst St; 8pm-2am Tue-Sat; streetcar 501

Next door to the **Paddock** (p120), the 300-person Healey's club has an idiosyncratic line-up of rock, as well as blues, soul and roots music. Stop by when the owner Jeff Healey (p27), a Canadian music icon, audiophile and radio DJ, gets up on the stage with his house band. Tuesday open-jam nights and Saturday matinees are no cover, currently.

HORSESHOE TAVERN Map pp226-7

☎ 416-598-4753; Queen Street, 370 Queen St W; streetcar 501

Past its 50th birthday, the legendary Horseshoe with its long-ass country-and-western bar is still showcasing 'roots, rock and alt nu music.' The Police played here to an almost empty house on their first North American tour when Sting did an encore in his underwear. Tuesday is usually a no-cover music night.

LEE'S PALACE Map pp236-7

☎ 416-532-1598; The Annex, 529 Bloor St W; subway Bathurst

Lee's Palace has set the stage for Dinosaur Jr, Buffalo Tom and the Cure. Kurt Cobain started an infamous bottle-throwing incident when Nirvana played here in 1990. With booming acoustics, it's definitely still a viable alt-rock concert venue. Upstairs is the **Dance Cave** (p126).

nia Map pp228-30

☎ 416-867-9499; Old York, 19 Church St; 🕒 from 9:30pm; streetcar 504

Around the corner from **C'est What** (p117), this slender music lounge catapults a new act onto the stage nearly nightly. Open your ears to Toronto singer-songwriters or international pop, roots, rock, funk, ambient and world grooves. Even the Barenaked Ladies have played here.

Artful Tunes

An avant-garde venue that defies classification is the **Music Gallery** (Map pp228-30; ☎ 416-204-1080; www.musicgallery.org; Entertainment District, Church of St George the Martyr, 197 John St; tickets $5-20; streetcar 501), which showcases experimental music, including chamber groups, electronica, jazz, acoustic and world beats. Acts with names like the Offensive Love Consort appear alongside a large helping of improvisation and performance art. Look especially for free lunchtime concerts and mini-festivals.

JAZZ, BLUES & FOLK

On the Danforth, **Dora Keogh** (p117) has superb Celtic jam sessions (even the Chieftains have dropped by) on Thursday evenings at 9pm and Sunday afternoons at 5pm, while next-door **Allen's** (p117) has live Celtic and East Coast music on Tuesday and Saturday nights. Jazz, blues and folk musicians often shake the rafters at **Healey's** (p121), the **Pilot Tavern** (p117), **Hemingway's** (p119), **Graffiti's** (p121) and **James Joyce Traditional Irish Pub** (p117).

Tickets & Festivals

Covers are unusually low except at top-flight places, where you'll find yourself paying over $20 (and reservations may be required). Go to www.jazzintoronto.com for club links and a full calendar of gigs, concerts and festivals, including the summertime **Beaches International Jazz Festival** (p10) and the **du Maurier Downtown Jazz Festival** (p9).

CHICAGO'S DINER Map pp226-7

☎ 416-977-2904; Queen Street, 335 Queen St W; streetcar 501

No cover is charged for blues, funk and jazz sounds at this Queen St restaurant. It's a good mix of folks, with a very casual attitude. The bar has pool tables, foosball and local brews on tap. The kitchen is open late (till 2am on weekends).

FREE TIMES CAFE Map pp234-5

☎ 416-967-1078; Kensington Market, 320 College St; streetcar 506

Maintaining a hippie Jewish vibe, this small back-room venue at **Bella's Bistro** is the oldest folk club in the city, with music almost nightly and good drink specials. Open stage usually happens on Monday.

GROSSMAN'S Map pp226-7

☎ 416-977-7000; Chinatown, 379 Spadina Ave; streetcar 510

Inside of a grubby 1940s tavern near Kensington Market, the emphasis is on singin' the blues, but acoustic rock and folk acts also appear. Incidentally, Dan Akroyd first worked on *The Blues Brothers* routine in here. Grossman's has music nightly – the Sunday night jam session has been raising the roof for nearly two decades – but rarely a cover charge.

MONTRÉAL BISTRO & JAZZ CLUB
Map pp238-9
☎ 416-363-0179; East Toronto, 65 Sherbourne St; closed Sun; streetcar 504
Top-notch local and international jazz cats play in front of the petite table lamps at elegant Montréal Bistro; for a full review of the romantic restaurant, see p95. Monday is for one-off events, while headliners perform Tuesday through Saturday.

ORBIT ROOM Map pp236-7
☎ 416-535-0613; Little Italy, 580 College St; 6pm-2am Tue-Sat; streetcar 506
By Bar Italia (p105), this upstairs hideaway has a vibe as hard to define as the club is to find. Here cocktail lounge lizards mix with music aficionados, and they all listen to a potent and unpredictable line-up of funk, swing, fusion jazz and hip-hop that's all over the musical map.

RESERVOIR LOUNGE Map pp228-30
☎ 416-955-0887; Old York, 44 Wellington St E; 8pm-2am Mon-Sat; streetcar 504
This seductive supper club is jumpin' with swing and boogie-woogie, so reservations are a must. If these bands don't get your feet tapping, you're probably dead. Decent Southern soul food is served, and the bartenders are famously friendly.

REX Map pp226-7
☎ 416-598-2475; Queen Street, 194 Queen St W; streetcar 501
Be sure to make a beeline for the Rex hotel, which has risen out of its down-at-the-heel past to become a renowned venue for live jazz and blues. Over a dozen different Dixieland, experimental and other local and international acts knock over the joint each week. Drinks are cheap, and the cover is $6 maximum.

SILVER DOLLAR ROOM Map pp234-5
☎ 416-763-9139; Kensington Market, 486 Spadina Ave; streetcar 506, 510
True blues reign supreme at the legendary Silver Dollar, where big-name touring acts from down south (ie Detroit and Chicago) kick up ticket prices, sometimes above $30 on weekends. There's no cover charged for midweek bluegrass jams and Saturday afternoon shows.

TOP O' THE SENATOR Map pp226-7
☎ 416-364-7517; Dundas Sq, 253 Victoria St; 8:30pm-2am Tue-Sat, 8pm-1am Sun; subway Dundas
Located in a historic building just east of Eaton Centre, this wonderfully hypnotic stage is like a fine jazz standard. Musicians (and bartenders) fill patrons' tall orders every night except Monday. The no-cover **Torch Lounge** (Map pp226-7; 8:30pm-1am Tue-Sun) above Torch Bistro lets you eavesdrop on the club for free while you swirl your swizzle stick.

Top Five Quirky Nights on the Town

- **Matador** (p127)
- **El Convento Rico** (p126)
- **Pirate Video Cabaret** (p128)
- **Theatre Passe Muraille** (p125)
- **Cineforum** (p115)

THEATER

There is plenty of first-rate theater (p25) in Toronto. Big-time Broadway musicals have their tryouts, indefinite runs and encore engagements year-round on downtown's Theatre Block and near Dundas Square. Upstart companies favor smaller venues around the Harbourfront and in the Distillery Historic District. Go to www.onstagetoronto.ca, or check newspapers and alternative weeklies, for current listings. The main season runs from September through June.

Tickets

Tickets for major productions are sold through **TicketKing** (☎ 416-872-1212, 800-461-3333; www.ticketking.com). For half-price tickets, you can go to **T.O. Tix** (p114) or inquire about 'rush' tickets at theater box offices. Discounted tickets are normally available for students, seniors and arts workers. Many smaller nonprofit theaters stage at least one PWYC (Pay What You Can) performance per week, usually a Sunday matinee.

Festivals

High-flying theater festivals at **Stratford** (p187) and **Niagara-on-the-Lake** (p189) are a day trip away from Toronto. During summer, the **du Maurier World Stage Festival** goes on stage at **Harbourfront Centre** (p129), while the eccentric **Toronto Fringe Theatre Festival** (☎ 416-966-1062; www.fringetoronto.com) takes place at miscellaneous venues – know that the sexier the title, the worse the play tends to be. **Native Earth Performing Arts** (☎ 416-531-1402; www.nativeearth.ca) sponsors an autumn festival of new Aboriginal plays and dances from Canada and the USA.

BUDDIES IN BAD TIMES THEATRE

Map pp231-3

☎ 416-975-8555; www.buddiesinbadtimestheatre.com; Church-Wellesley Village, 12 Alexander St; tickets around $20; subway College

An innovative venue for lesbigay and Canadian plays since 1979, original plays here may weave in Canadian themes, contemporary dance or jazz. It's tiny – only 300 seats for the main stage, and there are even fewer in **Talullah's Cabaret** (p127), a performance space for comedians, writers and singers.

Elgin & Winter Garden Theatre Centre (right)

CANADIAN STAGE COMPANY

Map pp238-9

☎ 416-368-3110; www.canstage.com; East Toronto, 26 Berkeley St; tickets $25-50; box office 10am-6pm Mon-Sat; streetcar 503, 504

Contemporary CanStage produces top-rated Canadian and international plays by the likes of David Mamet and Tony Kushner. Plays are staged at its own theater and the **St Lawrence Centre for the Arts** (Map pp228-30; ☎ 416-366-7723, 800-708-6754; Old York, 27 Front St E; subway Union).

DREAM IN HIGH PARK Map p225

☎ 416-367-1652 ext 500; High Park, 1873 Bloor St W; admission by donation $15; 8pm Tue-Sun Jul & Aug; streetcar 506 High Park

From July until Labour Day, CanStage's wonderful mid-summer presentation of Shakespeare happens under the stars in High Park. Show up early and take a blanket. Admission is PWYC, but donations are appreciated.

ELGIN & WINTER GARDEN THEATRE CENTRE Map pp226-7

☎ 416-872-5555; www.mirvish.com; Dundas Sq, 189 Yonge St; tickets $25-100; box office 11am-5pm Mon, 11am-8pm Tue-Sat, noon-2pm Sun; subway Queen

The restored double-decker **Elgin & Winter Garden Theatre Centre** (p124) stages high-profile productions. Nearby the **Canon Theatre** (☎ 416-872-1212, 800-461-3333; 244 Victoria St; tickets $25-120; box office 10:30am-6pm Mon, 10:30am-8pm Tue-Sat, 11am-3pm Sun), a 1920s-era Pantages vaudeville hall, is a hot ticket for new musicals like *The Producers*.

FACTORY THEATRE Map pp234-5

☎ 416-504-9971; www.factorytheatre.ca; Queen West, 125 Bathurst St; tickets $20-35, previews $12; box office noon-8pm Tue-Sat; streetcar 511

Inside an off-the-beaten-path Victorian home, this innovative theater company premieres Canadian and international plays, as well as new playwrights' scribblings during the independent **SummerWorks Theatre Festival** (☎ 416-410-1048; www.summerworks.ca).

LORRAINE KIMSA THEATRE FOR YOUNG PEOPLE Map pp238-9

☎ 416-862-2222; www.lktyp.ca; Old York, 165 Front St E; tickets $18-28; bus 75

Toronto's oldest nonprofit theater delivers enlightening children's plays from Canada and around the world, such as storytelling dramas, musical adaptations and comedies. Themes are timely, diverse and multicultural. Some shows are signed for the hearing-impaired.

ROYAL ALEXANDRA THEATRE

Map pp228-30

☎ 416-872-1212, 800-461-3333; www.mirvish.com; Theatre Block, 260 King St W; tickets $25-100; ⌚ box office 10:30am-6:30pm Mon-Tue, 10:30am-8:30pm Wed-Sat, 11am-7pm Sun; streetcar 504

Familiarly known as the 'Royal Alex,' it's one of the most impressive theaters in the city, found on Toronto's Theatre Block. Nearby the lavish **Princess of Wales Theatre** (300 King St W; ⌚ box office 10:30am-6:30pm Mon-Fri) is also owned by Ed Mirvish (p26). At either theater, you can catch splashy Broadway musicals.

THEATRE PASSE MURAILLE Map pp234-5

Theater Beyond Walls; ☎ 416-504-7529; www.passemuraille.on.ca; Queen West, 16 Ryerson Ave; tickets $20-35, previews $16; streetcar 501

Alternative Theater Beyond Walls is housed in the old Nasmith's Bakery & Stables buildings. Since the 1960s, its cutting-edge productions have focused on radical new plays (over 400 of 'em so far, and still counting) with contemporary Canadian themes. Ask about post-performance chats with the cast and producers, usually held on the first Tuesday evening after the show opens.

CLUBBING

No matter whether it's a big-floored dance club or a hole-in-the-wall underground spot, what's in vs what's not changes in the blink of an eye. Cover charges of $5 to $12 apply on weekends, although early birds and ladies may get in free some nights. Hats, sportswear, ripped jeans and under-19s are usually not allowed. You can put yourself on the VIP list (no waiting, no cover) at individual club websites or via www.clubdistrict.com and www.clubcrawlers.com, both of which have events listings and reviews. Toronto's rave scene was once out in the open, until city officials started cracking down. Look for flyers still at record shops. Most clubs open their doors around 9pm or 10pm (some don't really get going until even later) and close around 4am.

Club Strips & Neighborhoods

Mainstream dance clubs crowd the Entertainment District, also nicknamed 'Clubland,' between Queen and King Sts W, mostly along the smaller streets of Duncan, John and Peter. The whole area is jammed on weekends; check out the beautiful people queuing and find a club that suits your taste. In the gay Church-Wellesley Village, many bars have DJ nights. Alternative dance clubs lie along Queen West. An emerging strip nearby is King St, where venues like **Tangerine** (☎ 416-361-9111; Queen West, 647 King St W; streetcar 504, 511) lead the pack. Restaurants, bars and lounges in Little Italy are also known for their nightlife grooves. Yorkville offers a few dance floors, as do independent concert venues, including **Phoenix** (p121) and the **Opera House** (p121).

5IVE Map pp231-3

☎ 416-964-8685; Church-Wellesley Village, 5 St Joseph St; ⌚ Wed-Sun; subway Wellesley

Electronica and progressive house music dominate this upmarket gay spot, where go-go boys shine like angels and women clubbers are in the mix. Avoid a cover charge before midnight some nights, or attend 'Sunday morning worship' starting after dawn until noon. Small **Fly** (Map pp231-3; ☎ 416-410-5426; Yonge Street Strip, 8 Gloucester St; ⌚ usually Sat) has an aquatic dance lounge.

ALTO BASSO Map pp236-7

☎ 416-534-9522; Little Italy, 718 College St; ⌚ closed Tue; streetcar 506

A modish Little Italy crowd often heads to this restaurant and lounge, which spins anything from rare grooves to Brazilian house and keeps cover charges low. Meanwhile the **Lava Lounge** (Map pp236-7; ☎ 416-966-5282; 507 College St) may be yesterday's news, but a varied line-up still includes electronica, retro sounds, live R&B bands, funk and hip-hop.

BABALÚU Map pp231-3

☎ 416-515-0587; Bloor-Yorkville, 136 Yorkville Ave; ⌚ Wed-Sun; subway Bay

Yorkville's sizzling tapas bar is a cool Latin dance destination, with Tiki-esque décor thrown in for flavor. Expect Afro-Cuban beats, Latin American

Gay & Lesbian Nightlife

During **Pride Week** (p9) in June, about a million visitors descend on the Church-Wellesley Village. For information on Toronto's gay-friendly neighborhoods, queer happenings and even marriage licenses at City Hall, turn to p202. Otherwise the best source for finding out what's on now is the free alternative weekly *Xtra!* (p204). Locals' favorite spots include:

5IVE (p125)

Babylon (p118)

Black Eagle (p119)

Buddies in Bad Times Theatre (p124)

Crews/Tango/The Zone (p119)

El Convento Rico (right)

Pegasus Billiard Lounge (p131)

Pope Joan (p120)

Red Spot (p120)

Slack Alice (p120)

Talullah's Cabaret (p127)

Woody's/Sailor (p120)

Mainstream venues with queer-friendly vibes are **Allen's** (p117), **Cameron House** (p121) and **Ciao Edie** (p119). Also seek out **It's a Boy's Life** (www.itsaboyslife.com) dance events at koolhaus inside the **Guvernment** (below).

salsa, mambo, Brazilian and some rare vinyl. Show up early for free dance lessons (call first to check schedules).

COMFORT ZONE Map pp234-5

☎ 416-763-9139; Kensington Market, 480 Spadina Ave; Thu-Sun; streetcar 510

An eclectic mix of live reggae, hip-hop, fusion jazz, techno and trance DJs net folks with a cover of under $10. Detractors may label this place grungy, but the dance floor still packs a punch in the wee hours and the all-day 'Divine Sunday' party.

DANCE CAVE Map pp236-7

☎ 416-532-1598; The Annex, 529 Bloor St; subway Bathurst, streetcar 511

Upstairs from **Lee's Palace** (p122), the alternative Dance Cave has retro '80s grooves, Brit Pop, garage rock and '60s soul tunes, with no cover except on weekends. Crowds here are baby-faced.

DOCKS Map p225

☎ 416-469-5655; www.thedocks.com; East Toronto, 11 Polson St, off Cherry St; Thu-Sun; P free-$10

A lakeshore entertainment complex, the Docks has multiple nightclubs, all with huge dance floors, and a breezy outdoor patio. It's primed at the height of summer, when 2000 people can fit on special event nights.

EL CONVENTO RICO Map pp236-7

☎ 416-588-7800; Little Italy, 750 College St; Thu-Sun; streetcar 506

Inside a former church, this queer Latin dance palace sees as many straight as gay clientele these days, but drag shows still triumphantly go on stage Friday and Saturday night.

EL RANCHO Map pp236-7

☎ 416-921-2752; Little Italy, 430 College St; Thu-Sun; streetcar 506, 511

On the edge of Kensington Market, show up early for Latin dance lessons either here or at **Plaza Flamingo** (Map pp236-7; ☎ 416-603-8884; 423 College St; Tue-Sat), which is an empty barn on weeknights, but where the queue on Friday and Saturday is enormous.

ELEMENT Map pp234-5

☎ 416-359-1919; Queen West, 553 Queen St W; streetcar 501

It's not just another pretty hipster bar, since bi-level Element imports local and international DJs. Expect to hear progressive house, techno and trance tunes at this open-minded spot.

FILM LOUNGE Map pp226-7

☎ 416-887-9304; Chinatown, 393 Dundas St W; 10am-6pm Thu-Sat; streetcar 505

Intense beats don't stop throbbing until the break of dawn at this night owls' spot. It's just an upstairs room on the fringes of Chinatown, but the bouncers are outrageously picky.

GUVERNMENT Map pp228-30

☎ 416-869-0045; www.theguvernment.com; Harbourfront, 132 Queens Quay E; usually Thu-Sat; bus 6, 75

For a diversity of venues, nothing beats the 4500-sq-ft Guv. Although critics say it's too mainstream and full of suburbanites, DJs spin hip-hop, R&B, progressive house and trance music to satisfy all appetites. Rooftop skyline views are as impressive as the Arabian fantasy lounge and art-deco bar.

HOOCH Map pp234-5

☎ 416-703-5069; Queen West, 815 Queen St W; streetcar 501

Found upstairs from **Gypsy Co-op** (p106), Hooch lounge heats up during many nights of the week, often with no cover charge, for DJs spinning soul, jazz, house, drum 'n bass and much, much more. Think of rare grooves and hipster moves. Its sister club, **B-Side**, over at the Entertainment District's **Fez Batik** (p121) has a 'jazzanova' vibe and resident DJs.

MATADOR Map p225

☎ 416-533-9311; Greater Toronto, 466 Dovercourt Rd, west of Ossington Ave; 🕒 1:30am-5:30am Fri & Sat; streetcar 506

For three decades there has been after-hours madness on the huge dance floor of the Matador, just west of Little Italy. Live bands play honky-tonk and classic rock, though the owner once wrangled Leonard Cohen into a surprise show.

NASA DANCE BAR Map pp234-5

☎ 416-504-8356; Queen West, 609 Queen St W; 🕒 till 3am; streetcar 501, 511

Serious groovin' goes on at this no-cover spot, where soulful house, drum 'n bass, garage, funk, acid jazz and hip-hop collide. It's a chilled-out space with a relaxed door policy.

SYSTEM SOUNDBAR Map pp228-30

☎ 416-408-3996; Entertainment District, 117 Peter St; 🕒 Wed-Sat; streetcar 510

Resident house and drum 'n bass DJs drive a powerful vibe, with guest appearances by UK and European turntablists. Diversity is key for the crowd, with ravers, club prowlers and dance diva angels dying for progressive and trance grooves. Also check out **Sound Emporium** (Map pp228-30; ☎ 416-408-2646; 360 Adelaide St W; 🕒 Thu-Sun), formerly Turbo.

TALULLAH'S CABARET Map pp231-3

☎ 416-975-8555; Church-Wellesley Village, 12 Alexander St; 🕒 Fri & Sat; subway College, Wellesley

No pretense here, since it's all about the grooves at **Buddies in Bad Times Theatre** (p124), where the crowd is entirely mixed (queer and straight, male and female) and a miniscule cover is charged. Punk, art rock, indie bands, retro tunes – you just never know what you'll find on the weekends.

COMEDY & SPOKEN WORD

The alternative weekly *Now* knows what's on in the comedy clubs, and lists all of the readings at libraries, universities and bars like the **Red Spot** (p120), **Castro's Lounge** (p119) and **Free Times Cafe** (p122). Note most clubs and bars do not admit under-19s. **Insomniac Press** (☎ 416-504-9313; www.insomniacpress.com) tracks the city's reading series and literary events in *Word*, a monthly literary calendar. Pick up a free copy at **Pages Books & Magazines** (p148).

Top Five Comedy, Theater & Spoken Word Venues

- Second City (p128)
- Harbourfront Reading Series (right)
- Dream in High Park (p124)
- Glenn Gould Studio (p129)
- Factory Theatre (p124)

ALT.COMEDY LOUNGE Map pp226-7

☎ 416-977-9596; The Rivoli, 334 Queen St W; streetcar 501

Big laughs liven up the Rivoli on Monday nights, where local stand-up comics and international acts perform new material in a cabaret-like setting at the Alt.Comedy Lounge. As an added bonus, admission is PWYC (Pay What You Can).

HARBOURFRONT READING SERIES Map pp228-30

☎ 416-973-4000; www.readings.org; Harbourfront, York Quay Centre, 235 Queens Quay W; 🕒 box office 1pm-8:30pm Tue-Sat; streetcar 509, 510

If you want to hear the new voice of Canada's writers, this is the place. For more than 30 years, literary giants have headlined at Toronto's Harbourfront Centre. Tickets for Wednesday night readings cost $8, but you'll pay more for special events and October's **International Festival of Authors** (p127).

LAUGH RESORT Map pp228-30

☎ 416-364-5233; Entertainment District, 370 King St W; tickets $7-15; 🕒 8:30pm Tue-Sat, 8:30pm & 10:30pm Fri & Sat; streetcar 504, 510

Squeeze inside the Laugh Resort, where Ellen DeGeneres and Adam Sandler once cracked jokes. New talent takes the stage on Tuesday and Wednesday nights. This comedy club is conveniently located in Toronto's mainstream nightlife district.

PIRATE VIDEO CABARET Map pp236-7

☎ 416-535-9541; Koreatown, Clinton's, 693 Bloor St W; cover $5; 🕑 9pm Sun, doors open 8:30pm; subway Christie

The very cool Pirate Video Cabaret happens in the back room of Clinton's bar. A merry band of bohemians always entertains scenesters with stand-up and sketch comedy, film, video, music and poetry.

SECOND CITY Map pp228-30

☎ 416-343-0011, 800-263-4485; www.secondcity.com; Entertainment District, 56 Blue Jays Way; mainstage shows $15-30; 🕑 mainstage shows 8pm Sun-Fri, 8pm & 10:30pm Sat; streetcar 504

Sharing its name with a comedy club in Chicago, the club's moniker dates from when each city played second fiddle in the past, Chicago to the Big Apple (New York City) and Toronto to Montréal (in the eyes of Montréalers, that is). But Second City is legendary, and many *Saturday Night Live* comics started here (p21). Sunday night 'best of' shows drawn from the national touring acts are good bets. Improv performances (often held right after the last show ends) are absolutely free.

THEATRESPORTS TORONTO Map pp238-9

☎ 416-491-3115; Greektown, Bad Dog Theatre, 138 Danforth Ave; tickets $6-10; 🕑 mainstage shows 8pm Tue-Sat, 8pm & 10pm Fri & Sat; subway Broadview

Cooking up hilarious improv for over two decades, Theatresports is a multifaceted troupe that also offers special guest comedy nights, workshops and Saturday afternoon 'Puppy Posse' children's shows (family admission is $20).

YUK YUK'S Map pp228-30

☎ 416-967-6425; Entertainment District, 224 Richmond St W; cover $10-20; 🕑 Tue-Sun; subway Osgoode

Live acts are sometimes funny or are sometimes just a joke – just like Jim Carrey (p21), the Toronto native who cut his teeth here. Canadian and international touring acts appear regularly, with famous faces on some weekends. On 'Toonie Tuesdays,' admission costs just $2.

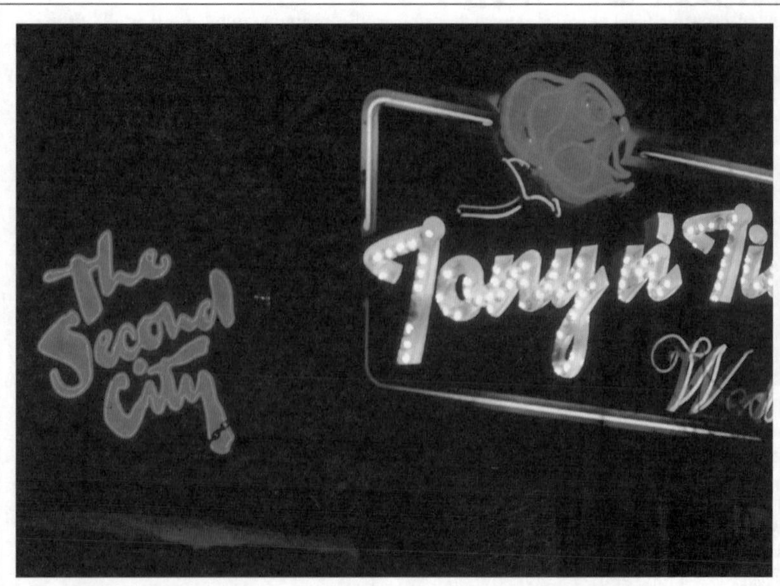

Second City (above)

CLASSICAL MUSIC & OPERA

The main performance season starts in September and runs straight through until spring. Venues include **Roy Thomson Hall** (Map pp228-30; ☎ 416-872-4255; www.roythomson.com; Theatre Block, 60 Simcoe St; box office 10am-6pm Mon-Fri, noon-5pm Sat; subway St Andrew), which also sells tickets for performances at **Massey Hall** (Map pp228-30; www.masseyhall.com; Dundas Sq; 178 Victoria St; subway Queen). Together they present a world of music, from opera tenors to chamber groups to the Girls Choir of Harlem. Other performances take place at the **Hummingbird Centre for the Performing Arts** (Map pp228-30; ☎ 416-393-7469; www.hummingbirdcentre.com; Old York; 1 Front St E; box office 10am-6pm Mon-Fri, 10am-1pm Sat; subway Union), perhaps by the national ballet or the Lincoln Center Jazz Orchestra. Construction of downtown's magnificent **Four Seasons Centre for the Performing Arts** (Map pp226-7; University Ave, cnr Queen St) is under way, but this grand new opera house and ballet theater won't open until summer 2006.

Tickets & Festivals

Buy tickets for major events through Ticketmaster's **Artsline** (☎ 416-872-1111; www.ticketmaster.ca). During summer, very affordable (even free) performances take place at various churches and outdoor venues, as well as during major festivals (p21). Go to www.newmusicconcerts.com for avant-garde performances by Canadian and international composers, including at the **Music Gallery** (p122).

CANADIAN OPERA COMPANY

Map pp228-30

☎ 416-363-8231, 800-250-4653; www.coc.ca; Old York, Hummingbird Centre for the Performing Arts, 1 Front St E; tickets $20-160; box office 10am-6pm Mon-Fri, 10am-1pm Sat; subway Union

In business for over half a century, Canada's national opera company can claim to have invented Surtitles, which projects text translations visible to the audience over a proscenium arch. Advance single tickets sell out quickly; check the website about a month before opening night for details.

CHURCH OF THE HOLY TRINITY

Map pp226-7

☎ 416-598-4521 ext 222; www.holytrinitytoronto.org; Eaton Centre, Trinity Sq; admission by donation $5; 12:15pm Mon late May–early Sep; subway Queen

Nestled behind **Eaton Centre** (p148), the welcoming Church of the Holy Trinity opens its doors on summer Music Mondays for wonderful medieval, classical, folk and modern music performances. Other houses of worship, including magisterial **St James Cathedral** (Map pp228-30; ☎ 416-364-7865; www.stjamescathedral.on.ca; 65 Church St; streetcar 504), offer a variety of free concerts year-round.

GLENN GOULD STUDIO Map pp228-30

☎ 416-205-5555; http://glenngouldstudio.cbc.ca; Canadian Broadcasting Centre, 250 Front St W; tickets $15-40; box office 11am-6pm Mon-Fri, during summer 11am-5pm Tue-Thu; streetcar 504

Free noontime concerts are given in the Glenn Gould Studio, where the soundtrack for *Schindler's List* was recorded. You'll need to purchase advance tickets for highly esteemed evening concerts of classical and contemporary music by soloists, chamber groups, choirs and sinfonia between September and June. Young international artists are often featured.

HARBOURFRONT CENTRE Map pp228-30

☎ 416-973-4000; www.harbourfront.on.ca; Harbourfront Centre box office, York Quay Centre, 235 Queens Quay W; box office 1-8pm Tue-Sat; streetcar 509, 510

The vibrant Harbourfront Centre puts on a variety of world-class musical performances throughout the year, including Sunday family shows (tickets $8, family admission $20) and free outdoor summer concerts in the **Toronto Music Garden** (p43). Subsidiary box offices at the **Harbourfront Centre CIBC Stage** (Map pp228-30) and **Premiere Dance Theatre** (Map pp228-30; Queen's Quay Terminal, 207 Queens Quay W, 3rd fl) open two hours before performance.

TORONTO CENTRE FOR THE ARTS

Map p224

☎ 416-250-3708; www.tocentre.com; North York, 5040 Yonge St; tickets from $10; box office 11am-6pm Mon-Sat, noon-4pm Sun; subway North York Centre

The marvelous 1000-seat George Weston Recital Hall presents concerts by the world's top musicians and vocalists. You can also catch ballet and theater performances at the 1700-seat Main Stage Theatre and the intimate Studio Theatre. It's far from downtown, though.

TORONTO SYMPHONY ORCHESTRA

Map pp228-30

☎ 416-593-4828; www.tso.on.ca; customer service centre box office; 212 King St W; tickets $30-100; 🕑 box office 10am-6pm Mon-Fri, noon-5pm Sat; subway St Andrew

A range of classics, Cole Porter–era pops and new music from around the world are presented by the TSO at Roy Thomson Hall, Massey Hall and the Toronto Centre for the Arts. Younger patrons aged 15 to 29 can buy 'tsoundcheck' (www.tsoundcheck.com) tickets for $10; these tickets usually go on sale the Monday of the performance week.

TRINITY-ST PAUL'S CENTRE Map pp236-7

☎ 416-964-6337; The Annex, 427 Bloor St W; 🕑 box office 10am-1pm & 2-6pm Mon-Fri; subway Spadina

The world-renowned **Tafelmusik** (www.tafelmusik.org; tickets $25-100) baroque orchestra and chamber choir performs most of the time at atmospheric Trinity-St Paul's United Church, as does the excellent **Toronto Consort** (www.torontoconsort.org; tickets $15-45) for early medieval and renaissance music. Check schedules of pre-concert lectures, family matinees, meet-the-musician nights and the annual holiday sing-along to Handel's *Messiah* at Massey Hall.

UNIVERSITY OF TORONTO FACULTY OF MUSIC Map pp231-3

☎ 416-978-3744; www.utoronto.ca/music; box office: St George campus, Edward Johnson Bldg, 80 Queen's Park; tickets $12-26; 🕑 box office noon-5pm Mon-Fri; subway Museum

UT's scholarly and professional music faculty presents a series of concerts – orchestral, chamber, wind ensembles, jazz and new music – at various venues around the university's St George campus. An afternoon of tea and opera at the MacMillan Theatre costs less than $30. Vocal performance classes and select concerts at Walter Hall are free.

DANCE

Keep an eye out for unique productions by the city's multicultural dance troupes, including Middle Eastern **Arabesque Dance Company** (☎ 416-920-5593; www.arabesquedance.ca), Chinese-inspired **Xing Dance Theatre** (☎ 416-413-0957; www.xingdancetheatre.com) and Afro-Caribbean **Ballet Creole** (☎ 416-960-0350; www.balletcreole.org).

Festivals

During August the **Fringe Festival of Independent Dance Artists** (☎ 416-410-4291; www.ffida.org; tickets $10-25, festival passes $100-120) happens at various venues, including Harbourfront Centre, **Buddies in Bad Times Theatre** (p124) and the **Distillery Historic District** (p146). Over half of the performing artists are from Toronto, with many others hailing from abroad.

DANCEMAKERS Map pp238-9

☎ 416-367-1800; Distillery Historic District, Case Goods Bldg, 55 Mill St, studio 313; tickets $15-40; streetcar 503, 504

An adventurous contemporary dance troupe, Dancemakers is emotive, expressionist and minimalist by turns. The repertoire emphasizes works by French director Serge Bennathan, with passion-driven Canadian themes.

HARBOURFRONT CENTRE Map pp228-30

☎ 416-973-4000; Harbourfront, Premiere Dance Theatre, Queen's Quay Terminal, 207 Queens Quay W, 3rd fl, box office: York Quay Centre, 235 Queens Quay W; tickets $5-40; 🕑 box office 1-8pm Tue-Sat; streetcar 509, 510

A focal point for Canadian dance companies, the Harbourfront Centre hosts a kaleidoscopic array of international touring troupes, too. Classical Indian dances, traditional folk performances and modern French comedies are among the productions staged here, mostly between October and May. Dancespeak, a chance to talk with the dancers, usually takes place on the second night of the performance run.

NATIONAL BALLET OF CANADA

Map pp228-30

☎ 416-345-9595, 866-345-9595; www.national.ballet.ca; Old York, Hummingbird Centre for the Performing Arts, 1 Front St E; tickets $35-120; 🕑 box office 10am-6pm Mon-Fri, 10am-1pm Sat, regular season Oct-May; subway Union

The National Ballet actively commissions new and experimental works by choreographers from across Canada, the USA and around the world. It also performs traditional ballets, such as *The Nutcracker*. Ask about free Ballet Talk introductory lectures given one hour before curtain time.

TORONTO DANCE THEATRE Map pp238-9

☎ 416-967-1365; www.tdt.org; Cabbagetown, 80 Winchester St; tickets $16-40; streetcar 506

Called kinetic and poetic, this contemporary dance troupe performs at a restored church in Cabbagetown and the Harbourfront Centre's Premiere Dance Theatre during winter and early spring. The annual Four at the Winch event spotlights four works by emerging Canadian choreographers.

Billiards

Academy of Spherical Arts (Map p225; ☎ 416-532-2782; Greater Toronto Area, 38 Hanna Ave, off Atlantic Ave; noon-2am Mon-Fri, 5pm-2am Sat; streetcar 504) Not quite as imposing as it sounds, but some of the antique billiards tables inside this old Brunswick Billiards Factory are hand-carved (one was even owned by the Prince of Wales).

andy poolhall (Map pp236-7; ☎ 416-923-5300; Little Italy, 489 College St; 6pm-2am Mon, 2pm-2am Tue-Sat, 7pm-2am Sun; streetcar 506, 511) A swingin' spot to shoot some stick, with DJs right next door at **Ciao Edie** (p119).

Charlotte Room (Map pp228-30; ☎ 416-598-2882; Entertainment District, 19 Charlotte St; 4pm-1am Mon-Wed, 4pm-2am Thu-Sat; streetcar 504, 510) For more mannered ladies and gents, this clubby spot has customized tables and an in-house pro.

Pegasus Billiard Lounge (Map pp231-3; ☎ 416-927-8832; Church-Wellesley Village, 489B Church St; 2pm-2am; subway Wellesley) Above the *Xtra!* offices in the gay village.

Rivoli Pool Hall (Map pp226-7; ☎ 416-596-1501; Queen Street, 334 Queen St W; 2pm-2am; streetcar 501) Upstairs from the Rivoli live music and comedy club (p127).

COFFEEHOUSES

Besides the following coffee shops, many restaurants and cafés will let you linger over a cup of coffee and dessert. Our favorites include **Le Gourmand** (p98), **Dufflet Pastries** (p107), **Future Bakery & Café** (p104) and **Mercatto** (p94), as well as Little Italy's **Sicilian Sidewalk Café** (p106).

JET FUEL Map pp238-9

☎ 416-968-9982; Cabbagetown, 519 Parliament St; 7am-8pm; streetcar 506

So arty and self-consciously cool, this hangout is for east-end gentrifiers, cyclists and literati who like to jeer at the beautiful people of Yorkville. Coffee is sinfully rich.

KALENDAR KOFFEE HOUSE Map pp236-7

☎ 416-923-4138; Little Italy, 546 College St; 11:30-10pm Mon-Wed, 11:30am-11pm Thu, 11:30am-midnight Fri, 10:30am-midnight Sat, 10:30am-10pm Sun; streetcar 506

Darkly lit booths are filled with cooing couples, so you'll have to scramble for a seat. Kalendar's kitchen creates delicious pastry-wrapped scrolls,' nan pizzas and orange-ginger-carrot soup, as well as generous desserts.

LETTIERI Map pp231-3

☎ 416-515-8764; Yorkville, 94 Cumberland St; 10am-9pm Sun-Thu, 10am-11pm Fri & Sat; subway Bay

An Italian chain of coffee shops, Lettieri serves good breakfast specials, light lunches and dessert pastries. Other locations include **Queen St** (Map pp226-7; ☎ 416-592-1360; 441 Queen St W; streetcar 501, 510) and the **Annex** (Map pp236-7; ☎ 416-516-1655; 581 Bloor St W; subway Bathurst), inside **Honest Ed's** (p153).

LOUIE'S COFFEE STOP Map pp234-5

Kensington Market, 235 Augusta Ave; hours vary; streetcar 510

Standing on a busy corner of Kensington Market since 1965, Louie's coffee shack is a mellow oasis, where vintage jazz abides. With just a few stools inside, think about getting your Italian soda, fruit or espresso shake to go.

MIOFRIO! JUICE+JAVA Map p240

☎ 416-693-6370; The Beaches, 2169 Queen St E; 7am-9pm Mon-Fri, 8am-9pm Sat & Sun; streetcar 501

Not that the Beaches needed yet another coffee shop, but this small chain seems to do everything right, from making rich, foamy cappuccinos to fresh-squeezed juices, with sinfully comfy chairs and free wi-fi Internet access for laptop users. Another handy branch is in **Rosedale** (Map p225; ☎ 416-960-1430; 1219 Yonge St; 7am-7pm Mon-Fri, 8am-7pm Sat & Sun; subway Summerhill).

MOONBEAN CAFE Map pp234-5

☎ 416-595-0327; Kensington Market, 30 St Andrews St; 7am-10pm; streetcar 510

'Nothing here is just ordinary,' says the man behind the counter, and that's true. Although it's a bit short on elbow room, Moonbean has organic and fair trade coffees, all-day breakfasts for $5 or less, and Bite Me vegan cookies.

REMARKABLE BEAN Map p240

☎ 416-690-2420; The Beaches, 2242 Queen St E; 7am-10pm; streetcar 501

More substantial sandwiches are made at the Beaches' **Best Coffee** (p110), but this neighborhood favorite serves you up shepherd's pie and still-in-the-pan homemade desserts. It's just steps from the **Fox** (p116).

TANGO PALACE COFFEE COMPANY

Map pp238-9

☎ 416-465-8085; Leslieville, 1156 Queen St E; 7am-11pm Sun-Thu, 7am-midnight Fri & Sat; streetcar 501, 502, 503

En route to the Beaches, this elegant coffeehouse lies among the antiques and design shops of Leslieville. Linger on sunny sidewalk chairs over a rich croissant and a dark-roasted brew – ah, heaven.

TEQUILA BOOKWORM Map pp234-5

☎ 416-504-7335; Queen West, 490 Queen St W; 10am-11pm; streetcar 501, 511

Tequila Bookworm approaches the platonic ideal of a coffee shop: high bookshelves and magazine racks lining a room of overstuffed chairs, couches and low tables. It's also got healthy sandwiches and juices for refueling.

Sports, Health & Fitness

Sports, Health & Fitness

Torontonians are passionate about the active life, and we don't just mean hockey. Outdoor activities are definitely where it's at, with folks cycling, blading and running along lakeshore trails, hiking up the city's river ravines and paddling on Lake Ontario during summer. In winter, ice-skating is a favorite pastime, with opportunities for skiing and snowboarding within the city limits, as well as excursions to ski resorts around Ontario. Don't be surprised if you see hard-core enthusiasts cycling when there's snow on the sidewalks, or hockey players skating on artificial ice in the middle of July.

But you don't have to get so intense; the lakefront beaches and trails will keep you happy, whether you choose to walk one kilometer or cycle several dozen more. Then head over to SkyDome or the Air Canada Centre to watch the fortunes of T.O.'s pro sports teams rise and fall. Even if you're not a sports maven, you'll likely get a thrill from joining the crowds at a fast-paced lacrosse game or placing a few bets at the track.

Torontonians are quick to adopt the latest fitness and healthy lifestyle crazes. Whatever they're doing in Los Angeles or Vancouver these days, you're sure to find it here, too. The city is also the perfect place to treat yourself to a Thai massage, unwind with yoga, indulge in an organic spa or artfully add a new tattoo.

WATCHING SPORTS

Tickets & Reservations

Toronto is a sports mad town (p14) and ticket prices for major events go through the roof. **Ticketmaster** (☎ 416-872-5000; www.ticketmaster.ca) sells advance tickets, as do the box offices at the **Air Canada Centre** (Map pp228-30; ☎ 416-815-5500; www.theaircanadacentre.com; 40 Bay St; subway Union) and **SkyDome** (Map pp228-30; ☎ 416-870-8000; www.skydome.com; 1 Blue Jays Way; subway Union). The illegal practice of 'scalping,' in which independent operators resell prime tickets outside venues around the game start time, happens around Union Station.

BASEBALL

TORONTO BLUE JAYS

☎ 416-341-1234, 888-654-1000; www.bluejays.com; tickets from $7; regular season Apr-Sep

Toronto's professional baseball team plays in the American League at **SkyDome** (Map pp228-30; ☎ 416-870-8000; www.skydome.com; 1 Blue Jays Way; subway Union). Tickets can be bought with a credit card by phone, on-line or through **Ticketmaster** (☎ 416-872-5000; www.ticketmaster.ca) for a fee; you can buy tickets for cash at the Sky Dome box office near Gate 9. Note the cheapest seats are a long way above the field. Instead try the 500-level seats (from $22) behind home plate.

BASKETBALL

TORONTO RAPTORS

☎ 416-815-5500; www.nba.com/raptors; tickets from $11; regular season Oct-Apr

During hockey season, the Toronto Raptors of the professional National Basketball Association (NBA) also play at the **Air Canada Centre** (Map pp228-30; ☎ 416-815-5500; www.theaircanadacentre.com; 40 Bay St; subway Union). Single game tickets, which cost up to hundreds of dollars, are sold through **Ticketmaster** (☎ 416-872-5000; www.ticketmaster.ca).

FOOTBALL

TORONTO ARGONAUTS

☎ 416-341-2700; www.argonauts.ca; tickets $15-50; regular season Jun-Oct

The Toronto Argonauts of the fast-paced professional Canadian Football League (CFL) play at **SkyDome** (Map pp228-30; ☎ 416-870-8000; www.skydome.com; 1 Blue Jays Way; subway

Top Five Places to Get Fit, Healthy & Beautiful Indoors

- **Coupe Bizzarre** (p141)
- **Sudi's the Spa** (p141)
- **Diesel Fitness** (p138)
- **Body Clinic** (p140)
- **Yoga Studio** (p139)

nion). Over the past 130 years, Toronto's foot-all team has brought home more Grey Cup hampionships than any other city in Canada. ou should bring a jacket, as things cool off at ight when SkyDome's roof is open.

IOCKEY

'ORONTO MAPLE LEAFS

☎ 416-815-5500; www.mapleleafs.com; tickets $25-00; ⏲ regular season Oct-Apr

n winter the National Hockey League (NHL) Maple Leafs play at the **Air Canada Centre** (Map pp228-30; ☎ 416-815-5500; www.theairca adacentre.com; 40 Bay St; subway Union). very game is pretty well sold out in advance, ut a limited number of same-day tickets go n sale through **Ticketmaster** (☎ 416-872-5000; www.ticketmaster.ca) at 10am and then later t the Air Canada Centre's ticket wicket start-ng around 5pm. Hockey tickets are costly, vith even the 'cheap' seats going for $30.

)THER SPORTS

'ORONTO ROCK

☎ 416-596-3075 ext 223; www.torontorock.com; ickets $10-50; ⏲ regular season Jan-Apr

acrosse may not be what you first think of vhen it comes to Canadian sports, but the 0-team **National Lacrosse League** (www.nll.com) as been building momentum for two lecades. Toronto's lacrosse team is red hot, aving won the league's championship title n 2003. You can watch them play at the Air Canada Centre.

VOODBINE RACETRACK Map pp224

☎ 888-675-7223; www.woodbineentertainment.com; 55 Rexdale Blvd, Rexdale; admission free, binocular ental $2; ⏲ live races held Mar-Nov; P

Secretariat's last race was run at Woodbine Racetrack, where the action revolves around horoughbreds and standardbreds (harness acing). Millions have been spent to turn it into flashy entertainment complex à la Niagara. ook for the bronze statue of Canada's famous acehorse Northern Dancer.

The racetrack is northwest of downtown oronto off Hwy 427, near Hwy 27. By public ransport, take the subway to Kipling, then atch the direct express Woodbine shuttle us that picks patrons up before post time usually 12:05pm, except 6:45pm for Wednes-lay races) and returns them 20 minutes after he last race.

OUTDOOR ACTIVITIES

Most outdoor activities are best done in summer, between late May and early September. Winter sports pick up toward the end of November and last until March. Contact **Toronto Parks & Recreation** (☎ 416-392-8186; www.city.toronto.on.ca/parks) for a seasonal activity Toronto fun guide, or browse its voluminous website for all kinds of activities listed here. Equipment rentals are available at **Europe Bound Outfitters** (p147), where baby carriers, binoculars, backpacks, trekking poles, ice-climbing gear and snow shoes can be hired for under $10 per day. Their discount 'weekend' rentals are a great deal, beginning at 6pm Thursday night and ending at 6pm on Monday. **Mountain Equipment Co-op** (p147) and **Hogtown Extreme Sports** (p147) are nearby. For specialist outdoor activity guides, drop by **Open Air** (p146) travel bookstore.

CYCLING, IN-LINE SKATING & RUNNING

For cyclists, in-line skaters and runners, the **Martin Goodman Trail** (Map pp225) is the place to go. This paved recreational trail stretches from the Beaches along the downtown Harbourfront to the Humber River, in the west end. Along the way you can connect to the paved and single-track mountain bike trails of the **Don Valley** system at Cherry St (Map pp238-9). On the **Toronto Islands** (p64) the boardwalk on the south shoreline and all of the interconnecting paved paths are car-free zones. You can also cycle or skate around hilly **High Park** (p77) for a challenge. If you fancy a longer trek, the Martin Goodman Trail is part of the **Lake Ontario Waterfront Trail** (www.waterfronttrail.org), which already stretches 350km from east of Toronto to near Niagara-on-the-Lake, where you can pick up the paved recreational trail alongside the **Niagara Parkway** (p178).

Recommended maps for serious cyclists include MapArt's *Toronto Bicycle Map* ($3.95) and the *Official Lake Ontario Waterfront Trail Mapbook* ($9.95). A recreational cycling club, the **Toronto Bicycling Network** (TBN; ☎ 416-760-4191; http://tbn.on.ca) is an excellent informational resource, with organized rides open to nonmembers for a $5 fee. Check the website or call for in-line skating events.

Rentals

Toronto's **Community Bicycling Network** (Map pp234-5; ☎ 416-504-2918; www.communitybicyclenetwork.org; Queen West, 761 Queen St W; streetcar 501) runs **BikeShare** (www.bikeshare.org). For $25 per year, members can borrow a single-speed yellow bike from any of a dozen centrally located hubs for up to three days.

Europe Bound Outfitters (p147) rents mountain bikes and tandems with helmets for $30 per day. Outside of the off-season (ie winter), bicycles and in-line skates can also be rented from the following.

Beaches Cyclery (Map p240; ☎ 416-699-1461; The Beaches, 1882 Queen St E; 🕑 vary; streetcar 501)

Centre Island Bicycle Rental (Map p241; ☎ 416-203-0009; Toronto Island Park; bicycles per hr $6, tandems $13, quadricycles $15-25; 🕑 seasonal hr vary; ferry Centre I)

High Park Cycle & Sports (Map pp225; ☎ 416-614-6689; 2878 Dundas St W; 🕑 hr vary; subway Keele)

McBride Cycle (Map pp225; ☎ 416-763-5652; 2923 Dundas St W; 🕑 hr vary; subway Keele)

Wheel Excitement (Map pp228-30; ☎ 416-260-9000; Harbourfront, 249 Queens Quay W; bicycles & in-line skates per hr/day $12/27, 2-day $36, each additional day $14; 🕑 10am-6pm Mon-Fri, 10am-7pm Sat & Sun late Apr-Oct; streetcar 509, 510)

GOLF

Excellent public golf courses abound in the Niagara region, for example the **Whirlpool Golf Course** (p180) at Niagara Falls. The **Docks** (p126) also has a driving range. There's also a Frisbee (disc) golf course on **Ward's Island** (p66). Closer to the city, try the following.

CITYCORE GOLF & DRIVING RANGE Map pp228-30

☎ 416-640-9888; Financial District, 2 Spadina Ave 🕑 7am-11:30pm mid-Apr–Oct, 10am-4pm Nov–mid-Apr; P

West of SkyDome, CityCore has a triple-decker heated driving range with views of the CN Tower. A par-three, nine-hole seasonal course is less exciting, however.

GLEN ABBEY GOLF CLUB Map p174

☎ 905-844-1811, 800-288-0388; www.glenabbey.com; 1333 Dorval Dr, Oakville; green fees from $125

Golfers may have already heard of Glen Abbey, the first course to be designed solely by Jack Nicklaus. It's where the pros play during the Bell Canadian Open. The club is a 40-minute drive west of downtown via the QEW, past Hwy 407 in the suburb of Oakville.

WOODEN STICKS Map pp174

☎ 905-852-4379; www.woodensticks.com;off Elgin Park Dr, Uxbridge; green fees from $160

West of the city proper, eclectic Wooden Sticks club boasts an 18-hole course that pays homage to many famous PGA tour stops, from Scotland to Florida.

HIKING

Though short on city parks, Toronto does have some substantial nature reserves in the numerous ravines formed by rivers and streams that empty into Lake Ontario. You can join up with the **Toronto Bruce Trail Club** (☎ 416-763-9061; www.torontobrucetrailclub.org) or the **Toronto Bicycling Network** (TBN; ☎ 416-760-4191; http://tbn.on.ca) for hardy day hikes.

Toronto Parks & Recreation (☎ 416-392-8186; www.city.toronto.on.ca/parks) oversee the city's self-guided **Discovery Walks.** The **Don Valley Hills & Dales** walk begins at Broadview subway station. Follow the signs down into the urban jungle and walk south past **Riverdale Farm** (p62) and the **Necropolis** (p62) in Cabbagetown and Chester Springs Marsh farther south. Before reaching Gerrard St, loop back north through Rosedale to connect to the **Central Ravines, Belt Line & Gardens** walk through Mt Pleasant Cemetery (p76) to Eglinton West subway station. Outside Old Mill subway station, on the Bloor-Danforth line, is the start of the two-hour **Humber River, Old Mill & Marshes** walk, which loops south to Lake Ontario and Hunber Bay, much of the way through woodland, then back north past a 1700s French settlement site.

ICE-SKATING, SKIING & SNOWBOARDING

In winter there are scenic places to ice-skate downtown, including **Nathan Phillips Square** (Map pp226-7; ☎ 416-338-7465; Queen Street, 100 Queen St W; 🕑 10am-10pm) outside City Hall and at the **Harbourfront Centre** (Map pp228-30; ☎ 416-973-4000; 235 Queens Quay W; 🕑 10am-10pm Sun-Thu, 10am-11pm Fri & Sat), both with artificial ice rinks open mid-November to

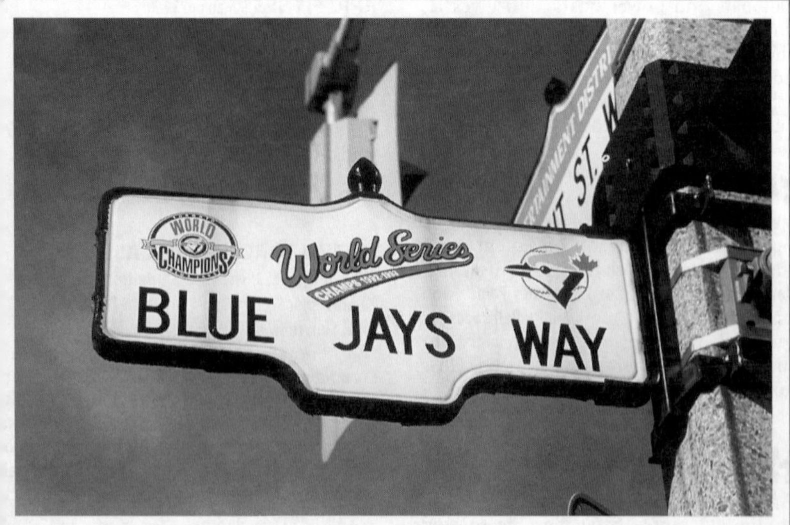

Blue Jays Way in the baseball team's hometown (p134)

Iarch, weather permitting. Admission is ree; rental skates cost from $6. Contact oronto Parks & Recreation (☎ 416-392-8186; vww.city.toronto.on.ca/parks) for information on other artificial rinks around town, ncluding at **Kew Gardens** (Map p240) and **Trinty Bellwoods Park** (Map pp234-5). If it has been uite cold recently, there's a natural ice rink t **Grenadier Pond** (p77) in High Park.

In winter, the family-friendly ski centers t **Earl Bales Park** (Map pp224; ☎ 416-395-934; 4169 Bathurst St; subway Sheppard, hen bus 84) and **Centennial Park** (Map pp224; ☎ 416-394-8750; 256 Centennial Park Rd; ubway Royal York, then bus 48) offer tame lownhill skiing and snowboarding (including rentals). The **Toronto Bicycling Network** (TBN; ☎ 416-760-4191; http://tbn.on.ca) organzes group skates (nonmembers $5) every riday, usually from December through Iarch, with dinner afterward. TBN also ffers **cross-country skiing excursions** (☎ 416-760-191 ext 1; nonmembers $25, plus trail fees x rental) from January through March. For nore downhill skiing and snowboarding pportunities, see p191.

SWIMMING & WATERSPORTS

eople tend not to swim in Lake Ontario, ven though there are over a dozen lifeguard beaches, which are open in July and August. Water quality is often poor, especially after rainstorms, so check with Toronto's **Beach Water Quality Hotline** (☎ 416-392-7161; www.city.toronto.on.ca/beach) first.

Free outdoor swimming can be found at the municipal pool in **High Park** (p77) or at **Gus Ryder Pool** (Map pp225; ☎ 416-392-6696), aka Sunnyside, on Lake Shore Blvd south of High Park. West of the Annex, the pool at **Christie Pitts Park** (Map pp240; ☎ 416-392-0745) has water slides, and there is the Olympic-sized **DD Summerville Pool** (Map pp240; ☎ 416-392-0740; Woodbine Park) at the Beaches.

Rentals & Lessons

The **Harbourfront Canoe & Kayak Centre** (Map pp228-30; ☎ 416-203-2277, 800-960-8886; www.paddletoronto.com; 283A Queen's Quay W; canoes per hr/day $15/40, kayaks $18/50, tandem kayaks $30/65; streetcar 509, 510) rents crafts for paddling around its pond or going out to Toronto Islands. There are private and group lessons, as well as evening and weekend paddles. There's also an on-site sailing school for people with disabilities. **Harbourfront Boating Centre** (Map pp228-30; ☎ 416-203-3000; Harbourfront; 283 Queens Quay W) rents sailboats and power boats, and gives lessons. Windsurfing rental is available at the Ashbridge's Bay area, near the western edge of the Beach boardwalk; contact the **Toronto Windsurfing Club** (www.torontowindsurfingclub.com) for details.

TENNIS

Municipal tennis courts (☎ 416-392-1111) are open April to October. Convenient courts include those at **High Park** (p77), beachside **Kew Gardens** (Map p240), **Hanlan's Point** (p66) on Toronto Islands and **Trinity Bellwoods Park** (Map pp234-5). Permits are necessary during busy times. There's also a Frisbee (disc) golf course on **Ward's Island** (p66).

HEALTH & FITNESS

An abundance of gyms, yoga and Pilates studios guarantee you'll be able to work out, no matter how cruel the weather is outside. Most large hotels have a fitness center and swimming pool for guests' use, and sometimes these facilities are made available to nonguests for a fee.

GYMS & HEALTH CLUBS

Private gyms usually charge $15 to $20 for a day pass; ask about weekly or monthly membership deals. Municipal recreation centers charge $10 or less per day; some offer pay-as-you-go fitness classes. The **St Lawrence CRC** (Map pp238-9; ☎ 416-392-1347; Old York, 230 The Esplanade; streetcar 503, 504) and **Beaches RC** (Map p240; ☎ 416-392-0740; The Beaches, 6 Williamson Rd; streetcar 501) both have indoor swimming pools. Contact **Toronto Parks & Recreation** (☎ 416-392-8186; www.city.toronto.on.ca/parks) for all other locations.

DIESEL FITNESS Map pp228-30

☎ 416-595-9900; www.dieselfitness.ca; 99 Spadina Ave; 6am-11pm Mon-Thu, 6am-9pm Fri, 8am-8pm Sat & Sun; streetcar 504, 510

Around the corner from the Theatre Block, this gym's in-house DJ booth and 'fuel bar' (juice, espresso and high-speed Internet access) are staffed by friendly pros. It has been voted the city's best gym, offering yoga, spin, Pilates, capoeira, urban funk and even Kick-Cardio Combat classes. Massage and spa services are available.

EPIC FITNESS Map pp231-3

☎ 416-960-1705; 9 St Joseph St; 6am-midnight Mon-Thu, 6am-11pm Fri, 7:30am-8pm Sat, 7:30am-7pm Sun; subway Wellesley

A boutique gym in the city center, Epic's three story loft is perfect for doing yoga, Pilates, spin cardio and weight training. Its location near the Church-Wellesley Village means a mostly male, often gay clientele.

METRO TORONTO YMCA

☎ 416-975-9622; www.ymcatoronto.org; 20 Grovesnor Sq; 6am-11pm Mon-Fri, 7am-8pm Sat & Sun; subway: College

The nonprofit YMCA's enormous downtown complex houses two full-sized gyms, racquetball courts, indoor and outdoor tracks and a 25m pool. Fitness classes (over 130 per week) are led by volunteers. International YMCA affiliate members are eligible for guest privileges here or at six other city campuses. For details call ☎ 416-928-9622 or ☎ 800-223-8024.

MILES NADAL JEWISH COMMUNITY CENTRE Map pp236-7

Bloor JCC; ☎ 416-924-6211; www.milesnadaljcc.ca; 750 Spadina Ave; 5:30am-10pm Mon-Thu, 5:30am-6:30pm Fri, 10am-7pm Sat, 7am-7pm Sun; subway Spadina

Next to the UT campus, the Bloor JCC is a community institution that's open to all. Recently

Exercising the Soul

Yoga and other Asian traditions have often been divorced from their spiritual roots in North America, but Toronto still has a few spots to calm your inner demons. When you feel like the urban jungle is closing in, **Zen Buddhist Temple** (Map pp236-7; ☎ 416-658-0137; www.zenbuddhisttemple.org; Kensington Market, 297 College St; streetcar 506, 510), founded by the Buddhist Society for Compassionate Wisdom, offers beginners' meditation retreats, relaxation workshops and free Sunday morning and afternoon Zen practice sessions. You can also open your heart to the dharma at **Tengye Ling Tibetan Buddhist Temple** (Map pp231-3; ☎ 416-966-4656; www.tengyeling.ca; The Annex, 11 Madison Ave; discourse 7:30pm Tue; subway Spadina), where English-language discourses are followed by breathing and walking meditation. The **Sivananda Yoga Vedanta Centre** (Map pp236-7; ☎ 416-966-9642; www.sivananda.org/toronto; The Annex, 77 Harbord St; streetcar 510) hosts free 90-minute introductory yoga classes on Sunday afternoons, usually at 4pm.

multimillion dollar renovation upgraded the acilities, which include a gigantic gym, swimning pool, fitness classrooms, an on-site coffee hop and juice bar. Members of affiliated North merican JCCs are eligible for guest privileges.

JNIVERSITY OF TORONTO ATHLETIC CENTRE Map pp231-3

☎ 416-978-3437; www.utoronto.ca; 55 Harbord St; 7am-11pm Mon-Fri, 10am-5pm Sat & Sun; treetcar 510

On the St George campus, this high-quality thletic center sells monthly memberships or just $70. Together its two buildings hold a 25m pool, an indoor track, sports gymnasiums, ardio/weight rooms and a dance studio.

YOGA & PILATES

Mainstream yoga studios are scattered round the city; some offer Pilates mat vork classes, too. See also **Diesel Fitness** (p138). For a perfectly trendy yoga outfit, top by **Lululemon Athletica** (p156).

Prices & Schedules

Single yoga classes cost around $15, but discounts are available. Sometimes your first class costs just $5, or is even completely free. A one-week introductory pass, for example, nay cost just $20. 'Community' classes, which are usually taught at off-peak times by nstructors in training, are half-price. Some places charge a nominal fee for mat rental. Schedules vary, but most are open daily.

BIKRAM YOGA Map pp238-9

☎ 416-778-7744; www.bikramyogadanforth.com; Greektown, Carrot Common, 348A Danforth Ave; subway Chester

Dynamic yoga performed in a heated room – t's said to increase flexibility and prevent inury. This Greektown studio also has a unique cork-padded floor. Massage and alternative esthetics are available on some days.

DOWNWARD DOG YOGA CENTRE Map pp234-5

☎ 416-703-8805; www.downwarddog.com; Queen West, 735 Queen St W; streetcar 501

n the bohemian Queen West area, this studio focuses on Ashtanga yoga, emphasizing forceful flow series. Check the website for special events like improvisational 'yoga jams,' musical performances and wellness workshops.

YOGA SANCTUARY Map pp231-3

☎ 416-928-3236; www.theyogasanctuary.net; Yonge Street Strip; 2 College St; subway College

Yoga classes are taught inside a lovely 19th-century ballroom, which was also used for painting by the **Group of Seven** (p27). Ashtanga is the focus, although Hatha, pre- and postnatal exercises, and Pilates are also scheduled.

YOGA STUDIO Map pp236-7

☎ 416-923-9366; www.yogastudio.net; The Annex, 344 Bloor St W, suite 400; subway Spadina

This inspiring place has it all: Ashtanga, Hatha, Kripalu, Pilates, even Thai massage. Karma Yoga classes are taught for a donation of $6 or more, paid directly to the teacher after class. Special workshops in stress reduction, tantra and belly dancing are detailed on the website, which has excellent city-wide links for holistic health.

ROCK CLIMBING

Across the Don River, the **Toronto Climbing Academy** (Map pp238-9; ☎ 416-406-5900; www.climbingacademy.com; East Toronto; 100A Broadview Ave; admission $10-15, shoes or harness rental $5; noon-11pm Mon-Fri, 10am-10pm Sat & Sun; streetcar 501, 502, 503, 504) has 50 different indoor routes over multidimensional terrain. Rates are about the same at famous **Joe Rockhead's Climbing Gym** (Map p225; ☎ 416-538-7670; www.joerockheads.com; Greater Toronto Area, 29 Fraser Ave; streetcar 509, 511), north of Exhibition Place. It's owned by Canadian climbing champ Joe Bergman.

PERSONAL CARE & WELLBEING

Toronto is the place to indulge in a little treat for your body, especially given the city's vivacious sense of style. Check the alternative weeklies (p204) for salon and day spa coupons, special promotions and new openings.

MASSAGE & DAY SPAS

Most day spas offer registered massage therapy (RMT), facials, manicures and pedicures, waxing and tanning services. Both men and women are welcome, unless otherwise stated. Appointments are always advised. Expect to pay upwards of $65 for an hour-long massage, at least $35 for a 'quickie' facial and $15 or more for any other miscellaneous services.

BODY CLINIC Map pp231-3

☎ 416-324-8999; www.bodyclinic.ca; Bloor-Yorkville, 17 Yorkville Ave; 🕑 9am-9pm Mon-Fri, 10am-8pm Sat, 11am-5pm Sun; subway Bloor-Yonge

An upscale holistic wellness center, the Body Clinic is famed for its healing hot stone massage (30-minute session $50). Acupuncture, naturopathic medicine, reflexology, shiatsu and Thai massage also fit with its motto of 'urban body healing.'

CHI SPA Map p225

☎ 416-515-8288; Greater Toronto Area, 1 Balmoral Ave; 🕑 hr vary; subway St Clair

Offering Eastern ideas and contemporary esthetic services, this alternative spa has just a few treatment rooms, along with organic fresh-squeezed juices, an aromatherapy bar and custom music. Nouveau 'Zen shiatsu' can intensively work out anybody's aches and pains.

ELIZABETH MILAN HOTEL DAY SPA

Map pp228-30

☎ 416-350-7500; www.elizabethmilanspa.com; Financial District, Fairmont Royal York, 100 Front St W; 🕑 9am-7pm Mon-Wed, 8:30am-8pm Thu-Fri, 8:30am-7pm Sat, 10am-5pm Sun; subway Union

This professional day spa offers services fo men, women, couples and even teens. Its determined owner has searched the world fo exotic beauty regimens, and also created some of her own, such as the 90-minute Chocolate Body Indulgence featuring a fondue body wrap ($190). Hotel chefs prepare spa lunches upon request.

ELMWOOD SPA Map pp226-7

☎ 416-977-6751, 877-284-6348; www.elmwoodspa.com; Yonge Street Strip, 18 Elm St; 🕑 9am-9pm Mon-Fri, 9am-8pm Sat, 10:30am-6:30pm Sun; subway Dundas; P $10

Open for two decades, this award-winning spa for men and women is a luxurious escape. A spa lunch can be enjoyed at the terrace restaurant in one's bathrobe. Champagne manicures are de rigueur. A one-time pass to the swimming

Hockey Hall of Fame (p45)

pool, whirlpool, steam room and sauna costs $20 (half-price with a visit to the hair salon or any other esthetic service).

IODINE & ARSENIC Map pp234-5

☎ 416-681-0577; Queen West, 867 Queen St W; 🕑 noon-6pm Mon-Tue, 11am-7pm Wed-Fri, 11am-6pm Sat, noon-6pm Sun; streetcar 501

Is it a fetish shop? A medical supply store? No, dear. This bold Queen West neighborhood fixture offers full esthetic services, including pedicures with lemongrass or lavender lotion from its signature line of organic bath and body products. Treatment rooms are spacious. Complimentary wine, coffee and juices are offered.

SHIATSU SCHOOL OF CANADA

Map pp236-7

☎ 416-323-1818; www.shiatsucanada.com; Little Italy, 547 College St; 🕑 call for appointment; streetcar 506

At the professional school's student clinic, your 75-minute shiatsu treatment costs just $30 (or sometimes $40 for two people as an introductory special). Ten-minute shiatsu tune-ups cost just $10. Acupuncture is also available. Workshops are open to the public.

STILLWATER Map pp231-3

☎ 416-926-2389; www.stillwaterspa.com; Bloor-Yorkville, Park Hyatt, 4 Avenue Rd; 🕑 9am-10pm Mon-Fri, 8am-10pm Sat, 10am-5:30pm Sun; subway Museum

The Park Hyatt hotel's serene spa has made a splash with its aquatherapies and specialty treatments, such as mother-to-be massage, honey and mandarin orange exfoliations and underwater shiatsu. At once refreshing and energizing, a full range of modern esthetic services are offered for men and women. Spa lunches are taken in the tea lounge.

SUDI'S THE SPA Map pp231-3

☎ 416-922-0813; www.sudis.com; Bloor-Yorkville, 97 Scollard St; 🕑 9am-8pm Mon-Fri, 9am-6pm Sat, 10am-5pm Sun; subway Bay

Run by an Iranian immigrant who built her business from the ground up, Sudi's spa is richly furnished with Middle Eastern carpets and Louis XVI chairs. Its 'cosmopolitan exotica' shines in aromatherapy body massage, Persian body scrubs and even body piercing. Seasonal specials at this full-service, award-winning spa are normally available Monday to Wednesday.

SUTHERLAND-CHAN CLINIC

Map pp225

☎ 416-924-1107 ext 10; www.sutherland-chan.com; The Annex, 330 Dupont St; 🕑 by appointment; subway Dupont

Students of Swedish massage will apply their healing hands by appointment only (one-hour massage $32). Specialty clinics are offered for pregnant women, seniors, sports players, the disabled and dancers at off-site locations around the city.

Lighten Up

For a real gas, drop by Canada's first **O_2 Spa Bar** (Map pp225; ☎ 416-322-7733, 888-206-0202; www.o2spabar.com; Bloor-Yonge, 2044 Yonge St; 🕑 noon-6pm Sun-Tue, 11am-9pm Wed-Fri, 10am-9pm Sat; subway Davisville). Modeled after Japan's 'I-need-a-boost' stations, patrons are hooked up to a pure oxygen hose for 20 minutes ($20). You can even add a flavor (grapefruit, anyone?). Private lounge rooms have mood lighting and reclining leather seats.

HAIR SALONS

Expect to pay at least $40 for a haircut and style. Try to make appointments at least a day in advance. Many of the spas listed in the previous section offer hair stylist services.

COUPE BIZZARRE Map pp234-5

☎ 416-504-0783; Queen West, 704 & 710 Queen St W; streetcar 501

Cutting-edge Coupe Bizzarre, a radical import from Montréal, is the DJ's choice. If you're open to a brave new look, volunteer to be a model and get a free haircut (coloring surcharge $20). It stocks Black & White pomade, the same powerful stuff that Elvis used.

HOUSE OF LORDS Map pp231-3

☎ 416-962-1111; Yonge Street Strip, 639 Yonge St; subway Bloor-Yonge

This UK import has treated the tresses of David Bowie and Alice Cooper. Although less than punk these days, it still does dreadlocks. Basic haircuts cost just $15 for men ($21 for women). Walk-ins are accepted. Upscale **Toni & Guy** (Map pp231-3; ☎ 416-920-7775; Bloor-Yorkville,

102 Bloor St W; subway Bloor-Yonge) also hails from England.

SALON JIE Map pp231-3

☎ 416-926-0026; Bloor-Yorkville, 38 Avenue Rd; subway Bay

At Salon Jie, hairdressing is elevated to a high art, with prices to match. Don't reveal your shock if some fashion model, A-list celebrity or even a real-life princess is being coiffed right next to you. The minimalist space is impressive, with a white interior accents with gun metal tones and hints of green tea and ocean blue. Sometimes the master stylist, Jie Matar, is on hand. The salon also offers esthetic services.

PIERCINGS & TATTOOS

You'd run out of body parts before running through all of Toronto's tattoo and piercing shops. A few locals' favorites include:

New Tribe (Map pp226-7; ☎ 416-977-2786; www.newtribe.ca; Queen Street, 232 Queen St W, 2nd fl; 11am-8pm Mon-Thu, 11am-10pm Fri & Sat, noon-6pm Sun; streetcar 501) Standard and custom body jewelry.

Tat-a-Rama (Map p240; ☎ 416-693-2331; www.tat-a-rama.com; The Beaches, 2219 Queen St E; noon-midnight Mon-Sat, noon-8pm Sun; streetcar 501) Custom tattoo artwork designs, with portfolios available on-line.

Way Cool Tattoos (Map pp234-5; ☎ 416-603-0145; Queen West, 679 Queen St W; noon-midnight Mon-Sat, noon-8pm Sun; streetcar 501, 511) A biker-style shop that also does piercing.

Shopping

Shopping

Toronto is a city of sinfully unrepentant shopaholics. Nearly every ethnic neighborhood and major thoroughfare has its own grab bag of shops, enough to satisfy even the least conventional of shoppers. New fashion, vintage wear, bookstores and quality artisan crafts are the city's shopping strengths. The city may not be a bargain shopping paradise, especially once taxes are figured in, but visitor refunds are possible and exchange rates tend to happily favor US and European visitors, so go wild!

Tax Refunds

Visitors are eligible for refunds of the 7% federal goods and services tax (GST) paid on nonconsumable goods and short-term accommodation, provided they spend at least $200 and that each eligible receipt totals over $50 before taxes. All original receipts (credit-card slips are not sufficient) must be stamped by customs before leaving the country, whether at the airport or a land-border crossing, when you'll need to make your goods available for inspection.

Drivers can obtain instant cash refunds for claims of less than $500 at participating land border duty-free shops, including at Sarnia, Windsor, Niagara Falls and Queenston. Otherwise mail your stamped receipts within one year of the purchase date, along with boarding passes and a completed GST rebate booklet available at tourist offices or directly from the federal **Visitor Rebate Program** (☎ 902-432-5608, 800-668-4748; www.ccra-adrc.gc.ca/visitors). Allow four to six weeks for processing.

Don't be misled by private companies that distribute 'official tax refund' booklets at visitor centers and duty-free stores. These companies offer to obtain your refund for you and then take up to 20% (minimum $10) for their 'services'. But it's usually just as fast and just as easy to do it yourself.

Shopping Strips

On youthful, schizophrenic Queen St, running east of Spadina Ave as far as the Eaton Centre mall, urban streetwear shops rub shoulders with predictable giants like Roots. Eclectic Queen West, a historic garment district lying west of Spadina Ave toward Trinity-Bellwoods Park, has the lion's share of radical music and clothing shops, many operated by vintage collectors or designers themselves. For correct sizes, check the clothing size chart on p157.

Chichi Bloor-Yorkville is the city center's most exclusive shopping district. This day-spa mecca was once 'Flower Power' central for hippies during the 1960s. Nothing is free here nowadays, least of all love from the haughty sales clerks. Fine-arts and antiques dealers set up shop on Yorkville's laneways and on Yonge St, north of Bloor St, in Rosedale. The beauty of the pieces – and their accompanying price tags – will make you gasp.

Off Chinatown, Kensington Market is worth a look. This is where Toronto's young bohemians buy their Rastafarian and retro clothing, along with superhero lunchboxes. Every house, it seems, hides a few racks of vintage clothing. Little Italy, west of the market along College St, is where traditional grocers hawk their produce as young *belle* seek out the latest imported Italian fashions and Canadian boutiques' sleek designs.

West of the University of Toronto's St George campus, students frequent the Annex for its specialized bookstores, used-music shops and a hodgepodge of artistic shops, especially along Harbord St and on Markham St. Unique Markham Village is a treasure trove of artists' workshops and galleries, bookstores and alt.culture shops found south of Bloor St, just west of Bathurst St. Landmark Honest Ed's is your first stop for bargain shopping, albeit with an overdose of kitsch.

Back downtown the underground PATH (p198) shops are literally bargain basements for discount clothing, everyday goods and services. Artisan shops abound by the Harbourfront, outdoors outfitters stand on King St west of the Theatre Block and there are fringe shops to suit all tastes on the Yonge Street Strip and in the Church-Wellesley Village.

Canadian and international design shops line King St W between Jarvis and Parliament Sts, an area known as the **Design Strip**. Also near downtown, the burgeoning Distillery Historic District is a major draw, with its design shops, art galleries and craft studios all inside a Victorian-era factory. East of the Don River, Leslieville is known for its antiques, retro furnishings and modern design shops along Queen St E. Greektown's the Danforth has old-world grocers, bakers and gyros shops, but also hip boutiques and a healthy lifestyle mini-mall, the Carrot Common.

North of downtown near the intersection of Yonge St and Eglinton Ave, nicknamed 'young and eligible,' some extraordinarily specialized shops serve the whims of the affluent. Second-hand riding gear? Belly-dancing jewelry? It's all there.

Opening Hours

Typical retail shopping hours are 10am until 6pm Monday to Saturday, noon to 5pm Sunday. But this varies depending on the season, the neighborhood and the amount of foot traffic. Prime shopping areas and malls may stay open until 9pm, especially from Thursday onward. Some shops are closed Sunday, a holdover from the days of 'Toronto the Good,' when Eaton's department store drew its curtains to discourage 'sinful' window-shopping. Where no opening hours appear with the following reviews, assume that the usual hours described here apply.

HARBOURFRONT

During weekends in summer, the **Harbourfront Centre** (Map pp228-30; ☎ 416-973-3000) sponsors an outdoor International Marketplace with vendors selling crafts, jewelry and home décor from the Americas, Africa and Asia.

ARCTIC NUNAVUT

Map pp228-30 *Art & Crafts*

☎ 416-203-7889, 800-509-9151; www.ndcorp.nu.ca; Queen's Quay Terminal, 207 Queens Quay W, ground fl; 🕓 10am-6pm; streetcar 509, 510; Ⓟ 2hr free with $50 purchase

Carved Inuksuk figurines, hand-crafted jewelry, embroidered vests, polar footwear and Arctic-related books, videos and DVDs are all sold at Arctic Nunavut. Proceeds benefit the Nunavut Development Corporation, which supports artisans from Canada's Aboriginal-run territory.

PROUD CANADIAN DESIGN & FIRST HAND CANADIAN CRAFTS

Map pp228-30 *Art & Crafts*

☎ 416-603-7413; Queen's Quay Terminal, 207 Queens Quay W, ground fl; 🕓 10am-6pm; streetcar 509, 510; Ⓟ 2hr free with $50 purchase

These adjoining shops blend national pride with tongue-in-cheek humor. Expect to find whimsically hip designs, maybe maple wood furniture, beeswax candles, sassy pillows or festive barware, with something for all budgets.

TILLEY ENDURABLES

Map pp228-30 *Outdoors Equipment*

☎ 416-203-0463, 800-363-8737; www.tilley.com; Queen's Quay Terminal, 207 Queens Quay W, ground fl; 🕓 10am-6pm; streetcar 509, 510; Ⓟ 2hr free with $50 purchase

This Canadian company turns out some of the finest, toughest, low-maintenance threads imaginable (admittedly they're geeky, but they do last) complete with Give 'Em Hell washing instructions. Tilley's signature hats have been worn by everyone from famous explorers to royalty.

YORK QUAY CENTRE

Map pp228-30 *Art & Crafts*

☎ 416-973-4000; www.harbourfront.on.ca; 235 Queens Quay W; 🕓 noon-6pm Tue & Thu-Sun, noon-8pm Wed; streetcar 509, 510

Walk west from Queen's Quay Terminal to discover **Bounty** (☎ 416-973-4993; 🕓 11am-6pm Tue, Sat & Sun, 11am-8pm Wed-Fri), a shop for contemporary Canadian crafts. Artisans in the adjacent **Craft Studio** (☎ 416-973-4963; 🕓 10am-6pm Tue & Sun, 10am-8pm Wed-Sat) blow hot glass, mold clay, weave textiles, design jewelry and teach classes (p200).

FINANCIAL DISTRICT

BAY OF SPIRITS GALLERY

Map pp228-30 *Art & Crafts*

☎ 416-971-5190; 156 Front St W; 🕓 10am-6pm Mon-Fri, 11am-5pm Sat; subway Union

St Lawrence Sunday Antique Market (below)

Apart from the **McMichael Canadian Art Collection** (p187), Bay of Spirits is about the only place to see works by West Coast First Nations artists. This atmospheric art gallery specializes in high-quality Aboriginal carvings and prints, as well as handcrafted jewelry, blankets and embroidered goods. Beware, some less-expensive items are not made in Canada.

GAME TREK Map pp228-30 *Toys & Collectibles*
☎ 416-597-0149; Fairmont Royal York, 100 Front St W, arcade level; 🕒 9am-9pm Mon-Fri, 9am-8pm Sat, 9am-7pm Sun; subway Union
This shop has everything to amuse you and any kids you might have in tow. Staff sell all the classics, such as Yahtzee and Scrabble, along with sci-fi and fantasy games, 3D jigsaw puzzles, model toys, crossword puzzle books and more.

OLD YORK

ARTS ON KING Map pp228-30 *Art & Crafts*
☎ 416-777-9617; 164 King St E; 🕒 10am-6:30pm Mon-Fri, 9am-6pm Sat, 11am-5pm Sun; streetcar 504
Affordable one-of-a-kind gifts by Canadian artisans – featuring folk to fine art, especially hand-blown glass, ceramics and jewelry – are brightly colored and imaginative. The gallery also hosts exhibitions by solo artists.

DISTILLERY HISTORIC DISTRICT
Map pp238-9 *Art & Crafts*
☎ 416-364-1177; www.thedistillerydistrict.com; 55 Mill St; 🕒 daily; streetcar 503, 504
In a restored Victorian-era factory complex, you'll be delighted at an abundance of art and design. Jewelry, pottery and fine-arts studio stores inhabit the **Pure Spirits Building**, just beyond the main gates. More idiosyncratic weavers, embroiderers, glass blowers and silversmiths set up shop in the **Case Goods Building** further south. Tucked off narrow Case Goods laneway, **Pikto** (☎ 416-203-3443; 9am-7pm Mon-Wed, 9am-9pm Thu & Fri, 10am-9pm Sat, noon-7pm Sun) is a unique professional photo lab, gallery and bookshop. Contemporary design shops and art galleries hold sway further west, along the railroad tracks.

OPEN AIR Map pp228-30 *Books & Maps*
☎ 416-363-0719, 800-360-9185; 25 Toronto St; 🕒 10am-6pm Mon-Fri, 10am-5:30pm Sat; subway King
Open Air has a wealth of travel guidebooks, literature, naturalists' field guides, outdoor activity books and maps, all tightly squeezed together. You could browse for hours. Look for a subterranean entrance on the south side of Adelaide St.

ST LAWRENCE SUNDAY ANTIQUE MARKET Map pp228-30 *Antiques & Collectibles*
☎ 416-410-1310; 92 Front St E; 🕒 5am-5pm Sun; streetcar 504
Every Sunday the North Market is overrun by salt-of-the-earth antique dealers with mixed bags of treasures and flea-market kitsch. Show up early. Across the street is the regular ol' **St Lawrence Market** (p47).

Top Five Canadian Art, Craft & Design Shops

- **Distillery Historic District** (p46)
- **Bay of Spirits Gallery** (p145)
- **Proud Canadian Design & First Hand Canadian Crafts** (p145)
- **York Quay Centre** (p145)
- **Guild Shop** (p150)

THEATRE BLOCK & ENTERTAINMENT DISTRICT

Roy Thomson Hall (p48) has its own music store (Map pp228-30 ☎ 416-593-4822 ext 358; 60 Simcoe St; 🕑 11am-6pm Tue-Fri, noon-5pm Sat; subway St Andrew). Hockey fans, don't leave town without your 'Property of Wayne Gretzky' T-shirts or replica team jerseys from **Wayne Gretzky's** (p97).

EUROPE BOUND OUTFITTERS

Map pp228-30 *Outdoors Equipment*

☎ 416-205-9992; www.europebound.com; 383 King St W; 🕑 10am-9pm Mon-Fri, 9am-6:30pm Sat, 11am-5:30pm Sun; streetcar 504

Across from **Mountain Equipment Co-op** (see following), this store carries name-brand gear, such as the North Face and Columbia. Whether you're looking for winter jackets, hydration day-packs, cycling accessories, maps or travel guidebooks, you're in luck here. There's a smaller branch in **Old York** (Map pp228-30; ☎ 416-601-1990; 47 Front St E; 🕑 10am-7pm Mon-Wed, 10am-8pm Thu & Fri, 10am-6pm Sat, 11am-5pm Sun).

HOGTOWN EXTREME SPORTS

Map pp228-30 *Outdoors Equipment*

☎ 416-598-4192; www.hogtownextreme.com; 401 King St W; 🕑 11am-8pm Mon-Fri, 10am-6pm Sat, 11am-5pm Sun; streetcar 504

Upstairs this skate-and-snowboard shop is the hottest place for fans of extremely cool sports. It sells BMX bikes, off-road skateboards, motorized scooters, awesome-looking safety accessories and footwear; ask about rentals.

MOUNTAIN EQUIPMENT CO-OP

Map pp228-30 *Outdoors Equipment*

☎ 416-340-2667, 888-847-0770; www.mec.ca; 400 King St W; 🕑 10am-7pm Mon-Wed, 10am-9pm Thu & Fri, 9am-6pm Sat, 11am-5pm Sun; streetcar 504

A wonderland of quality gear, Canadian-born MEC sells an affordable in-house line of backpacks. Lifetime membership costs $5, and entitles you to weekend privileges on the rock-climbing wall. Workshops, equipment rentals and repair services are available.

TORONTO ANTIQUE CENTRE

Map pp228-30 *Antiques & Collectibles*

☎ 416-345-9941; 276 King St W; 🕑 10am-6pm Tue-Sun; streetcar 504

Formerly at the Harbourfront Antique Market, high-end vendors here deal in Victorian, Edwardian, art-nouveau and art-deco antiques. Attention-grabbing deals include Canadian prints, Tibetan and Nepalese imports at Jewel of Tibet and Mexican silver at Girlztown.

QUEEN STREET & DUNDAS SQUARE

Independent music shops include **Second Vinyl** (Map pp226-7; ☎ 416-977-3737; 2 McCaul St; 🕑 11am-8pm Mon-Fri, 11am-6pm Sat; streetcar 501) and neighboring **Penguin Music** (Map pp226-7; ☎ 416-597-1687; 🕑 11am-8pm Mon-Fri, 11am-7pm Sat, 11am-6pm Sun). Nearby **ChumCityStore** (Map pp226-7; ☎ 416-591-5757 ext 2523; 277 Queen St W; 🕑 9am-6pm Mon-Tue, 9am-8pm Wed, 9am-9pm Thu, 9am-11pm Fri, 10am-6pm Sat, noon-5pm Sun) sells Canadian TV souvenirs.

Top Five Vintage Fashion Shops

- **Courage My Love** (p153)
- **Preloved** (p156)
- **Brava** (p155)
- **Cabaret Nostalgia** (p155)
- **Black Market** (p147)

BAY

Map pp228-30 *Department Store*

☎ 416-861-9111; 176 Yonge St; 🕑 10am-9pm Mon-Fri, 9:30am-7pm Sat, noon-6pm Sun; subway Queen

Victorian-era entrepreneur Robert Simpson's successful department store merged with the historic Hudson's Bay Company to create what is now known simply as The Bay. Notice the broad yellow stripe across the entrance doors that echoes the blue stripes used to measure animal pelts on the original Hudson's Bay traders' blankets. There's another branch in **Bloor-Yorkville** (Map pp231-3; ☎ 416-972-333; 44 Bloor St E; 🕑 10am-7pm Mon-Wed, 10am-9pm Thu & Fri, 9:30am-6pm Sat, noon-6pm Sun; subway Bloor-Yonge).

BLACK MARKET

Map pp226-7 *Vintage Fashion*

☎ 416-591-7945; 319 Queen St W; 🕑 11am-7pm Mon-Fri, 10am-7pm Sat, 11am-6pm Sun; streetcar 501

On the prowl for retro 1970s and '80s T-shirts with icons like Atari and ET? Look no further. Basement-level **Black Market Megawarehouse**

(Map pp226-7; ☎ 416-599-5858; 256A Queen St W; ⏰ 11am-7pm) has thrift store-worthy deals on Levi's, jackets and Western shirts.

DECIBEL Map pp226-7 *Fashion*
☎ 416-506-9648; 200 Queen St W; ⏰ 11am-7pm Mon-Sat, noon-6pm Sun; streetcar 501
So hip there's no need for a sign on the door, Decibel vends faux retro fashions for men. Aloha shirts, art-deco cigarette cases and funky toques (that's Canadian for 'hats,' ya know) are sold.

EATON CENTRE Map pp226-7 *Shopping Mall*
☎ 416-598-8560; 220 Yonge St; ⏰ 10am-9pm Mon-Fri, 9:30am-7pm Sat, noon-6pm Sun; subway Queen, Dundas
Just a few years ago, historic Eaton's department store went bankrupt (and was later bought by the Sears chain), but not before spawning this immense everyday-people's mall with hundreds of Canadian and international chain stores.

JOHN FLUEVOG Map pp226-7 *Shoes*
☎ 416-581-1420; www.fluevog.com; 242 Queen St W; ⏰ 11am-7pm Mon-Wed, 11am-8pm Thu & Fri, 10am-7pm Sat, noon-6pm Sun; streetcar 501
Creating one-of-a-kind shoes with attitude, this Vancouver-based designer attributes '50s furniture design and anything vintage as his inspirations. The website has previews of Fluevog's latest whimsies, costing up to a few hundred dollars per fantastic pair. Shoes come as tough-girl chunky or sex-kitten pointy as you like, with equally hip selections for men.

LE CHÂTEAU Map pp226-7 *Fashion*
Chateâuworks; ☎ 416-971-9314; 336-40 Queen St W; ⏰ 9:30am-9pm; streetcar 501, 510
Montréal-based chains such as Le Château sell sinfully affordable French-inspired fashions, albeit spray-painted with Québecois urban attitude. **Bedo** (Map pp226-7; ☎ 416-506-1580; 318 Queen St W; ⏰ 10am-6pm), nearby, has sexy snakeskin-print cocktail dresses and slim men's suits, all priced to impress.

LUSH Map pp226-7 *Specialty*
☎ 416-599-5874; 312 Queen St W; ⏰ 10am-8pm Mon-Thu, 10am-9pm Fri & Sat, noon-7pm Sun; streetcar 501, 510
This UK-based organic body, bath and beauty store does a huge Internet business, but you can get special products – Sex Bomb bath ballistics or Black Magic massage bars – for half-price in person. Just inhale the scents as you walk by...ahhhh. Also in **Bloor-Yorkville** (Map pp231-3; ☎ 416-960-5874; 116 Cumberland St; ⏰ 10am-8pm Mon-Sat, noon-6pm Sun; subway Bay).

MISDEMEANOURS Map pp231-3 *Fashion*
☎ 416-351-8758; 322½ Queen St W; ⏰ 10am-7pm Mon-Wed & Sat, 10am-8pm Thu & Fri, noon-6pm Sun; streetcar 501
An unbelievably cool clothing store for girls, Misdemeanors carries princess dresses and rock star outfits fitted for toddlers to teens. Its big sister, **Fashion Crimes** (☎ 416-592-9001; 395 Queen St W; ⏰ 10am-8pm Mon-Wed & Sat, 10am-9pm Thu & Fri, 11am-6pm Sun), sells antique-styled wear that's beloved by alt-fashionistas.

MODROBES Map pp226-7 *Fashion*
☎ 416-597-9560; 239 Queen St W; ⏰ 10am-7pm Mon-Wed, 10am-8pm Thu & Fri, 11am-8pm Sat, noon-6pm Sun; streetcar 501
The guiding motto is 'postmodern functional lounge wear.' Signature pants, skirts, shirts and hoodies are so comfy you could take final exams (or long plane flights) in them, which explains this Canuck designer's popularity with university students and backpackers.

NOISE Map pp226-7 *Fashion*
☎ 416-971-6479; 275 Queen St W; ⏰ 11am-7pm Mon-Sat, noon-6pm Sun; streetcar 501
Guys get stoked on skater gear, club wear and rave fashions here. A few doors down, **Noisy Girls** (Map pp226-7; ☎ 416-598-1183; 271 Queen St W; ⏰ 11am-7pm Mon-Sat, noon-6pm Sun) caters to the opposite sex.

PAGES BOOKS & MAGAZINES
Map pp226-7 *Books & Magazines*
☎ 416-598-1447; www.pagesbooks.ca; 256 Queen St W; ⏰ 9:30am-10pm Mon & Wed, 9:30-11pm Thu & Fri, 10am-11pm Sat, 11am-8pm Sun; streetcar 501
Open your mind at what is arguably Toronto's finest independent bookstore. Pages stocks new literature and nonfiction titles, small press editions, chapbooks and 'zines that cover the weird outer limits. This is Not a Reading Series happens here.

ROOTS Map pp226-7 *Fashion*
☎ 416-593-9640; Eaton Centre, 220 Yonge St; ⏰ 10am-9pm Mon-Fri, 9am-7pm Sat, 11am-6pm Sun; subway Dundas

Basically a maple leaf–emblazoned version of the Gap, Roots designs athletic streetwear that's unmistakably Canadian. In season, look for NHL hockey and Toronto International Film Festival souvenir merchandise here. Branches around town include **Bloor-Yorkville** (Map pp231-3; ☎ 416-323-3289; 101 Bloor St W; subway Bay).

SILVER SNAIL COMIC SHOP

Map pp226-7 *Toys & Collectibles*

☎ 416-593-0889; 367 Queen St W; 🕑 10am-6pm Mon & Tue, 10am-8pm Wed-Fri, 10am-7pm Sat, noon-6pm Sun; streetcar 501

A fun-o-rama playground of rare and new comic books, action figures, sci-fi collectibles and Japanese *anime* toys satisfies eager patrons from six to 60 years old. Cases displaying the most valuable vintage items are smudged with telltale nose-prints.

YONGE STREET STRIP & CHURCH-WELLESLEY VILLAGE

FASTBALL SPORTSCARDS

Map pp231-3 *Toys & collectibles*

☎ 416-323-0403; 624 Yonge St; 🕑 11am-7pm Mon-Wed, 11am-8pm Thu & Fri, 11am-6pm Sat, noon-4pm Sun; subway Wellesley

If an autographed hockey puck (from $40), rare 20th-century sports cards (mostly football, baseball and hockey) or retro sci-fi collectibles are what you seek, just ask the enthusiastic owner here.

GLAD DAY Map pp231-3 *Books & Magazines*

☎ 416-961-4161, 877-783-3725; 598A Yonge St; 🕑 10am-7pm Sat-Wed, 10am-9pm Thu & Fri; subway Wellesley

Fighting for the right to import politically (and erotically) hot lesbigay material since the early 1970s, Canada's oldest queer bookstore Glad Day stocks 'everything under the rainbow,' including videos, magazines and music.

NORTHBOUND LEATHER

Map pp231-3 *Specialty Fashion*

☎ 416-972-1037; www.northboundleather.com; 586 Yonge St; 🕑 11am-7pm Mon-Wed, 10am-9pm Thu & Fri, 10am-6pm Sat, noon-5pm Sun; subway Wellesley

Unshakably cool customers no longer opt for the discreet back door entrance at family-owned Northbound Leather. Although times have changed, the quality of custom-crafted fetish gear and fantasy fashion has not. Check the website for ideas.

PLAY DE RECORD Map pp226-7 *Music*

☎ 416-586-0380; 357A Yonge St; 🕑 noon-8pm Mon-Wed, noon-10pm Thu & Fri, noon-9pm Sat, 1pm-6pm Sun; subway Dundas

'Keepin' It Real Since 1990.' Aimed at DJs and underground music lovers, this record shop at the back of an electronics store is all vinyl, all the time. It specializes in rare and out-of-print records, with all sorts of dance and underground tunes.

RELEASE RECORDS Map pp231-3 *Music*

☎ 416-962-1400, 877-512-1400; www.releaserecords.com; 527 Yonge St; 🕑 noon-8pm Mon-Fri, noon-6pm Sat, noon-4pm Sun; subway Wellesley

A DJ's haven for house, progressive, techno, nu breaks, drum 'n bass and more. Vinyl and CD new releases include US, UK and European imports. The website has encyclopedic MP3 downloads, charts as well as streaming radio. Nearby **Refried Beats** (Map pp231-3; ☎ 416-920-2417; 599 Yonge St; 🕑 10am-9pm Mon-Sat, 11am-7pm Sun) sells used CDs and DVDs.

SAM THE RECORD MAN

Map pp226-7 *Music*

☎ 416-646-2775; 347 Yonge St; 🕑 9am-10pm Mon-Thu; 9am-midnight Fri & Sat, 9am-7pm Sun; subway Dundas

As part of a gargantuan neon chain, neon-emblazoned Sam's is where you'll find extensive selections of imports and Canadian tunes, from East Coast traditional to indie rock. This multi-level branch seems like a lab rat maze, but with patience you'll discover great bargains.

THIS AIN'T THE ROSEDALE LIBRARY

Map pp231-3 *Books & Magazines*

☎ 416-929-9912; 483 Church St; 🕑 10am-10pm Sun-Thu, 10am-11pm Fri & Sat; subway Wellesley

At this lesbigay community institution, the staff really know their stuff, which means novels, modern first editions, nonfiction titles, children's books and piles of magazines. Nearby **Out on the Street** (Map pp231-3; ☎ 416-967-2759; 551 Church St; 🕑 10am-8pm Mon-Wed, 10am-9pm Thu-Sat, 11am-6pm Sun) sells Pride paraphernalia.

Top Five Quirky Shops

- **Suspect Video & Culture** (p153) Where Hollywood of the North ferrets out rare videos, DVDs and more
- **Come as You Are** (p155) A delicious training ground for life's bedroom pursuits
- **Design Exchange** (DX; p45) Whimsical and technical design goods for everyday life
- **Beguiling** (p151) Nirvana for fans of indie comics
- **Iodine & Arsenic** (p141) A Queen West spa that could be easily mistaken for a fetish shop

BLOOR-YORKVILLE

CHAPTERS Map pp231-3 *Books & Magazines*
☎ 416-920-9299; www.chapters.indigo.ca; 110 Bloor St W; 🕑 9am-10pm Sun-Thu, 9am-11pm Fri & Sat; subway Bay
Chapters-Indigo is Canada's corporate bookselling juggernaut. This four-story branch has self-service Internet terminals, two Starbucks and also sells music and DVDs. Nearby **Indigo** (Map pp231-3; ☎ 416-591-3622; Manulife Centre, 55 Bloor St W; 🕑 10am-9:30pm Mon-Fri, 10am-7:30pm Sat, noon-6pm Sun) spotlights Canadian writers with in-store displays and author events.

CLUB MONACO Map pp231-3 *Fashion*
☎ 416-591-8837; 157 Bloor St W; 🕑 10-7pm Mon-Wed, 10am-8pm Thu & Fri, 11am-7pm Sat, noon-6pm Sun; subway Museum
Club Monaco's refined modern basics for men and women are often on sale. This grandiose building once housed the UT Department of Household Sciences, which explains the amusing Ionic columns over the entryway. The attached **Colony Kitchen** (p102) is a hot spot.

GUILD SHOP Map pp231-3 *Art & Crafts*
☎ 416-921-1721; www.craft.on.ca; 118 Cumberland St; 🕑 10am-6pm Mon-Wed, 10am-7pm Thu, 10am-6pm Fri & Sat, noon-5pm Sun; subway Bay
The Ontario Crafts Council has been promoting artisans for over 70 years. Ceramics, jewelry, glassworks, prints and carvings make up most of the displays, but you could catch a special exhibition of Pangnirtung weaving or Cape Dorset graphics. Staff are knowledgeable about First Nations art.

HOLT RENFREW
Map pp231-3 *Department Store*
☎ 416-922-2333; 50 Bloor St W; 🕑 10am-6pm Mon-Wed & Sat, 10am-8pm Thu & Fri, noon-6pm Sun; subway Bloor-Yonge
It aims to be the sleekest, most luxurious department store in Toronto. You may stumble upon

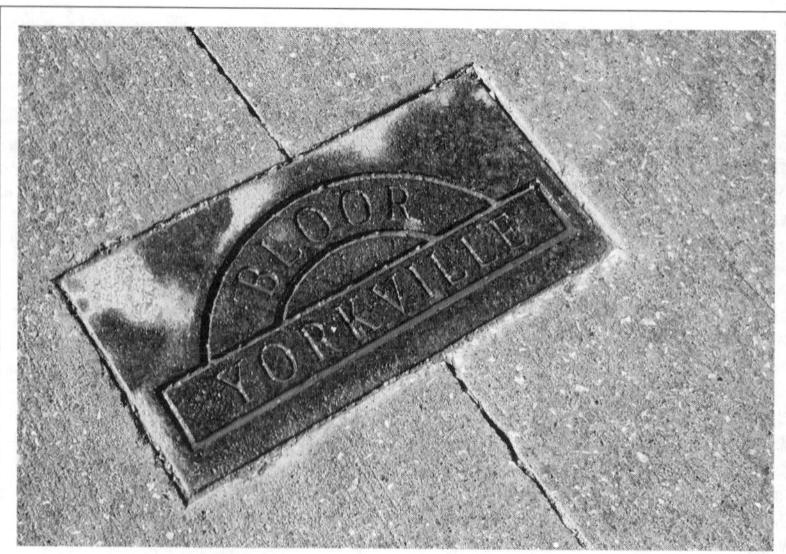

Cumberland St, Bloor-Yorkville (p55)

a trunk show or a famous designer making an appearance. The department store anchors the Holt Renfrew Centre, a shopping mall with over two dozen high-end and specialty shops.

KIDDING AWOUND

Map pp231-3 *Toys & Collectibles*

☎ 416-926-8996; 91 Cumberland St; 🕙 10:30-6pm Mon-Sat, noon-5pm Sun; subway Bay

Whether you want amusements for your hotel room, children's toy box or next cocktail party, Kidding Awound has it all: yo-yos, wind-up gizmos, vintage collectibles, board games and retro novelty items, all stuffed into a joyfully tumbled space.

L'ATELIER GRIGORIAN Map pp231-3 *Music*

☎ 416-922-6477; 70 Yorkville Ave; 🕙 10am-6pm Mon-Thu & Sat, 10am-8pm Fri, noon-5pm Sun; subway Bay

Aficionados of classical, jazz and new-world music should visit this shop for its new releases and listening stations. Staff can be snooty, but their taste is impeccable.

LA MAISON DE LA PRESSE INTERNATIONALE

Map pp231-3 *Books & Magazines*

☎ 416-928-2328; 124-126 Yorkville Ave; 🕙 8:30am-11pm; subway Bay

This upmarket newsstand sells an array of magazines, international newspapers and French-language guidebooks. Presse Internationale shops include: **Yonge Street Strip** (Map pp226-7; ☎ 416-260-0480; 363 Yonge St; subway Dundas); the **Annex** (Map pp236-7; ☎ 416-531-1187; 537 Bloor St W; subway Bathurst); **Little Italy** (Map pp236-7; ☎ 416-535-9666; 622 College St; streetcar 506); and the Beaches (Map p240; ☎ 416-690-6333; 2068 Queen St E; streetcar 501).

PEACHY FRESH Map pp231-3 *Fashion*

☎ 416-513-9884; 111 Yorkville Ave, 2nd fl; 🕙 11:30am-6pm Mon-Sat, noon-5pm Sun; subway Bay

Another cooperative venture by the folks behind Kensington Market's **Fresh Baked Goods** (p154) and Queen West's **Fresh Collective** (p156), local designers here display light-hearted clothing inventions in the upper-story windows.

SCIENCE CITY

Map pp231-3 *Toys & Collectibles*

☎ 416-968-2627, 877-260-8433; www.sciencecity.ca; Holt Renfrew Centre, 50 Bloor St W, concourse level; 🕙 10am-6pm Mon-Wed, 10am-8pm Thu & Fri, 11am-6pm Sat; subway Bloor-Yonge

Science City has games, gear and puzzles for geeks, both young and young-at-heart. Peruse the rooftop astronomy gear, optical illusion books, anti-gravity space pens, do-it-yourself educational kits and brain teasers galore.

THEATREBOOKS Map pp231-3 *Books*

☎ 416-922-7175; www.theatrebooks.com; 11 St Thomas St; 🕙 10am-7pm Mon-Fri, 10am-6pm Sat, noon-5pm Sun; subway Bay

No subject is neglected here. Original scripts, music, film, dance, drama theory, comedy, opera and costume design books are shelved alongside the latest screenwriting software, various DVDs and videos. Events feature readings by playwrights, actors and movie critics.

THOMAS HINDS TOBACCONIST

Map pp231-3 *Specialty*

☎ 416-927-7703; 800-637-5750; www.thomashinds.ca; 8 Cumberland St; 🕙 9am-7pm Mon-Tue, 9am-9pm Wed-Fri, 9am-6pm Sat, noon-5pm Sun; subway Bloor-Yonge

It's doing quite a business today out of its walk-in humidor, especially with US citizens who can't get Cuban cigars back home. Thomas Hinds' flagship store also has a smoking lounge.

UNIVERSITY OF TORONTO & THE ANNEX

Charming Markham Village (p58) is full of workshops and galleries, some of which are inside artists' houses. Most are closed Monday.

BEGUILING Map pp236-7 *Books & Magazines*

☎ 416-533-9168; 601 Markham St; 🕙 11am-7pm Mon-Thu & Sat, 11am-9pm Fri, noon-6pm Sun; subway Bathurst

It's the kind of crowded, mixed-up place that Robert Crumb would drop by (and in fact, he has). Be mesmerized by original 'zines, indie comics, pop culture books, limited edition artworks and posters. Check the associated website (www.torontocomics.com) for events across the city.

CEDAR BASKET Map pp236-7 *Art & Crafts*

☎ 416-964-9087; 16 Spadina Ave; 🕙 10am-6pm Mon-Wed & Fri, 10am-8pm Thu, 10am-4pm Sat; subway Spadina

A Bibliophile's Treasure Trove

Torontonians seem to be an awfully literate bunch. Many first-rate independent bookstores are found downtown and the student-dominated Annex neighborhood, but others pop up just about anywhere across the city. Our picks are:

A Different Booklist (Map pp236-7; ☎ 416-538-0889; The Annex, 746 Bathurst St; 🕑 10am-6pm Mon-Wed & Sat, 10am-7pm Thu & Fri; subway Bathurst, streetcar 510, 511) 'Live literature from the *third world*,' including books for kids.

Abelard Books (Map pp234-5; ☎ 416-504-2665; 519 Queen West, Queen St W; 🕑 11am-6pm Mon-Sat, noon-5pm Sun; streetcar 501) Mostly second-hand books in all genres, with a Canadiana section.

Another Man's Poison (Map pp226-7; ☎ 416-593-6451; Queen Street, 29 McCaul St; 🕑 10am-5pm Mon-Sat; streetcar 501) Used, rare and out-of-print books on art, design, architecture and antiques.

Another Story Bookshop (Map pp238-9; ☎ 416-462-1104; Greektown, 164 Danforth Ave; 🕑 11am-7pm Mon-Fri, 10am-6pm Sat, noon-6pm Sun; subway Broadview) Books about diversity, equity and social justice. Has a kids' section.

Bakka (Map pp231-3; ☎ 416-963-9993; Yonge Street Strip, 598 Yonge St; 🕑 11am-7pm Mon-Thu, 11am-8pm Fri, 11am-6pm Sat, noon-5pm Sun; subway Wellesley) New sci-fi, horror and fantasy volumes.

Balfour Books (Map pp236-7; ☎ 416-531-9911; Little Italy, 601 College St; 🕑 noon-11pm; streetcar 506) A good, dependable used bookstore in Little Italy.

Ballenford Books on Architecture (Map pp236-7; ☎ 416-588-0800; Markham Village, 600 Markham St; 🕑 noon-5pm Sun & Mon, 10am-6pm Tue-Sat; subway Bathurst, streetcar 510, 511) Architectural drawings hang on the walls here.

Cookbook Store (Map pp231-3; ☎ 416-920-2665, 800-268-6018; www.cook-book.com; Bloor-Yorkville; 850 Yonge St; 🕑 10am-7pm Mon-Fri, 10am-6pm Sat, noon-5pm Sun; subway Bloor-Yonge) Check the website for guest chef appearances and free recipes, maybe for moose stew.

David Mirvish Books (Map pp236-7; ☎ 416-531-9975; Markham Village, 596 Markham St; 🕑 10am-6pm Mon-Wed, 10am-7pm Thu & Fri, 11am-6pm Sat & Sun; subway Bathurst, streetcar 510, 511) Owned by 'Honest Ed' Mirvish's son. Over 80% of its stock is dedicated to the fine arts.

Librarie Champlain (Map pp238-9; ☎ 416-364-4345; East Toronto, 468 Queen St E; 🕑 10am-6pm Mon-Sat; streetcar 501) It's the largest French-language bookstore in Toronto, selling magazines, language-learning materials, videos and Montréal jazz festival recordings.

Omega Centre Bookstore (Map pp231-3; ☎ 416-975-9086, 888-663-6377; Bloor-Yorkville, 29 Yorkville Ave; 🕑 10am-9pm Mon-Fri, 10am-6pm Sat, 11am-5pm Sun; subway Bay) A serene mecca for alternative religions and out-there philosophies. Have your tarot cards read while you're here.

Parentbooks (Map pp236-7; ☎ 416-537-8334, 800-209-9182; The Annex, 201 Harbord St; 🕑 10:30am-6pm Mon-Sat; streetcar 511) Thousands of multicultural books and videos aimed at families.

Seekers Books (Map pp236-7; ☎ 416-925-1982; The Annex, 509 Bloor St W; 🕑 till midnight; subway Bathurst) Enlightenment may come tumbling down from the shelves of used academic and popular titles.

Sleuth of Baker Street (Map p225; ☎ 416-483-3111; Greater Toronto Area, 1600 Bayview Ave, south of Eglinton Ave; 🕑 10am-6pm Mon-Sat, 10am-8pm Fri, noon-4pm Sun; bus 11) Mystery books: out-of-print, first editions and Sherlockiana.

Some others to look out for:

Beguiling (p151)

Chapters (p150)

Dragon Lady Comics & Paper Nostalgia (p154)

Glad Day (p149)

La Maison de la Presse Internationale (p151)

Open Air (p146)

Pages Books & Magazines (p148)

Silver Snail Comic Shop (p149)

TheatreBooks (p151)

This Ain't the Rosedale Library (p149)

Toronto Women's Bookstore (p153)

The Native Canadian Centre of Toronto's nonprofit gift shop sells original works by First Nations artists, including beaded moccasins, bone choker necklaces, porcupine quill boxes, dreamcatchers, pottery, carvings and jewelry. It also carries Aboriginal music CDs.

CLAY DESIGN Map pp236-7 *Art & Crafts*

☎ 416-964-3330; 170 Brunswick Ave; 🕓 11am-6pm Tue-Fri, 10am-6pm Sat, noon-5pm Sun; bus 94

This potters' studio and gallery stands among a row of unique shops on Harbord St. When we last dropped by, it was exhibiting teapots, anything from calm Zen-inspired designs to fantastical Dr Seuss–like towers. **Things Japanese** (Map pp236-7; ☎ 416-967-9797; 159 Harbord St; 🕓 11am-6pm Mon-Sat, 11am-7pm Fri, noon-5pm Sun) is nearby.

GOOD FOR HER Map pp236-7 *Specialty*

☎ 416-588-0900, 877-588-0900; www.goodforher.com; 175 Harbord St; 🕓 11am-7pm Mon-Thu, 11am-8pm Fri, 11am-6pm Sat, noon-5pm Sun, women & transgender patrons only 11am-2pm Thu, noon-5pm Sun; bus 94

This low-key sex shop is owned, operated and patronized by women (although men are welcome outside of women-only shopping hours). A discriminating selection of erotic art, signature massage oils, how-to books and videos is rounded out by lesbian-friendly and Japanese-made toys. Check on-line for weekly schedules of sex-positive workshops.

HONEST ED'S

Map pp236-7 *Department Store*

☎ 416-537-1574; 581 Bloor St W; 🕓 10am-9pm Mon-Fri, 10am-6pm Sat, 11am-6pm Sun; subway Bathurst

Landmark Honest Ed's is a discount bonanza of clothes, household items and low-cost outdoor gear. In business for over 50 years, it's now quite a spectacle with the marquee lights reminiscent of a three-ring circus. Call Ed's answering machine to check opening hours.

SUSPECT VIDEO & CULTURE

Map pp236-7 *Specialty*

☎ 416-588-6674; www.suspectvideo.com; 605 Markham St; 🕓 noon-11pm Mon-Sat, noon-10pm Sun; subway Bathurst

Renowned Suspect Video is the place to buy or rent hundreds of eclectic, independent and rare videos and DVDs, from '70s kung-fu flicks to new art-house films. It also stocks alternative books, 'zines, comix and bizarre toys. This T.O. legend has another branch on **Queen West** (Map pp234-5; ☎ 416-504-7135; 619 Queen St W; 🕓 noon-11pm Mon-Sat, 1-10pm Sun; streetcar 511).

TORONTO WOMEN'S BOOKSTORE

Map pp236-7 *Books & Magazines*

☎ 416-922-8744, 800-861-8233; www.womensbookstore.com; 73 Harbord St; 🕓 10:30am-6pm Mon-Wed & Sat, 10:30am-8pm Thu & Fri, noon-5pm Sun; streetcar 510

Books authored by women of all backgrounds, including First Nations, African and Caribbean communities, are found beside queer and feminist theory texts. This nonprofit bookstore also sponsors readings, workshops and other events.

TROVE Map pp236-7 *Fashion*

☎ 416-516-1258; 793 Bathurst St; 🕓 11am-7pm Mon-Fri, 10am-6pm Sat, noon-5pm Sun; subway Bathurst

Quirky metal trees are filled with all kinds of brightly colored urban handbags, jewelry, gloves, belts and hats. Most of these items are Canadian-made designs and the staff are in the know about the local fashion scene.

KENSINGTON MARKET

COURAGE MY LOVE

Map pp234-5 *Vintage Fashion*

☎ 416-979-1992; 14 Kensington Ave; 🕓 11:30am-6pm Mon-Fri, 11am-6pm Sat, 1-5pm Sun; streetcar 505, 510

Vintage clothing stores have been around Kensington Market for decades, but Courage My Love still amazes fashion mavens with its second-hand slip dresses, retro pants and white dress shirts in a cornucopia of styles. The beads, buttons, leather goods and silver jewelry for sale are hand-picked.

EXILE Map pp234-5 *Fashion*

☎ 416-596-0827; 20 Kensington Ave; 🕓 9am-7pm Mon-Sat, 10am-6pm Sun; streetcar 505, 510

More outrageously glam than the rest of Kensington Ave, Exile has outrageous outfits, platinum blonde wigs, rock-star sunglasses and other riot girl accessories. It also stocks new designs by the likes of Porn Star Clothing.

Kensington Market (p153)

FRESH BAKED GOODS
Map pp234-5 *Fashion*
☎ 416-966-0123; 274 Augusta Ave; 🕓 11:30am-7pm Mon-Sat, noon-6pm Sun; streetcar 506
This shop's colorful knitwear is as lighthearted as it is one-of-a-kind. It's all the rage, too, with celebs stopping by for a sexy off-the-shoulder mohair or 'technofur' sweater. Sassy embroidered T-shirts and underwear sell out fast.

PHO-PA Map pp234-5 *Fashion*
☎ 416-979-9444; 160 Baldwin St; 🕓 11am-6pm; streetcar 510
This block of Baldwin St is an up-and-coming address for urban streetwear. It's more cutting-edge than Kensington Ave, with this particular shop owned by a twenty-something designer. If Pho-pa isn't here by the time you arrive, something else is sure to have taken its place.

ROACH-O-RAMA Map pp234-5 *Specialty*
☎ 416-203-6990; 191A Baldwin St; 🕓 hr vary; streetcar 510
Turn off your brain at revered Roach-o-Rama, a head shop that has been proudly 'serving potheads since, ah, I forget.' A chill-out garden patio at the back, Hot Box Cafe, serves hemp-baked goodies and smoothies.

LITTLE ITALY

DRAGON LADY COMICS & PAPER NOSTALGIA Map pp236-7 *Toys & Collectibles*
☎ 416-536-7460; 609 College St; 🕓 noon-8pm Sun-Thu, noon-10pm Fri & Sat; streetcar 506
A rare destination, Dragon Lady sells authentic and reprinted classic comic books, original art, collectible toys and vintage magazines. Display cases that safeguard the most priceless items have been known to hypnotize window shoppers.

GIRL FRIDAY Map pp236-7 *Fashion*
☎ 416-531-1036; 776 College St; 🕓 noon-7pm Mon-Sat, noon-5pm Sun; streetcar 506
Clothing for women moves beyond straight lines, but the look is still smooth as silk. Annual collections capture trends for modish fashionistas; wide-legged pants, tie-back dresses and svelte tops can be worn right from the office into Little Italy's lounge scene.

LILLIPUT HATS
Map pp236-7 *Specialty Fashion*
☎ 416-536-5933; 462 College St; 🕓 10am-6pm Mon-Fri, 11am-5pm Sat; streetcar 506, 511
Whether you would like something worthy of Katharine Hepburn, a nouveau cowboy hat or

a leopard-print velveteen creation, shop here. The milliner's annual hat collections for men and women are even sold at Toronto's top department stores.

SIM & JONES Map pp236-7 *Fashion*
☎ 416-920-2573; 388 College St; 11am-6pm Mon-Wed, 11am-7pm Thu-Sat, noon-5pm Sun, closed Mon Jan-Mar; streetcar 506

Nearer to Kensington Market than Little Italy, but closer to the latter in spirit, this local designers' gallery offers clothing for men and women. Personalized service compliments the sexy accessories, including leather goods, jewelry and handbags.

SOAPSCOPE Map pp236-7 *Specialty*
☎ 416-588-8621; www.soapscope.com; 828 College St; 10am-7pm Mon-Fri, 10am-6pm Sat; streetcar 506

Learn how to make a bath-time wonderland with do-it-yourself bath-bomb kits, soap-making instructions and supplies including essential oils, fragrances and colorants. Green tea lotions or grapefruit-scented candles, anyone? Check the website for upcoming workshops.

SOUNDSCAPES Map pp236-7 *Music*
☎ 416-537-1620; 572 College St; 10am-11pm Mon-Sat, 11am-10pm Sun; streetcar 506

This is an audiophile's spot that stocks new CDs in varied genres. Whether it's indie rock, alt-country or club sounds, the after-dark crowd is very happening. Staff can be music geeks, but if you speak their language, this is the place.

QUEEN WEST

Atmospheric **Red Tea Box** (p107) sells Southeast Asian crafts and tea ware. Stop by **Tequila Bookworm** (p132) for magazines, books and java. Sleek **Heel Boy** (Map pp234-5; ☎ 416-362-4335; 682 Queen St W; streetcar 501) is one of Queen West's many shoes stores.

ANNIE THOMPSON STUDIO
Map pp234-5 *Fashion*
☎ 416-703-3843; 674 Queen St W; 11am-6pm Tue-Sat, 1-5pm Sun; streetcar 501

Internationally famous designer Annie Thompson's shop presents local clothing creations with a bold, yet relaxed urban modish look for both sexes. Her personal motto: 'Personality is a terrible thing to waste.' Pieces are individually numbered like limited-edition artwork.

Top Five Local Fashion Designers' Shops

- Annie Thompson Studio (p155)
- Eza Wear (p156)
- Fresh Collective (p156)
- Girl Friday (p154)
- Modrobes (p148)

An honorable mention goes to Vancouver-born **John Fluevog** (p148) shoes, too.

BRAVA Map pp234-5 *Vintage Fashion*
☎ 416-504-8742; 483 Queen St W; 10:30am-7:30pm Mon-Sat, 1-6pm Sun; streetcar 501

Brava is a brilliant array of vintage wear that could give Kensington Ave a run for its money. Both guys and gals can afford to find the outfit of their dreams here, so perhaps this shop should call itself 'Bravo!'

CABARET NOSTALGIA
Map pp234-5 *Vintage Fashion*
☎ 416-504-7126; 672 Queen St W; 11am-6pm Mon-Sat, 11am-7pm Thu & Fri, 1-5pm Sun; streetcar 501

Cabaret Nostalgia has everything that swings: big-band gowns, old-time suits and pearl-buttoned silk gloves. **Circa Forty** (Map pp234-5; ☎ 416-504-0880; 456 Queen St W; 11am-6pm Mon-Sat, noon-5pm Sun) nearby also carries vintage clothes; its motto is 'lighten up and dress right.'

COME AS YOU ARE Map pp234-5 *Specialty*
☎ 416-504-7934, 877-858-3160; www.comeasyouare.com; 701 Queen St W; 11am-7pm Mon-Wed, 11am-9pm Thu & Fri, 11am-6pm Sat, noon-5pm Sun; streetcar 501

Catering to both sexes and all kinds of orientations, Canada's pioneering co-op sex shop sells books, toys, videos and DVDs. You may even be inspired to sign up for a workshop on erotic photography or Bondage 101!

COSMOS RECORDS Map pp234-5 *Music*
☎ 416-603-0254; 607A Queen St W; noon-8pm Tue-Sun; streetcar; 501

A vinyl specialty shop offering jazz, Latin, African and soul beats is a rare find. Cosmos' collections of rare Brazilian and Blue Note jazz are priced sky-high, but justifiably so.

EZA WEAR Map pp234-5 *Fashion*

☎ 416-975-1388; 695 Queen St W; 🕒 noon-6pm Mon, 11am-6pm Tue-Thu, 11am-7pm Fri & Sat, noon-5pm Sun; streetcar 501

Dreamed up by two students from Montréal, Eza turns out a sophisticated line of affordable, extremely wearable designer clothes for women and men. Most pieces are softly tailored, often styled with prints of foreign flavors.

F/X Map pp234-5 *Specialty*

☎ 416-504-0888; 515 Queen St W; 🕒 10am-7pm Mon-Sat, noon-6pm Sun; streetcar 501

Eclectic F/X sells sock monkeys, kitsch collectibles, hip designer accessories, vintage clothes, fairy-tale shoes, candy-flavored lip gloss and ice cream. It's absolutely eye-catching, even without the outdoor plastic-flower collage sign.

FLEURTJE Map pp234-5 *Fashion*

☎ 416-410-4948; 917 Queen St W; 🕒 11am-6pm Tue-Sat; streetcar 501

Designer Nicole Fleur has made a name for herself at Fleurtje, which means 'little flower.' Bold and stylish urban handbags have specialized pockets for cell phones, PDAs etc; her signature 'flip-flap' bags will last far longer than a season.

FRESH COLLECTIVE Map pp234-5 *Fashion*

☎ 416-594-1313; 692 Queen St W; 🕒 11am-7pm Mon-Fri, 11am-6pm Sat, noon-5pm Sun; streetcar 501

Similar to Yorkville's **Peachy Fresh** (p151), this storefront showcases the most contemporary wearables by a dozen local Toronto designers, who you may find working on new creations behind the counter.

GALLERY SIX ONE ONE

Map pp234-5 *Art & Crafts*

☎ 416-364-5189; 611 Queen St W; 🕒 11am-6pm Mon-Thu, 11am-7pm Fri, 11am-6pm Sat, 12-5pm Sun; streetcar 501

Works by dozens of Canadian artisans are exhibited at this open-hearted gallery and gift shop. Stop by to browse the temporary exhibitions of original prints and paintings, ceramics, home décor and photography.

GRREAT STUFF Map pp234-5 *Fashion*

☎ 416-536-6770; 870 Queen St W; streetcar 501

This distinctive menswear shop sells faux-vintage casual fashions, as well as hip looks for the workplace and nightlife. Racks reveal a mi[x] of local designers and European imports.

JAPANESE PAPER PLACE

Map pp234-5 *Specialty*

☎ 416-703-0089; www.japanesepaperplace.com; 887 Queen St W; 🕒 10am-6pm Mon-Wed & Sat, 10am-8pm Thu & Fri; streetcar 501

Strikingly beautiful paper goods at this import shop include bound journals, organizer boxes, special occasion cards and do-it-yourself paper making kits. With the money needed to purchase more than a few sheets, you could practically buy a plane ticket to Japan.

LULULEMON ATHLETICA

Map pp234-5 *Fashion*

☎ 416-703-1399; 734 Queen St W; 🕒 10am-6pm Mon-Wed, 10am-7pm Thu-Sat, 11am-6pm Sun; streetcar 501

This trendy Vancouver-based athletic clothing line specializes in yoga wear. Incidentally it's perfectly comfortable for long plane flights too. There's another branch in **Bloor-Yorkville** (Map pp231-3; ☎ 416-964-9544; 130 Bloor St W; subway Bay).

METROPOLIS RECORDS

Map pp234-5 *Music*

☎ 416-364-0230; 162-164 Spadina Ave; 🕒 noon-7pm Mon-Thu, noon-9pm Fri & Sat, noon-6pm Sun; streetcar 510, 501

DJs look to Metropolis, a CD bar that supplies vinyl in categories so obscure that few truly comprehend the genius behind them. Serious turntablists and club music aficionados only need apply.

PEACH BERSERK Map pp234-5 *Fashion*

☎ 416-504-1711; www.peachberserk.com; 507 Queen St W; 🕒 10am-8pm Mon-Fri, 10am-7pm Sat, noon-5pm Sun; streetcar 501

Peach Berserk strikes a happy-go-lucky note with silk-screened girlie creations. Its tag line is: 'Crazy Print Couture,' which results in mix-and-match tops, pants and skirts. Take a peek at the workshop in the back or bring in your own pattern for custom-made items.

PRELOVED Map pp234-5 *Fashion*

☎ 416-504-8704; 613 Queen St W; 🕒 11am-6pm Mon-Wed, 11am-7pm Thu & Fri, 10am-7pm Sat, noon-6pm Sun; streetcar 501

Movie stars are among the many devotees of Preloved's one-of-a-kind clothing re-designs of brave new cuts of vintage clothing. An aloha shirt might become a skirt, or a chrysanthemum kimono could be made into pajama pants – it's all original work here.

RED INDIAN ART DECO

Map pp234-5 *Antiques*

☎ 416-504-7706; 536 Queen St W; 10am-5pm Tue-Sat; streetcar 501

This antique dealer vends pieces seemingly pulled off an Agatha Christie BBC special set. You'll want to make room in your suitcase for one of its elegant rotary telephones, art-deco lamps or other vintage treasures.

ROTATE THIS Map pp234-5 *Music*

☎ 416-504-8447; 620 Queen St W; 11am-7pm Mon-Thu & Sat, 11am-8pm Fri, noon-6pm Sun; streetcar 501

Rotate This is perfect for those who always know of cutting-edge bands before anyone else does. The staff throw around tons of attitude, but audiophiles gravitate here for no-frills racks of vinyl and CD finds.

Clothing Sizes

Measurements approximate only, try before you buy

Women's Clothing						
Aus/UK	8	10	12	14	16	18
Europe	36	38	40	42	44	46
Japan	5	7	9	11	13	15
USA	6	8	10	12	14	16
Women's Shoes						
Aus/USA	5	6	7	8	9	10
Europe	35	36	37	38	39	40
France only	35	36	38	39	40	42
Japan	22	23	24	25	26	27
UK	3½	4½	5½	6½	7½	8½
Men's Clothing						
Aus	92	96	100	104	108	112
Europe	46	48	50	52	54	56
Japan	S		M	M		L
UK/USA	35	36	37	38	39	40
Men's Shirts (Collar Sizes)						
Aus/Japan	38	39	40	41	42	43
Europe	38	39	40	41	42	43
UK/USA	15	15½	16	16½	17	17½
Men's Shoes						
Aus/UK	7	8	9	10	11	12
Europe	41	42	43	44½	46	47
Japan	26	27	27½	28	29	30
USA	7½	8½	9½	10½	11½	12½

SIREN: A GOTHIC EMPORIUM

Map pp234-5 *Fashion*

☎ 416-504-9288; 463 Queen St W; 11am-7pm Mon-Sat, noon-6pm Sun; streetcar 501

All-female staff smile as they stock wicked clothes and accessories in purple, black or blood-red. Fetishists are willing to pay top-dollar for the designs, especially for absolutely wild choices in footwear or 'Dark Ware,' but the sale rack beckons.

EAST TORONTO

BUTTERFIELD 8 Map pp238-9 *Fashion*

☎ 416-406-5664; 235 Danforth Ave; 10am-6pm Mon-Fri, noon-4pm Sun; subway Broadview

Named after a movie starring Elizabeth Taylor, this store has a fabulous collection of jewelry, handbags, knickknacks, personal care products and things to make your house beautiful, as Oscar Wilde might say. Not far away is **El Pipil** (Map pp238-9; ☎ 416-465-9625; 267 Danforth Ave) that vends boutique fashions and charmingly priced accessories by local designers.

GRASSROOTS Map pp238-9 *Specialty*

☎ 416-466-2841, 888-633-5833; Carrot Common, 327 Danforth Ave; 10am-7pm Mon-Fri, 10am-6pm Sat, noon-6pm Sun; subway Chester

Environmentally friendly shampoos, toiletries and everyday supplies are sold here – a biodegradable pen or a book bag made out of recycled tires, anyone? – along with a great selection of baby items. Another branch in the **Annex** (Map pp236-7; ☎ 416-944-1993; 408 Bloor St W; 10am-8pm Mon-Fri, 10am-7pm Sat, noon-6pm Sun; subway Bathurst).

THE BEACHES

ART² Map pp240 *Art & Crafts*

2357 Queen St E; streetcar 501

Hidden down by the beach, this contemporary art space is all about fantastic jewelry and accessories. After-hours you can peer in the windows at abstract beaded necklaces, carved silver rings, semi-precious pendants, hand-woven scarves and knit hats.

DISCOVERY USED & COLLECTORS' RECORDS Map pp238-9 *Music*

☎ 416-778-6394; 1140 Queen St E; 11am-6pm Mon-Thu & Sat, noon-5pm Sun; streetcar 501, 502, 503

Collectors go gaga for blues, rock, reggae, folk and country tunes at this gold mine for out-of-print and rare vinyl. It also carries soundtracks, comedy and spoken word recordings

YOKA Map p240 *Fashion*

☎ 416-686-0836; 2116 Queen St E; ⌚ 10am-6pm Mon-Wed, 10am-7pm Thu-Sat, 11am-5pm Sun; streetcar 501

Comfy urban styles for women are the imprint here. Buy something hip and woolen if the lakefront winds are chilling your bones, or a slip of a sundress in balmy spring weather. Sidewalk sale racks hold yoga wear to cocktail dresses.

GREATER TORONTO AREA

Holt Renfrew Last Call (☎ 905-886-7444; 370 Steeles Ave W, Thornhill; ⌚ 10am-9pm Mon-Fri, 10am-6pm Sat, noon-6pm Sun; subway Finch, then bus 60) Head here for up to 70% off the same name-brand fashions carried by Bloor-Yorkville's exclusive department store, **Holt Renfrew** (p150).

A SHOW OF HANDS/PETROFF GALLERY Map p225 *Art & Craft*

☎ 416-782-1696, 877-542-3600; www.ashowofhands.com; 1016 Eglinton Ave W, west of Bathurst St; ⌚ 10am-6pm Mon-Wed, Fri & Sat, 10am-8pm Thu, noon-5pm Sun; subway Eglinton West

A superb gallery of both contemporary Canadian and international crafts is made even better by its focus on three-dimensional works, including blown glass, ceramics, textiles, carvings, wire sculpture as well as kaleidoscopes.

MADE YOU LOOK Map p225 *Fashion*

☎ 416-463-2136; 1338 Queen St W, west of Dufferin St; ⌚ 10am-6pm; streetcar 501

A dozen local jewelry designers work on-site at this gallery, where cases display pieces made of silver, handmade glass beads and more experimental materials. Custom designs for women and men are accepted. Ring the bell to enter.

Sleeping

Sleeping

Booking good-value accommodations is likely to be the thorniest issue in planning your trip to Toronto. Except for during the deep-freeze winter months, reservations are absolutely necessary. From Victoria Day through Labour Day – and beyond that for as long as the summer weather holds – decent places to stay will be full, night after night. Even the less-desirable hotels and B&Bs will have 'No Vacancy' signs on Friday and Saturday nights. If you're arriving during Caribana, Toronto Pride celebrations or the Toronto International Film Festival rooms will be booked out months in advance. See p8 for a list of major holidays and special events. Typical cancellation fees range from $20 to the entire first night's charge.

At hotels rates fluctuate wildly from day to day, and many places charge double or triple the off-peak rates in summer and on major holidays. Some hostels, guesthouses and B&Bs may not charge tax, but hotels certainly will, so be prepared. Always ask if parking, local phone calls and high-speed Internet access are included, as well as inquiring about discounts for students, seniors, CAA/AAA members and long-term (eg multinight, weekly or monthly) stays. Many hotels offer discounts for Internet bookings and special package deals via their own websites. At smaller hotels, B&Bs and guesthouses, you may able to negotiate a good deal during slow periods, if you ask politely.

Cheap Sleeps (budget options) are listed at the end of each neighborhood section. This category typically includes hostels and guesthouses offering dormitory beds from $20 to $25 and private rooms (usually with bathroom) starting under $60. Ask about weekly discounts. All of the downtown hostels offer Internet access, luggage storage, common kitchens, shared bathroom and laundry facilities.

Some hostels may unfairly pull the rug out from under you and renege on booked rooms or overstuff the corridors with extra bunk beds at busy times. Many hostels, guesthouses and B&Bs do not have air-conditioned rooms, which can quickly become a problem during the city's sweltering summer months.

You can't say Toronto and budget hotels in the same breath. Cheaper chain hotels like Howard Johnson or Days Inn have 'doubles' (which may mean two beds, not just double occupancy) starting near $100, as do Toronto's older independent hotels. Most mid-range and above downtown hotels are practically interchangeable, as the Hilton and Westin proved when they simply swapped their respective establishments in the late '80s.

Booking B&Bs

Be forewarned that some B&Bs require a two-night minimum stay, especially on weekends. A great place to start looking on-line is www.bbcanada.com, which has nearly 100 listings in the city. A few independent B&B operators belong to the **Toronto Guild of Bed & Breakfasts** (www.torontoguild.com).

B&B reservations agencies check, list and book rooms in the participating members' homes. When you indicate your preferences, all attempts will be made to find a particularly suitable host. If you're in town and want to check last-minute availability, it may be able to help during normal business hours. If you're planning on staying for more than a few days, these agencies also rent out suites and apartments on a weekly or monthly basis, which can work out to be a very good deal. It's almost always better value than staying at hotels.

Reliable agencies include:

Across Toronto Bed & Breakfast Reservation Service (☎ 705-738-9449, 877-922-6522; www.torontobandb.com) The oldest association in town has about a dozen members in central Toronto and on the Toronto Islands.

Bed & Breakfast Homes of Toronto (☎ 416-363-6362; www.bbcanada.com/associations/toronto2) Handles residential area B&Bs, anything from modest family homes to deluxe suites.

Downtown Toronto Association of Bed and Breakfast Guest Houses (☎ 416-410-3938; www.bnbinfo.com) Rooms in various neighborhoods, mostly in renovated Victorian houses.

Anxious for something with a little character? Downtown also offers historic hotels, boutique digs and lakefront properties, albeit at higher prices than almost any other neighborhood. At luxury hotels around town, you'll pay upwards of $150 for fully-equipped and more spacious accommodations. All of these top-end establishments have swimming pools, fitness rooms, valet parking, bars and fine restaurants, as well as concierges who can assist your every whim. Meanwhile luxury B&Bs serving full, hot breakfasts charge over $100 per night for rooms and suites that are outfitted with all the amenities, including bathroom, telephone and cable TV.

HARBOURFRONT

RADISSON PLAZA HOTEL ADMIRAL

Map pp228-30 *Hotel*

☎ 416-203-3333, 800-333-3333; www.radisson.com; 249 Queens Quay W; d from $115; streetcar 509, 510; P $15

The oft-forgotten Radisson has a quirky nautical theme. Situated right on the lakeshore, it's convenient to the **Martin Goodman Trail** (p145) and has an outdoor pool. Look for Internet booking specials, which may include business-class deals with full breakfast and a free nightly in-room movie.

WESTIN HARBOUR CASTLE

Map pp228-30 *Hotel*

☎ 416-869-1600, 800-937-8461; www.westin.com; 1 Harbour Sq; d from $160; streetcar 509, 510; P $17-28

On the waterfront, the 1000-room Westin is popular with business travelers and families. Some standard rooms enjoy lake views and the hotel's revolving restaurant overlooks Lake Ontario and the Toronto Islands.

FINANCIAL DISTRICT

BOND PLACE Map pp226-7 *Hotel*

☎ 416-362-6061, 800-268-9390; www.bondplacehoteltoronto.com; 65 Dundas St E; d from $90; subway Dundas; P $12

A modest high-rise east of Eaton Centre, Bond Place is a pleasant, if admittedly aging downtown hotel. Summer rates are good value, dropping in winter (when you should ask about 'stay two nights, get the third night free' specials).

CAMBRIDGE SUITES HOTEL

Map pp228-30 *Hotel/Extended Stay*

☎ 416-368-1990, 800-463-1990; www.cambridgesuitestoronto.com; 15 Richmond St E; d $220-500; subway Queen; P $12-16

This polished executive hotel offers two-room suites with in-room VCRs and free high-speed Internet access. Guests enjoy a deluxe breakfast buffet, full-service business center and penthouse fitness room with city skyline views. Ask about special weekend packages and B&B deals.

Top Five Downtown Sleeps

- **Best historic hotel** Fairmont Royal York (below); Le Royal Meridien King Edward (p162)
- **Best luxury boutique hotel** Hôtel Le Germain (p163)
- **Best lobby eatery** SoHo Metropolitan Hotel (p163)
- **Best guest services & amenities** Grand Hotel & Suites (p163)
- **Best views for sports fans** Renaissance Toronto Hotel (p162)

FAIRMONT ROYAL YORK

Map pp228-30 *Historic Hotel*

☎ 416-368-2511, 866-540-4489; www.fairmont.com/royalyork; 100 Front St W; d from $190; subway Union; P $30

Since 1929 the eminent Royal York has accommodated rock stars to royal guests. Built opposite Union Station by the Canadian Pacific Railway, its mock-chateau style adds character to Toronto's modern skyline. Rooms exude richness and style, with rates that rise depending upon demand. **Epic** (p92) and the **Library Bar** (p120) are both worth a second look.

HOTEL VICTORIA Map pp228-30 *Hotel*

☎ 416-363-1666, 800-363-8228; www.hotelvictoria-toronto.com; 56 Yonge St; d $100-170; subway King

One of the best small downtown hotels is the early 20th-century Hotel Victoria. Refurbished throughout, it still maintains a few old-fashioned features, such as its fine lobby. The multilingual, 24-hour reception desk warmly welcomes all guests. Rates include complimentary continental breakfast and health club privileges.

RENAISSANCE TORONTO HOTEL AT SKYDOME Map pp228-30 *Hotel*

☎ 416-341-7100, 800-468-3571; www.renaissance hotels.com; One Blue Jays Way; d/ste from $190/265; subway Union; Ⓟ $20-25

Only 70 of the most expensive rooms overlook the playing field, but if you request one of those, be prepared for floodlights and SkyDome noise at all hours. Mostly covered walkways connect this upmarket chain hotel with Union Station.

STRATHCONA Map pp228-30 *Hotel*

☎ 416-363-3321, 800-268-8304; www.thestrathcona hotel.com; 60 York St; d from $80; subway St Andrew

Convenient to Union Station, this familiar face offers all of the usual amenities (including Web TV), and yet, for the downtown area, is reasonably priced. Guests enjoy discounted privileges at the next-door fitness and racquet club.

Holiday Inn on King (right)

OLD YORK

LE ROYAL MERIDIEN KING EDWARD

Map pp228-30 *Historic Hote*

☎ 416-863-0888, 800-543-4300; www.lemeridien -kingedward.com; 37 King St E; tw/d from $125/190; subway King; Ⓟ $28

The glorious 'King Eddy' is Toronto's oldes hotel, named for King Edward VII, who gav it the royal seal of approval over a centur ago. This grand dame was built by none othe than Toronto's architect, EJ Lennox; today it's showpiece of baroque plasterwork, marble an etched glass. Standard rooms are well price (including twice-daily maid service), especiall on weekends. On site is **Café Victoria** (p95).

NOVOTEL TORONTO CENTRE

Map pp228-30 *Hote*

☎ 416-367-8900, 800-668-6835; www.novotel.com; 45 The Esplanade; d from $150; subway Union, streetcar 503; Ⓟ $14

Adorned in grand French Renaissance style the Novotel gracefully perches near the wa terfront and the historic **St Lawrence Market** (p96) Apartment-sized luxury rooms are worth fa more than is charged.

Cheap Sleeps

HOSTELLING INTERNATIONAL TORONTO Map pp228-30 *Hoste*

HI Toronto; ☎ 416-971-4440, 877-848-8737; www.hihostels.ca; 76 Church St; dm $22-24, d $65, monthly rates incl taxes $520-675; reception 24hr; streetcar 504

This award-winning hostel gets votes fo renovations that include a rooftop deck, air-conditioning and electronic key locks. Beds in quad rooms may not cost any more than those in larger dormitories, so ask when making reservations. Check the website for HI cardholde discounts around town.

THEATRE BLOCK & ENTERTAINMENT DISTRICT

HOLIDAY INN ON KING

Map pp228-30 *Hote*

☎ 416-599-4000, 800-263-6364; www.hiok.com; 370 King St W; d from $130; streetcar 504; Ⓟ $18

Near the Theatre Block, this dazzlingly white hotel seems to have been airlifted straight of Waikiki Beach. Standard rooms enjoy lake or city views, while the seasonal rooftop poo

Hotel Hijinks

The SkyDome hotel became instantly notorious when, during one of the first Blue Jays baseball games, a couple in one of the upperfield side rooms – either forgetfully or rakishly – became involved in some sporting activity of their own with the lights on, much to the crowd's amusement. Such a scoring performance was later repeated at another game. After that, the hotel insisted on guests signing waivers that stipulated there would be no more such free double plays.

azes onto the CN Tower. Children under ge 20 stay and eat free when accompanied y a parent. Visit the website to pick up great iternet-only deals.

ÔTEL LE GERMAIN
ap pp228-30 *Boutique Hotel*
416-345-9500, 866-345-9501; ww.germaintoronto.com; 30 Mercer St; d $240-500, e $475-900; streetcar 504; P $25
ip and harmonious, this hotel has grown up ıst a short walk from the Entertainment District nd SkyDome. Clean lines, soothing spaces and en-inspired materials all deliver a promised cean of well-being.' Guests are pampered ith Aveda bath amenities, in-room Bose ereos, high-speed Internet access, a rooftop rrace and cathedral-ceilinged lobby library.

OHO METROPOLITAN HOTEL
ap pp228-30 *Boutique Hotel*
416-599-8800, 800-668-6600; ww.metropolitan.com/soho; 318 Wellington St W; from $275; streetcar 504; P $15-20
fresh boutique hotel and condominium omplex in the heart of downtown, the SoHo et effects flawless service. Exquisite amenies include Italian linens, marble bathrooms, ng-sized beds, remote-controlled lighting, i-fi Internet access, a spa and health club. on't miss epicurean **SenSes** (p97).

heap Sleeps

ANADIANA GUESTHOUSE & ACKPACKERS **Map pp228-30** *Hostel*
416-598-9090, 877-215-1225; www.canadianalo ing.com; 42 Widmer St; dm incl taxes $22-28, s/d 0/65; reception 8am-midnight; streetcar 504
ccupying a few charming Victorian townouses in the Entertainment District, this friendly air-conditioned hostel has only a few dozen dorm beds and a couple of private rooms. Although the hostel fills up regularly with European travelers, you're still more likely to find an empty bed here than anywhere else.

QUEEN STREET & DUNDAS SQUARE

DELTA CHELSEA TORONTO DOWNTOWN **Map pp226-7** *Hotel*
☎ 416-595-1975, 877-814-7706; www.deltachelsea.com; 33 Gerrard St W; d from $100; subway College; P $22-30
Who says one hotel can't be all things to all people? With nearly 1600 rooms, Toronto's largest and arguably best-value hotel bustles with tourists, business travelers and families. If you're traveling with children, you'll appreciate the apartment-style suites stocked with cookie jars, bunk beds and alphabet fridge magnets. Breakfast is often available in the Deck 27 skyline lounge.

GRAND HOTEL & SUITES
Map pp228-30 *Luxury Hotel/Extended Stay*
☎ 416-863-9000, 877-324-7263; www.grandhotel toronto.com; 225 Jarvis St; d/ste from $150/200; streetcar 505; P $17
Proffering perks that put other hotels to shame, the Grand Hotel & Suites retreat offers shuttle services, which partly make up for its slightly unsavory location. All of the rooms are equipped with free wi-fi Internet access, two TV/VCRs, dual phone lines, DVD and CD players, a kitchenette and a marble bathroom. The loft suites, a complimentary breakfast buffet and the 450 sq meter fitness club, indoor pool and spa are pure indulgence.

HILTON TORONTO **Map pp228-30** *Hotel*
☎ 416-869-3456, 800-445-8667; www.hilton.com; 145 Richmond St W; d/ste from $150/180; subway Osgoode; P $22
A surprisingly sleek high-rise, here even the standard rooms have Web TV, high-speed Internet access and an on-demand CD library. For cityscape views, book one of the 32nd-floor Crown Suites. Freshly Canadian Tundra restaurant sits off the lobby. Be sure to ask about B&B rates, weekend escapes and family-sized deals.

LES AMIS BED & BREAKFAST

Map pp226-7 *B&B*

☎ 416-591-0635; www.bbtoronto.com; 31 Granby St; s/d incl taxes from $65/80; subway College

Run by a Parisian couple, this cheery non-smoking B&B offers full, gourmet vegetarian (or vegan) breakfasts. Air-conditioned rooms have futon beds; bathrooms are shared. Its only drawback is a slightly sketchy location, despite being just steps from Eaton Centre. French, German and Japanese are spoken. Gay and lesbian travelers are welcome.

SHERATON CENTRE TORONTO

Map pp228-30 *Hotel*

☎ 416-361-1000, 800-325-3535; www.sheratontoronto.com; 123 Queen St W; d from $150; subway Osgoode, Queen; Ⓟ $28

Thoughtful perks such as guaranteed fast-response concierge and room service distinguish this downtown high-rise from its competitors. There's an Olympic-sized pool; Jacuzzi suites are available. Ask about discounted theater and festival packages.

CHINATOWN

GLOBAL VILLAGE BACKPACKERS

Map pp228-30 *Hostel*

☎ 416-703-8540, 888-844-7875; www.globalbackpackers.com; 460 King St W; dm incl taxes $22-28, d $56-60; 🕒 reception 24hr; streetcar 504, 511

This kaleidoscopically colored independent hostel was once the Spadina Hotel, where Jack Nicholson, the Rolling Stones, Leonard Cohen and the Tragically Hip stayed. It's in an optimal location and even has its own bar, hence the party atmosphere. There's also a **Travel CUTS** (p198).

YONGE STREET STRIP & CHURCH-WELLESLEY VILLAGE

Among all of the fly-by-night and better-established B&Bs in the gay neighborhood centered on Church and Wellesley Sts, these are our picks. Some may only accept male guests.

BURWOOD INN Map pp231-3 *B&B*

☎ 416-351-1503, 877-580-5015; www.geocities.com/burwoodinn; 10 Monteith St; s with/without bathroom $90/60, d $110/80; subway Wellesley; Ⓟ $10

In a simply sweet century-old home with a shiny red door, the Burwood Inn has a small garden, shared kitchen and original art and architectur prints hanging on the walls. Spanish, French an German are spoken. The owners also offer slightly cheaper B&B option on McGill St.

CROMWELL FURNISHED SUITES

Map pp231-3 *Serviced Apartments/Extended Sta*

☎ 416-962-5670; cromwellreservation@rogers.com; 55 Isabella St; ste $80-95, 1-bedroom apt $100-140; subway Wellesley; Ⓟ

This balconied high-rise is party central fo gay men, but the location can be iffy a night. Although the ho-hum décor is nothin special, even studio suites have a kitchen. Ai conditioning costs an extra $75 per mont Minimum rental is three days.

DAYS INN TORONTO DOWNTOWN

Map pp231-3 *Hot*

☎ 416-977-6655, 800-329-7466; www.daysinn.com; 30 Carlton St; d from $80; subway College; Ⓟ $18

Affordable accommodation is found at th Days Inn, which has a heated indoor pool an fitness facilities. Other locations of this cha around the city are not necessarily as reliab or convenient.

DUNDONALD HOUSE Map pp231-3 *B&*

☎ 416-961-9888, 800-260-7227; www.dundonaldhouse.com; 35 Dundonald St; s/tw/d from $85/110/135; subway Wellesley; Ⓟ $5

Voted a community favorite, this strikin black-gabled house has stained glass an flower gardens. Guest amenities include sauna and fitness room, complimentary b cycles and shiatsu massage services (for a added fee). Accommodations range fro no-frills single or twin bedrooms up to $17 for a double with bay windows and a priva balcony.

GLOUCESTER SQUARE BED & BREAKFAST INNS Map pp231-3 *B&*

☎ 416-966-3074, 800-259-5474; www.gloucestersquare.com; 10 Cawthra Sq; s $100-120, d $145-200, ste $225-450; subway Wellesley; Ⓟ

With two dozen rooms and suites in three hi toric buildings (one was designed by famou architect EJ Lennox), here by Cawthra Squa guests enjoy unabashed opulence. Most room have antique touches; some suites have hig speed Internet access. Ask about spa service A breakfast buffet is available until 1pm, ar Saturday afternoon teas are a communi social event.

MMACULATE RECEPTION *B&B*
☎ 416-925-4202, 800-335-9190; www.immaculate eceptionbb.com; 34 Monteith St; d $85-125; subway Vellesley
eside Cawthra Square Park, this Second Empire ownhouse set back from the hoopla of Church t has sunny common areas. Rates for very simle, but tasteful air-con rooms (most without athroom) include a full hot breakfast.

MANSION Map pp231-3 *B&B*
☎ 416-963-8385; www.themansion.ca; 46 Dundonald t; d $70-100; subway Wellesley; P $5
ind above-average ambience at this luxurious etreat. Rooms are furnished in Victorian, Edvardian or Regency styles; each has a balcony, idge and cable TV. Continental breakfast is erved.

VICTORIA'S MANSION INN & GUESTHOUSE Map pp231-3 *B&B*
☎ 416-921-4625; www.victoriasmansion.com; 68 loucester St; d $65-130; subway Wellesley; P $10
ward-winning Victoria's Mansion can acommodate budget travelers for short and ong-term stays in a renovated 1880s heritage uilding. Studio suites have kitchenettes. The wners are also known to be personable and iendly.

Top 10 Perks at Toronto Accommodations

- **An indoor 130ft waterslide** Delta Chelsea Toronto Downtown (p163)
- **Star-spotting during the Toronto International Film Festival** Four Seasons (p165)
- **Luxury suites with 24-hour butler service** Windsor Arms (p166)
- **Free in-room cookies and popcorn** Cambridge Suites Hotel (p161)
- **A complimentary cappuccino bar** Hôtel Le Germain (p163)
- **VIP billiards at the next-door pub** Madison Manor (p167)
- **Sleep where the Beatles, Teddy Roosevelt and the Duke of Windsor have slept** Le Royal Meridien King Edward (p162)
- **Sleep where 'Papa' Hemingway lived** Howard Johnson Selby Hotel & Suites (p169)
- **Toronto Downtown Bed & Breakfast** (p166)
- **A bar just steps away from your dorm bed** Global Village Backpackers (p164)

BLOOR-YORKVILLE

With rack rates at times exceeding what you'd pay at top-notch downtown hotels, the posh Bloor St and Yorkville neighborhoods will delight fine hotel lovers. More affordable rooms are scarce, however.

FOUR SEASONS Map pp231-3 *Luxury Hotel*
☎ 416-964-0411, 800-819-5053; www.fourseasons.com/toronto; 21 Avenue Rd; d from $350; subway Bay; P $30
Some of the city's most costly rooms are at the Four Seasons in the heart of Yorkville. Everyone here looks quite glamorous. Even 'moderate' rooms have antique desks and marble bathrooms, while superior rooms and suites have walk-out balconies. Also worth mentioning is an indoor/outdoor pool, boutiques and five-star French cuisine at Truffles restaurant.

HOWARD JOHNSON INN
Map pp231-3 *Hotel*
☎ 416-964-1220, 800-446-4656; www.hojo.com; 89 Avenue Rd; d from $110; subway Bay; P $10
Next to Hazelton Lanes shopping center, HoJo offers the cheapest accommodation in ritzy Yorkville. Rates for standard-issue rooms, which have down-to-earth wood and brick décor, include continental breakfast.

INTERCONTINENTAL TORONTO
Map pp231-3 *Hotel*
☎ 416-960-5200, 800-267-0010; www.toronto.intercontinental.com; 220 Bloor St W; d from $210; subway St George; P $30
Opposite the Royal Conservatory of Music, the glitzy InterContinental is convenient to museums and the University of Toronto's St George campus. Personalized attention from the multilingual staff compliments round-the-clock business services, high-speed Internet, an indoor pool and sauna.

PARK HYATT Map pp231-3 *Luxury Hotel*
☎ 416-925-1234, 800-233-1234; www.parktoronto.hyatt.com; 4 Avenue Rd; d from $200; subway Museum; P $29
Ideal for business or leisure travelers, the Park Hyatt has an impressive circular drive with fountains and a rooftop skyline lounge. The addition of the award-winning **Stillwater** (p141) spa makes an already excellent hotel even better. Some rooms have king beds, marble bathrooms and calming colors. Check the website for special weekend packages.

QUALITY HOTEL Map pp231-3 *Hotel*
☎ 416-968-0010, 877-424-6423; www.qualityinn.com; 280 Bloor St W; d from $120, ste from $145; subway St George; (P) $14

This high-rise chain hotel has a prime location near the museums and shopping. Especially good value are newer rooms that come with cathedral ceilings and king-sized beds and one-bedroom executive suites. Another perk is free admission to a nearby health club.

SUTTON PLACE HOTEL
Map pp231-3 *Luxury Hotel*
☎ 416-924-9221, 866-378-8866; www.suttonplace.com; 955 Bay St; d/ste from $145/245; subway Wellesley; (P) $18

This luxurious European-styled hotel is over the top, but remains popular with visiting dignitaries and Toronto International Film Festival stars. Carefully placed throughout the hotel are elegant antiques and tapestries, gilded mirrors and chandeliers. For those staying longer, La Grande Résidence apartments are fully furnished.

TORONTO DOWNTOWN BED & BREAKFAST Map p225 *B&B*
☎ 416-941-1524; www.tdbab.com; 57 Chicora Ave; d/ste from $100/200; bus 5; (P) $15

This lovely gay-owned B&B is a quick bus ride north of Yorkville. Enjoy fresh-baked cookies by the fireplace, or relax with a movie borrowed from the videotape and DVD library. Breakfast varies from continental to a full, hot gourmet meal by a French-trained chef.

WINDSOR ARMS Map pp231-3 *Historic Hotel*
☎ 416-971-9666; www.windsorarmshotel.com; 18 St Thomas St; ste from $300; subway Bay; (P) $25

The Windsor Arms is an exquisite piece of Toronto history, no matter whether you're staying the night or just dropping in for tea (p92). The 1927 neo-gothic mansion boasts a grand entryway, stained-glass windows, nearly faultless services and an on-site spa. All this can be yours with a price tag of up to $2000 for the luxury suites, which boast 24-hour butler service.

UNIVERSITY OF TORONTO & THE ANNEX

Quiet residential neighborhoods that surround the University of Toronto's St George campus offer the best-value B&Bs in the city, apart from some of those in Cabbagetown (p61).

CASA LOMA INN Map pp236-7 *Guesthouse*
☎ 416-924-4540; casalomainn@sympatico.ca; 21 Walmer Rd; s/d from $80/90; subway Spadina; (P) $10

When it's all lit up at night, this breathtaking turn-of-the-20th-century Victorian inn seems like a pint-sized version of its namesake (p58). Each of 23 nonsmoking rooms has a TV, fridge, microwave and air-conditioning. No breakfast.

CASTLEGATE INN
Map p225 *B&B/Extended Stay*
☎ 416-323-1657; www.castlegateinn.com; 203 Spadina Rd; s & d $60-100, weekly rates from $300; subway Dupont; (P)

One of the best budget travel bargains in Toronto, this casual B&B owned by avid travelers occupies three apartment houses, all within striking distance of the UT campus and Yorkville. If you're sensitive to noise, request a quiet upper-floor room facing away from the street. Continental breakfast and limited parking are free.

COACH HOUSE Map p225 *B&B*
☎ 416-899-0306; www.thecoachhouse.ca; 117 Walmer Rd; ste $150-175, weekly rates $800-900; streetcar 511; (P)

This small establishment offers you a one-bedroom coach house with a loft bedroom decorated in French country style or an apartment-style suite with kitchenette. Both accommodations have cable TV/VCR, air conditioning and high-speed Internet access. Breakfast provisions are provided in a cute welcome basket.

FEATHERS B&B Map p225 *B&B*
☎ 416-534-1923; www.bbcanada.com/1115.html; 132 Wells St; s/d without bath from $75/85; streetcar 511; (P)

Antique dolls, exotic textiles and Indonesian puppets are sometimes on display at this airy artistic B&B. Simple singles start at $75, rising to $100 for doubles with bathroom. Rates include continental breakfast. Dutch, French and some German are spoken.

LOWTHER HOUSE Map pp231-3 *B&B*
☎ 416-323-1589, 800-265-4158; www.lowtherhouse.ca; 72 Lowther Ave; d $70-160; subway St George; (P)

Equidistant from Yorkville, several museums and the University of Toronto's St George ampus, this restored century-old Victorian ansion charms guests with its gardens and ommon-area fireplace. Suites will spoil you ith a marble double Jacuzzi bathroom or a in room. French is spoken.

ADISON MANOR Map pp236-7 *B&B*
☎ 416-922-5579, 877-561-7048; www.madison enuepub.com; 20 Madison Ave; d $90-195; subway adina; (P) $10
uests at this boutique B&B inn enjoy day-me billiards parlor privileges at the nearby **adison Avenue Pub** (p117). All rooms have a athroom, air-con and Internet access; a few ave fireplaces or balconies, too. Continental eakfast is served.

ERRACE HOUSE BED & BREAKFAST
ap p225 *B&B*
☎ 416-535-1493; www.terracehouse.com; 52 Austin e; d $130-200; bus 7; (P)
avelers recommend this historic 1913 home, hich boasts North African rugs, a fireplace nd full, hot gourmet breakfasts. If you are cky, savor the quiche or the strawberry-and-cotta pancakes. Some rooms come without bathroom. Terrace House Bed & Breakfast a short walk to the west of Casa Loma, or ou can take the No 7 Bathurst bus to Austin e and walk east. There is limited parking ailable.

heap Sleeps

uring summer the UT campus area of-rs student housing to tourists. Other uesthouses are open year-round, but you ould still make reservations as far in ad-ance as possible.

AMPUS CO-OPERATIVE RESIDENCE IC Map pp231-3 *Extended Stay*
RI; ☎ 416-979-2161; www.campus-coop.org; 395 iron St; s & d per month $380-600, plus membership e $25; subway Spadina
ampus Co-operative Residence Inc (CCRI), n independent housing cooperative, owns ozens of semidetached Victorian houses, nging from sedate brownstones to frat-oy animal houses. Rates for furnished single oms (there are only a few doubles avail-ble) vary depending on room size, but all ave shared kitchen and bathroom facilities. nere's a one-month minimum stay and if you eed parking, get a reserved spot in writing. ets are allowed.

GLOBAL GUESTHOUSE
Map pp236-7 *Guesthouse*
☎ 416-923-4004; singer@inforamp.net; 9 Spadina Rd; s with/without bathroom $62/52, d $72/62; subway Spadina
This old-fashioned brick Victorian with beautiful carved gables and a balcony sits just north of Bloor St. Decently spacious rooms with cable TV fill up quickly and include shared telephone and minikitchen access.

HAVINN Map p225 *Hostel*
☎ 416-922-5220, 888-922-5220; http://home.eol.ca /~havinn; 118 Spadina Rd; dm $25, s/d without bathroom $50/65; subway Spadina; (P)
At modest Havinn, you get a bed in a co-ed room with one or two other people. It's both clean and convenient, and there are limited kitchen facilities. Rates here include a super-continental breakfast. Ask about discounted winter rates.

UT STUDENT HOUSING OFFICE
Map pp231-3 *University Housing/Extended Stay*
☎ 416-978-8045; www.utoronto.ca; 214 College St; s & d without bathroom from $45; streetcar 506
The university rents rooms by the day, week or month from early May through to late

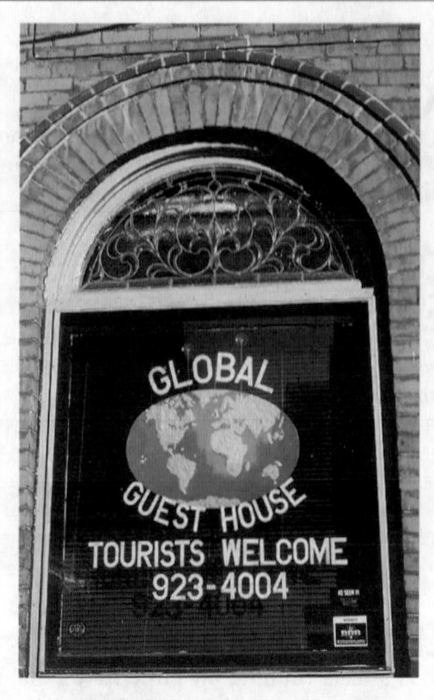

Global Guesthouse (above)

August. Of the many student dormitories, the **Innis Residence** (Map pp231-3) on the St George campus is very central. Prepaid room rates (around $2400 for the entire summer) may include both breakfast and maid service.

VICTORIA UNIVERSITY

Map pp231-3 *University Housing/Extended Stay*
☎ 416-585-4522, fax 416-585-4530; http://vicu.utoronto.ca; 140 Charles St; s/tw without bathroom $47/67, monthly rates from $950; subway Museum

Set in beautiful grounds, Victoria University opens its doors from early May until late August. Full complimentary breakfast is served in the old-world dining hall and local phone calls are free. One night's advance deposit required. Ask about reduced rates for students and seniors.

Top Five Bloor-Yorkville & the Annex Sleeps

- **Best luxury hotel** Park Hyatt (p165)
- **Best boutique Inn** Madison Manor (p167)
- **Best historic property** Windsor Arms (p166)
- **Best B&B** Lowther House (p166)
- **Best penny-pincher** Castlegate Inn (p166)

KENSINGTON MARKET

There are a few basic hostels in Kensington Market, although the majority serve down-on-their-luck clientele, not travelers.

Cheap Sleeps

COLLEGE HOSTEL Map pp234-5 *Hostel*

☎ 416-929-4777; www.affordacom.com; 280 Augusta Ave; dm $22-28, s/d incl taxes from $50/60; 24hr; streetcar 506; P

In bohemian Kensington Market, the friendly, no-frills College Hostel does not have the safest of locations, but backpackers rave about the perks: free lockers, free breakfast, free Internet, free local calls and an on-site sushi bar.

LITTLE ITALY

Side streets running off Little Italy's main drag are the scene for a burgeoning numbers of B&Bs.

LAKEVIEW VICTORIAN Map pp234-5 *B&*

☎ 416-821-6316, 416-535-6229; 42 Lakeview Ave; www.bbcanada.com/lakeviewbb; s & d from $70; streetcar 505; P

A stately white 1880s Victorian home in th Dovercourt neighborhood, just west of Litt Italy. All rooms have free local calls; some als have a sitting area with a fireplace. All roon are also without a bathroom. A breakfast bu fet includes fresh fruit and homemade bake goods.

PALMERSTON INN BED & BREAKFAS

Map pp236-7 *B&*
☎ 416-920-7842, 877-920-7842; www.palmerstoninn.com; 322 Palmerston Blvd; s $80 90, d $120-205; streetcar 506; P

This 1906 Georgian-style mansion has an ou door deck and library. All rooms come wi telephones, bathrobes and fresh flowers. Th single rooms are especially nice, with accen like stained glass, a skylight or an antiqu bed. Double rooms have air-conditionin some with a bathroom or a fireplace. A fu hot breakfast and afternoon sherry are serve here.

POSH DIGS Map pp236-7 *B&*

☎ 416-964-6390; posh_digs@yahoo.co; 371 Palmerston Blvd; d $100-135; streetcar 506; P

Each room inside of this eclectic red-bri mansion has its own bathroom, TV/VCR ar high-speed Internet access. Best of all, th Honeymoon suite has a whirlpool tub. Con nental breakfast is served.

EAST TORONTO

Many of Toronto's best B&Bs inhabit a chitectural gems around East Toronto. the historic Cabbagetown district, whic is conveniently served by both streetc and subway lines, most places are als gay-friendly.

1871 HISTORIC HOUSE B&B

Map pp238-9 *B&*
☎ 416-923-6950; www.1871bnb.com; 65 Huntley St s/d from $70/80; subway Sherbourne; P

What other property can claim both Buffalo B Cody and John Lennon as one-time guests? this historic Victorian home, which displays art and antiques in sunny common areas, rooms are without a bathroom, but the coac house suite has its own Jacuzzi.

INSLEY HOUSE Map p225 *B&B*
416-972-0533, 888-423-3337; 19 Elm Ave; d with/ thout bathroom from $70/50; subway Sherbourne; P
ery simple rooms are offered at this re- ored Rosedale mansion with an ivy-cov- ed facade. The locale is distinguished, yet eaceful. Rates include a full breakfast and ee parking.

LBERT'S INN Map pp238-9 *B&B*
416-929-9525; pimblett@attcanada.ca 263 Gerrard ; s/d from $65/85, ste $195; streetcar 505, 506; P
bove a restaurant and pub, this jovial uesthouse is run by a quirky English gentle- an who used to work at London's Mayfair otel. He describes his sense of humor as Monty Python,' so be prepared. Each room ome are without a bathroom) has air-con, V and a telephone, while the Balmoral uite has a working fireplace and kitchen. ne owner's other property, called **Pimblett's est** (www.pimbletts-rest.com), is resplend- nt with antiques, a library and mahogany replace.

LLENBY Map p225 *B&B*
416-461-7095; www.theallenby.com; 351 Wolver- gh Blvd; s with/without bathroom $85/45, d $95/55; bway Woodbine; P
t the eastern edge of Greektown is spotless llenby. All guests share bathrooms, a local lephone (free) and satellite TV. Rates include ontinental breakfast; ask about discounts in e off-season.

U PETIT PARIS Map pp238-9 *B&B*
416-928-1348; www.bbtoronto.com/aupetitparis; Selby St; s/d from $80/100; subway Sherbourne; P
ardwood floors mix with modern décor side this exquisite bay-and-gable Victorian ome. The Nomad's Suite has a skylight and avel photographs line the walls; the Artist's uite has garden views and an extra-large athtub. French is spoken.

ITY'S HEART GUEST HOUSE
ap pp238-9 *B&B*
416-935-0188; citys_heart@yahoo.com; 8 Linden ; s/d without bathroom from $35/60, 2-bedroom apt om $135; subway Sherbourne; P $5
uoted rates are higher in summer, but is cheery Victorian row house offers free gh-speed Internet access for guests and xtended-stay options. A bachelor apartment arts at $850 per month. Nearby is simple **Cavendish Guest House** (Map pp238-9; ☎ 416-921-3644; www.lizworks.com/cavendish; 5 Linden St; d $80).

COMFORT SUITES CITY CENTRE
Map pp238-9 *Hotel*
☎ 416-362-7700, 877-316-9951; www.clarionhotel.com; 200 Dundas St E; d/ste from $80/90; streetcar 505; P $14
This chain hotel tempts business travelers with its executive rooms, high-speed Internet access, indoor heated swimming pool and health club. Suites have a partial room divider and a sofa bed. Continental breakfast is free on weekdays.

HAMILTON HOUSE Map pp238-9 *B&B*
☎ 416-925-3061; www.bed-n-breakfast.to; 241 Seaton St; s $75-105, d $105-120; streetcar 505
Personable owners make the difference at this tree-shaded Cabbagetown property. Although not luxurious, some of the cozy rooms do have a bathroom. Ask ahead to arrange for an in-room telephone or parking. Breakfast is continental.

HOWARD JOHNSON SELBY HOTEL & SUITES Map pp238-9 *Historic Hotel*
☎ 416-921-3142, 800-446-4656; www.hotelselby.com; 592 Sherbourne St; d/ste from $75/200; subway Sherbourne; P $12
During the 1920s Ernest Hemingway resided at this turreted Victorian mansion while he worked as a reporter for the *Toronto Star* before heading off to Paris. Standard rooms are nothing special, except for the bargain rates, but two-room suites with high ceilings and fireplaces are found inside the original mansion. It's worth asking the friendly manager for weekend and multinight discounts. Continental breakfast is complimentary.

LAVENDER ROSE B&B Map pp238-9 *B&B*
☎ 416-962-8591; www.lavenderrosebb.com; 15 Rose Ave; d $95-125; streetcar 506; P
Cheerful, cozy rooms at this cream-colored Victorian all share a guest bathroom with a Jacuzzi; there's even a baby grand piano in the parlor. Weekday breakfasts are continental, but on weekends the spread is lavish. It's lesbian-owned.

MULBERRY TREE Map pp231-3 *B&B*
☎ 416-960-5249; http://bbtoronto.com/mulberrytree; 122 Isabella St; s/d from $80/100; subway Sherbourne; P $5

Quite a few artworks and antiques adorn this B&B. Two of the three rooms (each with a bathroom) are painted in berry tones. Full hot breakfasts (vegetarian options) are served. French and some German are spoken.

ROBIN'S NEST Map p225 *B&B*

☎ 416-926-9464, 877-441-4443; www.robinsnestbandbtoronto.com; 13 Binscarth Rd; d $95-225; subway Rosedale, then bus 82; P

The luxurious five-star Robin's Nest, a restored 1892 heritage home (it looks like a mansion), is your best shot at feeling like a million bucks. The Tree Tops Suite comes with mansard ceilings, an antique chesterfield and views of the formal garden. Breakfast is served on the veranda or on a silver tray delivered straight to your room.

VANDERKOOY BED & BREAKFAST
Map p225 *B&B*

☎ 416-925-8765; www.bbcanada.com/1107.html; 53 Walker Ave; s/d from $65/80; subway Summerhill; P

Artwork and stained glass are found all about the house, which has a communal fireplace. Rooms are bright and cheery; some don't have a bathroom. Breakfast is served overlooking the garden. It's quite convenient to the subway.

WILDSIDE HOTEL Map pp238-9 *Guesthouse*

☎ 416-921-6112, 800-260-0102; www.wildside.org; 161 Gerrard St E; s/d from $70/100; streetcar 506; P

This small hotel caters to transvestite, transsexual and cross-dressing clientele. All rooms have high-speed Internet access. A host of other amenities include a video library, shared kitchen, lounge, professional makeup studio and boutique.

Cheap Sleeps

City's Heart Guest House (p169) and **Allenby** (p169) have budget-priced single and double rooms without a bathroom; see those previous listings for details.

AMSTERDAM Map pp238-9 *Guesthouse*

☎ 416-921-9797; www.amsterdamguesthouse.com; 209 Carlton St; s/d from $55/65; streetcar 506

The Amsterdam is a polished Victorian house that's not at all stuffy, with a back balcony that has bird's-eye views of downtown. Simple rooms have air-con and cable TV. Although not large, the rooms are clean and comfy. Look for the flags flying out front.

NEILL-WYCIK COLLEGE HOTEL
Map pp226-7 *University Housing/Extended Sta*

☎ 416-977-2320, 800-268-4358; www.neill-wycik.com; 96 Gerrard St E; s/d/f/tr $40/60/66/80; May-Aug, reception 24hr; subway College

This budget traveler's favorite, near Ryerson Pc ytechnic University, operates from early May t late August. Private bedrooms with telephone are inside apartment-style suites that share kitchen/lounge and bathroom. There are laur dry facilities, lockers, TV lounges, a student-ru cafeteria for breakfast and incredible views fror the rooftop sundeck. The building isn't air-cor ditioned and there are no fans, so be prepare to sweat it out in mid-summer.

Top Five East Toronto Sleeps

- **Best historic hotel** Howard Johnson Selby Hotel & Suites (p169)
- **Best luxury B&B** Robin's Nest (p170)
- **Best French-speaking B&B** Au Petit Paris (p169)
- **Best quirky B&B** Albert's Inn (p169)
- **Best penny-pincher** Neill-Wycik College Hotel (p170)

THE BEACHES

ACCOMMODATING THE SOUL
Map p240 *B&*

☎ 416-686-0619, 866-686-0619; www.bbcanada.com/atsoul; 114 Waverley Rd; d $85-125; streetcar 501; P

An early 20th-century home boasting antique and delicious gardens, this will delight trave ers looking for tranquility. All rooms have bathroom and full, hot breakfasts are servec It's just a short walk from the lakefront. It's als gay-owned.

TORONTO ISLANDS

Check out the boxed text 'Booking B&Bs (p160) go to http://torontoisland.org t find more B&Bs and rental cottages o the islands.

TORONTO ISLAND BED & BREAKFAST Map p241 *B&*

☎ 416-203-0935, fax 416-203-2646; 8 Lakeshore Ave cnr 3rd St; d without bathroom from $70; ferry Ward's

For unforgettably unique accommodatior take the ferry over to Ward's Island, then wa about 300m toward the south shore, turn le nd look for this quaint white clapboard house. ooms fill up quickly during summer. Rates in-lude full breakfast and the use of bicycles.

Airport Alternatives

With 24-hour **Airport Express** (p195) bus services to downtown, most travelers won't need to stay near the airport. The Sheraton Gateway is very convenient if you do happen to need an airport hotel, but there are plenty of options in the airport vicinity that offer free shuttles to and from the airport, although these latter hotels only offer better deals than the Sheraton on weekdays.

Delta Toronto Airport West (☎ 905-624-1144, 800-737-3211; 5444 Dixie Rd; d from $100) Delta has spacious rooms, a fully equipped fitness center and indoor heated lap pool.

Sheraton Gateway (☎ 905-672-7000, 888-625-5144; d Sat & Sun from $110, Mon-Fri from $210) Attached to Pearson International Airport's Terminal 3, the Sheraton has a 24-hour fitness facility and indoor swimming pool. All rooms are soundproof, and some have views.

Wyndham Bristol Place (☎ 416-675-94444, 877-999-3223; www.wyndham.com; 950 Dixon Rd; d Fri & Sat from $120, Mon-Thu from $260) The posh Wyndham offers daytime rates of just $99.

REATER TORONTO AREA

 you don't mind spending slightly more me on public transport, it's worth seek-g out any one of these travelers' favorites. lthough High Park may not be central, r example, the surrounding neighbor-ood has some fine old homes that make triguing B&B options.

EACONSFIELD Map p225 *B&B*

☎ 416-535-3338; www.bbcanada.com/771.html; Beaconsfield Ave, east of Dufferin St; d without thhroom $85, ste $135-170; streetcar 501; P

Vith a jungle of a front garden almost ob-curing it from sight, lovely Beaconsfield is a ctorian-style boutique hotel owned by an tist–actress couple. Eclectic suites have a athroom and either one or two bedrooms. ll breakfasts are served.

ONNEVUE MANOR Map p225 *B&B*

☎ 416-536-1455; bonne@interlog.com; 33 Beaty Ave, est of Jameson Ave; d from $100; streetcar 501, 504, 8; P

Often voted one of the city's best B&Bs, this gay-owned hostelry is inside a restored 1890s red brick mansion that has lovely handcrafted architectural details. Over a dozen guest rooms all exhibit warm-colored interiors.

DRAKE HOTEL Map p225 *Boutique Hotel*

☎ 416-531-5042; www.thedrakehotel.ca; 1150 Queen St W, east of Dufferin St; d $120-190, ste $220-250; streetcar 501

Revamped to the tune of a cool $5 million, this century-old hotel presides beyond the edge of the Queen West strip. Beckoning to bohemians, artists and indie musicians, it has even lured famed chef David Chrystian into its kitchens. Artful rooms come with vintage furnishings, throw rugs, flat-screen TVs and Internet access.

FRENCH CONNECTION Map p225 *B&B*

☎ 416-537-7741, 800-313-3993; www.thefrenchconnection.com; 102 Burnside Dr, west of Bathurst St; s/d from $65/100, ste $85-150; subway St Clair West; P

It's a stand-out because of its fireplace, grand piano and gourmet French-inspired breakfasts. Elegant suites have king-sized beds and perhaps a private terrace or a whirlpool tub, too. Simpler single and double rooms, without bathrooms, at least have extra-long beds.

FOUR POINTS SHERATON LAKESHORE Map p225 *Hotel*

☎ 416-766-4392, 800-463-9929; www.fourpointstoronto.com; 1926 Lake Shore Blvd; d from $100; streetcar 501, 508; P

Close to the south gates of High Park, the Sheraton's multimillion dollar renovations have certainly paid off for guests, who enjoy a sauna, exercise rooms and easy access to paved recreational paths along the lakefront. It's about 8km west of downtown. Take the streetcar west to Windermere Ave, get off and walk south under the overpass.

GRAYONA TOURIST HOME Map p225 *Guesthouse*

☎ 416-535-5443, 800-354-0244; 1546 King St W, east of Roncesvalles Ave; s/d without bathroom $60/80; streetcar 504; P

This nonsmoking guesthouse is run by a friendly and reliable Australian. Every room has a fridge, telephone, TV and balcony access. More expensive family rooms have a bathroom (although it may down the hall), a children's cot and possibly cooking facilities. A surcharge applies for one-night stays.

INVERNESS Map p224 *B&B*

☎ **416-769-2028; ewleslie@sympatico.ca; 287 Humberside Ave, north of Bloor St W; d $75-95; subway High Park; P**

Possessing a more rural than urban atmosphere, this warm 1920s Arts-and-Crafts styled home is filled with antiques and hardwood furnishings. Rooms may or may not have a bathroom. Organic breakfasts are a plus.

RED DOOR BED & BREAKFAST

Map p225 *B&B*

☎ **416-604-0544; www.reddoorbb.com; 301 Indian Rd, south of Bloor St W; s/d from $90/115; subway Keele; P**

Near Roncesvalles Village, a predominantly Eastern European neighborhood, this B&B is just a short walk from High Park. Run by an artistic and musical couple, there's a grand piano in the living room and some French is spoken. Every room has air-con and a bathroom; the Oak Suite also has a sofa bed and a fireplace. Full, hot breakfasts are served.

TOADHALL BED & BREAKFAST *B&B*

☎ **905-773-4028; www.225toadhall.ca; Richmond Hill, 225 Lakeland Cres; s/d $95/125; P**

It's worth trekking north of downtown Toronto to stay in a solar-powered home on the shores of Lake Wilcox, which offers swimming, canoeing and windsurfing in fair weather. Although there's no air-conditioning, you can count on cool lake breezes and the owners also have a greenhouse. Gourmet breakfasts emphasize organic fare (vegetarian options by request).

Cheap Sleeps

CANDY HAVEN TOURIST HOME

Map p225 *Guesthouse*

☎ **416-532-0651; 1233 King St W, west of Dufferin St; s & d without bathroom $45; streetcar 504**

This one-of-a-kind guesthouse has been around for decades, so by now it's quaintly old-fashioned. All of the simple rooms share a bathroom. No breakfast is served. If you get lost, look for the front porch sign next to McDonald's.

Excursions

TORONTO EXCURSIONS
0 30 km
0 20 mi
81°W
80°W
79°W
45°N
44°N
43°N
Dyer's Bay
Cape Croker
Cape Croker
Georgian Bay
Lake Joseph
Lake Rousseau
Lake Muskoka
Bracebridge
Gravenhurst
Six Mile Lake
Honey Harbour
Gloucester Pool
Christian Island
Cedar Point
Penetanguishene
Midland
Port Severn
Sauble Falls Provincial Park
Sauble Beach
Owen Sound
Meaford
Nottawasaga Bay
Moonstone
Lake Couchiching
Orillia
Horseshoe Valley
Horseshoe Resort
Collingwood
Blue Mountain
Wasaga Beach
Lake Simcoe
Barrie
Durham
Shelburne
Uxbridge
Wooden Sticks
Falconry Centre
Mount Forest
Grand River
Luther Lake
Orangeville
Humber River
Aurora
Stouffville
David Dunlap Observatory
Richmond Hill
Unionville
Harriston
Palmerston
Arthur
Kleinburg
McMichael Canadian Art Collection
Thornhill
Paramount Canada's Wonderland
Rouge River
Credit River
Belwood Lake
Listowel
Conestogo Lake
Fergus
Brampton
Toronto
Elora
Lester B Pearson International Airport
Fast Ferry to Rochester, NY
Elmira
Acton
Mississauga
Milverton
St Clements
Guelph
Milton
Waterloo
Kitchener
Oakville
Glen Abbey Golf Club
Hydrofoil to Queenston
CANADA
USA
Nith River
Stratford
Shakespeare
New Hamburg
Cambridge
Lake Ontario
Waterdown
Burlington
St Mary's
Aldershot
Dundas
Hamilton
Stoney Creek
Niagara-on-the-Lake
Ancaster
Port Dalhousie
St Catharines
Grimsby
Woodstock
Brantford
Queenston
Niagara Falls
Ingersoll
Ohsweken
Caledonia
Ontario
Niagara Peninsula
Chippawa
London
Sarnia (100km)
Welland
Welland Canal
Niagara River
Cayuga
Grand River
Dunnville
Tillsonburg
Jarvis
Simcoe
Port Colborne
Windsor (175km)
Aylmer
St Thomas
Lake Erie
CANADA
USA
Long Point Bay
Port Stanley
Port Burwell
Long Point

Excursions

The name of the province 'Ontario' likely derives from an Iroquois or Huron word meaning 'beautiful, sparkling water,' which probably refers to the province's many lakes or mighty Niagara Falls. Although the famous falls surely deserve their millions of visitors (and honeymooners) each year, there is much more to be uncovered inside the province's 1 million sq km. Digging deeper into southwestern Ontario reveals the beautiful vineyards of the Niagara Escarpment, while the Stratford and Shaw theater festivals draw residents and travelers alike out into the countryside. Other quick escapes from the city include Canadian art collections and winter resorts for downhill skiing and snowboarding. All in all, it's enough to entertain anyone of any age. Peak summer season runs from Victoria Day in late May to Labour Day in early September. Note that opening hours are reduced out of season.

WINE TASTING & WATERFALLS

If you only have one day to spend outside Toronto, spend it all on the Niagara Peninsula. Start out early in the morning and drive through the **wine country** (p182), stopping off to taste some of the region's famous **ice wines** (p185). Have lunch in the vineyards, then hop back in the car and head straight for Niagara Falls. After ditching your car, launch straight onto a **Maid of the Mist** (p176) boat before exploring any of the other attractions around the falls, or those found further up the **Niagara Parkway** (p178). If you want to make an overnight trip of it, stay at a high-rise hotel right next to the falls or one of the quaint B&Bs standing along the parkway, then drive back to Toronto through the wine country the following day.

NATURE

The need to see 'green' is the impulse driving many visitors out of the city. That can mean leisurely cycling down the **Niagara Parkway** (p178) or the country laneways of the **wine country** (p182), exploring the **Niagara Glen Nature Preserve** (p179) and nearby Botanical Gardens (p179), whooshing down the Niagara River in a **Whirlpool Jet** (p190), ambling the gardens of **Stratford** (p187) or hiking the conservation lands of the **McMichael Canadian Art Collection** (p186). In winter, skiing areas are just a short drive northwest of Toronto at **Horseshoe Resort** and **Blue Mountain** (p191).

ART & ARCHITECTURE

The main draws are the **Stratford Festival** (p187) and Niagara-on-the-Lake's **Shaw Festival** (p189). Every year these theater festivals seem to get bigger, the seasons run longer, new venues are built and the attendant hullabaloo – including dramatic readings, behind-the-scenes tours, theater lectures, musical concerts and fringe festival performances – grows exponentially. Same-day rush tickets are often available at the main theater box offices in both towns, but a little advance planning will help you secure the best seats and, if you wish, overnight accommodations. In the town of **Stratford** (p187), you'll also find a few visual arts galleries and museums, as well as historic architecture worth noting, while Queenston's **RiverBrink Gallery** (p179) stands south of Niagara-on-the-Lake. Worth its own special trip is the phenomenal **McMichael Canadian Art Collection** (p186) of Canadian art, just a short drive from Toronto.

HISTORY

Toronto has its **Old York** (p46), but much of the early colonial history of Upper Canada took place in the Niagara region and you could easily visit all the sights in an afternoon's drive. Most of the sites left standing, some of which have been meticulously restored, are found in and around **Queenston** (p179), including the **Mackenzie Heritage Printery & Newspaper Museum** (p179), the **Laura Secord Homestead** (p179) and **monument to Major General Sir Isaac Brock** (p179) i Queenston Heights Park. History buffs shouldn't miss Niagara-on-the-Lake's fascinatin **Niagara Apothecary** (p190) and the **Niagara Historical Society Museum** (p190). Even kids will enjoy th ghost tours at **Fort George** (p190). If you end up at Niagara Falls, look for the wreck of th **Old Scow** (p176), too.

NIAGARA FALLS

Napoleon's younger brother and his new bride once rode in a stagecoach from New Orlean to view the falls, which have been a honeymoon attraction ever since. Spanning the Niagar River between Ontario and upper New York, the falls are one of Canada's top tourist destin ations, drawing over 13 million people annually. Although hundreds of the world's waterfal are actually taller than Niagara Falls, in terms of sheer volume, these are hard to beat: th equivalent of over a million bathtubs full of water goes over every minute. Even in winte when the flow is partially hidden and the edges frozen solid – like a freeze-framed film – it' quite a spectacle. Very occasionally ice jams stop the falls altogether. The first recorded in stance of this occurred on Easter Sunday 1848, and it caused some to speculate that the en of the world was nigh and others to scavenge the riverbed beneath the falls for treasure.

On the US side, the pretty **Bridal Veil Falls** (often referred to as the American Falls) cras down onto mammoth rocks that have fallen due to erosion. The grander, more powerfu **Horseshoe Falls**, on the Canadian side, plunge down into the Maid of the Mist pool, which i indeed misty and clouds views of the falls from afar. **Maid of the Mist** boats have been takin brave passengers close to the falls for a view from the bottom since 1846 – it's loud an wet and lots of fun. Everyone heads for the boats' upper deck, but views from either en of the lower deck are just fine, too.

Illuminating the falls has been a tradition since 1860, when the tightrope walker, 'Th Great Blondin,' first carried flares and shot off fireworks. Every night of the year, colore spotlights are turned on the falls, and in summer there are weekend fireworks. The annua **Winter Festival of Lights** is a season of concerts, fireworks and nighttime parades from the en of November until mid-January.

The town of Niagara Falls is split into two main sections. The 'normal' part of town where locals go about their business, is called 'old downtown.' The area around Bridge S near the corner of Erie Ave, has both the train and bus stations. Generally, however, ther is little to see or do in this part of town. About 3km south along River Rd (the Niagar Parkway) are the majestic falls and all the tourist trappings – a casino, hotels, artificial at tractions and flashing lights – producing a sort of Canadian Las Vegas.

Operating hours for individual attractions vary, so check with the Niagara Parks Com mission. This helpful provincial agency runs good, but busy information desks at **Table Ro Information Centre**, right next to the Horseshoe Falls, and at **Maid of the Mist Plaza.**

From near Table Rock Information Centre, you can **Journey Behind the Falls** by donning a plas tic poncho and walk down through rock-cut tunnels halfway down the cliff side – as close a you can get to the falls without getting in a barrel (or going over to the American side). It' open year-round, but be prepared to wait in line for your brief turn in the spray. Less tha 1km south of the Horseshoe Falls, the free **Niagara Parks Greenhouse** provides year-round flora displays. Opposite rusting away in the upper rapids of the river, the **Old Scow** is a steel barg that has been lodged on rocks and waiting to be washed over the falls since 1918.

At the north end of town, next to the Whirlpool Bridge, the **White Water Walk** is another wa to get up close and personal, this time on a 325m boardwalk suspended above raging whit water, just downstream from the falls. The jungly **Niagara Falls Aviary** has free-flying tropica bird exhibits from Australia, Africa and South America. Nearby the immensely successfu **Casino Niagara** never closes.

On a hilltop reached via a quaint **incline railway** meant for tourists, there's a fascinatin museum of Niagara Falls history attached to the **IMAX Niagara Falls**, which shows somewha outdated 45-minute shows about the history of the falls running almost continuously, al ternating with French versions and other current IMAX features. Adjacent is **Skylon Towe** a 520ft spire with yellow elevators crawling like bugs up the exterior. Virtually lording i

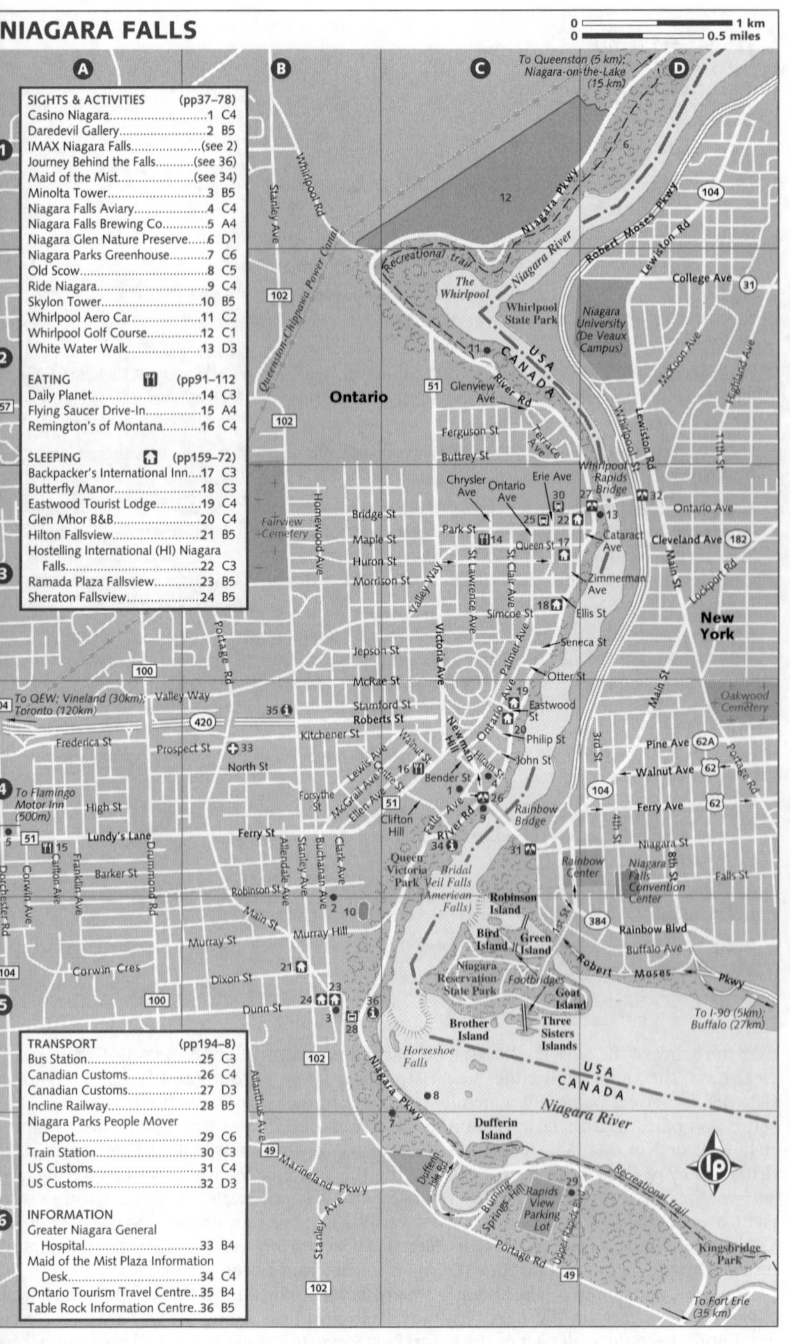
NIAGARA FALLS
0 1 km
0 0.5 miles
A
B
C
D
1
2
3
4
5
6
SIGHTS & ACTIVITIES (pp37–78)
Casino Niagara.....1 C4
Daredevil Gallery.....2 B5
IMAX Niagara Falls.....(see 2)
Journey Behind the Falls.....(see 36)
Maid of the Mist.....(see 34)
Minolta Tower.....3 B5
Niagara Falls Aviary.....4 C4
Niagara Falls Brewing Co.....5 A4
Niagara Glen Nature Preserve.....6 D1
Niagara Parks Greenhouse.....7 C6
Old Scow.....8 C5
Ride Niagara.....9 C4
Skylon Tower.....10 B5
Whirlpool Aero Car.....11 C2
Whirlpool Golf Course.....12 C1
White Water Walk.....13 D3
EATING (pp91–112)
Daily Planet.....14 C3
Flying Saucer Drive-In.....15 A4
Remington's of Montana.....16 C4
SLEEPING (pp159–72)
Backpacker's International Inn.....17 C3
Butterfly Manor.....18 C3
Eastwood Tourist Lodge.....19 C4
Glen Mhor B&B.....20 C4
Hilton Fallsview.....21 B5
Hostelling International (HI) Niagara Falls.....22 C3
Ramada Plaza Fallsview.....23 B5
Sheraton Fallsview.....24 B5
TRANSPORT (pp194–8)
Bus Station.....25 C3
Canadian Customs.....26 C4
Canadian Customs.....27 D3
Incline Railway.....28 B5
Niagara Parks People Mover Depot.....29 C6
Train Station.....30 C3
US Customs.....31 C4
US Customs.....32 D3
INFORMATION
Greater Niagara General Hospital.....33 B4
Maid of the Mist Plaza Information Desk.....34 C4
Ontario Tourism Travel Centre.....35 B4
Table Rock Information Centre.....36 B5
To Queenston (5 km); Niagara-on-the-Lake (15 km)
Ontario
New York
USA
CANADA
Niagara River
The Whirlpool
Whirlpool State Park
Niagara University (De Veaux Campus)
Recreational trail
Niagara Pkwy
Robert Moses Pkwy
Lewiston Rd
College Ave
Queenston-Chippawa Power Canal
Whirlpool Rd
Stanley Ave
Glenview Ave
River Rd
Terrace Ave
Ferguson St
Buttrey St
Chrysler Ave
Ontario Ave
Erie Ave
Whirlpool Rapids Bridge
Whirlpool St
Lewiston Rd
Ontario Ave
Cleveland Ave
Cataract Ave
Zimmerman Ave
Ellis St
Seneca St
Otter St
Main St
Lockport Rd
McKoon Ave
Highland Ave
11th St
Fairview Cemetery
Homewood Ave
Bridge St
Maple St
Huron St
Morrison St
Park St
Queen St
Valley Way
Victoria Ave
St Lawrence Ave
St Clair Ave
Simcoe St
Palmer Ave
Jepson St
McRae St
Stamford St
Roberts St
Kitchener St
Eastwood St
Philip St
John St
Oakwood Cemetery
Portage Rd
To QEW; Vineland (30km); Toronto (120km)
Valley Way
Frederica St
Prospect St
North St
Walnut St
Lewis Ave
Centre St
McGrail Ave
Ellen Ave
Forsythe St
Newman Hill
Hiram St
Bender St
Falls Ave
River Rd
Clifton Hill
Rainbow Bridge
3rd St
Pine Ave
Walnut Ave
Ferry Ave
4th St
Portage Rd
To Flamingo Motor Inn (500m)
High St
Lundy's Lane
Ferry St
Drummond Rd
Carlton Ave
Franklin Ave
Barker St
Corwin Ave
Dorchester Rd
Allendale Ave
Stanley Ave
Buchanan Ave
Clark Ave
Queen Victoria Park
Bridal Veil Falls (American Falls)
Robinson Island
Rainbow Center
Niagara Falls Convention Center
Niagara St
8th St
Falls St
Robinson St
Main St
Murray Hill
Murray St
Bird Island
Green Island
1st St
Rainbow Blvd
Buffalo Ave
Robert Moses Pkwy
Corwin Cres
Dixon St
Niagara Reservation State Park
Footbridges
Goat Island
Dunn St
To I-90 (5km); Buffalo (27km)
Brother Island
Three Sisters Islands
Horseshoe Falls
Niagara Pkwy
Atlantus Ave
Dufferin Island
Dufferin Isle Rd
Marineland Pkwy
Stanley Ave
Burning Springs Hill
Rapids View Parking Lot
Upper Rapids Blvd
Recreational trail
Portage Rd
Kingsbridge Park
To Fort Erie (35 km)

Transportation

Distance from Toronto Niagara Falls 125km.

Direction Southeast.

Travel time Two hours.

Car Follow the Queen Elizabeth Way (QEW) westbound from Toronto past St Catharines. Exit at Hwy 420 eastbound toward the Rainbow Bridge.

Parking There is limited metered parking around town, but plentiful pay parking lots (from $5 per 30 minutes, or $13 per day). The huge Rapids View parking lot is a little over 3km south of the falls off River Rd.

Bus station (☎ 905-357-2133; 4445 Erie Ave) This is in the old downtown area, away from the falls. Greyhound buses depart frequently for Toronto ($20, 1½ to two hours) and twice or three times daily for Buffalo, New York ($5.50, one to 1½ hours).

Casino Niagara shuttle bus (☎ 416-599-8892, 877-361-2888; www.itripmate.com) Passengers must be over 19 (ID required), and round-trip tickets cost $18. Note you must board a return bus from the casino within 24 hours. Call or check the website for schedules (daily runs) and pick-up information. Advance reservations are recommended.

Niagara Airbus (☎ 905-374-8111, 800-268-8111; www.niagaraairbus.com) Offers airport transfers from Toronto's Pearson International Airport.

Niagara Parks People Mover (day pass adult/child $6/3; 🕓 every 20min 9am-11pm Mar-Oct) Rely on the Niagara Parks Commission's economical and efficient bus system. The depot is in the huge Rapids View Parking Lot. Day passes can be purchased at most stops. Shuttles follow a 15km path from the Rapids View parking lot north past the Horseshoe Falls, Rainbow and Whirlpool Bridges, Whirlpool Aero Car and during peak season, to Queenston village.

Niagara Transit (☎ 905-356-1179; www.niagaratransit.com; shuttle rides adult/child $3/1, day pass for 1 adult & 2 children $6; 🕓 mid-May–Nov, departures every 30min 9-1:30am peak season) Niagara Transit provides a shuttle bus service around town. One route, the Red Line, goes around Clifton Hill and other falls attractions, then up Lundy's Lane to the motels and back. The Blue Line runs from the downtown bus and train stations to the falls area attractions, by Table Rock and down the Niagara Parkway to the Rapids View parking lot, then loops back around up Portage Rd and Stanley Ave. The Green Line goes from the Rainbow Bridge north to the Whirlpool Aero Car, then back down River Rd past the B&Bs to Clifton Hill. Out of season, Niagara Transit's regular city buses (adult/child $2.25/1) must be used.

Train VIA Rail runs daily trains from Toronto ($23.50, two hours), once in the morning and another in the late afternoon or early evening. Some Amtrak routes to/from the USA stop at Niagara Falls. The train station is opposite the bus station.

JoJo Tours (☎ 416-201-6465, 888-202-3513; http://home.interlog.com/~jojotour/; day trips $40-50) Friendly JoJo Tours offers day trips to the region which include a stop at a winery and Niagara-on-the-Lake.

Moose Travel (☎ 888-816-6673; www.moosenetwork.com; tours $40) Moose Travel runs tours to the falls from Toronto between May and October.

over the brink of the falls, the **Minolta Tower** has indoor and outdoor observation galleries. On clear days, the views from either tower stretch as far as Toronto and Buffalo, New York. **Clifton Hill** is a street name but generally refers to another slope near the falls given over to sense-bombarding artificial attractions in Disney-like concentration. You name it – Ripley's Believe It or Not, Madame Tussaud's Wax Museum, Criminals Hall of Fame (you get the drift) – they're all here. In most cases, paying the entrance fee will leave you feeling like a sucker. Air tour companies, such as **Fly Niagara** and **Niagara Helicopters**, take cashed-up visitors right over the falls, with departures from various locations around the Niagara Peninsula. Out on the Lundy's Lane motel strip, **Niagara Falls Brewing Co** gives cottage-brewery tours that let you sample its famous Eisbock (German for 'ice ram') beer.

The slow, pleasant two-lane **Niagara Parkway** runs for 56km, almost the length of the Niagara River, from Niagara-on-the-Lake past the falls to Fort Erie. Along the way are parks, picnic areas and viewpoints, all part of the **Niagara Parks Commission** system. A paved recreational trail for cycling, in-line skating or walking parallels the parkway and is marked with historic and natural points of interest. In season, fresh-fruit stands selling cold cherry cider pop up beside the trail.

About 4.5km north of Horseshoe Falls on the Niagara River, past the Great Gorge Adventure (don't bother), is the **Whirlpool Aero Car.** It was designed by Spanish engineer Leonardo Torres Quevedo and started operation in 1916. Here a gondola stretched 550m between two outcrops takes you above a deadly whirlpool, created by the falls, so you can peer at logs, tires and other debris spinning in the eddies below. The attraction is not wheelchair accessible. Next you'll pass the lush **Whirlpool Golf Course.**

A little further is the exceptional **Niagara Glen Nature Preserve**, the only place where you can gain a sense of what the area was like before the arrival of Europeans. There are 4km of walking trails winding down the gorge, past huge boulders, icy cold caves, wildflowers and woods where the falls were situated thousands of years ago. The Niagara Parks Commission offers daily guided nature walks during summer for a nominal fee. Take along your own water, as the Niagara is one river from which you do not want to drink – this region is one of the industrial centers of North America. Almost opposite the preserve are the finely trimmed **Botanical Gardens**, with 100 acres of herbs, vegetables and trees for browsing.

Nine kilometers north of the falls, you can step inside the glass-enclosed **Butterfly Conservatory**, where over 50 species make their way out of chrysalides and flutter about the over 130 species of flowers and plants. Since this is also a breeding facility, you can see new butterflies being released, usually around 9:30am, each morning. There's also an outdoor butterfly garden. Past the hideous floral clock and the 1950s **Sir Adam Beck power plant**, next to the Lewiston Bridge to the USA, is **Queenston Heights**, a national historic site known for its towering **monument to Major General Sir Isaac Brock**, 'Saviour of Upper Canada.' The winding stairwell inside takes you up over 50m to a fabulous view. Self-guided walking tours of the hillside recount the 1812 Battle of Queenston Heights, a significant British victory that helped Canada resist becoming part of the USA.

In the small village of **Queenston**, just beyond the Lewiston Bridge to the USA, is the historic **Mackenzie Heritage Printery & Newspaper Museum**, where William Lyon Mackenzie (p5) once edited the hell-raising *Colonial Advocate*. Nearby is the **Laura Secord Homestead**, which belonged to one of Canada's best-known heroines. During the War of 1812, she hiked over 30km to warn the British soldiers of impending attack by the USA – even though she was a US citizen by birth. Further north, the is the home of the Samuel E Weir Collection of Canadian art, which includes early landscapes of the Niagara Peninsula and works by the Group of Seven (p27).

Information

Accessible Niagara (www.accessibleniagara.com) This website provides advice for the mobility-impaired.

Discover Niagara (www.discoverniagara.com) This website offers travel deals and an events calendar.

Greater Niagara General Hospital (Map p177; ☎ 905-358-0171; 5546 Portage Rd) This has a 24-hour emergency room.

Info Niagara (www.infoniagara.com) This privately run website has helpful links.

Niagara Falls After Hours Walk-In Clinic (☎ 905-374-3344; 6453 Morrison St; 6-9pm Mon, Tue & Thu-Fri, 1-9pm Wed, 10am-3pm Sat & Sun) For nonemergencies only.

Niagara Falls & Great Gorge Adventure Pass (adult/child $32/19) This discount pass includes Maid of the Mist, Journey Behind the Falls and attractions along the Niagara Parkway and Queenston historical sites, as well as the Niagara Parks People Mover shuttle buses. Discount passes are available at Table Rock Information Centre as well as at various attractions.

Niagara Parks Commission (Map p177; ☎ 905-371-0254, 877-642-7275; www.niagaraparks.com; 9am-11pm summer, 9am-4pm rest of year) Runs information desks (open daily) at Maid of the Mist Plaza and Table Rock Information Centre.

Ontario Tourism Travel Centre (☎ 905-358-3221; 5355 Stanley Ave; 8:30am-6pm, later in summer) On the western outskirts of town. Look for free tourist booklets containing maps and discount coupons for attractions and rides.

Sights & Activities

Botanical Gardens (☎ 905-356-8554; 2565 Niagara Parkway; admission free; dawn-dusk)

Butterfly Conservatory (☎ 905-358-0025; 2405 Niagara Parkway; adult/child 6-12 $8.50/4; 9am-5pm, later in summer)

Casino Niagara (Map p177; ☎ 800-563-2557; www.casinoniagara.com; 5705 Falls Ave; 24hr; free shuttle buses run from hotels & attractions all over town)

Detour: Border Crossing

A few bridges run over the Niagara River to New York State, but only the Rainbow Bridge is open to tourists. You can walk or drive across to the falls from the American side, but both pedestrians and drivers have to pay a bridge toll. Foreign visitors should make sure their visas (p206) – both Canadian and US – are in order.

Daredevil Gallery (Map p177; ☎ 905-374-4629, 905-358-3611; 6170 Fallsview Blvd; admission free; ⏲ 10am-4pm)

Fly Niagara (☎ 877-359-2924; www.flyniagara.com; 30-minute flights $150) Fully narrated airplane tours over the falls and Lake Ontario. All passengers have window seats.

IMAX Niagara Falls (Map p177; ☎ 905-374-4629; www.imaxniagara.com; 6170 Fallsview Blvd; adult/child 4-12/senior $12/6.50/8.50)

Incline Railway (Map p177; rides $1; ⏲ Apr–mid-Oct, 9am-midnight summer) Weather permitting, it runs from nearby the Minolta tower down the hillside to the Table Rock complex by the falls area.

Journey Behind the Falls (Map p177; ☎ 905-354-1551; 6650 Niagara Parkway; adult/child 6-12 $7.50/3.75; ⏲ 10am-6pm Mon-Fri, 9am-6pm Sat & Sun, till 8pm summer)

Laura Secord Homestead (☎ 905-262-4851; 29 Queenston St, Queenston; adult/child 6-12 $2.50/1.50; ⏲ 10am-4pm May–mid-Oct)

Mackenzie Heritage Printery & Newspaper Museum (☎ 905-262-5676; 1 Queenston St, Queenston; adult/child 6-12 $2.50/1.50; ⏲ 10am-4pm May–mid-Oct)

Maid of the Mist (Map p177; ☎ 905-358-0311; www.maidofthemist.com; Maid of the Mist Plaza, 5920 Niagara Parkway; adult/child 6-12 $13/8; ⏲ every 15min, weather permitting 9:45am-4:45pm Mon-Fri, 9:45am-5:45pm Sat & Sun Apr-late Oct, 9:45am-7:45pm summer)

Minolta Tower (Map p177; ☎ 905-356-1501, 800-461-2492; adult/child 6-18/senior/family $7/5/5/20, day & night return ticket adult/child 6-18 $9/7; ⏲ hr vary)

Monument to Major General Sir Isaac Brock (14184 Niagara Parkway; admission free; ⏲ 10am-5pm summer)

Niagara Falls Aviary (Map p177; ⏲ 905-356-8888, 866-994-0090; www.niagarafallsaviary.com; 5651 River Rd; adult/child 6-12/senior $15/10/14; ⏲ 9am-9pm summer, 9am-5pm rest of year)

Niagara Falls Brewing Co (Map p177; ☎ 905-356-2739; 6863 Lundy's Lane; tours free, reservations required)

Niagara Helicopters (☎ 905-357-5672; www.niagara helicopters.com; 3731 Victoria Ave; 10-minute flights adult/child 2-11 $100/55; ⏲ 9am-sunset, weather permitting. Individual reservations noon-1pm)

RiverBrink Gallery (☎ 905-262-4510; www .riverbrink.org; 116 Queenston St, Queenston; adult/child under 12/senior $5/free/4; ⏲ 10am-5pm Wed-Sun Victoria Day–Thanksgiving)

Sir Adam Beck Power Plant (Niagara Parkway, at the Queenston-Lewiston Bridge; adult/child 6-12 $8/4; ⏲ 30min tours 10am-4pm mid-Mar–early Sep) Free parking and shuttle from the floral clock.

Skylon Tower (Map p177; ☎ 905-356-2651; www .skylon.com; 5200 Robinson St; adult/child under 13/senior $9.50/5.50/8.50; ⏲ 8am-midnight summer, 11am-9pm rest of year) Its revolving restaurant is more expensive than the Minolta Tower's, but the early-bird dinner special saves you some cash ($25 minimum food charge per person, plus elevator ride $2). Seatings are at 4:30pm and 5pm; reservations required.

Whirlpool Aero Car (Map p177; ☎ 888-255-1321; 3850 Niagara Parkway; adult/child 6-12 $6/3; ⏲ hr vary)

Daredevils

Surprisingly, more than a few people who have gone over Niagara Falls, suicides aside, do live to tell about it.

A schoolteacher named Annie Taylor first devised the padded-barrel method (successfully) in 1901, promoting a rash of barrel stunters that continued into the 1920s. In 1984 Karl Soucek revived the tradition with a bright red barrel at the Horseshoe Falls. He made it, but only to die just six months later in another barrel stunt at the Houston Astrodome, which certainly says something about tempting fate.

The first stuntman of the 1990s, witnessed and photographed by startled visitors, went over the edge in a kayak. He's now paddling the great white water in the sky. The US citizen who tried to jet ski over the falls in 1995 might have made it – if his rocket-propelled parachute had opened. Another American, Kit Carson, became the first person in recorded history to survive a trip over the falls unaided during 2003. After being charged by the Canadian government with illegally performing a stunt, he promptly joined the circus.

But there's no need to go to such extremes yourself when **IMAX Niagara Falls** (p176) allows everyone to try the plunge – virtually, that is.

Whirlpool Golf Course (Map p177; ☎ 905-356-1140, 866-465-3642; www.niagaraparksgolf.com; 3351 Niagara Parkway; green fees $65-70, cart rental $15-20, golf club rental $30; 🕒 Apr–mid-Nov)

White Water Walk (Map p177; 4330 Niagara Parkway; adult/child 6-12 $6/3; 🕒 10am-5pm late Apr-Oct, later in summer)

Eating

Daily Planet (Map p177; ☎ 905-371-1722; 4573 Queen St; meals $5-10; 🕒 till 2am) While finding food in Niagara Falls is no problem, the dining usually isn't great. That said, this is a good place to grab a brew and pub grub at nontourist prices, in the slow part of old downtown.

Flying Saucer Drive-In (Map p177; ☎ 905-356-4553; 6768 Lundy's Lane; meals $4-16; 🕒 6am-3am Mon-Thu, 6am-4am Fri & Sat) For 'out of this world' fast food, you can't miss this diner out on the Lundy's Lane motel strip. Famous 99¢ breakfast specials are served until noon.

Remington's of Montana (Map p177; ☎ 905-356-4410; 5657 Victoria Ave; mains $15-40; 🕒 dinner) Around Clifton Hill and along Victoria and Stanley Aves, scads of restaurants mostly focus on ever-popular Italian eateries. This steak and seafood restaurant is more stylish.

Sleeping

Accommodations are plentiful, but can be completely booked up sometimes. In summer, on weekends and for holidays (Canadian and American), prices spike sharply. Many B&Bs (peruse some of them on-line at www.bbniagarafalls.com) are found along River Rd, mid-way between the falls area and the old downtown. If you haven't made a reservation, just look for Vacancy signs.

Backpacker's International Inn (Map p177; ☎ 905-357-4266, 800-891-7022; 4219 Huron St, cnr Zimmerman Ave; dm/d $29/50) An independent hostel in a grand 19th-century home. Upstairs rooms, like those in a small European hotel, are particularly charming. Rates include taxes, morning coffee and muffin.

Butterfly Manor (Map p177; ☎ 905-358-8988; bbnotl@vaxxine.com; 4917 River Rd; d $110-160) An award-winning B&B. French, Italian, German and Spanish are spoken.

Eastwood Tourist Lodge (Map p177; ☎ 905-354-8686; www.theeastwood.com; 5359 River Rd; d $115-140, ste $150-175) A stately home with balconies overlooking the river. German and Spanish are spoken.

Flamingo Motor Inn (☎ 905-356-4646, 800-738-7701; 7701 Lundy's Lane; d peak/off-peak from $75/40) Millions of motels along Lundy's Lane offer enticements such as waterbeds, saunas and heart-shaped Jacuzzis – just like the kitschy Flamingo.

Glen Mhor B&B (Map p177; ☎ 905-354-2600; www.glenmhor.com; 5381 River Rd; d $80-130) Guest bicycles and pick-up available from the bus or train station. Japanese spoken.

Hilton Fallsview (☎ 905-354-7887, 800-445-8667; www.niagarafalls.hilton.com; 6361 Fallsview Blvd; d $65-400)

Hostelling International Niagara Falls (Map p177; HI; ☎ 905-357-0770, 888-749-0058; 4549 Cataract Ave; dm $19) A standby in the old downtown, close to the train and bus stations. Sheet rental is available at $2 per person.

Ramada Plaza Fallsview (Map p177; ☎ 905-356-1501, 800-272-6232; www.ramada.com; 6732 Fallsview Blvd; d $55-160) Hotel rooms by the falls tend to be new and expensive – $100 and up for rooms with views here, or at the nearby Sheraton or Hilton properties.

Sheraton Fallsview (☎ 905-374-1077, 877-353-2557; www.fallsview.com; 6755 Fallsview Blvd; d $75-240)

Niagara Falls (p176)

NIAGARA PENINSULA WINE COUNTRY

If it seems strange to find wine-making here in the Great White North, remember that the Niagara Peninsula sits on the 43rd parallel, similar in latitude to northern California and south of Bordeaux, France. The moderate microclimate created by Lake Ontario and the Niagara escarpment and the mineral-rich soil have contributed significantly to the area's viticultural success. Since the 1980s, Niagara's small cottage industry has really grown up and international award-winning vintners are now capably turning out international-caliber vintages.

Ongoing experimentation with different grape varieties results in erratic quality, but the predominant Riesling, Chardonnay and Gewürztraminer are steadily improving; reds like Cabernet Sauvignon, Pinot Noir and Baco Noir are so far, with very few exceptions, missable. But what you won't want to miss under any circumstances are the expensive late-harvest and ice dessert wines that have garnered the region a sterling international reputation, regularly beating French varieties in blind taste tests.

An ever-increasing number of wineries, now numbering over three dozen, use the vintner's quality alliance (VQA) designation. By the time you arrive here, at least half a dozen new wineries will have appeared, so be adventurous. Official wine route maps

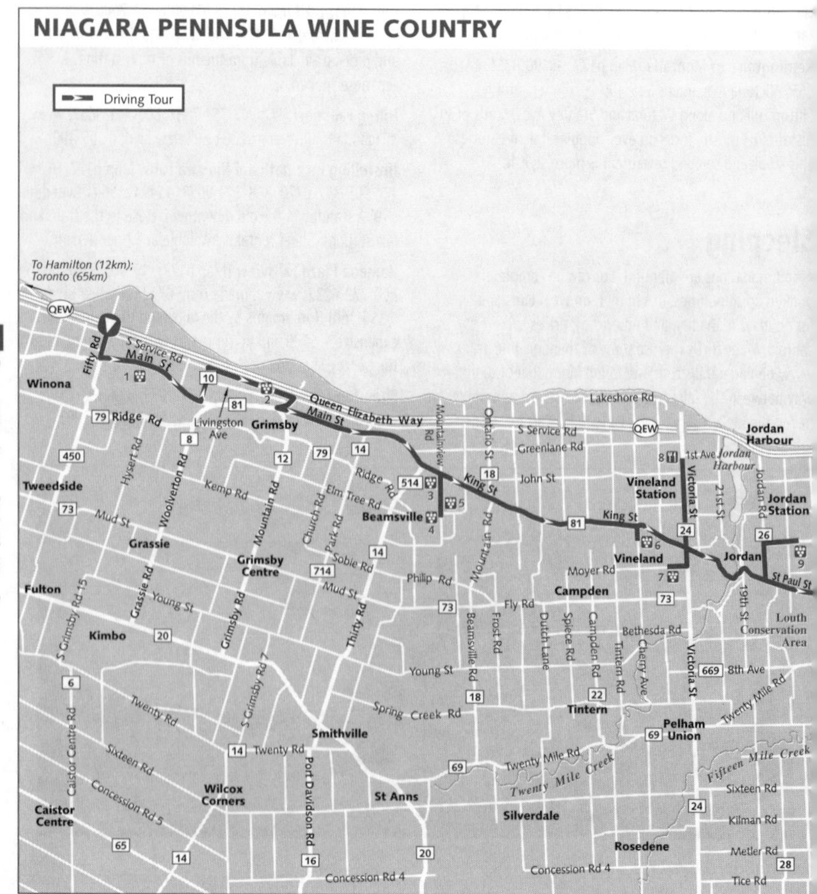

and helpful guide booklets are available free at many wineries' tasting rooms, or click on www.winesofontario.org. Most wineries are open daily until 4pm, but may closed earlier in winter. Tastings are often gratis, except for ice wines and other rare vintages (for which a nominal tasting fee applies). Some wineries offer free tours, even without reservations.

Driving Tour

The following drive hits the Niagara Peninsula's highlights, both for quality and style, of wineries and farm stands along the way to Niagara-on-the-Lake.

Coming from Toronto, get off the Queen Elizabeth Way (QEW) after about an hour at Exit 78/Fifty Rd, then follow signs to **Puddicombe Farms 1**, where you can pick your own cherries or raspberries (July) or apples (September/October). The café serves light lunches, afternoon tea and there's a general store. It also makes very good fruit wines.

Properly refreshed, loop back toward the expressway to **Kittling Ridge Estates Wines & Spirits 2**, which looks rather like a factory. But just one taste of its award-winning ice and late-harvest wines will win you over. Continue east on the service road, then cut south onto what eventually becomes rambling Hwy 81. Around Beamsville, look out for the photogenic **Peninsula Ridge Estates Winery 3**. The new wines taste unfinished, but the log-cabin tasting room

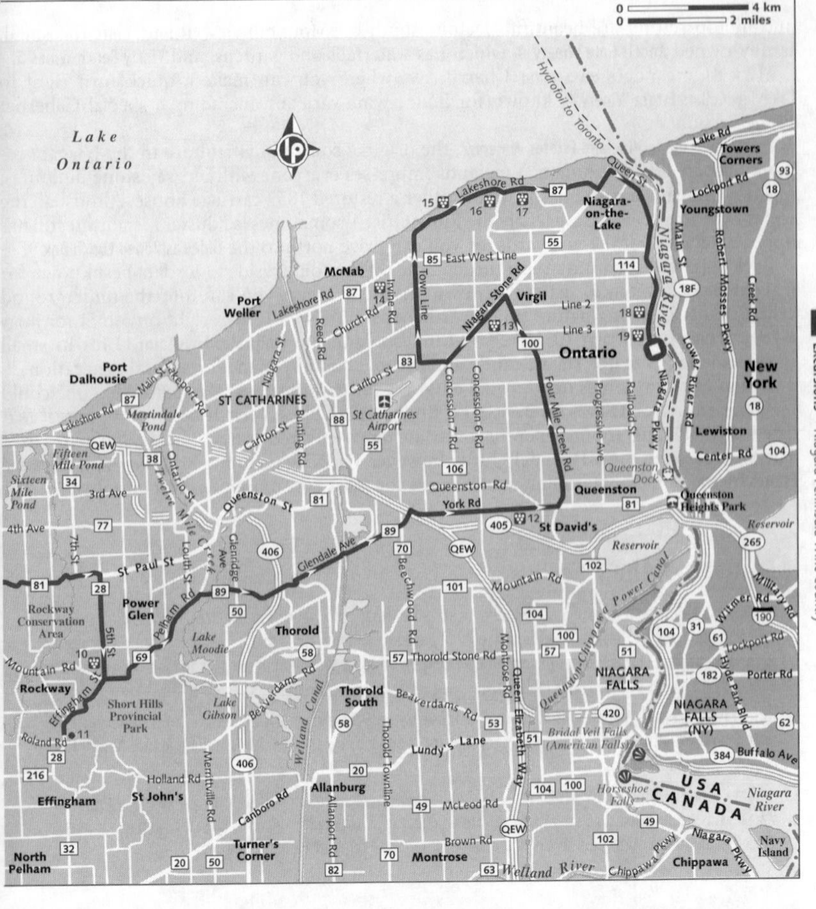

Transportation

Distance from Toronto Vineland 90km.

Direction Southwest.

Travel time One to 1½ hours.

Car Take the Queen Elizabeth Way (QEW) westbound past Hamilton. The official Wine Route is signposted at various exits off the QEW, on rural highways and along backcountry roads.

Crush on Niagara (☎ 905-562-3373, 866-408-9463; www.crushtours.com; tours $95-125) Crush on Niagara offers guided small-group van tours departing from various pick-up points in the Niagara region.

Niagara Airbus (☎ 905-374-8111, 800-268-8111; www.niagaraairbus.com;tours from Toronto $95-135, from Niagara Falls $50-85, from Niagara-on-the-Lake $35) Niagara Airbus stops at well-known wineries; some itineraries include vineyard tours, lunches and shopping in Niagara-on-the-Lake.

Niagara Wine Tours (☎ 905-468-1300, 800-680-7006; www.niagaraworldwinetours.com; 92 Picton St, Niagara-on-the-Lake; tours $80-120; 🕑 May-Oct) Niagara Wine Tours offers microregional cycle trips around the Niagara Peninsula, with tastings at local wineries and a private vineyard lunch. It also runs van tours of the Niagara-on-the-Lake wine region ($55 to $150).

and hilltop setting are beautiful. Detour south on Mountainview Rd to visit the small family-owned **Angels Gate Winery** 4, which has waterfalls and gardens, and **Thirty Bench Wines** 5.

Hwy 81 meanders east past Cherry Ave, where you can make a quick turn right to **Lakeview Cellars Estate Winery** 6, known for its ice wine varietals, including a special Cabernet Franc version.

Further east is **Vineland Estates Winery** 7, the original source of viticulture in the Niagara region. Like an elder statesman, Vinelands impresses everyone with its gray stone buildings, one now housing a petite B&B and the other a restored 1857 carriage house. Almost all the wines here are excellent, especially the Pinot Gris. A sometimes lackluster restaurant still has unbeatable views of the vineyards, or you can drive north to the **Olde Fashioned Lunch Box** 8.

Back on Hwy 81, continue east through the rolling countryside to Jordan, best known for its **Creekside Estate Winery** 9, just east of town on 4th St, where you can tour the underground cellars and stroll along nature trails. Further east on Hwy 81, turn right on 5th St for **Henry of Pelham Family Estate Winery** 10. Here you can also detour to **White Meadows Farm** 11 for its small store, which sells maple sugar, candy and syrup, all family made for several generations.

In another 20 minutes or so, you'll enter the Niagara-on-the-Lake region. No one could miss the grandiose **Château des Charmes** 12. Built to look like a French country manor, it features skylit tasting rooms opening onto a canopy-covered terrace facing the vineyards. The vintages aren't nearly so delightful, however. On Niagara Stone Rd (Hwy 55), **Hillebrand Estates Winery** 13 mostly ferments wines made for mass consumption, not connoisseurs. For

Festivals of the Vines

Ice Wine Celebration Although many wineries host ice-wine harvesting events in January (around $180), during which you can help pick grapes to make Ontario's 'liquid gold,' be forewarned that it's *really* cold out there; alternatively, **Hillebrand Estates Winery** (above) offers free ice wine tours, tastings and seminars indoors, as well as an ice wine bar on Niagara-on-the-Lake's main street.

Hillebrand Vineyard Jazz & Blues Twin summer music festivals come alive at **Hillebrand Estates Winery** (above) offering wine country cuisine, rare vintages for sale and the sounds of jazz in mid-July or blues in mid-August for about $25 per day.

Niagara Grape & Wine Festival (☎ 905-688-0212; www.grapeandwine.com) This festival takes place for 16 days starting the second Friday in September. It brings a bounty of activity to the region's vineyards. Stop by for musical concerts, gourmet picnics, wine seminars, artisan craft fairs and celebrity vintners' lunches.

those who've never visited a winery before, however, its introductory tours and tasting bar presentations are recommended. The presentations cost $5 and teach you how to identify regional taste and aroma essences.

Further north, near Lake Ontario, **Stonechurch Vineyards** 14 has a self-guided walking tour of its vineyards. **Konzelmann Estate Winery** 15 is one of the oldest around and the only one to take full advantage of the lakeside microclimate. The late-harvest Vidal tastes of golden apples, and the ice wines, helped along by freezing winter winds off the lake, are superb. Next on the right is the **Strewn Winery** 16, already producing medal-winning vintages and home to the popular **Wine Country Cooking School**, where one-day, weekend and week-long classes are all pure indulgence. At the winery, special ice wine tours require reservations. Closer to Niagara-on-the-Lake, **Sunnybrook Farm Estate Winery** 17 specializes in unique Niagara fruit and berry wines, such as spiced apple and blackberry.

After passing congested Niagara-on-the-Lake, the wine route continues down the Niagara Parkway to **Reif Estate Winery** 18. Situated between Line 2 and Line 3 Rds, this well-established winery has ice wines. Last on our drive, but one of the first Niagara-on-the-Lake wineries, award-winning **Inniskillin Wines** 19 is a master of the ice wine craft. Self-guided displays outline the history of wine-making in Niagara. Also on site is a 1920s barn, the design of which was influenced by Frank Lloyd Wright.

Liquid Gold

Niagara's regional wineries burst onto the scene at Vinexpo 1991 in Bordeaux, France. In a blind taste test, judges awarded one of the coveted gold medals to an Ontario ice wine, and international attendees' mouths fell open. These specialty vintages, with their arduous harvesting and sweet, yet multidimensional taste, continue to draw aficionados and the curious to the Niagara Peninsula wine country.

A certain percentage of grapes are left on the vines after the regular harvest season is finished. The vines are then covered with netting to protect them from birds. If storms and mold do not destroy them, the grapes grow ever more sugary and concentrated until three days of consistent, low winter temperatures, -8°C below, freeze them entirely during December or January.

When this happens, rapid harvesting of the fragile icy grapes must be done carefully by hand in the predawn darkness so that the sun doesn't melt the ice inside and dilute the resulting grape juice. The grapes are subsequently pressed and aged in barrels for several months, even up to a year. After decanting, the smooth ice vintages taste intensely of apples, or even more exotic fruits, and pack quite an alcoholic kick.

Why are ice wines so expensive? First, it takes 10 times the usual number of grapes to make just one bottle of ice wine. This, combined with labor-intensive production methods and the high risk of crop failure, often drives the price well above $40 per 375mL bottle. Late-harvest wines picked earlier in the year may be less costly (and less sweet), but just as full-flavored and aromatic.

Sights & Activities

Opening hours will be shorter during winter.

Angels Gate Winery (☎ 905-563-3942; www.angelsgatewinery.com; 4260 Mountainview Rd, Beamsville; 🕑 10am-5:30pm, weekend tours 11am & 3pm)

Château des Charmes (☎ 905-262-4219; www.chateaudescharmes.com; 1025 York Rd, Niagara-on-the-Lake; 🕑 10am-6pm, tours 11am & 3pm)

Creekside Estate Winery (☎ 877-262-9463; www.creeksideestatewinery.com; 2170 4th Ave, Jordan Station; 🕑 10am-6pm)

Henry of Pelham Family Estate Winery (☎ 905-684-8423; www.henryofpelham.com; 1469 Pelham Rd, St Catharines; 🕑 10am-6pm, tours 1:30pm summer)

Hillebrand Estates Winery (☎ 905-468-1723, 800-572-8412; www.hillebrand.com; 1249 Niagara Stone Rd, Niagara-on-the-Lake; 🕑 10am-6pm, tours hourly)

Inniskillin Wines (☎ 905-468-2187, 888-466-4754; www.icewine.com; Line 3, cnr Niagara Parkway, Niagara-on-the-Lake; 🕑 11am-5:30pm, tours 10:30am & 2:30pm, weekends only Nov-Apr, self-guided tours)

Kittling Ridge Estates Wines & Spirits (☎ 905-945-9225; www.kittlingridge.com; 297 South Service Rd, Grimsby; 🕑 10am-6pm Mon-Sat, 11am-5pm Sun, tours 2pm daily, 11:30am weekends Jun-Sep)

Konzelmann Estate Winery (☎ 905-935-2866; www.konzelmannwines.com; 1096 Lakeshore Rd, Niagara-on-the-Lake; 🕑 10am-6pm Mon-Sat, noon-6pm Sun, tours 2pm May-Sep)

Lakeview Cellars Estate Winery (☎ 905-562-5685; www.lakeviewcellars.on.ca; 4037 Cherry Ave, Vineland; 🕑 10am-5:30pm)

Peninsula Ridge Estates Winery (☎ 905-563-0900; www.peninsularidge.com; 5600 King St W, Beamsville; 🕑 10am-6pm, tours 11:30am & 3pm)

Puddicombe Farms (☎ 905-643-1015; www.puddicombefarms.com; 1468 Hwy 8; 🕑 9am-5pm, Wed-Sun only Apr-Jun & Nov-Dec)

Reif Estate Winery (☎ 905-468-7738; www.reifwinery.com; 15608 Niagara Parkway, Niagara-on-the-Lake; 🕑 10am-6pm, tours 1:30pm May-Oct)

Stonechurch Vineyards (☎ 905-935-3535; www.stonechurch.com; 1242 Irvine Rd, Niagara-on-the-Lake; 🕑 10am-6pm, self-guided tours)

Strewn Winery (☎ 905-468-1229; www.strewnwinery.com; 1339 Lakeshore Rd, Niagara-on-the-Lake; 🕑 10am-6pm, tours 1pm)

Sunnybrook Farm Estate Winery (☎ 905-468-1122; www.sunnybrookfarmwinery.com; 1425 Lakeshore Rd, Niagara-on-the-Lake; 🕑 10am-6pm)

Thirty Bench Wines (☎ 905-563-1698; www.thirtybench.com; 4281 Mountainview Rd, Beamsville; 🕑 10am-6pm)

Vineland Estates Winery (☎ 905-562-7088, 888-846-3526; www.vineland.com; 3620 Moyer Rd; 🕑 10am-6pm, tours 3pm, weekends only Nov-Apr, restaurant 11:30am-10pm May-Oct, 11:30-5pm Nov-Apr)

White Meadows Farm (☎ 905-682-0642; www.whitemeadowsfarms.com; 2519 Effingham St; 🕑 10am-5pm Mon-Sat, noon-5pm Sun)

Wine Country Cooking School (☎ 905-468-8304; www.winecountrycooking.com) Culinary vacations and wine country cooking classes.

Eating

Hillebrand Estates Winery, Peninsula Ridge Estates Winery, Puddicombe Farms and Vinelands Estates Winery (see Sights & Activities) have good restaurants.

Olde Fashioned Lunch Box (☎ 905-562-7669; 4630 Victoria Ave; meals $4-10; 🕑 8am-8pm Tue-Sun) Detour north of Vineland on Hwy 24. Signs warn customers that this isn't fast food; homemade sandwiches and burgers this tasty take time to make.

KLEINBURG

Kleinburg is a rather pricey retreat just north of Toronto. There are antique shops, small art galleries and places for a nosh, all squeezed into a few blocks of the main street. But the real draw is the **McMichael Canadian Art Collection**, a must-see for anyone interested in First Nations and modern Canadian art. The gallery's rustic handcrafted wooden buildings (including painter Tom Thomson's cabin, which was moved here from Rosedale Ravine) are set among walking trails that crisscross conservation-area wetlands. The McMichael gallery advertises itself as '100% Canadian.' It has extensive holdings of canvases by Canada's best-known landscape painters, the Group of Seven (p27), much of whose work was created in northern Ontario. Many visitors are equally captivated by the Inuit and British Columbian Aboriginal prints, photography and carvings, which are not as easily found at museums in downtown Toronto. In addition, the tasteful gallery shop sells art history books, high-quality crafts, musical CDs, videos and DVDs. Be forewarned, however, that the McMichael can be overrun with boisterous schoolchildren on weekday mornings, so time your visit accordingly.

Transportation

Distance from Toronto Kleinberg 34km.

Direction Northwest.

Travel time 45 minutes to one hour.

Car Take the Queen Elizabeth Way (QEW) west to Hwy 427, driving north past Hwy 401. Exit at Hwy 7, drive east (turn left) 6km, then turn north onto Hwy 27, then right onto Major Mackenzie Dr. At the next traffic light, turn left onto Islington Ave. Drive 1km north to the McMichael gallery gates, or continue into the town of Kleinburg.

Parking On-street parking is free in Kleinburg, from where you can backtrack on foot to the gallery gates.

Sights & Activities

McMichael Canadian Art Collection (☎ 905-893-1121, 888-213-1121; www.mcmichael.com; 10365 Islington Ave, Kleinburg; adult/child under 5/student/senior/family $15/free/12/12/30; 10am-4pm Nov-Apr, 10am-5pm May-Oct; P $5)

Eating

Mr McGregor's House (☎ 905-893-2508; 10503 Islington Ave; items $3-6) Hop on over for homemade quiche, soups and an afternoon tea table piled high with pies and cakes. In the backyard is a flower garden, where rabbits occasionally scamper.

STRATFORD

Stratford is a fairly typical slow-paced, rural Ontario town – except that it's home to a world-famous Shakespearean festival. There are also a number of smaller celebrations, including the beautiful Garden Festival which takes place in early March and the Stratford Summer Music, held in July to August, which sells tickets through the Stratford Festival box office.

Sir Alec Guinness played Richard III on opening night of the **Stratford Festival**, which began humbly in a huge tent at Queen's Park beside the Avon River. The festival, which recently celebrated its 50th season, has achieved international acclaim; the productions are first rate and feature respected actors. Aside from the plays, there are a number of other interesting programs, and some are free (for others, a nominal fee is charged and reservations are required). Among them are post-performance discussions with the actors, backstage tours, costume warehouse tours, lectures and luncheons, music concerts and dramatic readings by famous authors.

Surprisingly, the festival season runs from April through November. There are four theaters – all in town – that stage contemporary and modern drama and music, operas and, of course, works by the bard. Mainstage productions take place at the **Festival Theatre**, with its round, protruding stage in modern Elizabethan style. The **Avon Theatre** is the secondary venue, seating over a thousand theatergoers. The **Tom Patterson Theatre** is smaller than the Avon, with just under 500 seats. Attached to the Avon is the newly built **Studio Theatre**, an intimate 260-seat repertory venue.

Even though the play's the thing, pretty Stratford lures visitors with other pleasant ways to pass the time. The Avon River flows peacefully beside the town and adds to its charm.

Farmyard near Stratford (above)

Transportation

Distance from Toronto Stratford 145km.

Direction Southwest.

Travel time Two to three hours.

Car Take the Queen Elizabeth Way (QEW) west to Hwy 427, driving north to Hwy 401. Take Hwy 401 west to exit 278 (Kitchener), then follow Hwys 7/8 west to Stratford, past Shakespeare village.

Parking A free visitors' day pass for on-street parking is available from **Tourism Stratford** (below). The Festival Theatre parking lot in Queen's Park charges $6.

Bus For select summer weekend matinees, direct buses depart Toronto's Yorkdale Mall (subway Yorkdale) at 10am, returning from Stratford at 7pm ($35 round-trip); contact the Festival Theatre box office to check schedules and make reservations. Infrequent Greyhound buses from Toronto ($22, three hours) require a transfer in Kitchener.

Train VIA Rail operates two daily trains from Toronto ($30, 2½ hours). Some Amtrak trains to/from the USA also stop here. Stratford's train and bus station is at 101 Shakespeare St, off Downie St, eight blocks from the town centre.

On the river just west of the **Tourism Stratford visitors information centre**, the **Shakespearean Gardens** are on the site of an old woolen mill run along the waterfront. Near the bridge look for a bust of Shakespeare. You can get food to feed the mute and black swans (popcorn is easier to digest than bread) at the information centre.

Beside the Festival Theatre at the Discovery Centre, the **Stratford-Perth Museum** has collections of early-20th-century Canadiana and special historical and cultural exhibitions. Neighboring **Queen's Park** has good footpaths leading from the Festival Theatre and following the river past Orr Dam and a stone bridge, dating from 1885, to the formal **English flower garden**. In a renovated 1880s Victorian pump house you'll find **Gallery Stratford**, near **Confederation Park**. Featured inside the gallery are rotating shows of innovative contemporary art, emphasizing Canadian works and festival themes.

The city centre, with its almost too quaint shops and eateries, is ideal for ambling. Almost everything is close to Ontario St, where **Gallery Indigena** specializes in Canadian Aboriginal art and various bookshops vend festival-themed volumes. Queen's Park and the Festival Theatre are at the east end of town, just north of Ontario St. From the park, Lakeside Dr runs along the river back into town and meets York and Ontario Sts near the **Perth County Courthouse**, one of the town's most distinctive landmarks. A few blocks southeast along Downie St is the old-fashioned **City Hall**, a strikingly symmetrical construction in Queen Anne Revival style at the corner of Wellington St.

Information

Tourism Stratford (☎ 519-271-5140, 800-561-7926; www.city.stratford.on.ca; 47 Downie St; 9am-5pm Mon-Fri) Contact Tourism Stratford for a full calendar of arts, cultural and historical events.

Tourism Stratford visitors information centre (York St & Lakeside Dr; 9am-5pm May-Oct) Beside the river, off York St.

Sights & Activities

Boat tours & rentals (tours adult/child/student $6/2/4.50) Glide for 30 minutes past swans, parks and grand houses with even grander gardens. Tours depart from downstairs behind the Tourism Stratford visitor. Canoes, kayaks and paddleboats can also be rented ($15 to $25 per hour).

Gallery Indigena (☎ 519-271-7881; www.galleryindigena.com; 69 Ontario St; noon-4pm Sun & Mon, 10am-5:30pm Tue-Sat)

Gallery Stratford (☎ 519-271-5271; www.gallerystratford.on.ca; 54 Romeo St N; adult/student/senior $10/8/8; 9am-5pm Tue-Sun summer, closed Dec)

Stone Maiden Inn (☎ 519-271-7129; www.stonemaideninn.com; 123 Church St; bicycles per hr/day $8/25, deposit $200)

Stratford Festival & Festival Theatre Box Office (☎ 519-273-1600, 800-567-1600; www.stratford-festival.on.ca; Festival Theatre, Queen's Park, 55 Queen St; tickets $20-105) Call or go on-line to request the annual *Stratford Festival Visitors' Guide*. Tickets go on sale to the general public in early January, and by show time nearly every performance is sold out. Spring previews and fall end-of-season shows are discounted up to 50%. Students and seniors also qualify for reduced rates at some shows. A limited number of same-day rush tickets are available from the festival box office in person after 9am (or by phone after 9:30am).

Stratford Garden Festival (www.stratfordgardenfestival.com)

Stratford-Perth Museum (519-271-5311; www.cyg.net/~spmuseum; Discovery Centre, 270 Water St; adult/child 6-12/youth 13-18 $4.50/2/4; 10am-5pm Tue-Sat, noon-5pm Sun-Mon, 10am-4pm Tue-Sat Sep-Apr, closed weekends Jan & Feb)

Stratford Summer Music (www.stratfordsummermusic.ca)

Tours Free history walks depart from the tourist office at 9:30am Saturday from May until October, weather permitting, and also on weekdays during July and August. Tours of City Hall are given at 11am on Friday during July and August.

Eating

Church Restaurant (519-273-3424; 70 Brunswick St, cnr Waterloo St; lunch $8-25, dinner $15-45, prix fixe dinners from $70; 11:30am-1:30pm & 5-8:30pm Tue-Sun, Belfry Bar 9pm-midnight Fri & Sat) A grande dame of Stratford's culinary scene. It's inside the old Christ Church (1874), with organ and altar still intact. Reservations are essential.

Down the Street Bar & Cafe (519-273-5886; 30 Ontario St; lunch $8-12, dinner mains $18-25; 11am-1am) With whiffs of Parisian cafés and gilt mirrors, this place offers pre-theater dining, microbrews and wines by the glass.

Old Prune (519-271-5052; 151 Albert St; lunch $8.50-20, prix fixe dinner $65, cooking class $45; lunch 11:30am-1:30pm Wed-Sun, dinner 5-9pm Tue-Sun) From November until March, the famous Stratford Chef's School trains at this Edwardian house, where tables overlook a tranquil garden. Expect fresh, often organic and innovative contemporary food with just a hint of Québecois cuisine. Make reservations.

Principal's Pantry (519-272-9914; Discovery Centre, 270 Water St, basement level; meals $8-20; lunch & dinner) Across from the Festival Theatre, this dining room's proceeds support youth and community service projects.

Stratford's Olde English Parlour (519-271-2772; 101 Wellington St; meals $6-15; 11am-9pm) There are quite a few pubs about like this one, serving a hearty ploughman's lunch.

Tango Coffee Bistro (519-271-9202; 104 Ontario St; meals $4-10; 8am-8pm) Breakfast pastries, light lunches and hot dinners served in an artistic space. Fair-trade coffee blends include a light-roasted 'Sleepy Monk.'

York St Kitchen (519-273-7041; 41 York St; breakfast & lunch $5-8, dinner $10-15; 8am-8pm) Excellent sandwiches and home-style cooking dished out onto picnic plates. It's opposite the visitors' information centre.

Sleeping

Annex Inn (519-271-1407; 38 Albert St; d $125-225) Rooms have gas fireplaces and whirlpool tubs.

Bentley's Inn (519-271-1121, 800-361-5322; www.bentleys-annex.com; 99 Ontario St; ste $95-160) A modern, dark-wood furnished inn. Spacious bilevel suites have skylights and kitchenettes. The same folks run the Annex Inn, above.

Mercer Hall Inn (519-271-1888, 888-816-4011; www.mercerhallinn.com; 108 Ontario St; d $95-170, ste $125-200) Some of the uniquely artistic rooms and suites have kitchenettes, electric fireplaces or Jacuzzis. Bookshelves, CD racks and a DVD library are stocked with Canadiana.

Queen's Inn (519-271-1400, 800-461-6450; www.queensinnstratford.ca; 161 Ontario St; d $70-135, whirlpool ste $200) Near Waterloo St, it's the oldest lodging house in town.

Stratford Festival Visitor Accommodation Bureau (519-273-1600, 800-567-1600; www.stratfordfestival.ca; d from $50) The majority of rooms are in either B&Bs or residents' homes. The Tourism Stratford website also has an accommodations search engine.

Detour: Shakespeare

Some 12km east of Stratford along Hwys 7/8, the village of **Shakespeare** (www.hamlet.shakespeare.on.ca) has a tiny main street chockablock with antiques and craft shops. Quaint **Harry Ten Shilling Tea Room** (519-625-8333; 9 Huron Rd) serves lunch, afternoon tea and dinner daily. Descriptive cycling route pamphlets are available from Tourism Stratford; for bicycle rentals from Stratford, contact the **Stone Maiden Inn** (p188).

NIAGARA-ON-THE-LAKE

Originally a First Nations village, this small town 20km downstream (north) from Niagara Falls was founded by Loyalists from New York state after the American Revolution. It later became the first capital of Upper Canada. Today it's considered one of the best-preserved 19th-century towns in North America, although tour buses tend to ruin any charming effect. If it weren't for the acclaimed Shaw Festival, it wouldn't be worth more than the briefest of stops.

The town's main drag, **Queen St**, has many, many shops of the 'Ye Olde' variety selling antiques, British-style souvenirs and homemade fudge. The people at wonderful **Greaves Jams**

& Marmalades are fourth-generation jam-makers. Further east is the Victorian-era **Niagara Apothecary**, now a museum fitted with great old cabinets, remedies and jars. Special town events, mostly taking place in fair summer weather, include a tour of historic homes, outdoors musical concerts and art fairs. Victorian-style Christmas strolls, parades and caroling light up the streets in December.

The **Shaw Festival**, which is the only festival in the world devoted to producing the plays of George Bernard Shaw (1856–1950) and his contemporaries takes place between April and November at the **Court House Theatre**, the **Festival Theatre** and the **Royal George**, a one-time vaudeville house and cinema. Seminars, musical readings and informal Q&A conversations with cast members are held throughout the festival season.

South of Simcoe Park, the century-old **Niagara Historical Society Museum** has a vast collection relating to the town's past, ranging from First Nations artifacts to Loyalist and War of 1812 collectibles. Past the Festival Theatre at the southeastern edge of town, restored **Fort George** was a key battle site in the War of 1812; ghost tours, skills demonstrations and battle re-enactments occur throughout the summer. History buffs will also want to explore the village of **Queenston** (p179) along the Niagara Parkway.

The only Niagara Falls–like attractions in Niagara-on-the-Lake, the **Whirlpool Jet**, thrills passengers with a 29km trip through the rapids of the lower Niagara River. Reservations are required.

Transportation

Distance from Toronto Niagara-on-the-Lake 130km.

Direction Southeast.

Travel time Two hours.

Car Take the Queen Elizabeth Way (QEW) westbound past St Catharines to Exit 38/Niagara Stone Rd (Hwy 55), which follows onto Mississauga St intersecting Queen St downtown.

Parking Read the on-street parking signs carefully to avoid being fined. Metered spaces cost $2 or less per hour.

Bus & Taxi First go to Niagara Falls by bus or train, then transfer to a Niagara-on-the-Lake shuttle bus. Taxis from Niagara Falls (☎ 905-357-4000) cost around $35 each way.

Niagara-on-the-Lake shuttle bus (☎ 905-685-5463; one way/round-trip $10/15; 2-3 departures daily May-Sep).

Boat A high-speed hydrofoil (p195) from Toronto docks at Queenston, just south of Niagara-on-the-Lake.

Information

Niagara-on-the-Lake Chamber of Commerce (☎ 905-468-1950; www.niagaraonthelake.com; 26 Queen St, cnr King St; 🕑 10am-5pm Nov-Mar, 10am-7:30pm Apr-Oct) This helpful visitors' information centre is two blocks northwest of Simcoe Park.

Sights & Activities

Festival Tours (☎ 519-273-1652; adult/child under 17/student/senior $12/6/10/10; 🕑 10:30am, 12:30pm & 2pm Tue-Sun Jun-Sep, 10:30am Wed May & Oct) Narrated double-decker bus tours depart from York Lane, which is located near the Niagara-on-the-Lake Chamber of Commerce.

Fort George (☎ 905-468-4257; www.niagara.com/~parkscan; 26 Queens Pde, off Niagara Parkway; adult/child/senior $8/5/6.50; 🕑 10am-5pm Apr-Oct)

Ghost Tours (☎ 905-468-6621; www.friendsoffortgeorge.ca; 2hr tour adult/child under 13 $10/5) Reservations are advised for the fort's ghost tours.

Greaves Jams & Marmalades (☎ 905-468-7831; 55 Queen St, cnr Regent St; 🕑 9:30am-6pm Sun-Thu, 9:30am-6:30pm Fri & Sat)

Niagara Apothecary (☎ 905-468-3845; 5 Queen St; admission by donation; 🕑 noon-6pm mid-May–early Sep)

Niagara Historical Society Museum (☎ 905-468-3912; www.niagara.com/~nhs; 43 Castlereagh St, cnr Davy St; adult/child/student/senior $5/1/2/3; 🕑 10am-5:30pm, 1-5pm Nov-Apr)

Shaw Festival & Festival Theatre Box Office (☎ 905-468-2172, 800-511-7429; www.shawfest.com; 10 Queens Pde; tickets $20-77; 🕑 9am-5pm mid-Jan–Mar, 9am-8pm Apr-Nov) Request a complete Shaw Festival guidebook before tickets go on sale in January. Students can book

Prince of Wales Hotel (right)

half-price balcony seats for any performance; students and seniors may also attend specially priced matinees. Same-day discounted rush seats are sold from 9am.

Whirlpool Jet (☎ 905-468-4800, 888-438-4444; www.whirlpooljet.com; 61 Melville St; 45min tour adult/youth 6-14 $54/44; ⌚ Apr–mid-Oct) Bring a change of clothes. Pregnant women and children under age six are not allowed for safety reasons.

Zoom Leisure (☎ 905-468-2366; 275 Mary St, cnr Mississauga St; half-/full-day $15/25; ⌚ Apr-Oct) Price for bike rental includes a helmet, lock and map. Call in advance for bicycle rentals outside of the regular season.

Eating

Buttery (☎ 905-468-2564; www.thebutteryrestaurant.com; 19 Queen St; afternoon tea $9, lunch $8-16, dinner $26, feast $55; ⌚ 11am-11pm, afternoon tea 2-5pm) This pub-style place puts on a thoroughly kitschy Henry VIII-style dinner theater feast.

Epicurean (☎ 905-468-0288; 84 Queen St; lunch $6-9, dinner $17-21; ⌚ lunch daily, dinner Wed-Sun) For a quick counter lunch or upmarket Canadian bistro dinner with fresh berry pies, stop here.

Escabeche dining room (Prince of Wales Hotel; dinner $22-35; ⌚ breakfast, lunch & dinner) Fine Continental and Asian fusion cuisine is served.

Fans Court (☎ 905-468-4511; 135 Queen St; mains $12-18; ⌚ noon-9pm Tue-Sun) Cantonese, Sichuan and pan-Asian diversion in this most Anglo of towns.

Taste of Niagara tapas wine bar (Prince of Wales Hotel; ⌚ seasonally Apr-Oct)

Sleeping

Niagara-on-the-Lake Reservation Service (☎ 905-468-4263; www.niagaraonthelake.com; d from $60) The chamber of commerce offers a no-fee reservations service for most of the town's over 200 lovely B&Bs, inns, hotels and cottages. However, you will find that accommodations are generally quite expensive as well as often being booked out. They often require a two-night minimum stay on weekends.

Prince of Wales Hotel (☎ 905-468-3246, 888-669-5566; www.vintageinns.com; 6 Picton St, cnr King St; d $150-300, ste $350-400) This elegant Victorian hotel is opposite Simcoe Park and features some fine wining and dining options (left).

White Oaks Conference Resort & Spa (☎ 905-688-2550, 800-263-5766; www.whiteoaksresort.com; 235 Taylor Rd; d/ste from $200/280) A four-diamond resort hotel with chic modern design and a rejuvenating spa, fitness centre and racquet club.

Detour: Cycling Niagara

From downtown Niagara-on-the-Lake, you can cycle the rural laneways of the **Niagara Peninsula wine country** (p182) or ride south to historic **Queenston** (p179) and all the way to **Niagara Falls** (p176) on the paved recreational path alongside the **Niagara Parkway** (p178). You can rent your bicycle from **Niagara Wine Tours** (p184) for $20 per day or from **Zoom Leisure** (p191).

SKIING & SNOWBOARDING AREAS

Although Toronto is not Whistler by any stretch of the imagination, you can still find some fresh powder slopes within easy driving distance of the city. Depending on the weather, the ski season runs from early December to the middle of March. The nearest place to strap on a snowboard or skis is at **Horseshoe Resort**, which has cross-country trails, a tubing park and seven lifts leading to dozens of runs for skiers and snowboarders. Handily, it also has a hotel, spa, several eateries and a fireside lounge, all surrounded by wilderness just over an hour's drive from Toronto. If the weather is good, consider driving on to **Blue Mountain**, Ontario's largest mountain resort and run by Intrawest. Outside of Collingwood, here th resort's 25 acres feature 12 lifts (four of them are high-speed), three terrain parks, multi pipes and half-pipes and more than 30 assorted trails rated from beginner to double-diamond. Day or night, the surrounding village is full of shops, restaurants and entertainment. If you're not up for a long drive, turn to p136 for family skiing centers and ice skating within the city limits.

Transport

Distance from Toronto Horseshoe Resort 105km, Blue Mountain 160km.

Direction Northwest.

Travel time One to 2½ hours.

Car Follow the Queen Elizabeth Way (QEW) west to Hwy 427, driving north to Hwy 401. Take Hwy 401 eastbound to Hwy 400, which travels north to Barrie. Take Exit 117 East for Horseshoe Resort. For Blue Mountain, take Exit 98 and follow Hwy 26 for 11km to Craigleith, then turn left onto Blue Mountain Rd.

Bus Horseshoe Resort offers bus packages from Toronto ($60, including lift ticket).

JoJo Tours (☎ 416-201-6465, 888-202-3513; http://home.interlog.com/~jojotour/) JoJo offers day trips to both resorts, as well as dog sledding and snowmobile outings.

Sights & Activities

Blue Mountain (☎ 416-869-3799, 705-445-0231; www.bluemountain.ca; Blue Mountain Rd, off Hwy 26, Craigleith; lift tickets $30-50, ski & gear rentals $20-38, tube park ride $3) Daily lessons available.

Horseshoe Resort (☎ 416-283-2988, 800-461-5627; www.horseshoeresort.com; Horseshoe Valley Rd, Barrie; lift pass $22-44, cross-country trail pass $8-17, ski & gear rentals $13-27, tube park ride $3) Supervised kids' programs, daily lessons and discounts for on-line bookings.

Directory

Directory

TRANSPORTATION

AIRLINES

Major airlines serving Toronto's airports include:

Aeroflot (☎ 416-642-1653, 877-209-1935; www.aeroflotcanada.com)

Aeromexico (☎ 800-237-6639; www.aeromexico.com)

Air Canada (☎ 888-247-2262; www.aircanada.ca)

Air France (☎ 416-922-5024, 800-667-2747; www.airfrance.com)

Air New Zealand (ANZ; ☎ 800-663-5494; www.airnewzealand.com)

Air Transat (☎ 866-847-1112; www.airtransat.com)

Alaska Airlines (☎ 800-252-7522; www.alaskaair.com)

Alitalia (☎ 905-676-2886, 800-361-8336; www.alitalia.com)

All Nippon Airways (ANA; ☎ 800-235-9262; www.fly-ana.com)

America West Airlines (AWA; ☎ 800-363-2597; www.americawest.com)

American Airlines (AA; ☎ 416-283-2243, 800-433-7300; www.aa.com)

British Airways (☎ 416-250-0880, 800-247-9297; www.britishairways.com)

CanJet Airlines (☎ 800-809-7777; www.canjet.com)

Cathay Pacific (☎ 905-694-1100, 800-268-6868; www.cathaypacific.com)

Continental Airlines (☎ 800-523-3273; www.continental.com)

Cubana Airlines (☎ 416-967-2822; www.cubana.cu)

Czech Airlines (☎ 416-363-3174; www.csa.cz)

Delta Air Lines (☎ 800-221-1212; www.delta.com)

El Al Israel (☎ 416-967-4222, 800-361-6174; www.elal.co.il)

Finnair (☎ 416-222-0740, 800-950-5000; www.finnair.com)

Japan Airlines (JAL; ☎ 416-364-7229, 800-525-3663; www.jal.co.jp/en/)

JetsGo (☎ 514-733-0332, 866-448-5888; www.jetsgo.net)

Korean Air (☎ 800-438-5000; www.koreanair.com)

Lufthansa (☎ 416-360-3600, 800-563-5954; www.lufthansa.com)

Mexicana Airlines (☎ 905-612-8250, 866-281-3049; www.mexicana.com.mx)

Northwest Airlines/KLM (NWA; ☎ 800-441-1818, 800-225-2525; www.nwa.com)

Olympic Airways (☎ 416-920-2452; www.olympic-airways.gr)

Qantas (☎ 800-227-4500; www.qantas.com.au)

Scandinavian Airlines (SAS; ☎ 800-221-2350; www.scandinavian.net)

Singapore Airlines (☎ 416-860-0197, 800-387-0038; www.singaporeair.com)

Thai Airways International (☎ 800-426-5204; www.thaiair.com)

United Airlines (☎ 800-241-6522; www.united.com)

US Airways (☎ 800-428-4322, 800-943-5436; www.usairways.com)

Varig Brazil (☎ 416-926-7500, 800-468-2744; www.varig.com.br)

WestJet (☎ 403-250-5839, 877-937-8538; www.westjet.com)

ZOOM Airlines (☎ 613-235-9666, 866-359-9666; www.flyzoom.com)

AIRPORTS

Tickets for flights departing Canada, whether purchased in Canada or abroad, usually include departure taxes.

Canada's busiest airport, **Lester B Pearson International Airport** (YYZ; Map p224; ☎ 905-676-3506, Terminal 3 ☎ 905-612-5100; www.gtaa.com), is about a 27km drive northwest of downtown Toronto. Most Canadian airlines and major international carriers arrive at Pearson. Terminal assignments are subject to change, so call ahead or check the airport entrance signs carefully. Air Canada recently opened a new multibillion dollar terminal that eventually will replace Terminals 1 and 2. Except for Air Canada's Star Alliance partners, most other international carriers are assigned to Terminal 3. All terminals have food courts, duty-free stores, medical emergency clinics, baggage storage facilities, lost and found offices, ATMs, currency-exchange booths and information desks. Inter-terminal courtesy shuttle buses for transit passengers run frequently.

On the Toronto Islands, small **Toronto City Centre Airport** (YTZ; Map p241; ☎ 416-203-5942) is used by regional airlines, helicopter companies, charter and private flights. Air Canada Jazz commuter flights from Ottawa to TCAA rather than Pearson are quicker because you're already downtown – and you get a better look at the city, too.

Getting to/from the Airports

Airport Express (☎ 905-564-3232, 800-387-6787; www.torontoairportexpress.com) operates a 24-hour express bus service that connects Pearson International Airport with the Metro Toronto Coach Terminal and major downtown hotels, including the Westin Harbour Castle, Fairmont Royal York and the Delta Chelsea Toronto Downtown. Buses depart every 20 to 30 minutes; the one-way trip takes 40 minutes to an hour, depending on traffic. A one-way/round-trip ticket costs $15/26 (cash or credit card); students and seniors receive 10% off one-way fares.

If you are not carrying heavy luggage, the cheapest way to Pearson is via **TTC** (p198) subway and bus lines. At the time of writing, the fastest route was to take the Bloor-Danforth subway line west to Kipling station, then transfer to the No 192 Airport Rocket bus (5:30am to 2am daily); allow yourself at least an hour for the trip from downtown ($2.25). Night buses to the airport include the TTC's westbound No 300A Bloor-Danforth bus (every 15 minutes), which connects the airport with central Toronto in about 45 minutes.

A metered taxi from central Toronto to Pearson takes about 45 minutes, depending on traffic, and costs around $45. Fares from the airport are strictly regulated by drop-off zone, starting at $38 to downtown. If you're driving yourself, avoid using Hwy 401 during morning and evening rush hours; instead, take the Gardiner Expressway west from Spadina Ave and go north on Hwy 427. Parking at the airport garage costs $2.25 to $3.25 per half hour. Long-term parking at an off-site lot costs $13 per day or $59 per week, with free terminal shuttles available.

Ferries (Map p241; ☎ 416-203-6945) to TCCA leave from the foot of Bathurst St every 15 minutes from 6:15am until around 11pm, taking just seven minutes for the short sail. For Air Canada ticket holders, a free shuttle bus runs between the TCAA ferry slip and the Fairmont Royal York, opposite Union Station. Otherwise take the 509 Harbourfront or 510 Spadina streetcar from Union Station along Lake Shore Blvd W, then walk down to the ferry slip.

BICYCLE & IN-LINE SKATES

Toronto has 50km of on-street bicycle lanes and over 40km of marked routes for bicycles. In-line skaters can use sidewalks, but that's illegal for cyclists. The free *Toronto Cycling Map* is distributed by the **Toronto Cycling Committee** (☎ 416-392-7592; www.city.toronto.on.ca/cycling/index.htm) located at City Hall (p50), tourist offices (p226) and bicycle shops. Turn to p135 for more details about cycling and skating around Toronto, including equipment rentals.

Bicycles on Public Transport

Bicycles are permitted on TTC buses, streetcars and subways, except during weekday morning (6:30am to 9:30am) and afternoon (3:30pm to 6:30pm) rush hours or at other times when vehicles become heavily crowded. Bicycles are allowed on some, but not all, ferries to the Toronto Islands; restrictions usually apply during peak periods.

BOAT

From Toronto, speedy **Seaflight Hydrofoils** (Map pp238-9; ☎ 416-504-8825,877-504-8825; www.seaflight.com; 339 Queens Quay W) operates 70-minute boat trips to Queenston dock, along the Niagara Parkway. Fares (one way/round-trip $40/70) include a shuttle bus to either Niagara Falls (p176) or Niagara-on-the-Lake (p189). Make reservations three to five days beforehand. With advance notice, bicycles can be accommodated at no extra charge.

BUS

Long-distance buses are cheaper than trains, although not as fast or comfortable. Numerous bus lines covering Ontario, as well as buses within Canada and to US destinations, originate at the **Metro Toronto Coach Terminal** (Map pp226-7; ☎ 416-393-7911; Dundas Sq, 610 Bay St; subway Dundas), which has coin lockers and a **Travellers' Aid Society** (Map pp226-7; ☎ 416-596-8647) help desk. When making reservations, always ask for the direct or express bus. Advance tickets do not guarantee a seat.

Greyhound (☎ 416-367-8747, 800-661-8747; www.greyhound.ca) covers much of southwestern Ontario, including the Niagara region and Stratford. Discounts on standard one-way adult fares are given to ISIC cardholders, seniors, children and pairs traveling together. Purchase tickets at least a week in advance for the best fares. Long-distance routes include:

Destination	Cost	Duration
Buffalo	$32	3hr
Chicago	$114	11½-15hr
Detroit	$66	5½-6hr
Montréal	$80	8-9½hr
New York City	$114	10-13hr
Vancouver	$340	65-70hr

Fares offered by **Coach Canada** (☎ 800-461-7661; www.coachcanada.com) to Niagara Falls, Montréal, Buffalo and New York City are comparable.

CAR

Renting a car is only recommended for excursions outside Toronto. Driving in the city is nothing but a headache because urban expressways are continually congested and, except during winter, construction never ends.

Rental

Rates go up and down like the stock market, so it's worth phoning around or surfing the web to see what's available. Booking ahead usually ensures the best rates; the airport tends to be cheaper than downtown. Typically, a small car might cost $30 to $45 per day, or $200 to $300 per week. But after adding insurance, taxes, excess kilometers and any other fees, you could be handed a pretty surprising bill. Heavily discounted weekend rates (under $100) may include 'extra days,' say from noon Thursday until noon Monday.

Major international car-rental agencies have reservation desks at Pearson airport, as well as several city-wide offices, including:

Budget (☎ 416-622-1000, 800-268-9000; www.budget.com)

Di$count Car & Truck Rental (☎ 416-249-5800, 800-263-2355; www.discountcar.com)

National Car Rental (☎ 416-364-4191, 800-227-7368; www.nationalcar.com)

Thrifty Car Rental (☎ 416-947-1385, 800-847-4389; www.thrifty.com)

Smaller independent agencies offer lower rates, but may have fewer (and perhaps older) cars available. Try the following:

New Frontier Rent-A-Car (Map pp228-30; ☎ 416-979-5678, 800-567-2837; www.newfrontiercar.com; Theatre Block, Holiday Inn on King, 370 King St W; streetcar 504)

Wheels 4 Rent (Map pp234-5; ☎ 416-585-7782; www.wheels4rent.ca; Kensington Market, 77 Nassau St; streetcar 510)

Driving

In Ontario petrol (gasoline) averages 70¢ per liter, which equals nearly US$2 per US gallon. The use of seat belts is compulsory throughout Canada. You can turn right on a red light after first having made a full stop; flashing green lights at intersections signal protected left turns. All vehicles must stop for streetcars, behind the rear doors, while the streetcar is loading or unloading passengers. Drivers must also stop for pedestrians at crosswalks whenever the overhead crossing signals are flashing.

With few exceptions, you can legally drive in Canada as long as you have a valid driver's license issued by your home country. You may be required to show an International Driving Permit if your license isn't written in English (or French). Short-term US visitors can bring in their own vehicles without special permits, provided they have insurance. If you've rented a car in the USA and you are driving it into Canada, bring a copy of the rental agreement to save any possible hassle by border officials.

On weekends and holidays, especially during summer, major land border crossings with the USA quickly become jammed. You can check border wait times on-line at www.ccra-adrc.gc.ca/customs/general/times/menu-e.html before leaving. Smaller, secondary US–Canada border crossings are usually not busy; sometimes they are so quiet that the customs officers have nothing better to do than tear your luggage apart.

Parking

In Toronto, parking is expensive – usually $2.50 to $3.50 per half hour, with an average daily maximum of $10 or more (or a flat rate of around $5 after 6pm). Cheapest are the Toronto Parking Authority's municipal lots, which are scattered around the downtown area and marked by green signs. They cost the same as metered street parking, which (if you can find any) is usually $2 per hour. Some metered spaces may have a central payment kiosk for an entire row. Purchase the appropriate amount of time using cash or a credit card and be sure to display the receipt on your dashboard. Note it's not free to park next to a broken meter – it's illegal. Residential streets have only severely restricted on-street parking. Tow trucks show no mercy and getting your vehicle back will cost a bundle in cash and aggravation. In this book, the parking icon (P) is used for venues that have free parking; if on-site parking is available for a fee, this amount follows the icon. Otherwise ask about pay parking options nearby.

FERRY

During summer, Toronto Islands **ferries** (Map pp228-30; ☎ 416-392-8193;www.city.toronto.on.ca/parks/island/ferry.htm) run every 15 to 30 minutes from 8am to 11pm. Queues can be long on weekends and holidays, so show up early. Ferry services are greatly reduced the rest of the year, running every 30 to 45 minutes daily. During winter, ferries service only Ward's Island. The ferry dock is at the foot of Bay St, off Queens Quay, just west of the Westin Harbour Castle.

A high-speed international **ferry service** (☎ 585-227-2287, 877-825-3774; www.catsfastferry.com/hmpg.htm; adult/child US$20/10, plus bicycle/motorcycle/passenger car US$10/25/40) between Toronto and Rochester, New York, started in spring 2004. The fast ferry arrives in Toronto at Cherry St, about a mile east of the main Harbourfront area. The trip takes about 2¼ hours each way, with departures at least twice daily during summer.

PEDICAB

Deluxe bicycle rickshaws pedaled by fit young women and men can be hired around downtown during summer. Fares for longer trips should be negotiated with the driver before boarding. Tip generously.

TAXI

Metered fares start at $2.75; add $1.25 for each additional kilometer, depending on traffic. Taxi drivers will usually take you where you want to go without taking you for a ride. Just hail one on the street and watch them brake, U-turn or otherwise do whatever it takes to pick you up. Taxi stands are easily found outside of hotels, museums, shopping malls and entertainment venues.

Reliable companies include **Crown Taxi** (☎ 416-750-7878, 877-750-7878), **Diamond Taxicab** (☎ 416-366-6868) and **Royal Taxi** (☎ 416-777-9222; www.royaltaxi.ca), which has a fleet of wheelchair-accessible taxis.

TRAIN

Canadians feel a special attachment to the 'ribbons of steel' from coast to coast, although they don't take the train very often. Grand **Union Station** (Map pp228-30) downtown has currency exchange booths and a **Travellers' Aid Society** (Map pp228-30; ☎ 416-366 7788) help desk, but no left luggage lockers.

VIA Rail (☎ 416-366-8411, 888-842-7245; www.viarail.ca) services are excellent along the so-called Québec–Windsor corridor, an area of heavy traffic stretching from Québec City to Windsor, Ontario (just across the US–Canada border from Detroit, Michigan). Fares vary wildly, but are significantly cheaper if tickets are purchased at least one week in advance. The following table shows examples of one-way economy-class fares.

Destination	Cost	Duration
Montreal	$84	5hr
Niagara Falls	$22	2hr
Ottawa	$77	4hr

Overnight trains between Toronto and Montréal depart daily, except Saturday (double-occupancy sleeper cabins from $150 per person). VIA Rail's Corridor Pass ($235) is good for 10 days.

Amtrak (☎ 800-872-7245; www.amtrak.com) has several routes between the USA and Canada. The following table includes some of them.

Destination	Cost	Duration
Chicago-Toronto	US$94	14hr
NYC-Toronto	US$94	14hr
NYC-Montréal	US$68	10hr

International passengers are responsible for securing all documentation (ie passports and visas) prior to on-board customs and immigration procedures. Reservations are required. For fares and schedules, contact Amtrak or stop by the information desk inside Union Station.

The **GOTransit** (☎ 416-869-3200, 888-438-6646; www.gotransit.com) commuter train network serves the suburbs of Toronto. Service is fast and steady throughout the day.

TRAVEL AGENTS

Convenient branch offices of reputable budget, youth and student travel agencies include **STA Travel,** which has two branches: **Bloor-Yorkville** (☎ 416-925-5800; 200 Bloor St W; 10am-6pm Mon-Sat; subway Museum) and the **Annex** (Map pp231-3; ☎ 416-593-7240; 258B College St; 10am-6pm Mon-Fri; streetcar 506).

You can also try **Travel CUTS** with branches at **Union Station** (Map pp228-30; ☎ 416-365-0545; 65 Front St W; 10am-6pm Mon-Fri, 10am-7pm Wed-Thu; subway Union) and at the **Annex** (Map pp231-3; ☎ 416-979-2406; 187 College St; 9am-5pm Mon-Fri, 9am-7pm Wed, 10am-3pm Sat; streetcar 506).

Go to www.weekendtrips.com or phone ☎ 416-599-8747 for special bargains on weekend getaways to Ottawa, Montréal and other Canadian cities, as well as activity-based day trips to the Niagara Peninsula and other provincial destinations.

TTC SUBWAY, STREETCARS & BUSES

The **Toronto Transit Commission** (TTC; ☎ 416-393-4636; www.city.toronto.on.ca/ttc) runs an excel lent subway, streetcar and bus system throughout the city. A helpful, if basic *Ride Guide* is available from subway station attendants. Detailed route maps are posted at streetcar shelters, major bus stops and inside subway cars.

Subway lines operates from approximately 6am (9am on Sunday) until 1:30am daily, with trains every five minutes. Stations have clearly marked Designated Waiting Areas (DWAs) monitored by security cameras and equipped with a bench, pay phone and an intercom link to the station manager; they are located where the subway guard's car stops along the platform.

Streetcars are slower than the subway, but they stop more often (usually every block or two). Streetcars display their route number and final destination on both the front and rear cars. On weekdays they usually operate from 5am until 1:30am, with reduced service on weekends. Routes are numbered in the 500s and streetcars roll on St Clair Ave and College, Dundas, Queen and King Sts (all of which run east–west). Bathurst St and Spadina Ave streetcars mainly run north–south, then turn at the lakefront west toward the Canadian National Exhibition (CNE) grounds (511 Bathurst) or east toward Union Station (510 Spadina). The 509 Harbourfront streetcar travels from Union Station along Lake Shore Blvd west to the CNE grounds.

Visitors won't find much use for TTC buses, which are slow and get held up in traffic. Women traveling alone between 9pm and 5am can request special stops anywhere along regular bus routes; notify the driver in advance and exit via the front doors. Bus stops with blue-banded poles are part of the limited Blue Night Network operating basic routes around the city between 1:30am and 5am daily every 30 minutes or better.

For more far-flung travel, the TTC system connects with bus routes in surrounding suburbs such as Richmond Hill, Brampton and Hamilton. For information on these routes, contact **GO Transit** (☎ 416-869-3200, 888-438-6646; www.gotransit.com).

Fares & Passes

The regular adult TTC fare is $2.25 (student and senior $1.50, child under 13 50¢). You can transfer to any other bus, subway or streetcar at no extra charge, provided you obtain a paper transfer from the driver or automated dispensers near subway station exits. Exact change is required when boarding streetcars and buses. Day passes ($7.75) are valid for unlimited rides after 9:30am on weekdays (all day weekends) until 5:30am the following morning. On weekends and holidays, family passes ($7.75) are good for up to two adults and four children traveling together. Or buy 10 tokens for $19 (student and senior $12.50, child $4.25) from any subway station or local store displaying the TTC ticket agent sign.

WALKING

The city center is pedestrian friendly, with leafy residential neighborhoods as well as retail strips. In winter, denizens forego often icy sidewalks in favor of the downtown **PATH** (www.city.toronto.on.ca/path), an underground walkway system. Nearly 30km of mazelike tunnels ensure Torontonians never need see the grim light of a winter's day. If you become lost (as you almost certainly will), look up for cardinal directions posted on overhead signs and wall maps. With luck, you'll eventually surface at Union Station, Eaton Centre or wherever else you meant to go. Then again, you may end up in some anonymous, obscure downtown office building by mistake and never be heard from again!

PRACTICALITIES

ACCOMMODATIONS

Peak summer season runs from Victoria Day until Labour Day. Major special events (p8), such as the Toronto International Film Festival and Caribana, deem that you'll have trouble finding any type of accommodation or if you do, rates may be double or triple what you'd otherwise pay. For price ranges, special deals, advice on making reservations and a list of B&B booking services see p160.

Accommodations listings in this book are arranged alphabetically, with Cheap Sleeps (budget options) listed at the end of most neighborhood sections. Count on adding room taxes of about 12% to all rates quoted in this book – although visitors may be eligible for a refund of the 7% federal GST (p144). Places that offer valet or self-parking are marked with a Ⓟ icon.

BUSINESS

Despite cries of 'Buy Canadian!' foreign companies do quite well here. As the most popular Canadian city for conventions and trade shows, Toronto hosts over 100 events annually at the Metro Toronto Convention Centre and Exhibition Place. **Tourism Toronto** (p206) readily assists business travelers and offers corporate incentives.

Hours

Normal business hours are 9am to 5pm weekdays. Some postal outlets may stay open later and on weekends. Banks usually keep shorter hours, but close later on Friday; certain branches are open Saturday morning.

Typical retail shopping hours are 10am to 6pm Monday to Saturday, noon to 5pm on Sunday (although some shops are closed on Sunday). Shopping malls often stay open later, particularly on Thursday night.

Restaurants are usually open for lunch on weekdays from 11:30am until 2:30pm and serve dinner from 5pm until 9:30pm daily, later on weekends. If they take a day off, it's Monday. A few serve breakfast and weekend brunch.

Bars usually open late afternoon, but some unlock their doors before noon. Clubs may open in the evening around 9pm, but most don't get busy before 11pm. Bars serve liquor until 2am; a few dance clubs stay open officially until 4am.

It's not a problem finding 24-hour supermarkets, pharmacies or convenience stores. Tourist attractions may keep longer hours during summer, but some also close during winter.

Services

Check out the **Tourism Toronto** (p206) website for business services, including translation, secretarial and equipment rental. **Kinko's** (p202) offers you a full range of services, from on-site computer rental to high-quality color printing, and also accepts Fed Ex drop-offs. **Mail Boxes Etc** (p205) offers UPS courier services.

CHILDREN

Children are welcome almost anywhere. In traditional ethnic neighborhoods, such as Little Italy or Greektown, they'll be fussed over and even smilingly taken off your hands for a few minutes. There's rarely an extra charge for kids staying with their parents at motels and hotels. B&Bs may refuse to accept children under a certain age, while others brazenly charge full price for tots. The **Delta Chelsea Toronto Downtown** (p163) provides a supervized play center, kids' swim club and low-cost baby-sitting services. Car-hire companies rent car seats, which are legally required for young children. See p53 for a list of attractions that kids might enjoy. For more general information on enjoying travel with young ones, read Lonely Planet's *Travel with Children*.

Baby-sitting

Always ask for a licensed and bonded baby-sitting service. Rates typically start at $60 for three to five hours. Reputable agencies include:

Christopher Robin (☎ 416-483-4744; http://christopherrobin.homestead.com)

Improv Care (☎ 416-243-3285; www.improvcare.ca)

CLIMATE

Just how bad are the winters? January is the coldest month, with temperatures averaging several degrees below zero and plenty of snowfall. The windchill factor – a combination of temperature and wind speed off Lake Ontario – can result in much lower temperatures. Summers can be just as agonizing; the hottest month, July, sees average temperatures of up to 26°C. It feels more stifling due to the muggy humidity.

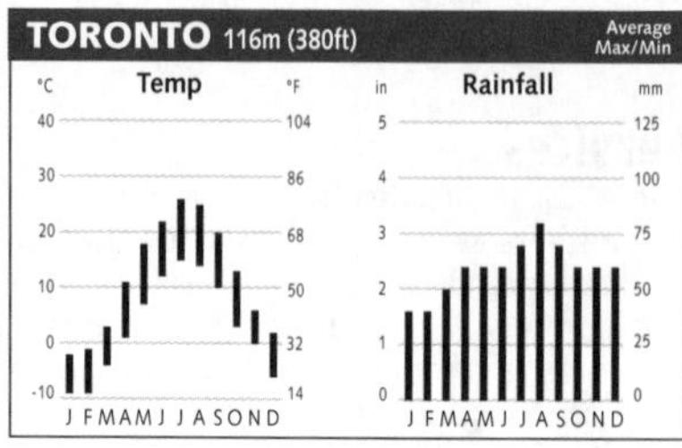

COURSES

With top-rated universities and hundreds of foreign-exchange students living in the city, Toronto is an excellent place to take a day or a week to study something new.

Arts & Crafts

Meet your inner artist at:

Clay Design (p153)

Craft Studio (Map pp228-30; ☎ 416-973-4963; Harbourfront, York Quay Centre, 235 Queens Quay W; streetcar 509, 510) Workshops in glass blowing (☎ 416-973-4951), textile art (☎ 416-973-4952), ceramics and jewelry (☎ 416-973-4994).

Gardiner Museum of Ceramic Art (p56)

Japanese Paper Place (p166)

Peach Berserk (p156) Silk-screening workshops.

Textile Museum of Canada (p52)

Toronto's First Post Office (p47) Papermaking, calligraphy and candlemaking classes.

Cooking

Other famous culinary schools are found in Niagara's wine country (p182) and Stratford (p187), both popular day-trip excursions from the city.

Big Carrot (p93)

Calphalon Culinary Centre (Map pp234-5; ☎ 416-847-2212, 877-946-2665; www.calphalonculinarycenter.com; Queen West, 425 King St W; streetcar 504, 510)

Dish Cooking Studio (Map p225; ☎ 416-920-5559; The Annex, 300 Dupont St; subway Dupont) Evening classes taught by local chefs and TV personalities, plus Kensington Market tours ($150).

Great Cooks (☎ 416-861-4727; www.greatcooks.ca; Queen Street, The Bay, 176 Yonge St, lower level; subway Queen)

Dance

Learn to get your groove on at:

Arabesque Academy (Map pp231-3; ☎ 416-920-5593; www.arabesquedance.ca; Old York, 20 College St, 2nd fl; subway College) Free bellydancing classes for new students.

Dancing on King (Map pp228-30; ☎ 416-955-0504; www.dancingonking.com; Yonge Street Strip, 79 King St E; subway King) Drop-in classes $10.

Toronto Dance Portal (www.torontodance.com)

Toronto Swing Dance Society (☎ 416-638-8737; www.dancing.org/tsds)

TOSalsa! (www.tosalsa.com)

Language

Toronto offers a whole world of language learning opportunities, including:

Alliance Française (Map pp236-7; ☎ 416-922-2014; www.alliance-francaise.ca; The Annex, 24 Spadina Rd)

Berlitz (Map pp231-3; ☎ 416-924-7773; www.berlitz.ca; 94 Cumberland St)

GEOS (Map pp226-7; ☎ 416-599-2120; www.geostoronto.com; Bloor-Yorkville, 415 Yonge St)

Goethe-Institut (Map pp228-30; ☎ 416-593-5257; www.goethe.de/uk/tor/enindex.htm; Yonge Street Strip, 163 King St W)

Italian Cultural Institute (Map pp231-3; ☎ 416-921-3802; www.iicto-ca.org/istituto1.htm; Financial District, 496 Huron St)

St George Business & Language School (Map pp231-3; ☎ 416-929-5553; www.stgeorgeschool.com; Bloor-Yorkville, 208 Bloor St W)

Spanish Centre (Map pp231-3; ☎ 416-925-4652; www.spanishcentre.com; Yonge Street Strip, 40 Hayden St)

CUSTOMS

Adults aged 19 and older can bring in 1.5L of wine or 1.14L of liquor (or a case of beer), 200 cigarettes, 50 cigars and 200g of tobacco. You can also bring in gifts valued up to $60 plus a 'reasonable amount' of personal effects, including cars, computers and outdoor equipment. Dispose of any perishable items, such as fruits, vegetables or plants, before crossing the border. Mace, pepper spray and many firearms are also prohibited. For the latest information on regulations, contact the **Canada Customs and Revenue Agency** (☎ 204-983-3500, 800-461-9999; www.ccra-adrc.gc.ca).

DISABLED TRAVELERS

Guide dogs may legally be brought into restaurants, hotels and other businesses. Many public service phone numbers and some payphones are adapted for the hearing-impaired. Larger private and chain hotels have suites for disabled guests. About 90% of curbs are dropped and most public buildings are wheelchair accessible.

Only some subway stations and city buses are wheelchair-equipped – look for specially marked stops displaying the blue wheelchair icon. The **TTC** (p198) also runs separate Community Routes that are fully accessible. **WheelTrans** (☎ 416-393-4111, reservations ☎ 416-393-4222, TTY ☎ 416-393-4555) offers door-to-door services at the cost of a regular bus ticket or subway token. VIA Rail and long-distance bus companies can accommodate wheelchairs if given sufficient advance notice.

Many car-rental agencies include hand-controlled vehicles or vans with wheelchair lifts without extra charge, but only with advance reservations; locally, contact **Kino Mobility Inc** (☎ 416-635-5873, 888-495-4455; www.kinomobility.com). Permits to use disabled parking spaces, including at blue-colored curbs, must be applied for in advance through the **Ontario Ministry of Transportation** (☎ 416-235-2999).

Other helpful resources include:

Access Toronto (☎ 416-338-0338, TTY ☎ 416-338-0889; www.city.toronto.on.ca/services/accesstoronto.htm)

Beyond Ability International (☎ 416-410-3748; www.beyond-ability.com)

Community Information Toronto (☎ 211, TTY ☎ 416-392-3778; www.211toronto.ca) Help line available 24 hours.

Mobility International USA (TTY ☎ 541-343-1284; www.miusa.org)

Society for Accessible Travel & Hospitality (☎ 212-447-7284; www.sath.org)

ELECTRICITY

Canada, like the USA and Mexico, operates on 110V, 60-cycle electric power. Gadgets built for higher voltage and cycles (such as 220/240V, 50-cycle appliances from Europe) will function poorly. North American electrical goods have plugs with two (flat) or three (two flat, one round) pins. Overseas visitors should bring an adapter, or buy one from an electronics store (try Future Shop), if they wish to use their own small appliances, such as razors or hair dryers.

EMBASSIES & CONSULATES

Most countries maintain embassies in Ottawa. Toronto consulates are generally open only during weekday mornings, although some are also open after lunch until 4pm or so.

Australia (Map pp231-3; ☎ 416-323-1155; Bloor-Yorkville, 175 Bloor St E, Suite 316)

Cuba (Map p224; ☎ 416-234-8181; Greater Toronto Area, Kipling Sq, 5353 Dundas St W, Suite 401-402)

Denmark (Map pp231-3; ☎ 416-962-5661; Bloor-Yorkville, 151 Bloor St W, Suite 310)

France (Map pp231-3; ☎ 416-925-8041; Bloor-Yorkville, 130 Bloor St W, Suite 400)

Germany (Map p225; ☎ 416-925-2813; The Annex, 77 Admiral Rd)

Italy (Map pp226-7; ☎ 416-977-1566; Queen Street, 136 Beverley St)

Japan (Map pp228-30; ☎ 416-363-7038; Financial District, Royal Trust Tower, 77 King St W, Suite 3300)

Mexico (Map pp228-30; ☎ 416-368-2875; Financial District, 199 Bay St, Suite 4440)

Netherlands (Map pp226-7; ☎ 416-598-2520; Dundas Sq, Eaton Centre, 1 Dundas St W, Suite 2106)

New Zealand (Map pp228-30; ☎ 416-947-0000; Financial District, 67 Yonge St, Suite 600)

Portugal (Map pp226-7; ☎ 416-217-0966; Dundas Sq, 438 University Ave, Suite 1400)

Spain (Map pp228-30; ☎ 416-977-1661; Financial District, Simcoe Place, 200 Front St W, Suite 2401)

Sweden (Map pp231-3; ☎ 416-963-8768; Bloor-Yorkville, 2 Bloor St W, Suite 504)

Switzerland (Map pp228-30; ☎ 416-593-5371; Financial District, 154 University Ave, Suite 601)

UK (Map pp231-3; ☎ 416-593-1290; Yonge Street Strip, 777 Bay St, Suite 2800)

USA (Map pp226-7; ☎ 416-595-1700, 800-529-4410; Queen Street, 360 University Ave)

EMERGENCY

police, fire & ambulance ☎ 911
police, nonemergency ☎ 416-808-2222, TDD ☎ 416-467-0493
SOS Femmes ☎ 416-487-6794, 800-287-8603
Toronto Rape Crisis Centre ☎ 416-597-8808, TTY ☎ 416-597-1214

SOS Femmes is primarily a French-speaking crisis line. The Toronto Rape Crisis Centre accepts collect calls and some counselors speak both French and Spanish. Both organizations are underfunded and under staffed, so if you happen to get a busy signal, keep trying. Counselors can make referrals to hospital sexual assault care centers. See Medical Services (p203) for hospital emergency rooms and clinics.

GAY & LESBIAN TRAVELERS

In the city's gay district located on Church St, called the Church-Wellesley Village or simply the 'gay village,' men's bars and clubs vastly outnumber lesbian venues, but grrrls should take heart because Toronto is home to drag kings, women-only bathhouse nights as well as queer reading series.

Other gay-friendly neighborhoods include the Annex, Kensington Market, Queen West and Cabbagetown.

In 2003 Toronto became famous for being the first city in North America to legalize same-sex marriage. Apply to **City Hall** (Map pp226-7; ☎ 416-363-9248, 416-363-0316; City Clerk's Office, 100 Queen St W; license $110; 🕑 8:30am-4:15pm Mon-Fri). The week-long celebrations of **Pride Toronto** (p9) attract one million folks annually.

Helpful local resources include:

519 Community Centre (Map pp231-3; ☎ 416-392-6874; www.the519.org; Church-Wellesley Village, 519 Church St; subway Wellesley)

Canadian Lesbian & Gay Archives (☎ 416-777-2755; www.clga.ca; Financial District, 56 Temperance St, Suite 20; subway Queen)

Glad Day (p149)

Lesbian & Gay Immigration Task Force (☎ 416-925-9872 ext 2211; www.legit.ca)

Siren (www.siren.ca) A free weekly for lesbians and bisexual women.

This Ain't the Rosedale Library (p149)

Toronto Women's Bookstore (p153)

Xtra! (p204)

HOLIDAYS

During national public holidays, all banks, schools and government offices (including post offices) are closed and transportation, museums and other services are on a Sunday schedule. Holidays falling on a weekend are usually observed the following Monday. See p8 for special events and peak travel seasons, and a list of public holidays.

INTERNET ACCESS

Major Internet service providers (ISPs), have dozens of dial-up numbers across Canada for those traveling with laptops. Some of these are:

AOL (☎ 800-265-6303; www.aol.ca)

CompuServe (☎ 800-848-8990; www.compuserve.com)

Earthlink (☎ 800-327-8454; www.earthlink.net)

Many motel, B&B and hotel rooms have phones equipped with data ports, and some offer high-speed Internet access. Deluxe hotels often have fully equipped business centers with computers, photocopiers, fax and Internet services.

Toronto's cheapest cybercafés are found along the Yonge Street Strip; Bloor St in the Annex and Koreatown; and Chinatown's Spadina Ave. Rates start at $2 per hour, with special multihour deals available. **Grey Region Comics** (Map pp231-3; ☎ 416-975-1718; Yonge Street Strip, 550 Yonge St; 🕑 9am-midnight; subway Wellesley) is convenient. A few coffee shops offer Internet access, either via pay kiosks or high-speed connections for laptop users. Check **HotSpotz** (www.hotspotz.ca) for free wi-fi locations around town.

Kinko's (www.kinkos.com) offers Internet access for 25¢ to 30¢ per minute. Many branches are open 24 hours, including **Kinkos** (Map pp228-30; ☎ 416-363-2705; Financial District, 357 Bay St; subway Queen) and the **Annex** (Map pp236-7; ☎ 416-928-0110; 459 Bloor St W; subway Spadina).

LEGAL MATTERS

The Canadian federal government permits the use of marijuana for medicinal purposes, but official prescription cannabis is strictly regulated. It's illegal to consume alcohol anywhere other than a residence or licensed premises, which puts parks, beaches and other public spaces off limits.

You could incur stiff fines, jail time and penalties if caught driving under the influence (DUI) of alcohol or any illegal substance (eg marijuana). The blood-alcohol limit over which you are considered legally drunk is .08%, which is reached after just two beers. Penalties include throwing you in jail overnight, followed by a court appearance, heavy fine and/or further incarceration.

If you are arrested, you have the right to remain silent. However, never walk away from law enforcement personnel without permission. After being arrested you have the right to an interpreter and one phone call. For low-cost legal advice, contact **Legal Aid Ontario** (Map pp226-7; ☎ 416-979-1446, 800-668-8258; www.legalaid.on.ca; Queen Street, 375 University Ave, Suite 404).

How Old is Old Enough?

Driving a car 16
Voting in an election 18
Drinking alcoholic beverages 19
Age of homosexual consent (for males) 18
Age of consent for other sexual activity 14

MAPS

The detailed neighborhood maps in this guide will certainly be enough for all but in-depth explorations. Lonely Planet's full-color, fold-out *Toronto City Map* has a handy street index and a laminated write-on, wipe-off surface. **Ontario Tourism** (p206) provides free provincial maps for excursions. **MapArt** (www.mapart.com) publishes an excellent series of affordable maps covering central Toronto, the Greater Toronto Area (GTA) and southwest Ontario; they're sold at many bookstores and newsstands. For specialist activity maps, drop by **Mountain Equipment Co-op** (p147) or **Europe Bound Outfitters** (p147).

MEDICAL SERVICES

There are no reciprocal healthcare arrangements between Canada and other countries. Non-Canadians must usually pay cash up front for treatment, so taking out travel medical insurance is strongly advised. Medical treatment in Canada is expensive, too; the standard rate for a bed is around $500 and up to $2500 a day for nonresidents. At emergency rooms expect to wait if your case isn't diagnosed as 'urgent.'

Clinics

Convenient clinics include:

Ambulatory Care Centre (ACC; Map pp231-3; ☎ 416-323-6400; Yonge Street Strip, 76 Grenville St; 🕒 24hr; subway Queens Park) Nonemergency medical services for women and their families.

Dental Emergency Clinic (Map p225; ☎ 416-485-7121; Greater Toronto Area, 1650 Yonge St; 🕒 8am-midnight; subway St Clair)

Hassle-Free Clinic (Map pp231-3; women ☎ 416-922-0566, men ☎ 416-922-0603; Church-Wellesley Village, 556 Church St, 2nd fl) Drop-in and appointment-only hours for STD/HIV testing and reproductive health services.

Emergency Rooms

Many of Toronto's major hospitals are clustered around University Ave (subway Queens Park), including:

Hospital for Sick Children (Map pp226-7; ☎ 416-813-1500, Telehealth line ☎ 866-797-0000; www.sickkids.on.ca; 555 University Ave)

Mount Sinai Hospital (Map pp226-7; ☎ 416-596-4200, emergency room ☎ 416-586-5054; www.mtsinai.on.ca; 600 University Ave)

Toronto General Hospital (Map pp226-7; ☎ 416-340-3111, emergency room ☎ 416-340-3946; www.uhn.ca; 200 Elizabeth St)

METRIC SYSTEM

Canada officially changed over from imperial measurement to the metric system in the mid-1970s, but the systems coexist in everyday life. For example, all speed-limit signs are in kilometers per hour and gasoline is sold by the liter, but produce is often sold by the pound. For help in converting between the two systems, use the chart found on the inside front cover.

MONEY

All prices quoted in this book are in Canadian dollars ($) and do not include taxes, unless otherwise noted. See also p205. Most Canadians do not carry large amounts of cash for everyday use, relying instead on credit cards, ATMs and direct debit cards. Personal checks are rarely accepted, unlike in the USA. See the inside front cover for exchange rates.

ATMs

Interbank ATM exchange rates usually beat traveler's checks or exchanging foreign currency. Canadian ATM fees are low (usually $1 to $1.50 per transaction), but your home bank may charge another fee on top of that.

Currency

Paper bills most often come in $5 (blue), $10 (purple), $20 (green) and $50 (red) denominations. Coins include the penny (1¢), nickel (5¢), dime (10¢), quarter (25¢), 'loonie' ($1) and 'toonie' ($2). The 11-sided, gold-colored 'loonie' coins feature the common loon, a North American waterbird.

Credit Cards

Visa, MasterCard, American Express and JCB cards are widely accepted in Canada. Credit cards can get you cash advances at bank ATMs, generally for a 3% surcharge. Beware: many US-based credit cards now convert foreign charges using highly unfavorable exchange rates and fees.

Changing Money

It's best to change your money at a recognized bank or other financial institution. Some hotels, souvenir shops and tourist offices exchange money, but rates aren't likely to be good. See the inside front cover for exchange rates.

After regular banking hours (p199), try **American Express** (Map pp231-3; ☎ 416-967-3411; Holt Renfrew Centre, 50 Bloor St W; 🕑 10am-6pm Mon-Wed, 10am-7pm Thu-Fri, 9am-4pm Sat; subway Bloor-Yonge), which also has another branch in the basement concourse of the **Fairmont Royal York** (p161).

You can also try **Money Mart** (Map pp231-3; ☎ 416-920-4146; www.moneymart.ca; 617 Yonge St; 🕑 24hr; subway Wellesley).

Thomas Cook has branches in the **Financial District** (Map pp228-30; ☎ 416-366-1961; www.thomascook.ca; 10 King St E; 🕑 9am-5pm Mon-Fri; subway King), **Bloor-Yorkville** (Map pp231-3; ☎ 416-975-9940; 1168 Bay St; 🕑 9am-6pm Mon-Fri; subway Bloor-Yonge) and **Financial District** (Map pp228-30; ☎ 416-979-9300; BCE Pl, 161 Bay St; 🕑 9am-6pm Mon-Fri; subway Union). Thomas Cook also has a booth at Pearson International Airport.

Traveler's Cheques

American Express, Thomas Cook and Visa traveler's checks in Canadian dollars are accepted as cash at many hotels, restaurants and stores. The savings you might make on exchange rates by carrying traveler's checks in a foreign currency (even US$) don't make up for the hassle of having to exchange them at banks or other financial institutions.

NEWSPAPERS & MAGAZINES

Most 'daily' newspapers are not published on Sunday; the hefty weekend edition appears on Saturday instead.

eye (www.eye.net) A free alternative weekly, focused on arts and entertainment.

Financial Post (www.nationalpost.com/financialpost) Canada's answer to the USA's *Wall Street Journal.*

Globe & Mail (www.globeandmail.ca) The elder statesman of national daily newspapers.

L'Express de Toronto (www.lexpress.to) French-language weekly newspaper, published on Tuesday.

MacLean's (www.macleans.ca) National monthly magazine of Canadian news and culture.

Now Toronto (www.nowtoronto.com) Outstanding alternative weekly, free every Thursday.

Toronto Life (www.torontolife.com) Toronto's upscale lifestyle, dining, arts and entertainment monthly magazine.

Toronto Star (www.thestar.com) The city's comprehensive daily newspaper of record.

Toronto Sun (www.canoe.com/NewsStand/TorontoSun/home.html) Sensational tabloid with good sports coverage.

Where Toronto (www.where.ca/toronto) The most informative of the free glossy tourist magazines.

Xtra! (www.xtra.ca) Toronto's gay-oriented alternative biweekly (free).

PASSPORTS

Visitors from almost all countries need a passport. For US citizens, a driver's license is often sufficient to prove residency when entering via land border crossings. However, a birth certificate or certificate of citizenship or naturalization may be required before admission is granted. Permanent residents of the US who aren't citizens should carry their green card.

PHARMACIES

One popular chain around town is **Shoppers Drug Mart**, which has stores at **Yonge Street Strip** (Map pp226-7; ☎ 416-979-2424; 700 Bay St; 🕑 24hr; subway College), **Yonge Street Strip** (Map pp231-3; ☎ 416-920-0098; 728 Yonge St; 🕑 8am-midnight Mon-Fri, 9am-midnight Sat, 11am-midnight Sun; subway Bloor-Yonge) and the **Annex** (Map pp236-7; ☎ 416-961-2121; 360 Bloor St W; 🕑 8am-midnight Mon-Sat, 10am-midnight Sun; subway Spadina).

POST

Canada Post/Postes Canada (☎ 800-267-1177; www.canadapost.ca) may not be remarkably quick, but it's reliable. Standard postcards or 1st-class air-mail letters (up to 30g) cost 48¢ to destinations within Canada, more to the US (65¢) or any other destination ($1.25). Post offices and postal outlets in drugstores are found throughout the city.

Poste-restante mail should be addressed as follows:

FAMILY NAME, First Name
25 The Esplanade
Toronto, ON M5W 1A1

Post restante will be held for 15 days before being returned. Mail can be picked up at the main post office (Map pp228-30; ☎ 416-365-0656; Old York, 25 The Esplanade; 🕑 8am-5:45pm Mon-Fri). Any packages sent to you in Canada will be ruthlessly inspected by customs officials, who will then assess duties.

Hotel concessions, newsstands and tourist shops also sell stamps, but usually for more than face value. Convenient shipping outlets include **Mail Boxes Etc/UPS Store** (Map pp228-30; ☎ 416-367-9171; Theatre Block, 157 Adelaide St W; 🕑 8am-7pm Mon-Fri, 10am-5pm Sat; subway St Andrew).

RADIO

In the Megacity, flip the dial to:

CBC1 (99.1FM; www.cbc.ca/webone) The CBC's other frequency, with music and news; 'Definitely Not the Opera,' a Canadian pop culture show, airs on Saturday afternoons.

CBC2 (94.1FM; http://toronto.cbc.ca) Classical music, with 'Saturday Afternoon at the Opera'.

CHIN (100.7FM; www.chinradio.com) Multicultural, multilingual programming.

CIUT (89.5FM; www.ciut.fm) 'Real Radio' from the UT campus; tune into 'Radio Music Gallery' (10am Friday).

CJRT (91.1FM; www.jazz.fm) All jazz.

CKLN (88.1FM) Ryerson University's eclectic music, news and talk radio.

Edge (102.1FM; www.edge.ca) Toronto's premier new-rock station, with breaking music news.

Radio Canada (90.3FM, 860AM; http://radio-canada.ca) National public broadcasting in French.

SAFETY

Downtown east of Yonge St (basically anywhere from the Gardiner Expressway north to Carlton St), women walking alone after dark are likely to be mistaken for prostitutes by curb-crawling johns. The southern section of Jarvis St, between Carlton and Queen Sts, especially around Allan Gardens, should be avoided by everyone late at night.

Because many social service agencies have recently closed, there are an increasing number of homeless people and street youths begging on the streets. Keep in mind that homeless people are more likely to be assaulted or harassed than to do so to you.

Although violent crime rates are steadily falling, property theft has increased slightly. Police estimate a total of at least 73 gangs operating in Toronto. Biker wars that have racked Québec have made their way into Ontario. If you see these biker gangs out on the highway, give them a wide berth.

SENIOR TRAVELERS

People over the age of 65 (sometimes 50) typically qualify for the same discounts as students. Any photo ID is usually sufficient proof of age. The **Canadian Association of Retired Persons** (CARP; ☎ 416-363-8748, 800-363-9736; www.fifty-plus.net; 1yr membership $20) has excellent cyber resources (free).

Elderhostel (☎ 877-426-8056; www.elderhostel.org) specializes in inexpensive, educational packages for people 55 years or older. Accommodation is in university dorms and the programs are so popular that a lottery is often conducted to decide which applicants can participate. **Routes to Learning Canada** (☎ 613-530-2222, 866-745-1690; www.routestolearning.ca) coordinates Elderhostel programs in Ontario.

TAX & REFUNDS

The federal goods and services tax (GST), variously known as the 'Gouge and Screw' or 'Grab and Steal' tax, adds 7% to nearly every product, service or transaction, on top of which usually follows an 8% Ontario retail sales tax. Visitors are eligible for refunds on GST paid for short-term accommodation and nonconsumable goods, although the refund process is inconvenient (p144).

TELEPHONE

Local calls cost 25¢ from public pay phones. Public pay phones are either coin- or card-operated; a few accept credit cards or have data ports for laptop Internet connections.

Dial all 10 digits of a given phone number, including the three-digit area code and seven-digit number, even for local calls. Downtown phone numbers take the 416 (and sometimes 647) area code, while telephone numbers within the Greater Toronto Area (GTA) typically have the 905 area code.

Always dial '1' before toll-free (800, 888, 877 etc) and domestic long-distance numbers. Some toll-free numbers are good anywhere in North America, others within Canada only. International rates apply for calls to USA, even though the dialing code (+1) is the same as for Canadian long-distance calls.

Phonecards

Sold at convenience stores, private prepaid phonecards often give rates far superior to the country's Bell networks. Beware those phonecards that advertise the cheapest per-minute rates may charge hefty connection fees for each call, especially for using the toll-free access number from payphones. You can avoid surcharges for the latter by depositing 25¢ and dialing the local access number instead.

Mobile Phones

North America uses various mobile phone systems, which are mostly incompatible with the GSM 900/1800 standard used in Europe, Asia and Africa. Check with your cellular service provider about using your phone in Canada. Calls may be routed internationally, and US travelers should beware of roaming surcharges (it can become very expensive for a 'local' call).

Faxes

To send faxes, visit **Kinko's** (p202) copy center or **Mail Boxes Etc** (p205). You'll pay $1 or $2 per page for local faxes, around $5 for international ones.

TIME

Toronto is in the Eastern time zone (EST/EDT), the same as New York City. This may seem odd to travelers coming from the USA, as the zone immediately south of the Ontario border is Central Standard Time (CST), which is one hour behind. At noon in Toronto it's:

9am	Vancouver
11am	Chicago
1pm	Halifax
5pm	London
6pm	Paris
3am (next day)	Sydney
5am (next day)	Auckland

During Daylight Saving Time (from the first Sunday in April to the last Saturday in October), the clock moves ahead one hour.

Useful Numbers

international dialing ☎ 011 + country code
international operator ☎ 00
local directory assistance ☎ 411
local operator ☎ 0

TIPPING

Tip restaurant servers 15%, which is equal to the total amount of tax on your bill, up to 20% for excellent service. If the restaurant automatically adds a 'service charge' (usually for groups of six or more), do not double tip. Bartenders get at least $1 per drink, 15% when buying a round. Tip taxi drivers about 10% of the fare, rounding up to the nearest dollar. Skycaps, bellhops and cloak-room attendants get around $2 per item; housekeepers are tipped $2 to $5 per night.

TOURIST INFORMATION

Tourism Toronto (Map pp226-7; ☎ 416-203-2600, 800-499-2514; www.torontotourism.com) has a summer kiosk staffed inside City Hall. Telephone agents are available year-round from 8:30am to 5:30pm weekdays. After hours, you can use their automated touch-tone information menu.

Ontario Tourism (Map pp226-7; ☎ 800-668-2746, French ☎ 800-268-3736; www.ontariotravel.net; Eaton Centre, 220 Yonge St, subway level; 🕑 10am-9pm Mon-Fri, 9:30am-7pm Sat, noon-5pm Sun) is staffed by knowledgeable people who speak eight languages. Stop by to browse the racks of activity, shopping and entertainment brochures.

Ontario Tourism Travel Centres are located at US–Canada border crossings. These offices provide information and currency-exchange services. They are open from 8:30am until at least 6pm daily during summer, closing earlier in the off-season.

Niagara Falls (Map pp177; ☎ 905-358-3221; 5355 Stanley Ave) West on Hwy 420 from the Rainbow Bridge.

Sarnia (☎ 519-344-7403; 1415 Venetian Blvd) At the Bluewater Bridge.

Windsor (☎ 519-973-1310; 1235 Huron Church Rd) East of the Ambassador Bridge.

VISAS

Short-term visitors from nearly all Western countries, except parts of Eastern Europe, normally don't require visas. As visa requirements change frequently, it's a good idea to check with the **Canadian Immigration Centre** (24hr call center ☎ 416-973-4444; www.cic.gc.ca) or the Canadian embassy or consulate in your home country to see if you're exempt.

A passport and/or visa does not guarantee entry. Proof of sufficient funds or possibly a return ticket out of the country may be required. Visitors with medical conditions may only be refused if they 'might reasonably be expected to cause excessive demand on health and social services' (ie they admit to needing treatment during their stay in Canada).

If you are refused entry but have a visa, you have the right of appeal at the port of entry. If you're arriving by land, the best course is simply to try again later (after a shift change) or at a different border crossing.

To/from the USA

Visitors to Canada who also plan to spend time in the USA should know that admission requirements are subject to rapid change. Under the US visa waiver program, visas are not currently required for citizens of the EU, Australia and New Zealand for visits up to 90 days. Check with US **Citizenship and Immigration Services** (www.uscis.gov) for the latest eligibility requirements. Even those visitors who don't need a visa are subject to a US$6 entry fee at land border crossings. Be sure to check that your entry permit to Canada includes multiple entries, too.

WOMEN TRAVELERS

Toronto sets high standards for women's safety, especially compared with major US cities. On the main streets, busy foot traffic continues past midnight, but there are still some neighborhoods to avoid (p205). The TTC makes excellent provisions for women riding public transport after dark (p198). Note it is illegal to carry pepper spray or mace in Canada. A few social service organizations for women operate out of the **519 Community Centre** (p202). See **Emergency** (p201) for other helpful resources, including sexual assault crisis lines. The **Toronto Women's Bookstore** (p153) has bulletin boards and flyers advertising woman-centered activities, classes, rallies and other happenings.

WORK

It is difficult to get a work permit because employment opportunities go first to Canadians. In most cases, you'll need to take a validated job offer from a specific employer to a Canadian consulate or embassy abroad.

Each year, a limited number of one-year **working holiday visas** are made available to Australians (A$165) and New Zealanders (NZ$195) between the ages of 18 and 30. Competition is stiff, so apply as early as possible. Application forms are available through Sydney's **Canadian Consulate General** (☎ 02-9364-3082; www.whpcanada.org.au) or the **Canadian High Commission** (☎ 04-473-9577) in Wellington.

Student Work Abroad Program (SWAP) facilitates additional working holidays for students and youths under 30 (sometimes 35). Participants come from nearly 20 countries, including Australia, France, Germany, Mexico, New Zealand, the UK and the USA. **SWAP Canada** (www.swap.ca) or **Travel CUTS** (p198) can tell you which student travel agency to contact in your own country for further details.

Behind the Scenes

THE LONELY PLANET STORY

The story begins with a classic travel adventure: Tony and Maureen Wheeler's 1972 journey across Europe and Asia to Australia. There was no useful information about the overland trail then, so Tony and Maureen published the first Lonely Planet guidebook to meet a growing need.

From a kitchen table, Lonely Planet has grown to become the largest independent travel publisher in the world, with offices in Melbourne (Australia), Oakland (USA), London (UK) and Paris (France).

Today Lonely Planet guidebooks cover the globe. There is an ever-growing list of books and information in a variety of media. Some things haven't changed. The main aim is still to make it possible for adventurous travelers to get out there – to explore and better understand the world.

At Lonely Planet we believe travelers can make a positive contribution to the countries they visit – if they respect their host communities and spend their money wisely.

THIS BOOK

This 2nd edition of *Toronto* was researched and written by Sara ('Sam') Benson, as was the 1st edition. Monica Bodirsky contributed the boxed text 'First Nations Foundations' (p33) to this edition. Regional publishing managers Maria Donohoe and David Zingarelli guided the development of this title. This guide was commissioned and developed in Lonely Planet's Oakland office and produced in Melbourne. The project team included:

Commissioning Editors Erin Corrigan, Sara Benson
Coordinating Editors Julia Taylor, Lou McGregor
Coordinating Cartographer Herman So
Assisting Editors Lara Morcombe, Susannah Farfor, Melissa Faulkner, Kate Evans, Jacquie Saunders, Steven Cann, Margie Jung
Assisting Cartographer Helen Rowley
Pre-layout Designer Nicholas Stebbing, Michael Ruff
Layout Designer Michael Ruff
Cover Designer Brendan Dempsey
Series Designer Nic Lehman
Series Design Concept Nic Lehman, Andrew Weatherill
Managing Cartographers Alison Lyall, Anthony Phelan
Managing Editor Kerryn Burgess
Mapping Development Paul Piaia
Project Manager Glenn van der Knijff
Regional Publishing Managers Maria Donohoe, David Zingarelli
Series Publishing Manager Gabrielle Green
Series Development Team Jenny Blake, Anna Bolger, Fiona Christie, Kate Cody, Erin Corrigan, Janine Eberle, Simone Egger, James Ellis, Nadine Fogale, Roz Hopkins, Dave McClymont, Leonie Mugavin, Rachel Peart, Ed Pickard, Michele Posner, Howard Ralley, Dani Valent
Thanks to Glenn Beanland, Ryan Evans, Wayne Murphy

Cover photographs by Lonely Planet Images CN Tower, Jon Davison (top); Toronto city skyline from Toronto Island, Cheryl Conlon (bottom); Skaters watching annual WinterCity Festival from Nathan Phillips Square, Corey Wise (back)

Internal photographs by Corey Wise/Lonely Planet Images except for the following: p8 (#4), p73 (#1) Cheryl Conlon/Lonely Planet Images; p67 (#1) Curtis Martin/Lonely Planet Images; p74 (#1), p137 Eoin Clarke/Lonely Planet Images; p70 (#2) Glenn van der Knijff/Lonely Planet Images; p187 Jim Wark/Lonely Planet Images; p8 (#2), p181 Jon Davison/Lonely Planet Images; p74 (#3), p191 Mark Lightbody/Lonely Planet Images; p73 (#4) Rick Gerharter/Lonely Planet Images; p74 (#2) Tony Wheeler/Lonely Planet Images. Many of the images in this guide are available for licensing from Lonely Planet Images: www.lonelyplanetimages.com.

ACKNOWLEDGEMENTS

Many thanks to the Toronto Transit Commission for use of the TTC Subway/RT Route map and the City of Toronto for the underground PATH map information.

THANKS

SARA BENSON

This book would not have been possible without the generous support of many Torontonians, including Stefania and David of the Castlegate Inn; journalist Jennie Punter and all of the other wonderful folks at the 2003 Toronto International Film Festival; and Monica Bodirsky for illuminating the city's First Nations history. Thank you to my parents for making the trip to the Great White North once again, and to Josh Lucas for being there.

OUR READERS

Many thanks to the travelers who used the last edition and wrote to us with helpful hints, useful advice and interesting anecdotes. Your names follow:

Daniel Abbott, Max Alavi, Travis Anderson, Wolfgang Angerer, Eileen Arandiga, Jorge Blanco, Chris Borthwick, Matthew Brady, J F Brouillette, M Brown, Paul-Antoine and Michelle Buer, Kat Burns, Taodhg Burns, Marianne Busch, Claudia Chritl, Antoni Cladera, Anna Clarke, Sara and Brian Cox, John Delfeld, Laura Delfeld, Martin Edwards, Erik Eskin, Boris Funke, Michael Stuart Garfinkle, Yang Guan, Jim Guthrie, Justine Hall, Lydia Han, Malcolm Hunt, Martin Hunt, Brent Irvine, Anna Keller, Steven Kerr, Eberhard Kloeber, Janet Komars, Maxime Lachance, Joanna Lyon, Judy MacIntosh, Hilary Marrinan, Steve McKay, Neil McRae, Sheila Meehan, Ruth Neilson,

Tom Neilson, Laure Perrier, Tony and Jill Porco, Simon Preece, Aljaz and Urska Prusnik, Paul Quayle, Glen Rajaram, Reinhard Reading, Thomas Regel, Ron Reid, Angela Reynolds, Shelagh M Rowan-Legg, Gladys Rubatto, Karl Rubin, Martina Schoefberger, Howard Schwartz, Ingrid Schweinhardt, Richard Semple, Norm Singer, Barney Smith, John Stigant, Joshua Taylor Barnes, Catherine Thomas, Desmond Vas, James Vieland, Kathryn Webster, Andrew Young, So Young

SEND US YOUR FEEDBACK

We love to hear from travelers – your comments keep us on our toes and help make our books better. Our well-traveled team reads every word on what you loved or loathed about this book. Although we cannot reply individually to postal submissions, we always guarantee that your feedback goes straight to the appropriate authors, in time for the next edition. Each person who sends us information is thanked in the next edition – and the most useful submissions are rewarded with a free book.

To send us your updates – and find out about LP events, newsletters and travel news – visit our award-winning website: www.lonelyplanet.com. Note: we may edit, reproduce and incorporate your comments in Lonely Planet products such as guidebooks, websites and digital products, so let us know if you don't want your comments reproduced or your name acknowledged. For a copy of our privacy policy, visit www.lonelyplanet.com/privacy.

Notes

Notes

Notes

Index

See also separate indexes for Eating (p220), Shopping (p220) and Sleeping (p221).

Index

000 map pages
000 photographs

Index

000 map pages
000 photographs

EATING

000 map pages
000 photographs

SHOPPING

SLEEPING

Index

000 map pages
000 photographs

MAP LEGEND

ROUTES
Tollway
Freeway
Primary Road
Secondary Road
Tertiary Road
Lane
Under Construction
Track
One-Way Street
Unsealed Road
Mall/Steps
Tunnel
Walking Tour
Walking Tour Detour
Walking Trail
Walking Path

TRANSPORT
Ferry
Metro
Monorail
Bus Route
Rail
Rail (Underground)
Tram
Cable Car, Funicular

HYDROGRAPHY
River, Creek
Intermittent River
Canal
Water

BOUNDARIES
International
State, Provincial
Disputed
Marine Park
Regional, Suburb
Cliff

AREA FEATURES
Airport
Area of Interest
Beach, Desert
Building, Featured
Building, Information
Building, Other
Building, Transport
Cemetery, Christian
Forest
Land
Mall
Park
Reservation
Sports
Urban

POPULATION
CAPITAL (NATIONAL)
Large City
Small City
CAPITAL (STATE)
Medium City
Town, Village

SYMBOLS

Sights/Activities
Beach
Buddhist
Castle, Fortress
Christian
Jewish
Monument
Museum, Gallery
Point of Interest
Winery, Vineyard
Zoo, Bird Sanctuary

Eating
Eating

Drinking
Drinking
Café

Entertainment
Entertainment

Shopping
Shopping

Sleeping
Sleeping

Transport
Airport, Airfield
Border Crossing
Bus Station
Cycling, Bicycle Path
General Transport
Taxi Rank

Information
Bank, ATM
Embassy/Consulate
Hospital, Medical
Information
Internet Facilities
Parking Area
Police Station
Post Office, GPO
Toilets

Geographic
Lighthouse
Lookout
Mountain, Volcano
National Park
Waterfall

Map Section

GREATER TORONTO AREA

0 — 4 km
0 — 2 miles

Toronto Zoo
Rouge Park
Cedarbrae Golf Course
Rouge River
Brookside Golf Course
East Point Park
To Montreal (540km)
Morningside Ave
Galloway Rd
Guild Inn
Guildwood Park
Guildwood Pkwy
Sylvan Park
Cathedral Bluffs Park
Neilson Rd
Finch Ave E
Highland Creek
Morningside Park
Scarborough Golf & Country Club
W Highland Creek
Markham Rd
Kingston Rd
2
48
Milliken Park
Steeles Ave E
McCowen Rd
Brimley Rd
Midland Ave
Kennedy Rd
Birchmount Rd
Warden Ave
Victoria Park Ave
Sheppard Ave E
Ellesmere Rd
Danforth Rd
Thomson Memorial Park
Eglinton Ave E
Bluffer's Park
Scarborough Bluffs
Pine Hills Cemetery
St Clair Ave E
Warden Woods
Toronto Hunt Club Golf Course
Lake Ontario
Macdonald-Cartier Fwy
Scarborough
Lawrence Ave E
401
To Wooden Sticks (45km)
404
Don Valley Pkwy
Charles Sauriol Conservation Reserve
O'Connor Dr
Taylor Creek Park
Taylor Ck
Danforth Ave
Kingston Rd
Eastern Beaches
Ashbridge's Bay Park
See Toronto Map (p225)
German Mills Creek
Leslie St
East Don Parkland
Don Mills Rd
Sunnybrook Park
Ernest Thompson Seton Park
Woodbine Ave
Coxwell Ave
Gerrard St E
Queen St E
Lake Shore Blvd E
Tommy Thompson Park
E Don River
Moatfield Farm Park
Wilket Creek
York Mills Rd
Windfields Park
Ontario Science Centre
Laird Dr
Don River
Pape Ave
Broadview Ave
North Shore Park
To David Dunlap Observatory & Holt Renfrew Last Call (10km); Toadhall Bed & Breakfast (15km)
Bayview Ave
Toronto Centre for the Arts & MOCCA
Don Valley Golf Course
W Don River
Mt Pleasant Cemetery
Don Valley Brick Works Park
Todmorden Mills
Parliament St
Yonge St
11
Finch Ave E
York Cemetery
Gibson House
Auberge du Pommier
Mt Pleasant Rd
Jarvis St
Yonge St
Toronto Inner Harbour
Toronto Outer Harbour
Bathurst St
Earl Bales Park
Lawrence Ave W
Avenue Rd
University of Toronto
University Ave
Spadina Ave
Upper Canada College
G Ross Lord Park
West Don Parkland
Dufferin St
North York
WR Allen Rd
Bathurst St
TORONTO
Christie Pits Park
Bloor St W
College St
Queen St W
Gardiner Expwy
Toronto City Centre Airport
Toronto Islands
Downsview Airport
Dufferin St
St Clair Ave W
Dufferin St
Ontario Place
To Paramount Canada's Wonderland (5km)
York University
Keele St
Derrydowns Park
401
Prospect Cemetery
High Park Cycle & Sports
Dupont St
St W
Keele St
High Park
Western Beaches
Humber Bay
Black Creek Pioneer Village
Finch Ave W
Jane St
Sheppard Ave
Downsview Dells Park
Wilson Ave
Eglinton Flats
Weston Rd
Smythe Park
Dundas McBride Cycle
Inverness
S Kingsway
400
West Humber Parkland
Oakdale Golf & Country Club
Black Creek
Lion's Park
Scarlett Rd
Etienne Brûlé Park
Humber Marshes Park
Humber Bay Park
Weston Rd
Steeles Ave W
Humber River
St George's Golf & Country Club
James Gardens Park
Royal York Rd
Rowntree Mills Park
Pine Point Park
Macdonald-Cartier Fwy
Etobicoke
Eglinton Ave W
Islington Golf Club
Montgomery's Inn
Islington Ave
Colonel Samuel Smith Park
The Queensway
407
Dixon Rd
Kipling Ave
Cuban Consulate
Lake Shore Blvd W
To Kleinburg (11 km)
Albion Rd
Rexdale Blvd
W Humber River
409
Wyndham Bristol Place
401
West Deane Park
Mimico Creek
Burnhamthorpe Rd
427
Bloor St W
MISSISSAUGA
Etobicoke Valley Park
Toronto Golf Club
Marie Curtis Park
27
Woodbine Racetrack
427
Lester B Pearson International Airport
Centennial Park
Queen Elizabeth Way
Lakeview Golf Club
Claireville Conservation Area
Claireville Reservoir
Sheraton Gateway
Dixon Rd
401
To Delta Toronto Airport West (1km); Kitchener & Waterloo (80km); Stratford (115km); Detroit, USA
Etobicoke Creek
Dixie Rd
Dundas St W
Cawthra Rd
To Glen Abbey Golf Club (20km); Vineland (70km); Niagara Falls (105km); Niagara-on-the-Lake (110km)

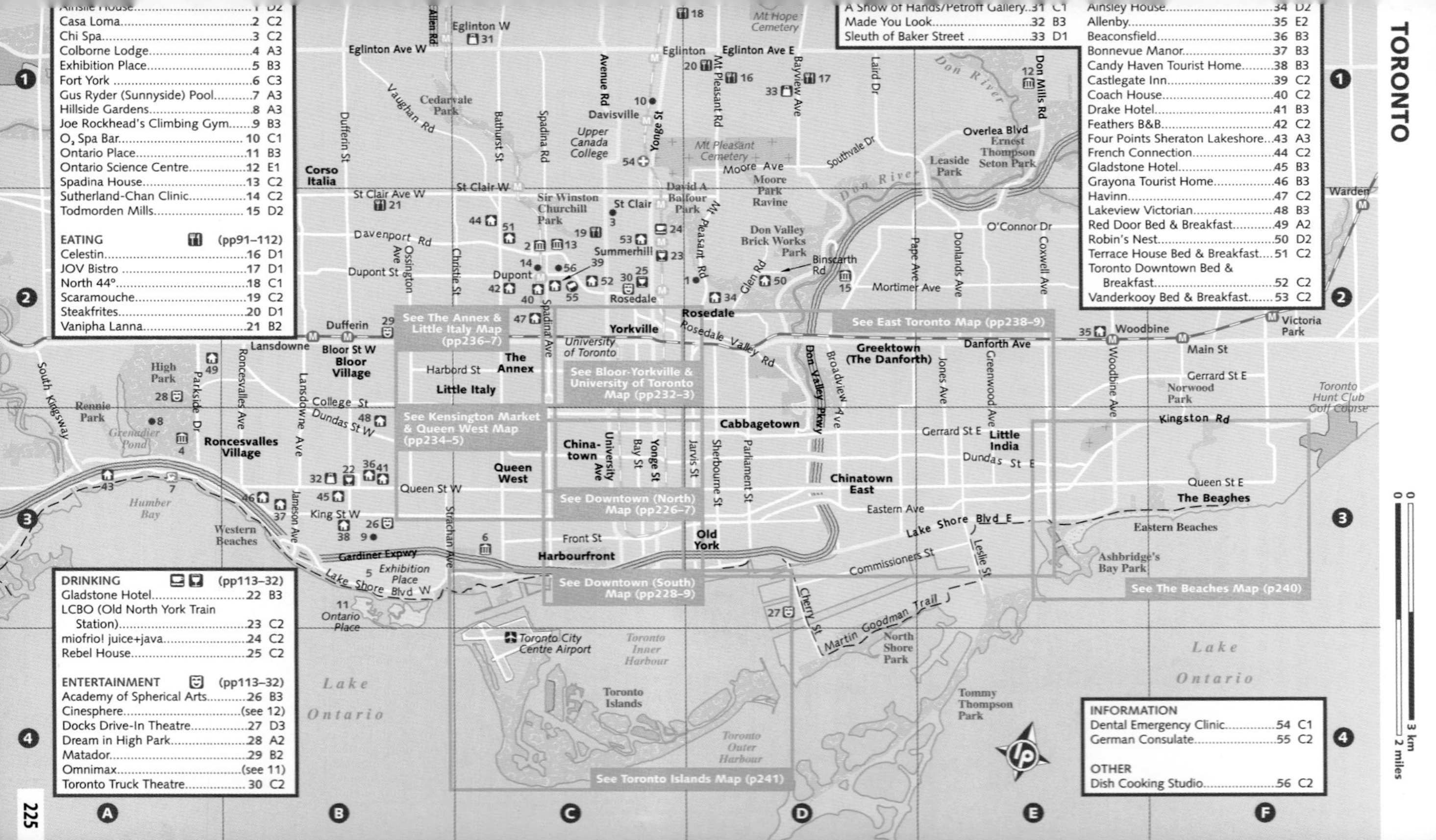
0 3 km
0 2 miles
Casa Loma 2 C2
Chi Spa 3 C2
Colborne Lodge 4 A3
Exhibition Place 5 B3
Fort York 6 C3
Gus Ryder (Sunnyside) Pool 7 A3
Hillside Gardens 8 A3
Joe Rockhead's Climbing Gym 9 B3
O, Spa Bar 10 C1
Ontario Place 11 B3
Ontario Science Centre 12 E1
Spadina House 13 C2
Sutherland-Chan Clinic 14 C2
Todmorden Mills 15 D2
A Show of Hands/Petroff Gallery 31 C1
Made You Look 32 B3
Sleuth of Baker Street 33 D1
Ainsley House 34 D2
Allenby 35 E2
Beaconsfield 36 B3
Bonnevue Manor 37 B3
Candy Haven Tourist Home 38 B3
Castlegate Inn 39 C2
Coach House 40 C2
Drake Hotel 41 B3
Feathers B&B 42 C2
Four Points Sheraton Lakeshore 43 A3
French Connection 44 C2
Gladstone Hotel 45 B3
Grayona Tourist Home 46 B3
Havinn 47 C2
Lakeview Victorian 48 B3
Red Door Bed & Breakfast 49 A2
Robin's Nest 50 D2
Terrace House Bed & Breakfast 51 C2
Toronto Downtown Bed & Breakfast 52 C2
Vanderkooy Bed & Breakfast 53 C2
EATING (pp91–112)
Celestin 16 D1
JOV Bistro 17 D1
North 44° 18 C1
Scaramouche 19 C2
Steakfrites 20 D1
Vanipha Lanna 21 B2
DRINKING (pp113–32)
Gladstone Hotel 22 B3
LCBO (Old North York Train Station) 23 C2
miofrio! juice+java 24 C2
Rebel House 25 C2
ENTERTAINMENT (pp113–32)
Academy of Spherical Arts 26 B3
Cinesphere (see 12)
Docks Drive-In Theatre 27 D3
Dream in High Park 28 A2
Matador 29 B2
Omnimax (see 11)
Toronto Truck Theatre 30 C2
INFORMATION
Dental Emergency Clinic 54 C1
German Consulate 55 C2
OTHER
Dish Cooking Studio 56 C2
See The Annex & Little Italy Map (pp236–7)
See Bloor-Yorkville & University of Toronto Map (pp232–3)
See Kensington Market & Queen West Map (pp234–5)
See Downtown (North) Map (pp226–7)
See Downtown (South) Map (pp228–9)
See East Toronto Map (pp238–9)
See The Beaches Map (p240)
See Toronto Islands Map (p241)
Lake Ontario

DOWNTOWN (NORTH)

SIGHTS & ACTIVITIES (pp37–78)

Art Gallery of Ontario (AGO)......... 1 C3
Campbell House........................... 2 D5
Canada Life Building..................... 3 D5
Chum/Citytv Complex.................. 4 C5
ChumCityStore........................(see 11)
Church of the Holy Trinity............. 5 F4
City Hall...................................... 6 E4
Elmwood Spa............................... 7 F3
Grange.. 8 B4
Henry Scadding House.................. 9 F4
Mackenzie House....................... 10 G4
MuchMusic Studios.....................(see 4)
MZTV Museum............................ 11 C5
Nathan Phillips Square................ 12 E4
New Tribe.................................. 13 C5
Old City Hall............................... 14 E5
Osgoode Hall............................... 15 D4
Speakers Corner.......................... 16 C5
Textile Museum of Canada.......... 17 D4

EATING (pp91–112)

Agora.......................................(see 1)
Baldwin Natural Foods................ 18 C2
Bright Pearl................................ 19 A3
Eating Garden...........................(see 30)
Freckle Bean Cafe....................... 20 C3
Fresh by Juice for Life.................. 21 A5
Furama Cake & Dessert
Garden....................................... 22 A4
Goldstone Noodle House............ 23 A4
Jodphore Club...........................(see 26)
John's Italian Caffe...................... 24 C2
Kim Thanh.................................. 25 A3
Konnichiwa................................ 26 C2
La Maison du Croissant Tree........ 27 F3
Le Commensal............................ 28 E3
Le Select Bistro..........................(see 49)
Lee Garden................................. 29 A2
Marchelino Mövenpick..............(see 56)
Mata Hari Grill............................ 30 B2
Oro.. 31 E3
Phở' H'ung................................. 32 A2
Queen Mother Café..................... 33 C5
Senator Restaurant..................... 34 F4
Swatow...................................... 35 A3
Ten Ren's Tea & Ginseng............ 36 A3
Tiger Lily's Noodle House........... 37 C5

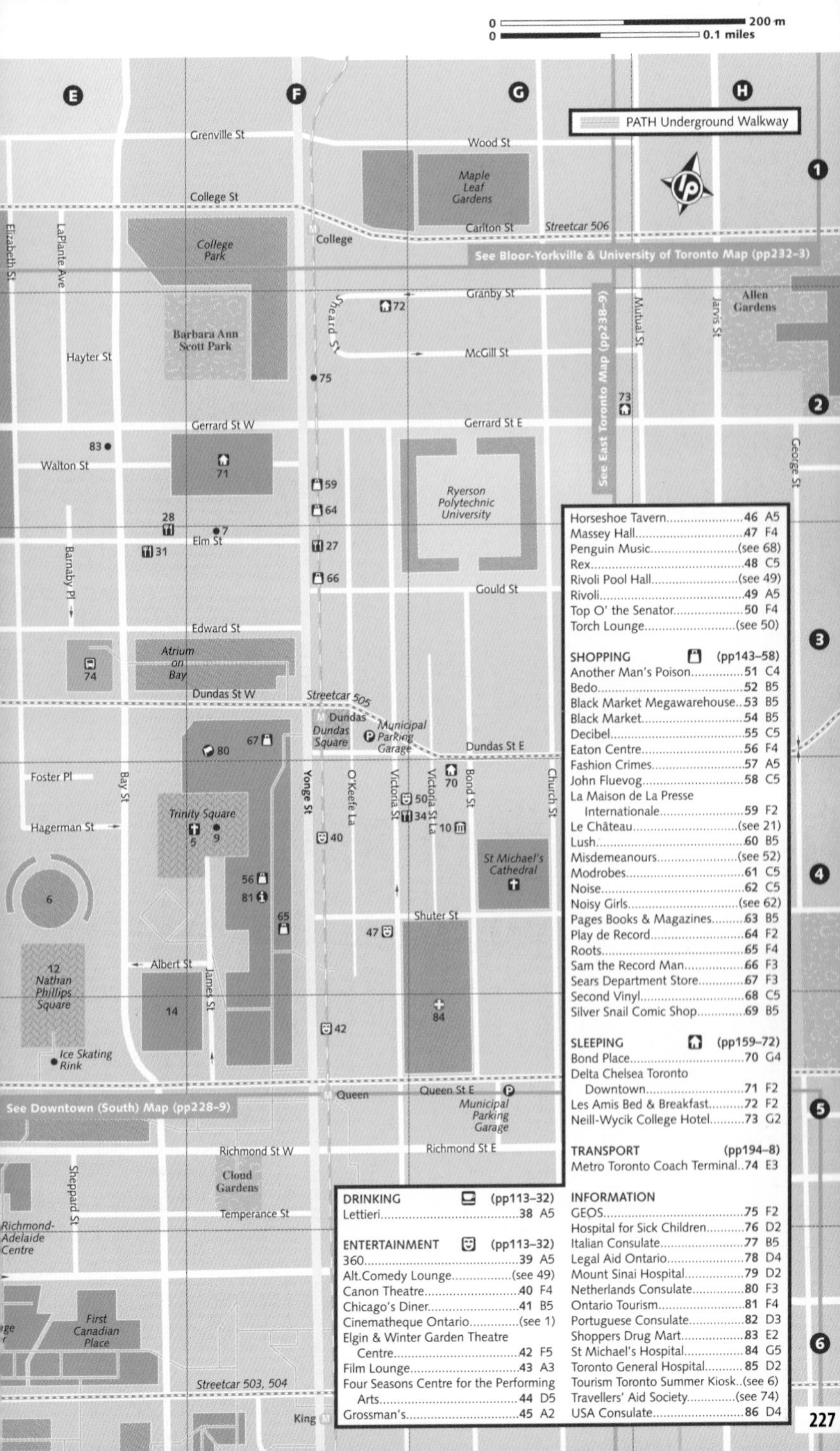

0 200 m
0 0.1 miles
PATH Underground Walkway
Grenville St
Wood St
Maple Leaf Gardens
College St
Carlton St
Streetcar 506
College
College Park
See Bloor-Yorkville & University of Toronto Map (pp232-3)
Elizabeth St
LaPlante Ave
Granby St
Sheard St
McGill St
Barbara Ann Scott Park
Hayter St
Mutual St
Jarvis St
Allen Gardens
See East Toronto Map (pp238-9)
Gerrard St W
Gerrard St E
George St
Walton St
Ryerson Polytechnic University
Elm St
Barnaby Pl
Gould St
Edward St
Atrium on Bay
Dundas St W
Streetcar 505
Dundas
Dundas Square
Municipal Parking Garage
Dundas St E
Foster Pl
Bay St
Yonge St
O'Keefe La
Victoria St
Victoria St La
Bond St
Church St
Trinity Square
Hagerman St
St Michael's Cathedral
Shuter St
Albert St
James St
Nathan Phillips Square
Ice Skating Rink
Queen
Queen St E
Municipal Parking Garage
See Downtown (South) Map (pp228-9)
Richmond St W
Richmond St E
Cloud Gardens
Sheppard St
Temperance St
Richmond-Adelaide Centre
First Canadian Place
Streetcar 503, 504
King

Horseshoe Tavern....46 A5
Massey Hall....47 F4
Penguin Music....(see 68)
Rex....48 C5
Rivoli Pool Hall....(see 49)
Rivoli....49 A5
Top O' the Senator....50 F4
Torch Lounge....(see 50)

SHOPPING (pp143–58)
Another Man's Poison....51 C4
Bedo....52 B5
Black Market Megawarehouse..53 B5
Black Market....54 B5
Decibel....55 C5
Eaton Centre....56 F4
Fashion Crimes....57 A5
John Fluevog....58 C5
La Maison de La Presse Internationale....59 F2
Le Château....(see 21)
Lush....60 B5
Misdemeanours....(see 52)
Modrobes....61 C5
Noise....62 C5
Noisy Girls....(see 62)
Pages Books & Magazines....63 B5
Play de Record....64 F2
Roots....65 F4
Sam the Record Man....66 F3
Sears Department Store....67 F3
Second Vinyl....68 C5
Silver Snail Comic Shop....69 B5

SLEEPING (pp159–72)
Bond Place....70 G4
Delta Chelsea Toronto Downtown....71 F2
Les Amis Bed & Breakfast....72 F2
Neill-Wycik College Hotel....73 G2

TRANSPORT (pp194–8)
Metro Toronto Coach Terminal..74 E3

DRINKING (pp113–32)
Lettieri....38 A5

ENTERTAINMENT (pp113–32)
360....39 A5
Alt.Comedy Lounge....(see 49)
Canon Theatre....40 F4
Chicago's Diner....41 B5
Cinematheque Ontario....(see 1)
Elgin & Winter Garden Theatre Centre....42 F5
Film Lounge....43 A3
Four Seasons Centre for the Performing Arts....44 D5
Grossman's....45 A2

INFORMATION
GEOS....75 F2
Hospital for Sick Children....76 D2
Italian Consulate....77 B5
Legal Aid Ontario....78 D4
Mount Sinai Hospital....79 D2
Netherlands Consulate....80 F3
Ontario Tourism....81 F4
Portuguese Consulate....82 D3
Shoppers Drug Mart....83 E2
St Michael's Hospital....84 G5
Toronto General Hospital....85 D2
Tourism Toronto Summer Kiosk..(see 6)
Travellers' Aid Society....(see 74)
USA Consulate....86 D4

DOWNTOWN (SOUTH)

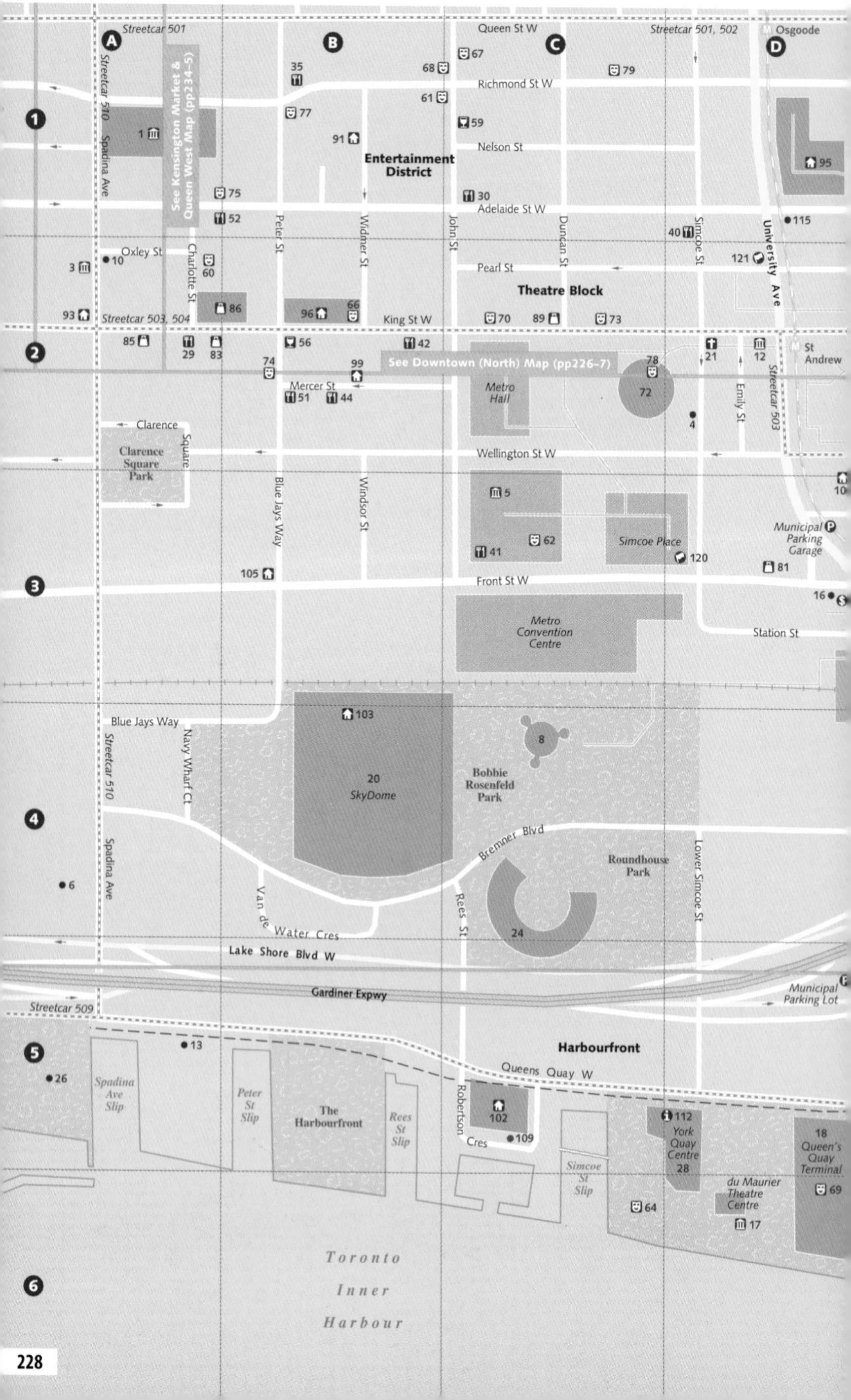

Streetcar 501
Queen St W
Streetcar 501, 502
Osgoode
Richmond St W
Spadina Ave
Streetcar 510
See Kensington Market & Queen West Map (pp234–5)
Entertainment District
Nelson St
Adelaide St W
Peter St
Widmer St
John St
Duncan St
Simcoe St
University Ave
Oxley St
Charlotte St
Pearl St
Theatre Block
Streetcar 503, 504
King St W
St Andrew
See Downtown (North) Map (pp226–7)
Mercer St
Metro Hall
Emily St
Streetcar 503
Clarence Square
Clarence Square Park
Wellington St W
Blue Jays Way
Windsor St
Simcoe Place
Municipal Parking Garage
Front St W
Metro Convention Centre
Station St
Blue Jays Way
Navy Wharf Ct
SkyDome
Bobbie Rosenfeld Park
Bremner Blvd
Roundhouse Park
Lower Simcoe St
Van de Water Cres
Rees St
Lake Shore Blvd W
Gardiner Expwy
Municipal Parking Lot
Streetcar 509
Harbourfront
Queens Quay W
Spadina Ave Slip
Peter St Slip
The Harbourfront
Rees St Slip
Robertson Cres
Simcoe St Slip
York Quay Centre
Queen's Quay Terminal
du Maurier Theatre Centre
Toronto Inner Harbour

0 200 m
0 0.1 miles
Queen St E
Queen
Richmond St E
Cloud Gardens
Temperance St
Lombard St
Sheppard St
Richmond-Adelaide Centre
Adelaide St E
First Canadian Place
Scotia Plaza
Bay St
Yonge St
Victoria St
Toronto St
Court St
Church St
St James Park
Jarvis St
George St
Streetcar 503, 504
King St E
King
Financial District
Jordan St
Melinda St
Colborne St
Leader La
St Lawrence Market (North)
Front St E
Commerce Court
Scott St
Wellington St E
Streetcar 503
Old York
BCE Place
Royal Bank Plaza
St Lawrence Market (South)
Market St
Farquars La
George St S
Scott La
Union
Front St E
The Esplanade
St Lawrence Garage
Wilton St
See East Toronto Map (pp238–9)
Gardiner Expwy
Harbour St
Lake Shore Blvd E
Streetcar 509, 510
Freeland St
Cooper St
Lower Jarvis St
Harbour St
See Toronto Islands Map (p241)
Queens Quay E
Martin Goodman Trail
Bay St
Queens Quay
Streetcars 509, 510
Yonge St Slip
Jarvis St Slip
Harbour Square
Harbour Square Park
Hanlan's Point Ferry
Centre Island Ferry
Ward's Island Ferry
PATH Underground Walkway

DOWNTOWN (SOUTH) (pp228–9)

SIGHTS & ACTIVITIES (pp37–78)
401 Richmond....1 A1
Air Canada Centre....2 E4
Art at 80....3 A2
Canada's Walk of Fame....4 D2
Canadian Broadcasting Centre & Museum..5 C3
Citycore Golf & Driving Range....6 A4
Cloud Forest Conservatory....7 F1
CN Tower....8 C4
Design Exchange (DX)....9 E2
Diesel Fitness....10 A2
Elizabeth Milan Hotel Day Spa....(see 92)
Flatiron (Gooderham) Building....11 G2
Goethe-Institut Gallery....12 D2
Great Lakes Schooner Company....(see 18)
Harbourfront Boating Centre....(see 13)
Harbourfront Canoe & Kayak Centre....13 A5
Hockey Hall of Fame....14 F3
Mariposa Cruise Lines....(see 18)
Market Gallery....15 H2
Nicholby's Sports & Souvenirs....16 D3
Power Plant....17 D6
Queen's Quay Terminal....18 D5
Redpath Sugar Museum....19 G5
SkyDome....20 B4
St Andrew's Presbyterian Church....21 D2
St James Cathedral....22 G2
St Lawrence Hall....23 H2
Steam Whistle Brewing....24 C4
Toronto Dominion Gallery of Inuit Art....25 E3
Toronto Music Garden....26 A5
Union Station....27 E3
York Quay Centre....28 D5

EATING (pp91–112)
Asakusa....29 A2
Avalon....30 C1
Biff's....31 F3
Bymark....32 E2
Café Victoria....(see 100)
Canoe....33 E2
Courthouse Market Grille....34 G1
Fez Batik....35 B1
Harbour Sixty Steakhouse....36 E5
Kubo DX....(see 9)
Marche Mövenpick....37 F3
Mercatto....38 G2
Mercatto....39 E1
Monsoon....40 D1
Mövenpick Palavrion....41 C3
Mövenpick's Caffé Bar & Masquerade..(see 37)
N'Awlins....42 B2
Nami....(see 34)
Nutty Choclatier....43 F1
Rain....44 B2
Rosewater Supper Club....45 G2
Sen5es....(see 105)
Spring Rolls....46 H2
St Lawrence Market (South Market)....47 H3
Tasting Rooms....48 E2
Temperance Society Breadspreads Bar....49 F1
Terroni....50 F1
Wayne Gretzky's....51 B2
YYZ Restaurant & Wine Bar....52 A1

DRINKING (pp113–32)
B-Side....(see 35)
beerbistro....53 F2
C'est What....54 G3
Esplanade BierMarkt....55 G3
Indian Motorcycle Cafe & Lounge....56 B2
Irish Embassy Pub & Grill....57 F2
Library Bar....58 E3
Reds....(see 48)
Smokeless Joe's....59 C1

ENTERTAINMENT (pp113–32)
Canadian Opera Company....(see 65)
Charlotte Room....60 A2
Famous Players Paramount....61 B1
Glenn Gould Studio....62 C3
Guvernment....63 H5
Harbourfront Centre Box Office....(see 112)
Harbourfront Centre CIBC Stage....64 C6
Harbourfront Reading Series....(see 28)
Hummingbird Centre for the Performing Arts....65 F3
IMAX....(see 61)
koolhaus....(see 63)
Laugh Resort....66 B2
Music Gallery....67 C1
National Ballet of Canada....(see 65)
National Film Board (NFB) Mediatheque.68 B1
nia....(see 54)
Premier Dance Theatre....69 D6
Princess of Wales Theatre....70 C2
Reservoir Lounge....71 G2
Roy Thomson Hall....72 C2
Royal Alexandra Theatre....73 C2
Second City....74 B2
Sound Emporium....75 A1
St Lawrence Centre for the Arts....76 G3
System Sandbar....77 B1
Toronto Symphony Orchestra Box Office....78 C2
Yuk Yuk's....79 C1

SHOPPING (pp143–58)
Arctic Nunavut....(see 18)
Arts on King....80 H2
Bay of Spirits Gallery....81 D3
Bay....82 F1
Europe Bound Outfitters....83 A2
Europe Bound Outfitters....84 G3
Game Trek....(see 92
Hogtown Extreme Sports....85 A
Mountain Equipment Co-op....86 A
Open Air....87 G
Proud Canadian Design & First Hand Canadian Crafts....(see 18
St Lawrence Market (North Market)....88 H
St Lawrence Sunday Antique Market....(see 88
Tilley Endurables....(see 18
Toronto Antique Centre....89 C

SLEEPING (pp159–72
Cambridge Suites Hotel....90 F
Canadiana Guesthouse & Backpackers...91 B
Fairmont Royal York....92 E
Global Village Backpackers....93 A
Grand Hotel & Suites....94 H
Hilton Toronto....95 D
Holiday Inn on King....96 B
Hostelling International (HI) Toronto....97 G
Hotel Victoria....98 F
Hôtel Le Germain....99 B
Le Royal Meridien King Edward....100 G
Novotel Toronto Centre....101 G
Radisson Plaza Hotel....102 C
Renaissance Toronto Hotel at SkyDome....103 B
Sheraton Centre Toronto....104 E1
SoHo Metropolitan Hotel....105 B
Strathcona....106 D
Westin Harbour Castle....107 F

TRANSPORT (pp194–8
New Frontier Rent-a-Car....(see 96
Toronto Island Ferry Terminal....108 F
Wheel Excitement....109 C

INFORMATION
American Express....(see 92
Citibank....110 D
Craft Studio....(see 18
Dancing on King....111 G
Harbourfront Centre Information Desk....112 D
Japan Consulate....113 E
Kinko's....114 E1
Mail Boxes Etc/UPS Store....115 D
Main Post Office....116 F
Mexican Consulate....117 F
New Zealand Consulate....118 F
Shoppers Drug Mart....119 F
Spanish Consulate....120 D
Swiss Consulate....121 D
Thomas Cook....122 F
Travel CUTS....(see 27
Travellers' Aid Society....123 E
Travellers' Aid Society....(see 27)

BLOOR-YORKVILLE & UNIVERSITY OF TORONTO (pp232–3)

SIGHTS & ACTIVITIES (pp37–78)

- AIDS Memorial 1 G4
- Bata Shoe Museum 2 B2
- Body Clinic 3 F2
- Canadian Boxing Hall of Fame 4 F2
- Epic Fitness 5 F4
- Eric Arthur Gallery 6 B6
- Firehall No 10 7 E2
- Gardiner Museum of Ceramic Art 8 D3
- Japan Foundation 9 D2
- Maple Leaf Gardens 10 G6
- Metro Toronto Police Museum 11 E6
- Metro Toronto YMCA 12 F5
- Provincial Legislature 13 D5
- Royal Ontario Museum 14 C3
- Salon Jie 15 D2
- Stillwater (see 100)
- Sudi's the Spa 16 E1
- Toni & Guy 17 E2
- Toronto Heliconian Club 18 D1
- Toronto Public Library – Lillian H Smith Branch 19 A6
- Toronto Public Library – Yorkville Branch 20 F2
- Toronto Reference Library 21 F2
- University of Toronto Athletic Centre 22 A4
- UT Art Centre 23 C4
- Yoga Sanctuary 24 F6

EATING (pp91–112)

- 7 West Café 25 F3
- à la Carte (see 8)
- Bistro 990 26 E4
- Bloor Street Diner (see 73)
- Byzantium 27 G5
- Café L'Express (see 73)
- Carman's Dining Club 28 G5
- Colony Kitchen (see 68)
- Duke of York 29 C2
- Ethiopian House 30 F4
- Fire on the East Side 31 F4
- Fran's 32 F6
- Friendly Thai 33 F4
- Greg's Ice Cream 34 C2
- Just Desserts 35 F5
- Mövenpick's Bistretto & La Pêcherie 36 D2
- Okonomi House 37 F3
- Papaya Hut 38 F5
- Phõ' Hu'ng (see 34)
- Retro Rotisserie 39 F5
- Saigon Sister 40 F3
- Sassafraz 41 E2
- Summer's Ice Cream 42 E2
- Wanda's Pie in the Sky 43 F2
- Wish 44 F3
- Zelda's 45 G5

DRINKING (pp113–32)

- Babylon 46 G4
- Bar Mercurio 47 B2
- Bedford Ballroom 48 C2
- Black Eagle (see 54)
- Crews/Tango/The Zone 49 G5
- Hemingway's 50 D2
- Lettieri 51 E2
- Lobby 52 C2
- Panorama (see 73)
- Pilot Tavern 53 F2
- Red Spot 54 G5
- Rooftop Lounge (see 100)
- Slack Alice 55 G4
- Wilde Oscar's 56 G5
- Woody's/Sailor 57 G5

ENTERTAINMENT (pp113–32)

- 5IVE 58 F4
- Alliance Atlantis Cumberland 4 59 D2
- Babalúu 60 D2
- Buddies in Bad Times Theatre 61 F5
- Cineplex Odeon Carlton 62 F6
- Cineplex Odeon Varsity (see 73)
- Fly (see 31)
- Pegasus Billiard Lounge 63 G5
- Tallulah's Cabaret (see 61)
- University of Toronto Faculty of Music 64 D3

SHOPPING (pp143–58)

- Bakka 65 F4
- Bay 66 F2
- Chapters 67 D2
- Club Monaco 68 D2
- Cookbook Store 69 F2
- Fastball Sportscards 70 F4
- Glad Day (see 65)
- Guild Shop 71 E2
- Holt Renfrew 72 F2
- Indigo 73 E3
- Kidding Awound 74 E2
- L'Atelier Grigorian 75 E2
- La Maison de la Presse Internationale 76 D2
- Lululemon Athletica 77 D2
- Lush (see 71)
- Northbound Leather 78 F4
- Omega Centre Bookstore 79 E2
- Out on the Street (see 46)
- Peachy Fresh 80 D2
- Refried Beats 81 F4
- Release Records 82 F5
- Roots 83 E2
- Science City (see 72)
- TheatreBooks 84 E3
- This Ain't the Rosedale Library 85 G5
- Thomas Hinds Tobacconist 86 F2

SLEEPING (pp159–72)

- Burwood Inn 87 G4
- Campus Co-operative Residence Inc (CCRI) 88 B3
- Cromwell Furnished Suites 89 F3
- Days Inn Toronto Downtown 90 F6
- Dundonald House 91 G4
- Four Seasons 92 D2
- Gloucester Square Bed & Breakfast Inns 93 H4
- Howard Johnson Inn 94 D1
- Innis Residence 95 B3
- InterContinental Toronto 96 C2
- Lowther House 97 B1
- Mansion 98 G4
- Mulberry Tree 99 H3
- Park Hyatt 100 D2
- Quality Hotel 101 B2
- Sutton Place Hotel 102 E4
- UT Student Housing Office 103 B6
- Victoria University 104 D3
- Victoria's Mansion Inn & Guesthouse 105 G4
- Windsor Arms 106 E3

INFORMATION

- 519 Community Centre 107 G4
- Ambulatory Care Centre 108 F6
- American Express (see 72)
- Arabesque Academy 109 F6
- Australian Consulate 110 G2
- Berlitz 111 E2
- Danish Consulate 112 D2
- French Consulate 113 D2
- Grey Region Comics 114 F5
- Hassle-Free Clinic 115 G4
- Money Mart 116 F4
- Nona Macdonald Visitors Centre 117 B5
- Shoppers Drug Mart 118 F3
- Spanish Centre 119 F3
- St George Business & Language School 120 C2
- STA Travel 121 A6
- STA Travel (see 34)
- Swedish Consulate 122 F2
- Thomas Cook 123 E3
- Travel CUTS 124 C6
- UK Consulate 125 F6

OTHER

- House of Lords 126 F3
- Italian Cultural Institute 127 A2

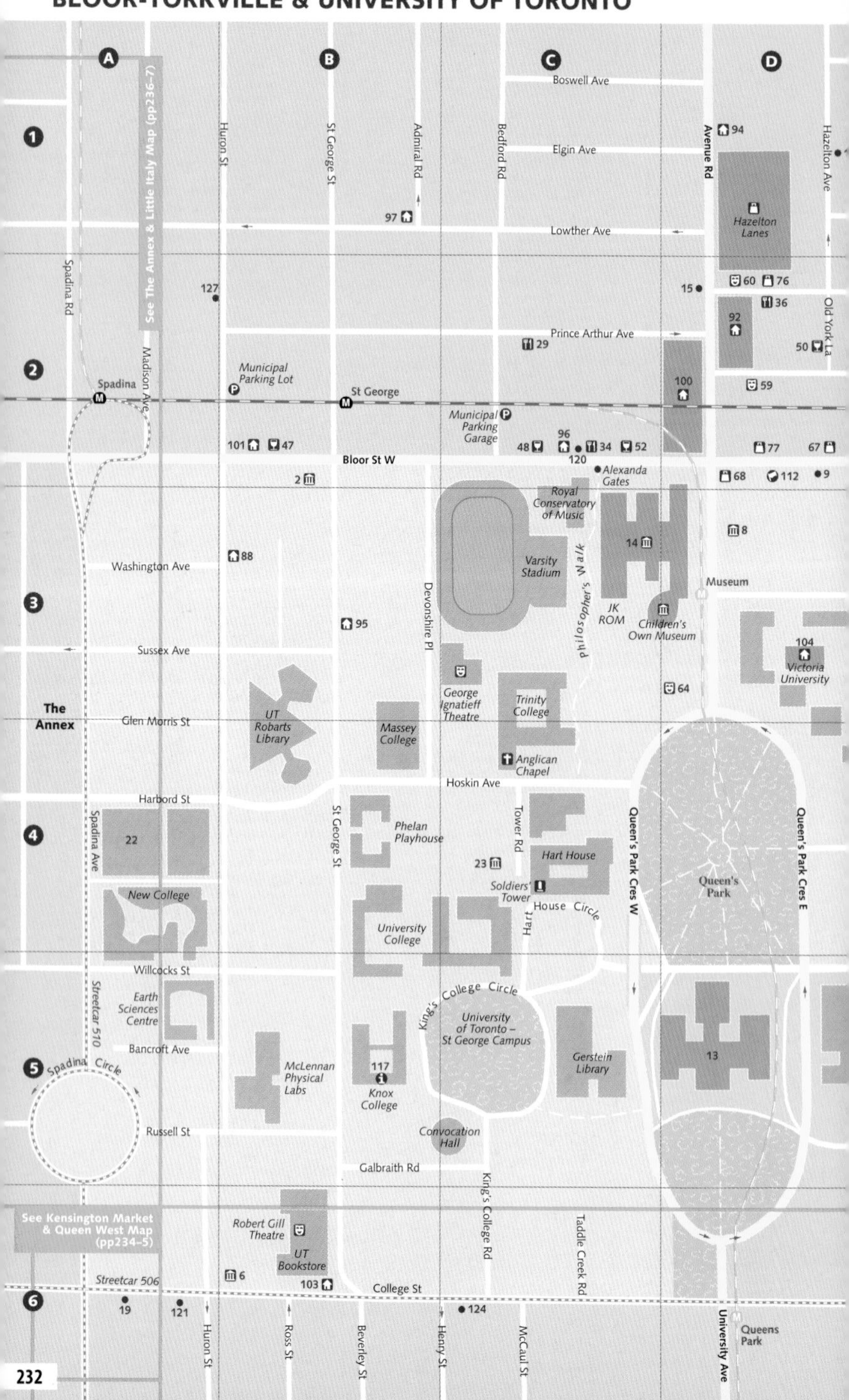
A
B
C
D
1
2
3
4
5
6
Boswell Ave
Elgin Ave
Lowther Ave
Prince Arthur Ave
Huron St
St George St
Admiral Rd
Bedford Rd
Avenue Rd
Hazelton Ave
Old York La
Spadina Rd
Madison Ave
See The Annex & Little Italy Map (pp236–7)
Hazelton Lanes
94
97
127
15
60
76
36
92
50
29
Municipal Parking Lot
Spadina
St George
Municipal Parking Garage
100
59
101
47
48
96
34
52
120
77
67
Bloor St W
2
Alexanda Gates
68
112
9
Royal Conservatory of Music
Varsity Stadium
14
8
88
Washington Ave
Philosopher's Walk
Museum
JK ROM
Children's Own Museum
Devonshire Pl
95
Sussex Ave
104
Victoria University
George Ignatieff Theatre
Trinity College
64
The Annex
Glen Morris St
UT Robarts Library
Massey College
Anglican Chapel
Hoskin Ave
Harbord St
Spadina Ave
22
St George St
Phelan Playhouse
Tower Rd
Queen's Park Cres W
Queen's Park Cres E
23
Hart House
Soldiers' Tower
House Circle
Hart
Queen's Park
New College
University College
Willcocks St
Streetcar 510
King's College Circle
Earth Sciences Centre
University of Toronto – St George Campus
Bancroft Ave
Gerstein Library
13
Spadina Circle
McLennan Physical Labs
117
Knox College
Russell St
Convocation Hall
Galbraith Rd
King's College Rd
Taddle Creek Rd
See Kensington Market & Queen West Map (pp234–5)
Robert Gill Theatre
UT Bookstore
6
Streetcar 506
103
College St
19
121
124
Huron St
Ross St
Beverley St
Henry St
McCaul St
University Ave
Queens Park

0 200 m
0 0.1 miles
E
F
G
H
Rosedale
Jesse Ketchum Park
McMurrich St
Davenport Rd
Aylmer Ave
Rosedale Rd
Pine Hill Rd
Severn St
Park Rd
Elm Ave
Scollard St
Bay St
Yonge St
Yorkville
Municipal Parking Garage
Yorkville Ave
Collier St
Church St
Rosedale Valley Rd
See East Toronto Map (pp238-9)
Bellair St
Asquith Ave
Cumberland St
St Paul's Square
Mt Pleasant Rd
Bay
Holt Renfrew Centre
Bloor-Yonge
Bloor St W
Bloor St E
Balmuto St
Sultan St
St Thomas St
Manulife Centre
Hayden St
Charles St W
Charles St E
La Scala La
St Mary St
Yonge St Strip
Inkerman St
Isabella St
St Nicholas St
Huntley St
Irwin Ave
Gloucester St
Earl St
St Joseph St
Monteith St
Dundonald St
Cawthra Square Park
Cawthra Square
Jarvis St
Phipps St
Church St
Wellesley
Church-Wellesley Village
Wellesley St W
Wellesley St E
Municipal Parking Lot
Ontario Government Ministry Buildings
Breadalbane St
Maitland St
Maitland Pl
Alexander Pl
Mutual St
Grosvenor St
Alexander St
See Downtown (North) Map (pp226-7)
Grenville St
Wood St
College St
College
Carlton St
Streetcar 506
College Park
Elizabeth St
LaPlante Ave

KENSINGTON MARKET & QUEEN WEST

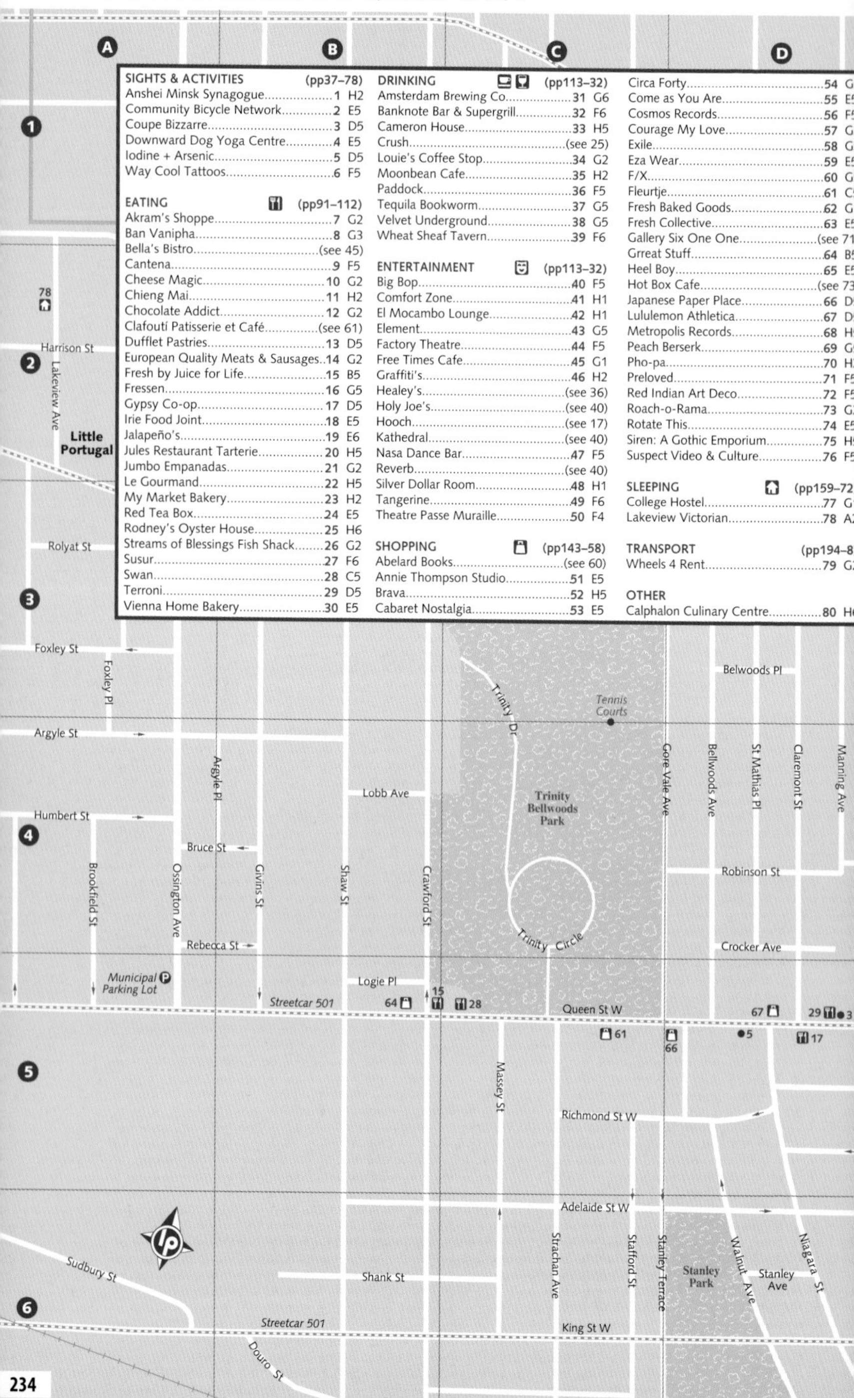

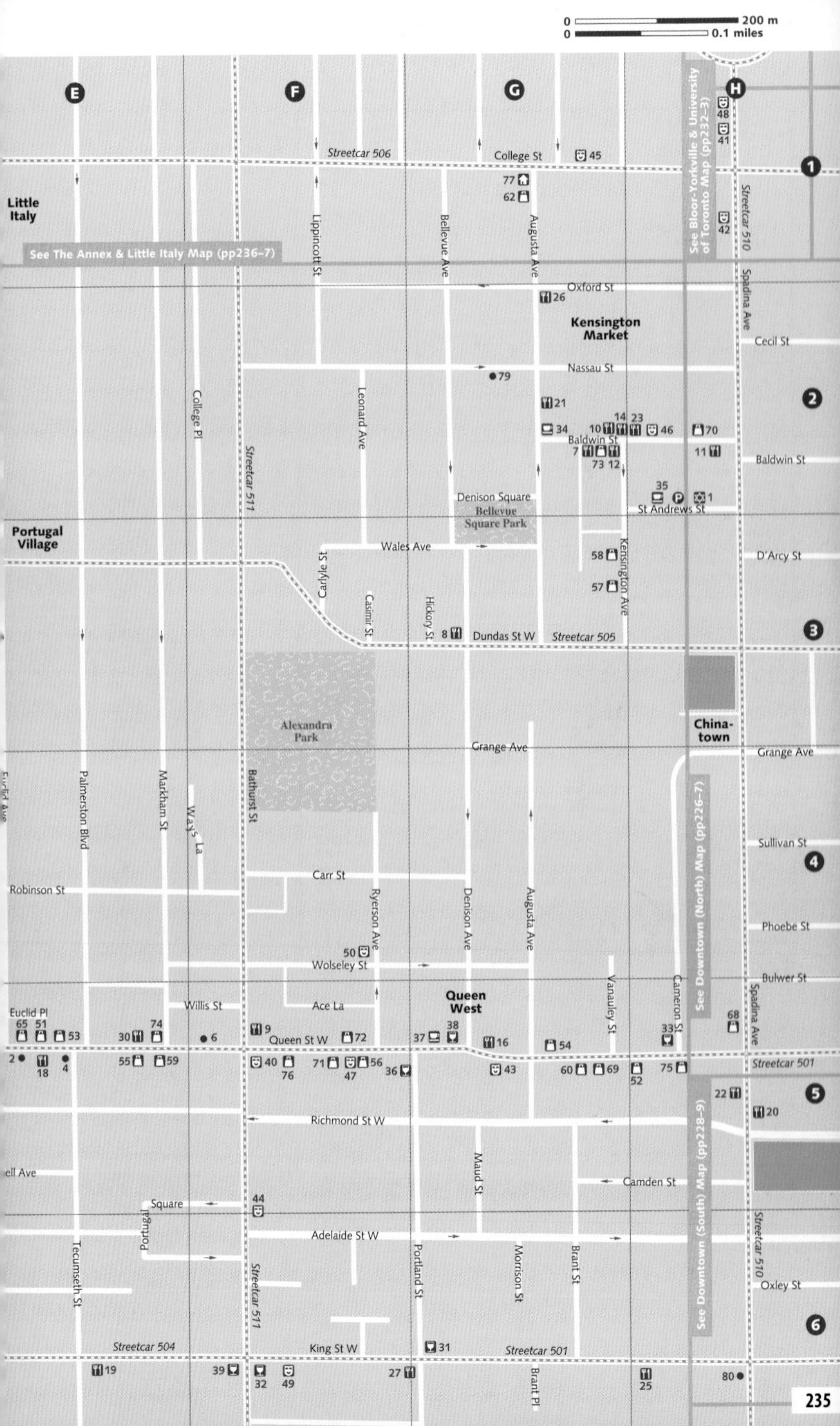

0 200 m
0 0.1 miles
E
F
G
H
Little Italy
See The Annex & Little Italy Map (pp236–7)
See Bloor-Yorkville & University of Toronto Map (pp232–3)
Streetcar 506
College St
Streetcar 510
Spadina Ave
Lippincott St
Bellevue Ave
Augusta Ave
Oxford St
Kensington Market
Cecil St
Nassau St
Leonard Ave
College Pl
Streetcar 511
Baldwin St
Denison Square
Bellevue Square Park
St Andrews St
Portugal Village
Wales Ave
D'Arcy St
Carlyle St
Casimir St
Hickory St
Kensington Ave
Dundas St W
Streetcar 505
Alexandra Park
China-town
Grange Ave
Palmerston Blvd
Markham St
Ways La
Bathurst St
Sullivan St
Robinson St
Carr St
Ryerson Ave
Denison Ave
See Downtown (North) Map (pp226–7)
Phoebe St
Wolseley St
Bulwer St
Queen West
Vanauley St
Cameron St
Euclid Pl
Willis St
Ace La
Queen St W
Streetcar 501
Richmond St W
See Downtown (South) Map (pp228–9)
Maud St
Camden St
Square
Portugal
Adelaide St W
Tecumseth St
Portland St
Morrison St
Brant St
Oxley St
Streetcar 504
King St W
Brant Pl
1
2
3
4
5
6

THE ANNEX & LITTLE ITALY

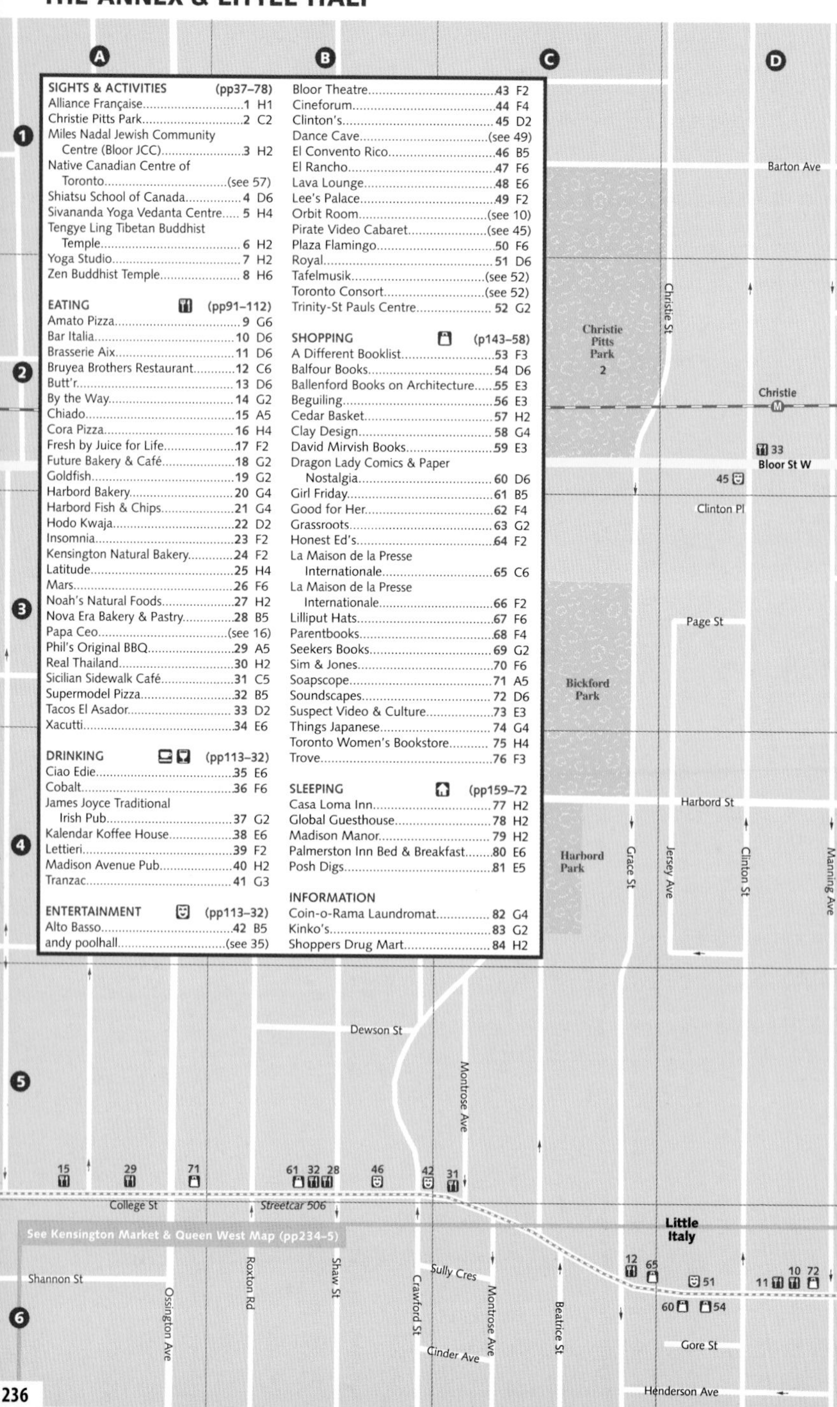

A
B
C
D
1
2
3
4
5
6
SIGHTS & ACTIVITIES (pp37–78)
Alliance Française....1 H1
Christie Pitts Park....2 C2
Miles Nadal Jewish Community Centre (Bloor JCC)....3 H2
Native Canadian Centre of Toronto....(see 57)
Shiatsu School of Canada....4 D6
Sivananda Yoga Vedanta Centre....5 H4
Tengye Ling Tibetan Buddhist Temple....6 H2
Yoga Studio....7 H2
Zen Buddhist Temple....8 H6
EATING (pp91–112)
Amato Pizza....9 G6
Bar Italia....10 D6
Brasserie Aix....11 D6
Bruyea Brothers Restaurant....12 C6
Butt'r....13 D6
By the Way....14 G2
Chiado....15 A5
Cora Pizza....16 H4
Fresh by Juice for Life....17 F2
Future Bakery & Café....18 G2
Goldfish....19 G2
Harbord Bakery....20 G4
Harbord Fish & Chips....21 G4
Hodo Kwaja....22 D2
Insomnia....23 F2
Kensington Natural Bakery....24 F2
Latitude....25 H4
Mars....26 F6
Noah's Natural Foods....27 H2
Nova Era Bakery & Pastry....28 B5
Papa Ceo....(see 16)
Phil's Original BBQ....29 A5
Real Thailand....30 H2
Sicilian Sidewalk Café....31 C5
Supermodel Pizza....32 B5
Tacos El Asador....33 D2
Xacutti....34 E6
DRINKING (pp113–32)
Ciao Edie....35 E6
Cobalt....36 F6
James Joyce Traditional Irish Pub....37 G2
Kalendar Koffee House....38 E6
Lettieri....39 F2
Madison Avenue Pub....40 H2
Tranzac....41 G3
ENTERTAINMENT (pp113–32)
Alto Basso....42 B5
andy poolhall....(see 35)
Bloor Theatre....43 F2
Cineforum....44 F4
Clinton's....45 D2
Dance Cave....(see 49)
El Convento Rico....46 B5
El Rancho....47 F6
Lava Lounge....48 E6
Lee's Palace....49 F2
Orbit Room....(see 10)
Pirate Video Cabaret....(see 45)
Plaza Flamingo....50 F6
Royal....51 D6
Tafelmusik....(see 52)
Toronto Consort....(see 52)
Trinity-St Pauls Centre....52 G2
SHOPPING (p143–58)
A Different Booklist....53 F3
Balfour Books....54 D6
Ballenford Books on Architecture....55 E3
Beguiling....56 E3
Cedar Basket....57 H2
Clay Design....58 G4
David Mirvish Books....59 E3
Dragon Lady Comics & Paper Nostalgia....60 D6
Girl Friday....61 B5
Good for Her....62 F4
Grassroots....63 G2
Honest Ed's....64 F2
La Maison de la Presse Internationale....65 C6
La Maison de la Presse Internationale....66 F2
Lilliput Hats....67 F6
Parentbooks....68 F4
Seekers Books....69 G2
Sim & Jones....70 F6
Soapscope....71 A5
Soundscapes....72 D6
Suspect Video & Culture....73 E3
Things Japanese....74 G4
Toronto Women's Bookstore....75 H4
Trove....76 F3
SLEEPING (pp159–72)
Casa Loma Inn....77 H2
Global Guesthouse....78 H2
Madison Manor....79 H2
Palmerston Inn Bed & Breakfast....80 E6
Posh Digs....81 E5
INFORMATION
Coin-o-Rama Laundromat....82 G4
Kinko's....83 G2
Shoppers Drug Mart....84 H2
Barton Ave
Christie St
Christie Pitts Park
2
Christie
33
Bloor St W
45
Clinton Pl
Page St
Bickford Park
Harbord St
Harbord Park
Grace St
Jersey Ave
Clinton St
Manning Ave
Dewson St
Montrose Ave
15
29
71
61
32
28
46
42
31
College St
Streetcar 506
Little Italy
See Kensington Market & Queen West Map (pp234–5)
Shannon St
Ossington Ave
Roxton Rd
Shaw St
Crawford St
Sully Cres
Montrose Ave
Cinder Ave
Beatrice St
12
65
51
10
72
11
60
54
Gore St
Henderson Ave

0 200 m
0 0.1 miles
E
F
G
H
1
2
3
4
5
6
Kendal Ave
Lowther Ave
Palmerston Square
London St
Streetcar 511
Bathurst St
Albany Ave
Howland Ave
Brunswick Ave
Dalton Rd
Walmer Rd
Spadina Rd
Madison Ave
Bathurst
Spadina
Bloor St W
atown
Markham Village
Lippincott St
Croft St
Lennox St
The Annex
Sussex Ave
Spadina Ave
Herrick St
Streetcar 510
University of Toronto – St George Campus
Harbord St
Palmerston Blvd
Markham St
Borden St
Major St
Robert St
Sussex Mews
Ulster St
Willcocks St
Spadina Circle
Van Koughnet St
Russell St
See Bloor-Yorkville & University of Toronto Map (pp232–3)
College St
Streetcar 506
College Pl
Bellevue Ave
Augusta Ave
Kensington Market

EAST TORONTO

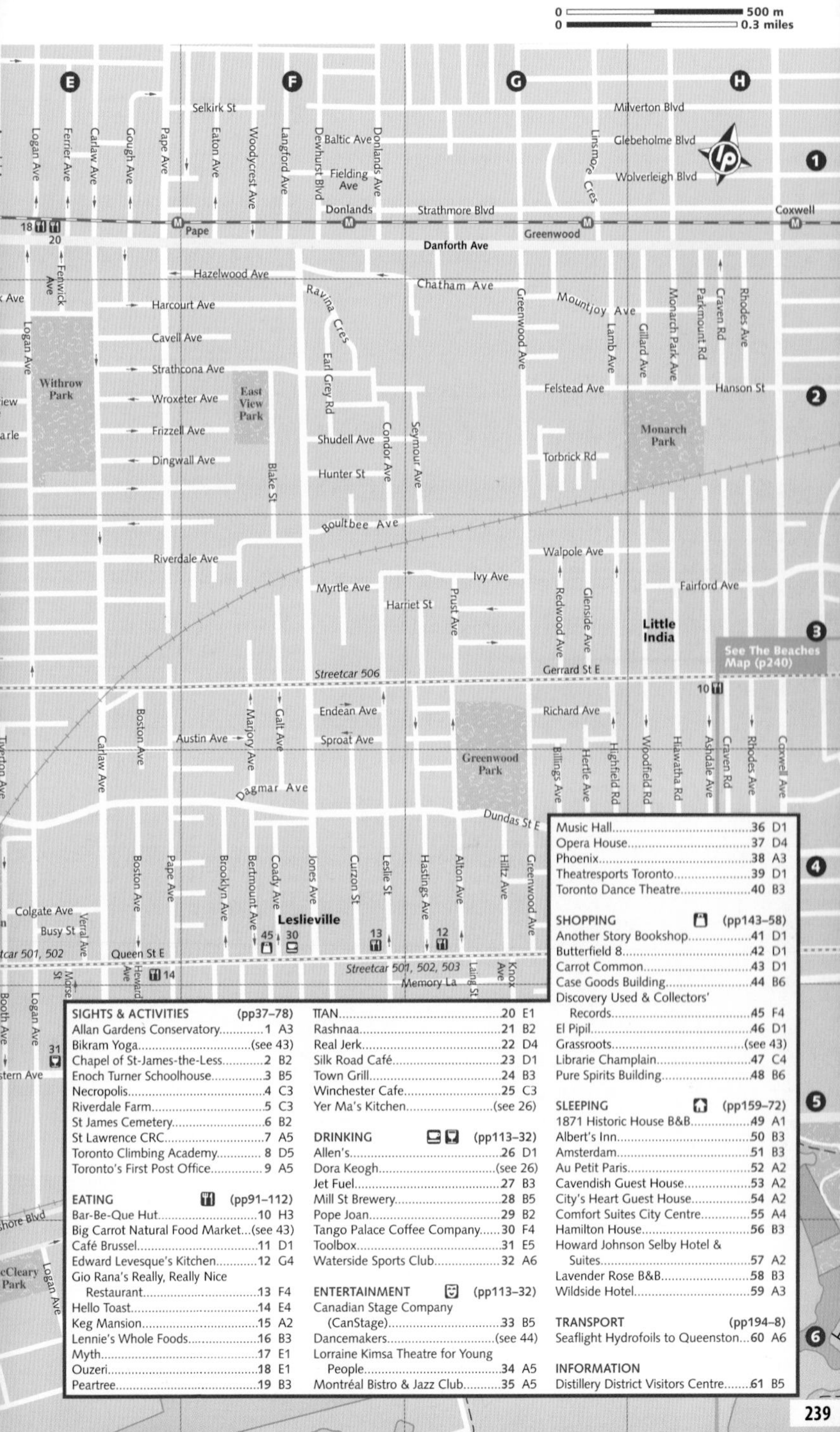
0 500 m
0 0.3 miles
E
F
G
H
1
2
3
4
5
6
Selkirk St
Logan Ave
Ferrier Ave
Carlaw Ave
Gough Ave
Pape Ave
Eaton Ave
Woodycrest Ave
Langford Ave
Dewhurst Blvd
Baltic Ave
Donlands Ave
Fielding Ave
Donlands
Strathmore Blvd
Milverton Blvd
Glebeholme Blvd
Wolverleigh Blvd
Linsmore Cres
Coxwell
Pape
Greenwood
Danforth Ave
Fenwick Ave
Hazelwood Ave
Chatham Ave
Ravina Cres
Harcourt Ave
Cavell Ave
Strathcona Ave
Wroxeter Ave
Frizzell Ave
Dingwall Ave
Withrow Park
East View Park
Earl Grey Rd
Shudell Ave
Hunter St
Condor Ave
Seymour Ave
Blake St
Greenwood Ave
Mountjoy Ave
Lamb Ave
Gillard Ave
Monarch Park Ave
Parkmount Rd
Craven Rd
Rhodes Ave
Felstead Ave
Hanson St
Monarch Park
Torbrick Rd
Boultbee Ave
Riverdale Ave
Walpole Ave
Myrtle Ave
Harriet St
Prust Ave
Ivy Ave
Redwood Ave
Glenside Ave
Fairford Ave
Little India
See The Beaches Map (p240)
Streetcar 506
Gerrard St E
Endean Ave
Sproat Ave
Richard Ave
Austin Ave
Boston Ave
Carlaw Ave
Marjory Ave
Galt Ave
Greenwood Park
Billings Ave
Hertle Ave
Highfield Rd
Woodfield Rd
Hiawatha Rd
Ashdale Ave
Craven Rd
Rhodes Ave
Coxwell Ave
Tiverton Ave
Dagmar Ave
Dundas St E
Pape Ave
Brooklyn Ave
Bertmount Ave
Coady Ave
Jones Ave
Curzon St
Leslie St
Hastings Ave
Alton Ave
Hiltz Ave
Greenwood Ave
Leslieville
Colgate Ave
Busy St
Verral Ave
Queen St E
Streetcar 501, 502
Streetcar 501, 502, 503
Memory La
Laing St
Knox Ave
Heward Ave
Marsh St
Booth Ave
Logan Ave
stern Ave
shore Blvd
McCleary Park
Logan Ave
MUSIC HALL / ENTERTAINMENT (cont.)
Music Hall....36 D1
Opera House....37 D4
Phoenix....38 A3
Theatresports Toronto....39 D1
Toronto Dance Theatre....40 B3
SIGHTS & ACTIVITIES (pp37–78)
Allan Gardens Conservatory....1 A3
Bikram Yoga....(see 43)
Chapel of St-James-the-Less....2 B2
Enoch Turner Schoolhouse....3 B5
Necropolis....4 C3
Riverdale Farm....5 C3
St James Cemetery....6 B2
St Lawrence CRC....7 A5
Toronto Climbing Academy....8 D5
Toronto's First Post Office....9 A5
EATING (pp91–112)
Bar-Be-Que Hut....10 H3
Big Carrot Natural Food Market...(see 43)
Café Brussel....11 D1
Edward Levesque's Kitchen....12 G4
Gio Rana's Really, Really Nice Restaurant....13 F4
Hello Toast....14 E4
Keg Mansion....15 A2
Lennie's Whole Foods....16 B3
Myth....17 E1
Ouzeri....18 E1
Peartree....19 B3
TTAN....20 E1
Rashnaa....21 B2
Real Jerk....22 D4
Silk Road Café....23 D1
Town Grill....24 B3
Winchester Cafe....25 C3
Yer Ma's Kitchen....(see 26)
DRINKING (pp113–32)
Allen's....26 D1
Dora Keogh....(see 26)
Jet Fuel....27 B3
Mill St Brewery....28 B5
Pope Joan....29 B2
Tango Palace Coffee Company....30 F4
Toolbox....31 E5
Waterside Sports Club....32 A6
ENTERTAINMENT (pp113–32)
Canadian Stage Company (CanStage)....33 B5
Dancemakers....(see 44)
Lorraine Kimsa Theatre for Young People....34 A5
Montréal Bistro & Jazz Club....35 A5
SHOPPING (pp143–58)
Another Story Bookshop....41 D1
Butterfield 8....42 D1
Carrot Common....43 D1
Case Goods Building....44 B6
Discovery Used & Collectors' Records....45 F4
El Pipil....46 D1
Grassroots....(see 43)
Librarie Champlain....47 C4
Pure Spirits Building....48 B6
SLEEPING (pp159–72)
1871 Historic House B&B....49 A1
Albert's Inn....50 B3
Amsterdam....51 B3
Au Petit Paris....52 A2
Cavendish Guest House....53 A2
City's Heart Guest House....54 A2
Comfort Suites City Centre....55 A4
Hamilton House....56 B3
Howard Johnson Selby Hotel & Suites....57 A2
Lavender Rose B&B....58 B3
Wildside Hotel....59 A3
TRANSPORT (pp194–8)
Seaflight Hydrofoils to Queenston...60 A6
INFORMATION
Distillery District Visitors Centre....61 B5

THE BEACHES

Kingston Rd
Queen St E
Streetcar 501
Streetcar 502, 503
Lake Shore Blvd E
Lake Ontario
Kew Gardens
Glen Stewart Ravine
St John's Cemetery Norway
Ashbridge's Bay Park
Ashbridge's Bay Yacht Club
Ashbridge's Bay
Coatsworth Cut
Scenic Lookout
Woodbine Beach
Kew Beach
Beaches Park
Balmy Beach
Boardwalk
Martin Goodman Trail
Municipal Parking Lot
Skating Rink
Little India
See East Toronto Map (pp238–9)
SIGHTS & ACTIVITIES (pp37–78)
Beaches Cyclery 1 B2
Beaches RC 2 C1
DD Summerville Pool 3 B3
Lawn Bowling Club 4 C2
Leuty Life Saving Station 5 A4
RC Harris Filtration Plant 6 F2
Silverbeach Boathouse 7 F2
EATING (pp91–112)
Akaneya 9 E2
Beacher Café 10 D2
Best Coffee House 11 E2
Blū Lobster Bistro 12 E2
La Tea Da Salon de Thé 13 D2
Nevada 14 C2
Otabe 15 E2
White Bros Fish Co 16 E2
DRINKING (pp113–32)
Castro's Lounge 17 D2
Lion on the Beach 18 C2
miofrio! juice+java 19 C2
Remarkable Bean 20 E2
ENTERTAINMENT (pp113–32)
Alliance Atlantis Cinema 21 A2
Fox 22 E2
SHOPPING (pp143–58)
Art² 23 D2
La Maison de la Presse Internationale 24 C2
Yoka (see 17)
SLEEPING (p159–72)
Accommodating the Soul 25 C2
OTHER
0 400 m
0 0.2 miles